DATE DUE			
Mar 27 '72			
May 15 '72			
Sep 21 '72			
Oct 28 '72			

GAYLORD M-2   PRINTED IN U.S.A.

Atomic Diplomacy: Hiroshima and Potsdam

THE USE OF THE ATOMIC BOMB
AND THE AMERICAN CONFRONTATION
WITH SOVIET POWER

GAR ALPEROVITZ
FELLOW OF KING'S COLLEGE IN
THE UNIVERSITY OF CAMBRIDGE

SIMON AND SCHUSTER - NEW YORK

FIRST PRINTING

Library of Congress Catalog Card Number: 65–15029
Manufactured in the United States of America
By American Book–Stratford Press, Inc., New York
Designed by Eve Metz

THE AUTHOR AND THE PUBLISHERS ARE GRATEFUL FOR PERMISSION TO INCLUDE IN
THIS BOOK MATERIAL FROM THE FOLLOWING SOURCES:

The Bobbs-Merrill Company, Inc., for material from *I Saw Poland Betrayed*, copyright 1948 by Arthur Bliss Lane.

Brandt & Brandt for material from *I Was There* by Admiral Leahy. Copyright 1950 by William D. Leahy, copyright 1950 by Curtis Publishing Company; published by McGraw-Hill Book Company.

W. Collins Sons & Co., Ltd., for material from *Triumph in the West, 1943–1946* by A. Bryant.

Columbia University Press for material from Harry S. Truman, *Truman Speaks*, 1960.

Doubleday & Company, Inc. for selections from *Crusade in Europe* by Dwight D. Eisenhower, copyright 1948 by Doubleday & Company, Inc., and from *The White House Years: Mandate for Change, 1953–1956* by Dwight D. Eisenhower, copyright © 1963 by Dwight D. Eisenhower.

Harper & Row for selections from J. F. Byrnes, *All in One Lifetime* and *Speaking Frankly*; F. Knebel and C. W. Bailey, *No High Ground*; R. E. Sherwood, *Roosevelt and Hopkins: An Intimate History*; H. L. Stimson and McGeorge Bundy, *On Active Service in Peace and War*.

Houghton Mifflin Company for material from Winston S. Churchill, *Triumph and Tragedy*, Vol. VI of *The Second World War*, and from J. C. Grew, *Turbulent Era*, Vol. II.

Life Magazine for selections from the Truman *Memoirs*, copyright © 1955 Time Inc.

J. B. Lippincott Company for material from *The Man of Independence* by Jonathan Daniels. Copyright 1950 by Jonathan Daniels.

The Pennsylvania State University Press for material from R. G. Hewlett and O. E. Anderson, Jr., *The New World 1939–1946*, Vol. I., *A History of the U. S. Atomic Energy Commission*, 1962.

Princeton University for material from *The Forrestal Diaries* by James Forrestal, edited by Walter Millis, The Viking Press, 1951.

Princeton University Press for material from four books by H. Feis: *Between War and Peace*, *The China Tangle*, *Japan Subdued*, and *Churchill, Roosevelt, Stalin*.

Stanford University Press for material from R. J. C. Butow, *Japan's Decision to Surrender*, 1957.

The Viking Press for material from J. R. Deane, *The Strange Alliance*.

John Wiley & Sons for material from E. J. Rozek, *Allied Wartime Diplomacy: A Pattern in Poland*, 1958.

World Peace Foundation for material from *Negotiating with the Russians* by R. Dennett and J. E. Johnson, 1951.

FOR
MY DAUGHTER KARI
AND IN MEMORY OF
A GREAT AMERICAN CONSERVATIVE,
HENRY L. STIMSON

ACKNOWLEDGMENTS

I wish to acknowledge and thank the following for the help they have given me, directly through advice, encouragement, material support, and the provision of information; and indirectly through their work: Emily and Julius Alperovitz, Oscar E. Anderson, P. M. S. Blackett, Sir Denis Brogan, Michael Brower, Naomi Burns, E. H. Carr, Benjamin V. Cohen, Daniel S. Greenberg, Joseph C. Grew, Paul Y. Hammond, Elinor and Christopher Jencks, King's College (Cambridge University), Admiral William D. Leahy, Mrs. Jacqueline Lushin, Archibald MacLeish, The Marshall Aid Commemoration Commission, George L. Mosse, Marcus G. Raskin, Joan V. Robinson, Alice Kimball Smith, The Henry L. Stimson Literary Trust, Arthur I. Waskow, William Appleman Williams.

—G. A.

CONTENTS

CONTENTS

PREFACE

Dear Mr. President,
I think it is very important that I should have a talk with you as soon
as possible on a highly secret matter. I mentioned it to you shortly
after you took office, but have not urged it since on account of the
pressure you have been under. It, however, has such a bearing on our
present foreign relations and has such an important effect upon all my
thinking in this field that I think you ought to know about it without
much further delay.

—*Secretary of War Henry L. Stimson*
to President Harry S. Truman,
April 24, 1945

THIS NOTE WAS WRITTEN twelve days after Franklin Delano Roosevelt's death and two weeks before World War II ended in Europe.[1] The following day Secretary Stimson advised President Truman that the "highly secret matter" would have a "decisive" effect upon America's postwar foreign policy. Stimson then outlined the role the atomic bomb would play in America's relations with other countries.[2] In diplomacy, he confided to his diary, the weapon would be a "master card."[3]

This book begins in the spring of 1945, a time when postwar problems unfolded as rapidly as the Allied armies converged in Central Europe. During the fighting which preceded Nazi surrender the Red Army conquered a great belt of territory bordering the Soviet Union. Debating the consequences of this fact, American policy makers defined a series of interrelated problems: What political and economic pattern was likely to emerge in Eastern and Central Europe? Would Soviet influence predominate? Most important, what power—if any—did the United States have to effect the ultimate settlement on the very borders of Russia?

Roosevelt, Churchill, and Stalin had attempted to resolve these issues of East-West influence at the February 1945 Yalta Conference.

With the Red Army clearly in control, the West was in a weak bargaining position. It was important to reach an understanding with Stalin before American troops began their planned withdrawal from the Continent. Poland, the first major country intensely discussed by the Big Three, took on unusual significance; the balance of influence struck between Soviet-oriented and Western-oriented politicians in the government of this one country could set a pattern for big-power relationships in the rest of Eastern Europe.

Although the Yalta Conference ended with a signed accord covering Poland, within a few weeks it was clear that Allied understanding was more apparent than real. None of the heads of government interpreted the somewhat vague agreement in the same way. Churchill began to press for more Western influence; Stalin urged less. True to his well-known policy of cooperation and conciliation, Roosevelt attempted to achieve a more definite understanding for Poland and a pattern for East-West relations in Europe. Caught for much of the last of his life between the determination of Churchill and the stubbornness of Stalin, Roosevelt at times fired off angry cables to Moscow, and at others warned London against an "attempt to evade the fact that we placed, as clearly shown in the agreement, somewhat more emphasis . . . [on Soviet-oriented Polish politicians in the government]."*

Roosevelt died on April 12, 1945, only two months after Yalta. When Truman met with Secretary Stimson to discuss the "bearing" of the atomic bomb upon foreign relations, the powers were deeply ensnarled in a tense public struggle over the meaning of the Yalta agreement. Poland had come to symbolize *all* East-West relations. Truman was forced to pick up the tangled threads of policy with little knowledge of the broader, more complex issues involved. How the new President faced this challenge, and how he approached the fundamental problem of postwar American-Soviet relations, are primarily themes of this book.

Herbert Feis, a noted expert on the period, has written that "Truman made up his mind that he would not depart from Roosevelt's course or renounce his ways."[4] Others have argued that "we tried to

---

* See Appendix I for a detailed review of the Polish problem.

work out the problems of the peace in close cooperation with the Russians."[5] It is often believed that American policy followed a conciliatory course, changing—in reaction to Soviet intransigence—only in 1947 with the Truman Doctrine and the Marshall Plan. My own belief is somewhat different. It derives from the comment of Truman's Secretary of State that by early autumn of 1945 it was "understandable" that Soviet leaders should feel American policy had shifted radically after Roosevelt's death:[6] It is now evident that, far from following his predecessor's policy of cooperation, shortly after taking office Truman launched a powerful foreign policy initiative aimed at reducing or eliminating Soviet influence from Europe. Much of the material in the following pages attempts to illuminate this conclusion.

The ultimate point of this study is not, however, that America's approach to Russia changed after Roosevelt. Rather it is that the atomic bomb played a role in the formulation of policy, particularly in connection with Truman's only meeting with Stalin, the Potsdam Conference of late July and early August 1945. Again, my judgment differs from Feis's conclusion that "the light of the explosion 'brighter than a thousand suns' filtered into the conference rooms at Potsdam only as a distant gleam."[7] I believe new evidence proves not only that the atomic bomb influenced diplomacy, but that it determined much of Truman's shift to a tough policy aimed at forcing Soviet acquiescence to American plans for Eastern and Central Europe. The weapon "gave him an entirely new feeling of confidence," the President told his Secretary of War.[8] By the time of Potsdam Truman had been advised on the role of the atomic bomb by both Secretary Stimson and Secretary of State Byrnes. Though the two men differed as to tactics, each urged a tough line. Part of the book attempts to define how closely Truman followed a subtle policy outlined by Stimson, and to what extent he followed the straightforward advice of Byrnes that the bomb (in Truman's words) "put us in a position to dictate our own terms at the end of the war."[9]

A study of American policy in the very early days of the Cold War must inevitably deal with Soviet actions and reactions. I wish to stress that this book is basically an analysis of *American* policy; it is not an attempt to offer a detailed review of *Soviet* policy. Stalin's approach seems to have been cautiously moderate during the brief few months here described. It is perhaps symbolized by the Soviet-sponsored free elections which routed the Communist Party in Hungary in the autumn of 1945. The book does not attempt to interpret this moderation, nor to explain how or why Soviet policy changed to the harsh totalitarian controls characteristic of the period after 1946.

The judgment that Truman radically altered Roosevelt's policy in mid-1945 nevertheless obviously suggests a new point of departure for interpretations of the Cold War. In late 1945 General Eisenhower observed in Moscow that "before the atom bomb was used, I would have said, yes, I was sure we could keep the peace with Russia. Now I don't know . . . People are frightened and disturbed all over. Everyone feels insecure again."[10] To what extent did postwar Soviet policies derive from insecurity based upon a fear of America's atom bomb and changed policy? The book stops short of this fundamental question, concluding that further research is needed to test Secretary Stimson's judgment that "the problem of our satisfactory relations with Russia [was] not merely connected with but [was] virtually dominated by the problem of the atomic bomb."[11]

Similarly, I believe more research and more information are needed to reach a conclusive understanding of why the atomic bomb was used. The common belief is that the question is closed, and that President Truman's explanation is correct: "The dropping of the bombs stopped the war, saved millions of lives."[12] My own view is that presently available evidence shows the atomic bomb was not needed to end the war or to save lives—and that this was understood by American leaders at the time. General Eisenhower has recently recalled that in mid-1945 he expressed a similar opinion to the Secretary of War: "I told him I was against it on two counts. First, the Japanese were ready to surrender and it wasn't necessary to hit them with that awful thing. Second, I hated to see our country be the first to use such a weapon . . ."[13] To go beyond the limited conclusion that the bomb was unnecessary is not possible at present. However, I have attempted to define the remaining questions with some precision. The issue is not why it was *decided* to use the bomb, but rather, how policy makers came to *assume* the bomb would be used, and why they never questioned this assumption as Eisenhower did.

The information and views here presented challenge many common opinions. I have made no attempt, however, to take up the various arguments offered by the great number of writers, both serious and casual, who have touched upon the subject. At certain points I have presented the ideas of one or two representative authors for comparison with new information. But so far as possible I have eschewed contention, and reduced debate and controversy to a minimum.

Looking back to the views I held when I began this study six years ago, I am deeply aware of how much my own understanding of the period has changed, and how my original ideas have been challenged by new facts. In the course of my research I have often been reminded of a comment made by the economist John Maynard Keynes. My experience has matched his insight, and Keynes's point may be useful as a word of introduction for others: "The difficulty lies, not in the new ideas, but in escaping from the old ones, which ramify, for those brought up as most of us have been, into every corner of our minds."[14]

G. A.

Washington, D.C., 1964

Let us re-examine our attitude toward the Cold War, remembering we are not engaged in a debate, seeking to pile up debating points. We are not here distributing blame or pointing the finger. We must deal with the world as it is . . .

—PRESIDENT JOHN F. KENNEDY
June 10, 1963

CHAPTER I

The Strategy of an Immediate Showdown

> *It was now or never. . . .*
> —PRESIDENT HARRY S. TRUMAN
> April 23, 1945

IT WAS A SHORT TWO WEEKS before the combined strength of Britain, the United States, and the Soviet Union forced the collapse of Nazi power and the end of the Second World War. Only eleven days had passed since the death of Franklin Delano Roosevelt. The new President of the United States prepared for his first meeting with a representative of the Soviet Union. Rehearsing his views on the subject of the negotiation—a reorganization of the Polish government—Truman declared that if the Russians did not care to cooperate, "they could go to hell."* A few hours later the President expressed the same view to Soviet Foreign Minister V. M. Molotov in language which, according to the President's Chief of Staff, was "not at all diplomatic."[1]

THE FIRM APPROACH

ALTHOUGH THIS ENCOUNTER is often overlooked by those who stress Truman's desire to continue his predecessor's policy of "cooperation with the Russians," the fiery and blunt language was not the result of a moment's flash of temper.[2] The new President had care-

---

* This is taken from Bohlen's notes. (Forrestal, *Diaries*, p. 50; see also Truman, *Year of Decisions*, p. 77.)

fully considered his approach to Molotov. By the third week of April 1945 he and most of his senior advisers had agreed that Roosevelt's policy of "cooperation" had to be reconsidered and that it would now be wise strategy to face the Russians with a firm negotiating position and strong language.

The immediate problem concerned a reorganization of the Polish government established under Soviet auspices as the Red Army drove the Germans to the banks of the Oder. Both Roosevelt and Churchill had promised support for a government "friendly" to the Soviet Union, one which would not open the way to a future German attack.[3] At Yalta it had been agreed that the Soviet-backed Warsaw government "now functioning in Poland" would be "reorganized" to form a "new" government by the addition of Western-oriented Polish political leaders.[4] After a considerable debate over a number of lesser points, following Yalta the "Polish question" had reduced to a three-way struggle over the allocation of power in the new government.* Each of the Big Three promoted his favored Poles. As Admiral Leahy put it, the power struggle was now "the nub of the issue."[5]

Just before Truman took office, Stalin attempted to define the problem more precisely by suggesting that the Yugoslav precedent be "more or less" followed in Poland—that is, that the Warsaw government be expanded by adding approximately one new minister for each four already in the Cabinet, to achieve a power ratio of one in five.† This would give the more Soviet-oriented Poles predominant influence. Almost immediately upon taking office, Truman rejected Stalin's proposal. Churchill thought it "remarkable" that the new President "felt able so promptly to commit himself" to a position totally opposed to the Russian view and very close to the Prime Minister's own stand.[6] Neither Truman nor Churchill wished to commit himself

---

* See Appendix I, for a detailed discussion of the post-Yalta negotiations.

† The actual precedent depends upon how one evaluates the political coloration of various Yugoslav Cabinet members. No attempt at such an independent assessment is made. The ratio 1 of 5 (20%) is taken from Churchill and Truman. It is possible to find various estimates of the ratio: Lane gives 1 of 5 (20%) (*I Saw Freedom Betrayed*, p. 65); Churchill gives 1 of 5 (20%) in one place, but 6 of 31 (19%), elsewhere (*Stalin's Correspondence*, I, pp. 340, 343); Truman endorsed both of these figures contained in Churchill's messages (*Stalin's Correspondence*, II, p. 224), Truman gives 6 of 31 (19%) elsewhere (*Year of Decisions*, p. 109); Stalin gives 4 of 18 or 20 (22% or 20%) (Sherwood, *Roosevelt and Hopkins*, p. 901); Feis gives 6 of 27 (22%) (*Churchill, Roosevelt, Stalin*, p. 576); Woodward gives 5 of 28, or 3 of 28 (18% or 11%) (*British Foreign Policy*, p. 507*fn.*); Mikolajczyk even gives 50% (*The Pattern of Soviet Domination*, p. 132).

to terms for the reorganization of the government and, in a joint message to Stalin on April 18, they urged that the Warsaw government meet on an equal basis with the group of Western-oriented Polish political leaders.[7] Such a meeting would give the same status to the Warsaw government and to the group of nongovernmental political figures. It would implicitly reject the Russian demand that the Warsaw government be recognized as the "core" of the reorganized government.

The struggle over power in the new Polish government stemmed in great part from the vagueness of the Yalta agreement itself. The Soviet interpretation could be sustained by certain sections of the protocol, the Anglo-American by others. The language was imprecise. The President's Chief of Staff, Admiral Leahy (who had opposed the Soviet view at Yalta), believed the agreed formula gave the Russians what they asked; it could be stretched "all the way from Yalta to Washington without ever technically breaking it." Roosevelt had agreed with this view.[8] In fact, the language was sufficiently favorable to Stalin's view so that, just before his death, Roosevelt felt it necessary to caution Churchill against attempting to "evade" the fact that "we placed, as clearly shown in the agreement, somewhat more emphasis" on the Warsaw government than on the Western-oriented political leaders.[9]

Despite the general thrust of this message, Roosevelt did not accept Stalin's view that the Warsaw government should hold four out of five posts in the new government. Unfortunately he did not have time to give more precision to American policy before his death. In mid-April between Stalin and Churchill there was a great and seemingly unbridgeable difference of views; between Stalin and Roosevelt, a lesser, but ill-defined difference.

When Truman took office he was fully aware of the limitations of the Yalta language. He complained to his Secretary of State that the vague wording did not give him firm footing in his stand against the Russians.[10] Thus, it was in spite of his understanding and in spite of Roosevelt's attempt to restrain Churchill, that Truman accepted the advice of the State Department and sided with Churchill in the dispute over the Polish government.

The importance of the Polish issue lies not so much in the details of the diplomatic dispute, however. The long war with Germany was in its final phase, and "in its larger aspects," as Truman stated at the time, the Polish question had become "a symbol of the future development of our international relations."[11] The matter had an importance which transcended the specific points at issue. It must be understood as a basic question involving primary matters of American policy and—as the President and his advisers believed—the fundamental structure of American-Soviet relations. Behind the firm approach Truman took to the Polish question was a new estimate of the requirements of diplomacy toward the Soviet Union: all of the President's important advisers, save two, felt it necessary to have a symbolic showdown with Russia which would clarify relationships and force the Russians to cooperate with American principles throughout Eastern and Central Europe. Thus, the Polish issue was seen as symbolic, not merely as another in a series of seemingly infinite negotiations. The reasoning which underlay this view can best be understood by reviewing the arguments presented to the President by his ambassador to the Soviet Union, W. Averell Harriman.[12] On April 20, eight days after Roosevelt's death, Harriman explained his belief that the leaders of the Soviet Union were following two policies at the same time. One was a policy of cooperation with the United States and Great Britain, the second a policy of extension of Soviet control over neighboring states by independent action. In Harriman's view, certain elements around Stalin had misinterpreted American generosity—especially in the matter of Lend-Lease aid—and America's desire for cooperation, as indications of "softness." They believed the Soviet government could "do as it pleased" in Eastern Europe without risking challenge from the United States.[13]

Harriman argued that Soviet domination in Eastern Europe was intolerable. He believed that the United States was faced with "a barbarian invasion of Europe." He was convinced that Soviet control over any country meant not only that its influence would be paramount in the country's foreign relations, but also that the Soviet system with its secret police and its extinction of freedom of speech would prevail. Faced with these "unpleasant facts," Harriman believed it was necessary to decide what America's attitude should be. He argued that a reconsideration of Roosevelt's policy was necessary. It was essential to abandon the illusion that the Soviet government was likely to act in accordance with the principles which the rest of the world held in international affairs.[14]

Earlier, Harriman had urged that the United States select "one or two cases" where Soviet actions were intolerable and "make them realize that they cannot continue their present attitude except at great cost to themselves."[15] Now he took up the Polish case with the President. He argued that a firm American line had to be taken in this instance in order to establish all relations with Russia on a new basis. A firm approach was the only way to achieve practical cooperation. Harriman told the President he believed Stalin had discovered that an honest execution of the Yalta decision would mean the end of the Warsaw government, and that he had therefore abandoned the Yalta agreement. Harriman did not feel that two interpretations of the Yalta decision were possible and urged support for his view in the Polish dispute. He admitted that a firm approach might possibly jeopardize the Charter meeting of the United Nations, set for April 25 at San Francisco.[16]

"I am . . . a most earnest advocate of the closest possible understanding with the Soviet Union," Harriman had commented a few days earlier, "so that what I am saying relates only to how best to attain such understanding."[17] Harriman was extremely confident that a strong stand would not precipitate a break with the Soviet Union. It is this confidence which is the most striking feature of the American attitude, for not only Harriman but almost every senior government official shared the same sense of the power relationships. Harriman and others judged that the United States had sufficient power to demand acceptance of its terms for Eastern Europe.

This estimate of the relative strengths derived primarily from a judgment regarding the economic positions of the two countries. Harriman, who had spent much of his time in Moscow dealing with the Lend-Lease program, had often advised of the "enormous" requirements of the invasion-devastated Russian economy. The Russians had already requested a large postwar credit, which Harriman estimated would amount to six billion dollars.[18] He now argued forcefully that the Soviet government would yield to the American position "because they needed our help in their reconstruction program." For this reason, the United States could "stand firm" on important issues "without running serious risks."[19]

Harriman reported that some quarters in Moscow believed it was a matter of life and death to American business to increase exports to Russia. He said that, of course, this was untrue, but that a number of Russian officials nevertheless believed it. A firm approach would dispel this illusion. Once more Harriman repeated that he was not pessimistic about the outcome of a confrontation based upon a firm stand. In fact, not only was there little to fear, but such an approach was the one way to arrive at a new "workable basis with the Russians."[20]

The strategy Harriman offered can be summarized in a few sentences: Soviet actions in Eastern Europe had to be opposed by the United States. Since America had overwhelming economic power, and the Soviet Union enormous reconstruction requirements, the United States was in an extremely favorable bargaining position. A reconsideration of Roosevelt's policy was necessary. A firm stand and an immediate symbolic showdown would make the Russians realize that they could continue their domination of Eastern Europe only at "great cost to themselves." Since American economic aid was so important to the Russians, the showdown was likely to bring favorable results and cooperation with American principles. There was only the slightest chance of failure and a break in relations.

STRONG WORDS ON A STRONG POSITION

THIS FIRST LONG MEETING between the President and Harriman—one of many similar high-level discussions of diplomatic strategy in mid-April 1945—exhibits four basic assumptions of policy. The first was opposition in principle to Soviet desires in Eastern Europe and disgust at Soviet actions in the area. Most key American policy makers feared Soviet domination, the imposition of totalitarian governments, and the breakdown of economic interchange between Eastern and Western Europe.* Disturbed by their judgment of Soviet intentions, most American advisers agreed that the United States would have to take a more active role in demanding that the Soviet Union accept democratic-capitalistic governments in Eastern Europe. A favorable organization of the Polish government was the immediate

---

* See below, pp. 52–54, 77–80.

point at issue, but this was regarded only as a prerequisite to early elections which would establish democratically based authority in the country.[21] In fact, the single most important requirement of policy for each country in Eastern Europe, in the American view, was an early free election.*

A second point to remember is that in early 1945 American policy makers were thinking primarily about Eastern Europe. The fear of subversion in Western Europe was not great—Communist parties were not only cooperating with, but actively supporting, conservative regimes in Italy, France, and Belgium.† Nor were policy makers much worried about the possibility of military aggression in Western Europe; the immediate issue was the organization of Europe behind Red Army lines. Anxiety about this question reveals other assumptions common in policy-making circles in April 1945. One was a belief that America's own interest required active influence in Eastern Europe. What went on in the liberated areas had already been defined as "of urgent importance to the U.S." by the time Truman took office.[22] Though often overlooked, such interest in Eastern Europe was an abandonment in principle of the ideal of isolation.

Finally, another assumption was that the United States had sufficient economic and military power to persuade or force the Soviet Union out of the area, or at the very least, to achieve cooperation with American policies and a substantial reduction in Soviet influence. Since this goal was accepted by almost all major advisers, the most important questions were those of strategy; the focal point of policy was the judgment of the relative bargaining power available to each side in any confrontation over Eastern Europe. It is to this question that Harriman had addressed himself, urging that American economic power was so great that a symbolic diplomatic showdown would force the Russians to yield to the American position. "Russia is really afraid of our power or at least respects it," he told Secretary of War Stimson,

---

* See below, pp. 131–132, 148, 211–216.

† See below, pp. 131–132, for a discussion of this point. It is true, of course, that there was some fear of Communist subversion in Western Europe. Harriman warned of this at times. (*Forrestal Diaries*, pp. 39–40.) There was also a brief flurry of concern in the State Department associated with the "Duclos letter." (See *Conference of Berlin*, I, pp. 267–80.) However the immediate points at issue were all in Eastern Europe and by and large policy makers assumed they could control the situation in Western Europe. (See, for example, Truman, *Year of Decisions*, pp. 236–37.)

and he confidently asserted that although Russia might "try to ride roughshod" over her neighbors, "she really [is] afraid of us."[23]

The Ambassador was not alone in this judgment. His position has been delineated in some detail not only because of the obvious importance of arguments presented by an experienced ambassador to the Soviet Union, but precisely because Harriman's well-articulated view was supported in essentials by almost every important adviser consulted by the President.* In addition to Harriman the chief figures involved were Acting Secretary of State Joseph C. Grew, Secretary of State Edward Stettinius, Chief of Staff to the President Admiral William D. Leahy, Secretary of War Henry L. Stimson, and Secretary of the Navy James V. Forrestal.

In a round of talks during April, Harriman discussed basic strategy with each of the above men. His consultations with the State Department were, of course, a matter of normal procedure. He found that the chief officials in the Department were in agreement that economic aid could and should be used to bring the Russians into line in Eastern Europe.[24] Admiral Leahy was also "canvassed" (to use his term) by Harriman on April 21. The Ambassador found Leahy sympathetic to his basic views and in agreement that economic aid to Russia now should be "limited exclusively to material that would assist in the common war effort."[25] Secretary of War Stimson also agreed with the concept of the strategy; his only objections—important ones—concerned the *timing* and method to be employed. Finally the day before he saw Truman, Harriman spoke at length with Secretary of the Navy Forrestal. He urged "much greater firmness" toward the Russians. Forrestal was enthusiastically in favor of the firm approach and, in fact, had long maintained contact with Harriman in Moscow; his private diaries were filled with Harriman's cables and his own favorable comments.[26]

Of course, Harriman's most important allies were in the State Department. Roosevelt often ignored the advice of the Department during his lifetime.[27] (He had not even bothered to read the briefs prepared for his use before the Yalta Conference.)[28] However, in the last weeks of Roosevelt's life, with his chief aide, Harry L. Hopkins,

---

* See below, pp. 51, 60–61, for disagreement by Stimson and Marshall over timing.

hospitalized and out of government, and the President's own health failing, the Department was increasingly called upon to take responsibility for policy decisions of ever greater importance.*[29] When Roosevelt was replaced by Truman—who admittedly knew very little about foreign affairs—officials in the Department of State were asked to join in making decisions of the highest importance. Joseph C. Grew was a key figure, for the Acting Secretary of State saw Truman regularly to brief him on diplomatic questions.[30] Secretary Stettinius was out of Washington for most of the remainder of his term of office, and Grew was the chief official of the Department.

The Acting Secretary was an extremely conservative State Department representative. Grew not only doubted the possibility of cooperation with the Russians (and was personally opposed to men like Hopkins), but was *already* convinced that "a future war with Soviet Russia is as certain as anything in this world can be certain."[31] It is a sign of the policy-making atmosphere in Washington after Roosevelt's death that Grew, who had formerly rarely reached the ear of the President with his firm advice, was able to write to a friend three weeks after Truman took office: "If I could talk to you about the new President you would hear nothing but the most favorable reaction. . . . He certainly won't stand for any pussyfooting in our foreign relations and policy. . . . You can imagine what a joy it is to deal with a man like that."[32]

When Harriman returned to Washington for consultations after Roosevelt's death, he found that Grew and others near to Truman were far more sympathetic to his strategy for dealing with Russia than Roosevelt and his chief aides had been. Harriman seems to have sensed the opportunity this gave him, for he undertook his round of policy discussions with great energy. Convinced that only a firm line could establish relations on a sound basis, the Ambassador pressed his case with vigor and intelligence. It is not accurate, however, to say that Harriman's efforts changed policy. As early as April 3, Secretary Stimson noted in his diary that "there has been growing quite a strain of irritating feeling between our government and the Russians"; and almost all the men Harriman spoke with in mid-April had come in-

---

* See Appendix I.

dependently to the conclusion that a firm line with Russia was necessary.[33] It is, therefore, more to the point to note that Harriman's
presence and activities in Washington during the first weeks of the
new Truman administration served to focus attention on the Soviet
problem, and to stimulate a new consensus on a precise strategy for
treating with Russia.

Thus, Harriman's fast-moving series of Washington discussions set
the stage for a new policy based upon already well-developed views.
The actual decision was taken just before Molotov's meeting with the
President on April 23. A few hours before receiving the Soviet Foreign Minister, Truman called in his senior advisers for a final review
of strategy. There was a short dispute over the meaning of the Yalta
agreement on Poland. Admiral Leahy held that the language "was
susceptible of two interpretations."[34] Although he opposed the Soviet
position on Poland, he believed the Russians were within the terms of
the Yalta agreement.* However, Secretary Stettinius argued that only
the view urged by the State Department was possible. More important
than the details of the discussion, however, was the general view accepted by the meeting. All of the senior advisers, with two important
exceptions, agreed with the President and Ambassador Harriman on
strategy. As Secretary Forrestal put it, "This difficulty over Poland
could not be treated as an isolated incident."[35] The matter had to be
seen in terms of the larger perspective. It was a symbolic issue. "For
some time the Russians had considered that we would not object if
they took over all of Eastern Europe."[36] Forrestal argued: "We had
better have a showdown with them now rather than later."[37] As Admiral Leahy summarized, "The consensus . . . was that the time had
arrived to take a strong American attitude toward the Soviet
Union . . ."[38]

The agreement that a symbolic showdown would be wise and ex-
pedient was almost unanimous. Only Stimson, who agreed with the
principle of such a showdown, but opposed immediate action, noted
that when Harriman and others "moved for strong words by the President on a strong position," there was only one person besides himself

---

* Leahy's position is curious. It appears
that he judged a showdown to be so important—it "would have a beneficial effect upon
the Soviet outlook"—that he was prepared to
ignore his own belief that the Russians were
advocating a legitimate interpretation of
Yalta. (*I Was There,* p. 352; Diary, April
23, 1945, p. 63.)

prepared to offer a different view.[39] The solid consensus derived not only from the preparatory work done by Harriman and the attitudes already accepted by the senior advisers; equally important, the new President had made it abundantly clear from almost the first days of his administration that he personally believed a "firm" line necessary. Even before his April 20 interview with Harriman, when Truman had heard of a new Soviet-Polish treaty he had decided to "lay it on the line" with Molotov.[40] At the long discussion of strategy with Harriman, the President had interrupted his ambassador before he got to the heart of his proposal to say that he "was not afraid of the Russians" and that he "intended to be firm." He reiterated this view at three separate points during the discussion.[41] Like Harriman and the others, Truman believed a showdown would risk very little. It was his opinion that "the Russians needed us more than we needed them."[42] Truman would make "no concessions" from American principles. He was quite aware of the strength economic aid gave to America's bargaining position, and he believed there was not much danger of a break. He planned to let Molotov know his feelings "in words of one syllable."[43]

Thus, Truman was in accord with his advisers, and, indeed, was enthusiastically in favor of a firm line. In fact, at the April 23 meeting, he did not wait to hear the consensus before offering his own view. Instead, he initiated the discussion by declaring that "our agreements with the Soviet Union so far had been a one-way street and that he could not continue." He believed it was necessary to set relations on a new basis; "it was now or never. . . ."[44]

REMOVING THE LAST OBSTACLE TO THE SHOWDOWN STRATEGY

AT FIRST READING, the showdown strategy appears as an inexplicable reversal of the policy that was being followed by Roosevelt only a few weeks earlier. American economic power was as great when Roosevelt lived as it was in the first weeks of the Truman administration; the leverage this fact gave to diplomacy was no less powerful. To understand fully the changes in American policy in mid-April, it is necessary to go beyond the discussion thus far presented. During the war three major obstacles had blocked those advisers who urged a firm line toward the Russians. The first—Roosevelt's strong belief that cooperation was possible—died with the President. Truman was personally far less sympathetic to the Russians and, indeed, at a time when Roosevelt was begging for support for Lend-Lease aid to the Russians in 1941, then Senator Truman was suggesting: "If we see that Germany is winning the war we ought to help Russia and if Russia is winning we ought to help Germany and that way let them kill as many as possible. . . ."[45]

The second obstacle to a firm line was a fear that American-Soviet cooperation might be destroyed and that a separate peace between Germany and the Soviet Union might be signed.[46] This objection was obviated by the collapse of German power. But there had been a third obstacle to the firm line: the fear that a showdown and tough approach might lose Soviet help in the war against Japan.[47] At the time of Roosevelt's death, this argument had lost none of its force in policy-making circles.

The need for Soviet help in the Japanese war had disturbed no individual more than General John R. Deane, Chief of the United States Military Mission in Moscow. Like Harriman, Deane had long been urging a tougher policy with the Russians;[48] and, like Harriman, he believed that American economic aid could be used to force the Russians to accept American policies, in both the military and the political fields.[49] Both Deane and Harriman had suffered innumerable personal frustrations in dealing with the suspicious Russians.[50] Deane reported to General Marshall at the end of 1944 that he had "become gradually nauseated by Russian food, vodka, and protestations of friendship."[51] Deane emphasized the great value of American aid to the war-torn Soviet Union, and he complained of the lack of cooperation on numerous minor requests. "We are in the position of being at the same time the givers and the suppliants," he wrote. "This is neither dignified nor healthy for U.S. prestige."[52] Deane joined his friend and colleague Harriman in the effort to convince Washington to adopt a much greater degree of firmness. "I feel certain we must be tougher," he wrote to Marshall.[53]

Despite his repeated urging, however, during Roosevelt's lifetime, Deane had met with as little success as Harriman.[54] The Joint Chiefs of Staff to whom he reported were even more concerned than the

President with the need for Soviet help against Japan. They wished to do nothing that might jeopardize future relations.[55] Frustrated by this unanswerable argument against the firm approach, Deane spent the winter months of early 1945 trying to find a way to reduce American dependence on Soviet help in the Far East.[56] In cooperation with General Frank N. Roberts, Deane produced a series of studies which showed that air bases in Siberia, sought by the United States for B-29 bombing operations against Japan, would actually be of little value; they would increase the total bomb tonnage delivered on Japan by only 1.39 per cent over what might be achieved by using available Pacific bases; the Siberian bases would certainly not be worth the logistical effort needed to establish and supply them.[57] Deane was also able to show that sufficient supplies could be delivered to meet all the requirements of Soviet participation in the Japanese war without having to clear a Pacific supply route.[58]

After the death of Roosevelt, Deane returned with Harriman to Washington for consultations. He took along his studies "to help sell my ideas to the Chiefs of Staff."[59] He urged that the United States "withdraw from all cooperative ventures that were not essential to winning the war and . . . stop pushing our proposals on the Russians and force them to come to us."[60] Thus, while Harriman urged Washington political advisers to adopt a tougher approach, Deane worked hard to convince the military authorities that Soviet help was less essential than had previously been thought. The advice from the two Moscow colleagues was completely complementary, and, at the same time that Harriman won approval for his showdown strategy, Deane was able to prove his case. On April 24 the Joint Chiefs canceled plans for B-29 bases in Siberia and put aside plans for clearing a Pacific supply route to the Soviet Union.[61]

It had also been thought that Soviet troops would be needed to hold down the Japanese Kwantung army so as to prevent reinforcement of the main islands during the actual invasion.[62] However, by mid-April the Joint Chiefs found they could accomplish this objective by other means. American control of the Japanese seas was now so well established that the movement of Japanese forces from the China mainland to the home islands could be prevented.[63] To be sure, Soviet participation in the war against Japan would be useful—especially the shock value of a declaration of war by the third major power—but, by

April 24, the Joint Staff planners advised the Joint Chiefs of Staff: "Early Russian entry into the war against Japan is no longer necessary to make the invasion feasible."[64] There was no objection to this report, and it was officially adopted by the Joint Chiefs on May 10.[65]

Deane was "elated" by these decisions: "As far as military collaboration was concerned, they cleared the decks of any dependence we were placing on Russian generosity."[66] At the April 23 meeting with the President, Deane was thus able to second Harriman's firm strategy with few qualms that the formerly unanswerable objection would be raised. Deane felt "we were in a position to be tough and indifferent," and he told Truman that in Moscow he had learned that "if we were afraid of the Russians we would get nowhere."[67] He concluded: "We should be firm."[68] Consequently, the summary consensus of the meeting, written by Admiral Leahy, which began, "The time had come to take a strong American attitude toward the Soviet Union," ended with the judgment, "No particular harm could be done to our war prospects if Russia should slow down or even stop its war effort in Europe and Asia."*[69]

Thus the President and most of his chief advisers were convinced that an immediate symbolic showdown would risk very little. It would make the Russians understand that they could not continue their policies in Eastern Europe "except at great cost to themselves" and would establish cooperation on a "realistic basis." When Truman met with Molotov, a few hours after the discussion with his advisers, he "went straight to the point."[70] The President indicated that the Soviet Union could not expect American economic assistance unless the Polish discussions continued on the basis of the American proposals. Truman pointedly remarked that the issue had become a matter of public concern and that it would not be possible to get congressional approval

---

* At the April 23, 1945, meeting two further arguments supplemented Deane's major point. Harriman noted that a year had passed since the Russians had agreed to start collaboration in the Far East, but none of the agreements had been carried out. Hence, the United States could not count on a Soviet commitment to enter the war. Deane also argued that "regardless of what happened" the Russians would enter the Pacific war as soon as they could because they had interests in the Far East and could not risk a letdown by their war-weary population. (Truman, *Year of Decisions*, p. 79.) Though these arguments conflicted in their estimate of Soviet intentions, they pointed to the same conclusion: a firm stand would not have major implications for the war against Japan. Despite the argument Harriman made at the April 23 meeting, his own views seem to have been more consistently in line with those of Deane. On other occasions he "was satisfied [the Russians] were determined to come in" the Japanese war because of their requirements in the Far East. (Forrestal, *Diaries*, p. 55; Leahy Diary, April 19, 1945, p. 82.)

for economic-assistance measures without public support. The Soviet government would do well to "keep these factors in mind" when considering the American proposals on Poland.[71]

Although he understood that the Yalta agreement was vague, Truman told Molotov that the American interpretation was the only one possible.[72] "All we were asking was that the Soviet Government carry out the Crimea decision," he declared. Molotov said that the Soviet government believed the remaining difficulties could easily be overcome, and he began to discuss the general problem of Allied cooperation. Truman responded "sharply" that an agreement had been reached on Poland and that "there was only one thing to do, and that was for Marshal Stalin to carry out that agreement."[73]

Molotov said that Stalin had offered his view of the agreement in previous messages, and he added that he personally could not understand why, if the three governments could reach an agreement on the composition of the Yugoslav government, the same formula could not be applied in the case of Poland.[74]

Once more Truman replied "sharply" that "an agreement had been reached. . . . It was only required to be carried out by the Soviet Government." Molotov again began to explain that he could not accept the view that the Yalta agreement had been broken. Again Truman declared that the United States asked only that the Soviet Union carry out its agreements. Molotov should clearly understand that American cooperation could be had only on this basis, not "on the basis of a one-way street."

"I have never been talked to like that in my life," Molotov declared.

"Carry out your agreements and you won't get talked to like that," Truman responded.[75]

AMERICA'S ECONOMIC LEVERAGE

TRUMAN'S DECISION to force the Polish issue to a showdown "was more than pleasing" to his Chief of Staff. Admiral Leahy believed that the blunt language "would have a beneficial effect on the Soviet outlook."[76] Along with the President and his other senior advisers, Leahy judged that "the Russians had always known that we had the power," and they should "know after this conversation that we had the determination. . . ."[77] The matter was one of basic principle; Leahy concluded that "the President's strong American stand at this meeting . . . leaves to the Soviet only two courses of action: either to approach more closely to our expressed policy to Poland, or to drop out of the Association of Nations."[78]

Despite Leahy's confident estimate of the force of the showdown, the Soviet Union did not choose either alternative. Within twenty-four hours parallel messages reached Truman and Churchill from Moscow. Stalin commented that "one cannot but recognize as unusual a situation in which two governments—those of the United States and Great Britain—reach agreement beforehand on Poland, a country in which the U.S.S.R. is interested first of all and most of all, and place its representatives in an intolerable position, trying to dictate to it." The Soviet Premier emphasized the importance of Poland to Soviet security: "You evidently do not agree that the Soviet Union is entitled to seek in Poland a government that would be friendly to it. . . . This is rendered imperative . . . by the Soviet people's blood freely shed on the fields of Poland. . . ." Stalin remarked that by "turning down the Yugoslav example as a model for Poland, you confirm that the [Warsaw] Provisional Government cannot be regarded as a basis for, and the core of, a future Government . . ." This meant there could be no progress. Stalin concluded that there was "only one way out of the present situation and that is to accept the Yugoslav precedent."[79]

Thus, the first response to the showdown strategy did not justify the hopes of the President and his advisers. Nevertheless, on the same day that Stalin's reply came in, Secretary of State Stettinius made another effort to make Molotov understand the stakes involved. In a discussion held at San Francisco, Stettinius once more affirmed the American position and emphasized that future economic aid would depend entirely upon the mood and conscience of the American people. He advised Molotov that he would have his last opportunity to prove that Russia deserved economic assistance.[80] Stettinius' efforts met with no success and on April 29 he reported to Truman that the Polish issue had reached an impasse.[81]

The crisis over Poland deepened when in the first week of May information reached Washington that the Warsaw government had already begun to administer territory taken from Germany on the Polish western border.[82] Though this had been accepted in principle at Yalta, no final settlement had been made; and the action indicated Russian determination to support the Warsaw government's claim to legitimacy and its right to a predominant role in a reorganized government.[83] Molotov also renewed an earlier request that the Warsaw government be represented at San Francisco,[84] and he confirmed reports that sixteen Polish underground leaders—some of them political figures—had been arrested on charges of obstructing the Red Army.[85] Although the American and British governments believed the extremely anti-Russian Poles could well have given cause for the Soviet charges, there was little information available, and the arrests seemed aimed at predetermining Polish political issues.[86] Much disturbed by the Soviet attitude, on May 5 the American and British governments jointly announced they would not continue discussions of the Polish issue until a full explanation of the arrests had been given.[87]

Thus the firm line of policy was maintained, as was the parallel position of the United States and Britain. The real issue, of course, still centered on the "Yugoslav precedent," and Truman cabled Stalin on May 4 to say that he supported a long message of Churchill's which had simultaneously rejected the Yugoslav precedent and urged a number of points of procedure.[88] The President said there could be no question of the Warsaw government coming to San Francisco and told Stalin that the American viewpoint had not changed.[89] However, again the President was unsuccessful. On May 7, the State Department reported the latest Russian response on the Polish question. "It was a turndown in every respect," Acting Secretary Grew told Admiral Leahy, "both as to setting up the government and also with regard to the sixteen Polish leaders . . ."[90]

It now was obvious that the showdown strategy had failed. Faced with a setback, Truman's advisers decided it was necessary to further emphasize and dramatize American determination. As early as April 11, Ambassador Harriman and the Department of State were in agreement that the United States "should retain current control of . . . credits [to the Russians] in order to be in a position to protect American vital interests in the formulative period immediately following the war."[91] Lend-Lease aid during the war had been provided according to Soviet requests and American resources, with very little question raised about supporting evidence for Soviet requirements.[92] Harriman believed that Lend-Lease shipments should now be limited exclusively to materials that could be directly related to the common war

35

effort.[93] General Deane had urged the same policy upon the Joint Chiefs of Staff.[94] Any Soviet request which might extend beyond the war period could then be processed in connection with arrangements for a large-scale Soviet credit which had been discussed at Yalta and which still figured in the administration's strategy.[95] Indeed, a limitation on Lend-Lease followed logically from the view that American diplomacy could gain if the Soviet Union were more dependent upon economic assistance. This would increase America's economic leverage and would "make the Soviet authorities come to us," as Deane had phrased it.[96]

Harriman had also pressed this view during his April round of consultations. By early May, Secretaries Stimson and Forrestal, Acting Secretary Grew, Admiral Leahy, and the Joint Chiefs of Staff had endorsed the strategy.[97] On May 8, the day of the German surrender and a day after the report of Stalin's rejection of the President's stand on the Polish issue, Acting Secretary Grew decided to move from consensus to action. Together with Assistant Secretary of State William L. Clayton and Lend-Lease Administrator Leo T. Crowley, he brought the President a draft order authorizing an immediate cutback of Lend-Lease shipments now that the war in Europe was over.[98] Truman agreed with the strategy and signed the order. Almost immediately ships on the high seas bound for the Soviet Union were ordered to turn back, instructions were given to discontinue the loading of ships in port, and goods already aboard ships in American harbors were unloaded.[99] The harshness of this action stirred considerable public protest, and on May 11 the President substituted a slightly modified instruction which allowed ships already at sea to continue and permitted the completion of loading operations already under way.[100] Despite this modification, however, Truman did not change the substance of the order.*

---

* Truman later disclaimed responsibility for the abrupt "*manner* in which the [cutback] order was executed," saying that he had not read the paper he signed. This seems dubious, since there was a great effort by at least four advisers to make sure the President understood what he was doing. But even if one accepts the President's report, the fact remains that Truman immediately substituted a slightly modified order which accomplished substantially the same purpose. The President, of course, has never disclaimed responsibility for this action. As to the harsh execution of the first order, even Harriman was taken aback by the thoroughness with which lower officials acted upon orders from above. (*Year of Decisions*, p. 228; Daniels, *The Man of Independence*, p. 271; Feis, *Between War and Peace*, p. 27*fn*.) On another occasion, Truman offered what, as will be shown, is probably the most accurate recollection; namely that the timing, but not the substance of the action, was a "mistake." (*New York Times*, Feb. 15, 1950.) See below, pp. 223–224.

The abrupt Lend-Lease cutback put great pressure on the Russians, especially as no warning had been given for an action which was bound to disrupt the careful plans of a scarcity wartime economy.[101] As is evident, the timing of the cutback—in the midst of the deadlock after the initial Polish showdown—was certain to be interpreted as economic pressure aimed at forcing the Russians to yield in the diplomatic confrontation. The full story of the Lend-Lease cutback has not been made public. Hitherto it has not been possible to demonstrate conclusively that the Lend-Lease cutback was designed primarily to put pressure on the Russians. However, fresh evidence on this matter indicates that the advisers who urged the action did so precisely for this reason. Moreover they understood their actions would be interpreted as pressure. That the President was fully informed of the strategy and party to it is also shown by reports of discussions among his top advisers.

Truman received complementary advice on the matter from two distinct sources. The State Department, in consultation with Harriman, had long been agreed upon the strategic value of close controls over aid to the Soviet Union.[102] Immediately before the final order was given, however, Lend-Lease Administrator Crowley telephoned Acting Secretary Grew to confirm his understanding of, and agreement with, the action. He particularly wanted the President to understand the implications of the cutback, and asked to accompany Grew when the order was explained to Truman; he wanted "to be sure the President thoroughly understands the situation and that he will back us up and will keep everyone else out of it." Crowley foresaw that "we would be having difficulty with the Russians, and he did not want them to be running all over town looking for help."[103]

At the same time that Crowley and Grew were preparing to explain the Lend-Lease order to the President, Secretary Stimson was at the White House. Stimson too wanted to be certain that the President fully understood the Lend-Lease problem; he had asked for an interview for the single purpose of advising "the necessity of a more realistic policy in regard to the Russians and the use of Lend-Lease towards them." Stimson thought the best approach would be to eliminate the Lend-Lease protocol. He found that the President agreed and, indeed, was "vigorously enthusiastic" in support of his viewpoint. Truman said it was "right down his alley." After his interview Stimson telephoned Grew to report on his conversation. The Acting Secretary was "very much pleased" at the President's attitude.[104] Two days later Stimson discussed strategy with Assistant Secretary of War John J. McCloy, explaining that the Russians had "rather taken [the lead] away from us because we have talked too much and been too lavish with our beneficencies." However, the Secretary of War was confident that America's power would bring the Russians into line: "They can't get along without our help and industries. . . ."[105]

After Truman endorsed the memorandum, Ambassador Harriman telephoned Grew to report that "the Lend-Lease thing was settled." Like Crowley, Harriman had few doubts about the effect of the order. He predicted that "we would be getting a good 'tough slash-back' from the Russians but that we have to face it."[106] For this reason, Crowley was asked to work out a statement to give to the press. On May 12, Crowley telephoned Grew to ask his opinion of a draft which read:

> In view of the end of hostilities in Europe a careful re-examination is being made of Lend-Lease programs with a view to allocating materials to theaters where they are most needed.

Grew approved the draft. He noted that "the statement did not seem to bring the Russians in directly," and commented approvingly: "That was good. . . ." Grew wanted to be sure the Russians were not named, "since this whole thing is full of dynamite. . . ." Crowley suggested that "it would be a good idea when the Russians came to us just to say to them that we were going to reconsider their request because we have to use some of these materials in other theaters." He remarked that "what had disturbed the White House apparently was that War Shipping felt that when the men quit loading ships for Russia, they would immediately start to talk and they felt that a statement should be made." Crowley explained that his draft "was as little as we could say. . . ."[107]

As these conversations show, there can be no doubt that the abrupt Lend-Lease cutoff was designed primarily with the Russians in mind. To be sure, the action was in accord with the terms of the law requiring an end to the program in Europe after Germany's defeat.[108] But this was not an overriding consideration, for the law allowed Lend-Lease aid for those assisting in the war against Japan and admitted of a wide range of interpretations for use in Europe even after the German surrender. The cutoff did not, in fact, eliminate the flow of goods specifically related to Soviet participation in the war against Japan, although there was now a more careful screening of requests.* The law also allowed a generous interpretation which provided supplies to British forces in Europe after the German surrender on the grounds that these forces freed other resources for Japan. A parallel interpretation, though equally justifiable under the law, was not applied to Soviet forces in Europe or elsewhere.[109] Thus, contrary to a commonly held opinion, the law did not require an immediate halt of Lend-Lease shipments to the Soviet Union after the defeat of Germany. As has been indicated, the primary motivation for the timing of the Lend-Lease cutback is to be found in the prevailing concepts which guided the showdown strategy.†

Despite the increased economic pressure which the Lend-Lease cutback created, and despite Stettinius' warning to Molotov, the Russians did not yield in the diplomatic confrontation. A brief message from Stalin on May 10 responded to Truman's last communication and noted that the American note still refused to accept the Warsaw government as the "basis" for the reorganized Polish government. The Soviet Premier concluded: "I am obliged to say that this attitude rules out an agreed decision on the Polish question."[110]

Once again the showdown strategy had failed to bring the promised results. Again there was a direct challenge to the theory that economic pressure would bring the Russians into line with American views. Most American policy makers responded to the challenge, not by reconsidering the assumptions of the strategy, but by following the pattern they had established after the initial setback: They decided that the showdown had to be continued and that the pressure on the Russians had to be increased. Truman's advisers converged upon him with the suggestion that the American position be reaffirmed and emphasized at the highest level, in a face-to-face confrontation with Stalin. On May 14 Admiral Leahy advised the President that an early meeting with Churchill and Stalin was an absolute necessity—"The

---

* After the order, Soviet requests were reduced by 50 per cent in many categories, the first time such screening had been applied since the initiation of the Lend-Lease program. (Feis, *Between War and Peace*, pp. 329–33; U.S. Defense Dept., "Entry of the Soviet Union into the War Against Japan," p. 75.)

† Feis attempts to argue that the provisions of the law were the main reason for this action (*Churchill, Roosevelt, Stalin*, p. 647). For further information on how little Truman felt himself restricted by the law, however, see *Conference of Berlin*, I, pp. 805–20 (especially p. 819), and II, pp. 341, 1184–85.

Polish issue had become a symbol of the deterioration of our relations with the Russians."[111] The next day Acting Secretary of State Grew and Ambassador Harriman emphasized the same point. Grew told Truman that "we all felt in the Department of State that it was of the utmost importance that the Big Three meeting should take place as soon as possible." Harriman then explained that Russia was "the number one problem affecting the future of the world and the fact was that at the present moment we were getting farther and farther apart. . . ." Harriman said that he felt the "establishment of a basis for future relations with Russia and the settlement of those immediate issues could only be done at a tripartite meeting, that the longer the meeting was delayed the worse the situation would get, and that while he assumed . . . that we were not prepared to use our troops in Europe for political bargaining, nevertheless, if the meeting could take place before we were in a large measure out of Europe he felt the atmosphere of the meeting would be more favorable and the chances of success increased. . . ."[112]

Similar views prevailed in London. Eden reported the breakdown of the Polish negotiations to Churchill and urged that the Soviet Union now had to be "brought up sharply against realities."[113] Churchill agreed, responding that the relationship with the Russians could now "only be founded upon their recognition of Anglo-American strength."[114] The Prime Minister believed that "the decisive, practical points of strategy" involved *above all* that a settlement must be reached on all major issues . . . *before the armies of democracy melted . . .*"[115] On May 6 he proposed an immediate heads-of-government meeting to the President. On May 11 and May 12 he sent further pleas to Truman: "Surely it is vital now to come to an understanding with Russia . . . before we weaken our armies mortally . . ."[116] To Eden, he confidentially advised: "It is to this early and speedy show-down and settlement with Russia that we must now turn our hopes."[117] On May 14 Eden told Truman that "no solution of the [Polish] problem could be expected until there could be a meeting between the President, the Prime Minister and Stalin."[118]

The Strategy of a Delayed Showdown

We shall probably hold more cards in our hands later than now.

—SECRETARY OF WAR
HENRY L. STIMSON
May 16, 1945

ALTHOUGH HIS DECISION to force a showdown with Russia had been taken with regard to the specific issue of Poland, Truman's resolve was not limited solely to this dispute. In fact, Poland had been chosen as a *symbolic* issue; the implications of the showdown were expected to affect the whole structure of Soviet-American relations.* It is not surprising, therefore, that in the last week of April Truman also decided to take a strong line on diplomatic problems in Central Europe. Here, however, it was not American economic aid which was central to the tough strategy, but the advantageous position of American troops in Germany.

Soviet-American disputes in Central Europe arose out of the special circumstances of German collapse. The Allies had hoped to avoid the bitter territorial struggle that had occurred in the last days of the First World War and by the late autumn of 1944 had prudently negotiated an agreement delineating zones of occupation to be established in Germany after the fighting.[1] However, the military situation had changed considerably after the agreements were signed. Apparently realizing the inevitable outcome of the war, Hitler reduced resistance

---

* See above, pp. 21–22.

to the Anglo-American advance in the west while he concentrated forces against the Russians in the east. He seemed to hope at least to give over more of Germany to troops whose homes had not been devastated by the Nazi invasion, and at most to sow suspicion and encourage a struggle for the control of German territory.[2]

As a consequence, the western armies found themselves deep within the Soviet zone of Germany, much farther to the east than had originally been expected. As a matter of course, early in April Eisenhower proposed a simple arrangement which would have allowed military commanders in Germany to arrange withdrawals to the agreed zones.[3] Eisenhower's suggestion was immediately opposed by Churchill. On April 5, the Prime Minister cabled Roosevelt urging a "stand fast" order. He noted that final agreement on occupation zones for Austria had not yet been negotiated and, since Russia would very likely occupy almost the whole of the country, he thought it might "be prudent for us to hold as much as possible in the north."[4] At the same time, Churchill directed General Ismay to oppose any major troop movements and to refer any suggested withdrawal to the President and himself.[5]

Churchill's strategy was not very complicated. Despite the existing protocol, which specifically required troop withdrawals after German capitulation, he believed it might be possible to obtain additional concessions from the Russians if he could maintain the extended troop positions. Realizing the relative weakness of the British bargaining position, he counted heavily on the value of the troop withdrawals in the next round of negotiations.[6] Although in communication with Roosevelt he linked the withdrawal only to the relatively minor unsettled Austrian zonal questions,* privately he informed Ismay that his purpose was far more general—before the armies were withdrawn, "political issues operative at that time should be discussed between the heads of Governments, and in particular . . . the situation should be viewed as a whole and in regard to the relations between the Soviet, American and British Governments."[7]

Churchill's approach to Roosevelt was made well in advance of the

---

* For more information on this dispute, see
Feis, *Between War and Peace*, pp. 65–69,
149–51.

war's end, before the time when large-scale troop movements would have to be made. In a parallel action, the British Chiefs of Staff proposed a temporary "stand fast" order. This was accepted by the Joint Chiefs of Staff, so that while the matter was being discussed between London and Washington, Eisenhower was directed to maintain the troop positions.[8] The temporary directive was issued on the day Roosevelt died (April 12), and Churchill moved immediately to exploit his advantage. On April 14 he reaffirmed the substance of his earlier instruction to Ismay,[9] and on April 18 he took the matter up with Roosevelt's successor. To achieve his end, the Prime Minister was now prepared to utilize whatever argument he thought most persuasive. Undoubtedly aware of American concern over the developing problems of scarcity in Central Europe, he abandoned the attempt to link the withdrawal to the Austrian zonal dispute and switched the basis of his attack.* "The Russian occupational zone has the smallest proportion of people and grows by far the largest proportion of food . . ." he cabled Truman. "Before we move from the tactical positions we have at present achieved," the Russians should be forced to agree that "the feeding of the German population must be treated as a whole and that the available supplies must be divided *pro rata* between the occupational zones."[10]

When this suggestion reached Washington, Truman referred the matter to the Joint Chiefs of Staff for advice.[11] He found them unwilling to use the troop positions for political purposes.[12] From London, Ambassador John G. Winant advised that an attempt to bargain the troop positions for better food distribution might jeopardize cooperative-control arrangements for Germany.[13] Unwilling to alter the direction of Roosevelt's policy less than a week after his death, the new President deferred to his advisers (as he tended to do on decisions involving military matters) and on April 21 responded to Churchill: "The fact that the Russian zone contained the greater portion of German food-producing areas . . . was well known" before agreement was reached on the zones. Acceptance of the agreement "was in no way made contingent upon the conclusion of satisfactory arrangements for an equitable distribution of German food resources." Truman suggested that Eisenhower be given discretion to make troop

---

* See below, pp. 52–54, 77–80.

adjustments, but that where time permitted, he should refer major movements to the Combined Chiefs of Staff.*

While Truman and Churchill debated a course of action, a further temporary directive was issued which continued to withhold discretion to make troop withdrawals.[14] With the movements still held up, Churchill returned to the struggle. Ignoring Truman's argument that food could not be bargained for, the Prime Minister once more switched his ground, reverted to the issue raised earlier with Roosevelt, and continued to urge his main point upon the President. On April 24 he noted that "all questions of our spheres in Vienna or arrangements for triple occupation of Berlin remain unsettled." He begged that the troops be held in place until the issues had been satisfactorily resolved.[15]

At about the time this message went out, Eisenhower wrote Marshall: "I do not quite understand why the Prime Minister has been so determined to intermingle political and military considerations in attempting to establish a procedure for the conduct of our own and Russian troops when a meeting takes place. My original recommendation . . . was a simple one. . . . One of my concerns was the possibility that the Russians might arrive in the Danish peninsula before we could fight our way across the Elbe and I wanted a formula that would take them out of that region at my request. . . . I really do not anticipate that the Russians will be arbitrary in demanding an instant withdrawal. . . ."[16]

THE FIRM APPROACH IN CENTRAL EUROPE

THE MESSAGES FROM Churchill and Eisenhower reached Washington shortly after Truman's April 23 confrontation with Molotov. Although Poland was the question the President discussed with the Soviet Foreign Minister on that date, the decision to force a showdown with Russia involved a fundamental change of course. Despite his earlier willingness to follow the advice of the Joint Chiefs, Truman

---

* This quotation is Leahy's paraphrase of Truman's message. (*I Was There*, p. 350.) There is disagreement on the date of this message. Leahy, Mosely, Feis, and Wilmot say April 21, 1945. (*I Was There*, p. 349; "The Occupation of Germany," p. 602; *Churchill, Roosevelt, Stalin*, p. 609; *The Struggle for Europe*, p. 795.) Churchill indicates it was between April 21 and April 24, 1945. (*Triumph and Tragedy*, p. 516.) Truman says April 23. (*Year of Decisions*, p. 214.)

now committed himself to the tough approach; he decided to maintain the American troop positions in the Soviet zone of Germany. Reversing himself completely, Truman rejected Eisenhower's view and accepted Churchill's. In a cable to the Prime Minister on April 26, he pointed out that even under the existing directives the Russians could not require a troop withdrawal without the approval of the heads of government.[17] The President suggested a joint message to Stalin which linked the troop withdrawals to a satisfactory solution of the remaining Austrian issues. Delighted at Truman's agreement with his firm strategy, Churchill approved the draft and parallel messages went American stand against Russia.†

Thus, despite the fact that he recognized "the Russians were in a strong position," Truman followed the showdown on Poland with a firm approach to the problem of cooperation in Central Europe.[18] He wanted acceptance of his proposals for the administration of Austria and believed that by refusing to fulfill the previous understanding on Germany he could force Stalin's acquiescence. His joint action with Churchill once more stressed his willingness to present a united Anglo-American stand against Russia.*

Again, various military authorities believed this handling of the troop issue would bring negative results. The Joint Chiefs of Staff had already raised their objections. In Britain, General Ismay, the chief of the Imperial General Staff, felt that "considering that we have already agreed with the Russians as to the Zones of Occupation in Germany, I consider Winston is fundamentally wrong in using this as a bargaining

---

* Truman obscures this point in his memoirs so as to make it appear that he refused to follow Churchill's approach. He does not quote the April 27, 1945, message, which quite clearly shows his change of position. Thus three extraneous issues were injected into the dispute: Truman made it clear that the troops would not be withdrawn from the Soviet zone of Germany until the Russians yielded on the delineation of the Austrian zones of occupation, the apportionment of zones and facilities in Vienna, and the establishment of a satisfactory Allied Control Council for Austria. In fact, the Churchill-Truman tactic utilized a heavy hammer to attempt to drive a small nail, for on none of these questions were there major differences. For this reason one wonders whether Truman, like Churchill, might not have been trying to use the Austrian issues as an excuse to

keep the troops in place until *all* political issues had been resolved with the Russians. (For Truman's recollection of what happened, see *Year of Decisions*, pp. 62, 214–16, 303–4; but also see Churchill, *Triumph and Tragedy*, p. 517; *Stalin's Correspondence*, I, pp. 337–38; II, p. 224; Ehrman, *Grand Strategy*, pp. 154–55. For more information on the disputed points, see Feis, *Churchill, Roosevelt, Stalin*, p. 622; *Between War and Peace*, p. 66.)

† This is another place where those who stress Truman's willingness to follow Roosevelt's policies miss the change in strategy after April 23, 1945. It is simply an error to say, as Feis does, that "Truman carefully carried out all the agreements which Roosevelt had entered." (*Churchill, Roosevelt, Stalin*, p. 600; see also p. 636, and Woodward, *British Foreign Policy*, p. 518*fn*.)

counter."[19] In Germany, Eisenhower believed it "indefensible" to use the troops to gain advantage on the Austrian issues. He was certain that "to start off our first direct association with Russia on the basis of refusing to carry out an arrangement in which the good faith of our government was involved would wreck the whole cooperative attempt at its very beginning."[20]

It appears that these judgments were correct, for immediately difficulties arose in Austria, where Soviet troops held a position almost as advantageous as the Anglo-American position in Germany. The Russians had already shown awareness of their own bargaining strength; on the day after Truman's showdown with Molotov, Andrey Y. Vyshinsky had informed American and British representatives that Karl Renner, a former Socialist chancellor of the Austrian Republic, had presented a plan for creating a provisional government. Vyshinsky had indicated that the Soviet government would favor such a development.[21] Shortly after linking the troop question to the Austrian issues, the British and American governments had responded that they wished to be consulted on the establishment of a new government. They had urged the Soviet Union to defer recognition of Renner. But the Russians showed little interest in this proposal, Renner proclaimed the establishment of a provisional government, and on April 29 Radio Moscow announced that the Soviet commander in Austria had recognized the new government.*[22]

The Russian armies were clearly in a position to determine the course of events in Austria, and this initial response to Truman's firm line was hardly encouraging. Although Renner's government appeared to represent all Austrian political elements, its establishment without Western consultation sidestepped the question of Allied administration and cooperative control of the country.[23] Truman had the American embassy file a protest emphasizing the need for joint responsibility: "We assume that it remains the intention of the Soviet Government that supreme authority in Austria will be exercised by the four powers acting jointly on a basis of equality . . . until the establishment of an Austrian government recognized by the four powers."[24]

---

* This indicated a practical working arrangement with the military. Moscow did not grant diplomatic recognition at this time. (*Conference of Berlin*, I, p. 334.)

Truman did not accompany this message with a suggestion that the Western troops might withdraw to the agreed zones so that the unresolved Austrian issues could be considered independently. Instead, he continued to hold to the American demand on the points at issue. Stalin's response was equally firm. Now he refused to allow Western representatives to enter Vienna until a satisfactory solution of the zonal questions had been achieved. He also indicated that Allied control of Austria would not be established until the Anglo-American tactic was abandoned.*[25]

Thus, by the first week of May there were grave doubts that the American plan for cooperative control of Austria would be fulfilled. Despite renewed protests from London and Washington, a stalemate had been reached and it appeared that Stalin would not yield to a firm approach in Central Europe any more than he was yielding to a similar approach regarding Poland.[26] Churchill's reaction was typical; he urged that the Anglo-American troops be held in position *even if* the Western position were accepted on the Austrian problems. Moreover, he was certain that an immediate confrontation with Stalin was essential. On May 4 the Prime Minister wrote to Eden: "The Allies ought not to retreat from their present positions to the occupational line until we are satisfied about Poland, and also about the temporary character of Russian occupation of Germany, and the conditions to be established in the Russianized or Russian-controlled countries in the Danube valley, particularly Austria and Czechoslovakia, and the Balkans."[27] Churchill followed this statement of intent with a series of messages to Truman. The Polish and Central European stalemates were now bound up together in an over-all crisis of confidence between the powers. Thus, in the same May 6 message in which he demanded an immediate meeting with Stalin, Churchill urged: "We should hold firmly to the existing position obtained or being obtained by our armies."[28]

Truman responded that he would "stand firmly on our present announced attitude toward all the questions at issue."[29] Although this reaffirmed the President's earlier message linking the troop withdrawal

---

* Apparently Stalin was more disturbed by the tactic of linking the troop withdrawal to the political issues than he was with the American position on the points in dispute. As will be seen, after the troops were withdrawn, he quite readily agreed to a satisfactory solution of all of the political problems. See below, pp. 83–84.

to the Austrian question, Churchill tried to get a commitment to his more general view that the troops be held in position until *all* issues were settled in a meeting with Stalin. On May 11, he cabled: "I earnestly hope that the American front will not recede."[30] On May 12 he appealed to the President again, reiterating the argument that it was essential to come to an understanding with Russia "before we . . . retire to the zones of occupation."[31] Truman's reply on May 14 neither refused nor accepted the general "stand still" order *and the President continued to maintain troops in position on the previous basis.**

This situation immediately had repercussions throughout the heart of Europe. In fact, Truman had tied his own hands. By making withdrawal from the Soviet zone in Germany dependent upon the resolution of the Austrian issues, he lost all initiative; the Russians rejected his stand on the points in dispute, and the troops held their positions. With the West refusing to fulfill the previous agreements for withdrawal, Stalin refused to establish joint control arrangements. It seemed that Truman's own strategy also prevented cooperative control of Germany.

Additional complications now arose. At Churchill's insistence, at the last minute a brief military-surrender document had been substituted for the longer surrender instrument which had previously been drawn up by the powers.† Consequently, no formal basis for establishing the Allied Control Council existed, nor were the principles of Allied administration embodied in the surrender agreement as had originally been planned.[32] On May 16 Eisenhower reported that Churchill refused to establish joint control procedures for Germany because this would offer an occasion for the Russians to demand that the troops be withdrawn to the agreed zones.[33] Eisenhower said he

---

* This has been emphasized because various accounts make it appear that because he refused a general "stand still" order Truman wished to withdraw American troops to their zones. In fact, there was no substantive change in the situation. (See Churchill, *Triumph and Tragedy*, p. 557; Feis, *Churchill, Roosevelt, Stalin*, p. 637; Truman, *Year of Decisions*, p. 248; *Conference of Berlin*, I, p. 11.)

† The reason for this substitution has never been adequately explained. Churchill's overriding interest at this time was to forestall troop withdrawals from the Soviet zone. It is probable that Churchill objected to the long surrender document because—as he explained to Eisenhower when the terms of the document had been written in declaration form— he feared the provisions establishing joint control would give Stalin a basis for demanding that the Anglo-American troops be removed to the agreed zones. (See Feis, *Between War and Peace*, pp. 76–77; Mosely, "Dismemberment of Germany," p. 497; Smith, *My Three Years in Moscow*, p. 20.)

was finding it difficult to carry out his orders without agreement on joint control. A week later he told Washington his mission could not be carried out unless the terms of surrender were made public and the Allied Control Council was proclaimed.[34]

Thus, by mid-May, Truman was faced with a direct challenge to the plan for cooperative control of Central Europe. There were no signs that Allied Control Councils would be established in either Austria or Germany. The President was forced to consider his future course of action.

SECRETARY STIMSON AND THE IMMEDIATE SHOWDOWN

To THOSE ADVISERS who had urged a firm line on all issues in dispute between Russia and the United States, there seemed no way out of the mid-May stalemate except an immediate face-to-face meeting with Stalin. Truman had now been urged to hold such a confrontation by Churchill and almost every important American adviser concerned with policy making. However, official opinion was not unanimous on the point. One influential member of the Cabinet not only opposed an early meeting but also objected on more fundamental grounds to the line of action being taken regarding Poland and Central Europe.

Almost alone among the presidential advisers at the April 23 discussion (at which a decision had been made to take a firm stand with Molotov), Secretary of War Stimson had argued against an immediate showdown over the Polish issue. Although Stimson believed in a "more realistic policy" utilizing Lend-Lease aid "toward" the Russians, he had not agreed with the group decision. He objected to the timing, the method, and the issue chosen for the symbolic confrontation. One reason for this was Stimson's belief that the Russians were not likely to yield on the specific point at issue. More important, however, was his conviction that much could be gained by delaying all diplomatic disputes.

At the April 23 meeting Stimson had presented a series of arguments to convince the President that a showdown over Poland had to be avoided. He thought it important "to find out what the Russians were driving at" in their interpretation of the Yalta agreement. He

49

pointed out that "in the big military matters" the Soviet government had kept its word, and the military authorities of the United States had come to count on it. "In fact, they had often done better than they had promised." On that account, he believed it was important to find out what motive they had in connection with these border countries and what their ideas of independence and democracy were in the areas they regarded as vital to the Soviet Union.[35]

Stimson was a leading American conservative. He had established a brilliant record as a Wall Street lawyer, had served as Secretary of War under President William Howard Taft, had acted as Secretary of State under President Herbert Hoover, and though an eminent Republican, had agreed to join President Franklin Roosevelt's war Cabinet.[36] His caution derived from no sympathy for the Soviet system. Rather, he prided himself on a realistic approach to world affairs, and he had long ago acknowledged the Soviet "claim that, in the light of her bitter experience with Germany, her own self-defense . . . will depend on relations with buffer countries like Poland, Bulgaria, and Rumania." Stimson understood that these relations would be "quite different from complete independence on the part of those countries,"[37] but he had come to the conclusion that facts had to be faced.

"The Russians perhaps were being more realistic than we were in regard to their own security," he told Truman at the April 23 meeting.[38] "We had to remember that the Russian conception of freedom, democracy, and independent voting was quite different from ours or the British."[39] When he returned from the discussion, Stimson dictated a caustic diary entry attacking an overly legalistic interpretation of the Yalta agreement: "Although at Yalta [Russia] apparently agreed to a free and independent ballot for the ultimate choice of the representatives of Poland, yet I know very well . . . that there are no nations in the world except the U.S. and U.K. which have a real idea of what an independent free ballot is."[40]

The essence of Stimson's view was a conservative belief that the postwar power structure in Europe had to be acknowledged so that a *modus vivendi* could be established with Russia. Although he wished to preserve American economic interests in Eastern Europe, he took for granted Soviet special interests in the border countries just as he accepted American special interests in Latin America—the two areas were "our respective orbits."[41] If the parallel Soviet interest in Eastern Europe were understood, Stimson believed "our position in the western hemisphere and Russia's in the eastern hemisphere could be adjusted without too much friction."[42] He believed this would require a fair acceptance of Soviet claims. He was critical of some policy makers who were "anxious to hang on to exaggerated views of the Monroe Doctrine and at the same time butt into every question that comes up in Central Europe."[43]

Stimson did not dwell on this point with Truman. He admitted that the Russians had made a good deal of trouble on minor military matters and that it had sometimes been necessary to "teach them manners." However, on the greater matter of the Polish question, he believed that without fully understanding how seriously the Russians felt we might be "heading into very dangerous waters." He noted that the Russian viewpoint was undoubtedly influenced by the fact that before World War I most of Poland had been controlled by Russia. Stimson said he would like to know how far the Russian reaction to a strong position on Poland would go. It was his opinion that the Russians would not yield. He urged that the President "go slowly and avoid an open break."[44]

Stimson knew that Truman had rejected his advice at the April 23 meeting. He confided to his diary that "nobody backed me up until it came round to Marshall."[45] The General still thought Soviet help might be of some use in the Japanese war, but this was not the only reason he had come to Stimson's defense on the Polish issue.[46] Two weeks before Roosevelt's death Stimson had sensed the increasingly tough view a number of advisers were taking toward Russia. As early as April 2 he thought this "a very serious matter, for we simply cannot allow a rift to come between the two nations without endangering the entire peace of the world."[47] Expecting trouble, Stimson had summoned Marshall so as to keep "close with him in order to have my power in my elbow for the conference that may come up."[48] With Marshall as an ally, Stimson had been prepared to enter the policy conflict over Poland. It was time, he noted in his diary, "for me to use all the restraint I can on these other people who have been apparently getting a little more irritated."[49]

Although he had prepared for the fight, after the meeting with the President, Stimson was aware that Harriman and Deane had outmaneuvered him. He attributed their energetic activities to the fact that they had "been suffering personally from the Russians' behavior on minor matters for a long time." He was disturbed that "they were evidently influenced by their past bad treatment," for he believed that the victory of the tough line set the stage for a severe test of Soviet-American relations.[50] "It was one of the most difficult situations I have ever had since I have been here. . . . We are at loggerheads with Russia on an issue which in my opinion is very dangerous and one which she is not likely to yield on in substance. . . . In my opinion we ought to be very careful and see whether we couldn't get ironed out on the situation without getting into a head-on collision."[51]

EUROPEAN STABILITY AND AMERICAN SECURITY

THE REASON STIMSON felt so strongly about this point was not, as is often supposed, that he feared the tough line would lose Soviet help in the Japanese war. Though this had indeed been an important point at an earlier stage, strategic plans no longer required Soviet assistance. To be sure, some military leaders still felt that an early Russian entry into the war would be of general value, but Stimson himself does not seem to have been particularly concerned about the point at this time, and, in fact, he had reasons for wishing to end the war before the Russians entered it.* The main reason Stimson believed a rift between the two nations would endanger the "entire peace of the world" was his conviction that cooperation with Russia was absolutely essential to the postwar stability of Europe; if the European economy collapsed, Stimson believed, chaos, revolution, and war would result. "All of this is a tough problem requiring coordination between the Anglo-American allies and Russia," he confided to his diary; "Russia will occupy most of the good food lands of Central Europe. . . . We must find some way of persuading Russia to play ball."[52]

Thus, Stimson's awareness of Soviet security interests was bolstered by his strong desire for Soviet cooperation in postwar Europe. He believed American interests were already involved, for Stimson had come to define American security as dependent upon European stabil-

---

* Stimson was worried that Soviet entry would mean Soviet domination of Manchuria. For the relationship between his fears and his strategy for ending the war, see Chapter IV.

ity.[53] The Secretary's reasoning was natural for a man who had been deeply involved in public affairs at the Cabinet level since 1911. Having lived through two European wars which had involved the United States, he concluded that world peace was "indivisible."[54] To avoid a future war it was necessary to lay the basis for a lasting European peace.* Stimson feared the disease and starvation in Central Europe which might be "followed by political revolution and communistic infiltration." He felt it "vital" to keep Western Europe "from being driven to revolution or communism by famine,"[55] and he concluded that "an economically stable Europe . . . is one of the greatest assurances of security and continued peace we [the United States] can hope to obtain."[56]

Stimson also wanted the "restoration of stable conditions in Europe" because he believed that "only thus can concepts of individual liberty, free thought and free speech be nurtured."[57] Despite his concern with the possibility of revolution, the Secretary was not pessimistic about the future. He believed wise policy could persuade the Russians to establish arrangements in Europe which would also redound to their benefit. Consequently, Stimson focused his attention on ways to promote cooperation in the heart of the Continent—Germany and Austria.

Throughout the war, Stimson had stressed the need for sound economic conditions in Central Europe.[58] He had led the fight against Secretary of the Treasury Henry Morgenthau's plan for destroying great sectors of German industry. He feared the consequences of eliminating such an important factor in the European economy. To accept Morgenthau's advice, he reasoned, would involve "poisoning the springs out of which we hope that the future peace of the world can be maintained." He urged that methods of "economic oppression . . . do not prevent war; they tend to breed war."[59] Instead of following such a plan it would be wise to restore German industry under careful controls.[60] "We should not remove [German] capacity for

---

* See also Byrnes's 1945 argument, "Two wars in one generation have convinced the American people that they have a very vital interest in the maintenance of peace in Europe." (Senate Committee on Foreign Relations, *A Decade of American Foreign Policy*, p. 55.) Again, Stimson's 1945 declaration that "the worst thing we did to break the chance of peace after the last war, and to tempt willful nations toward aggression, was to keep out." (*On Active Service*, p. 599.)

aiding in the restoration of stable conditions in Europe and the world."[61]

Stimson viewed the problems of Germany and Austria in exactly the same way as he saw the broader issues of the Continent. Since Soviet troops would be in control of the good food lands, cooperation would be essential to economic stability. As early as October 1943, Stimson stressed the need for open trading arrangements: "Central Europe after the war has got to eat. She has got to be free from tariffs in order to eat." Policy makers who did not understand this did not have "any grasp apparently of the underlying need of proper economic arrangements to make the peace stick."[62]

The problem was as important to the Secretary in 1945 as it was in 1943, but now the issue was more urgent. In mid-April, Assistant Secretary of War John J. McCloy returned from an inspection of Europe reporting "complete economic, social and political collapse" in both Germany and Austria.[63] Stimson summarized the situation to the Cabinet on April 20 as "chaos" and "near anarchy."[64] On May 16 he pressed Truman on the matter, strongly urging American efforts to create stability. "The eighty million Germans and Austrians in Central Europe necessarily swing the balance of that continent," he argued. "A solution must be found."[65]

Leaving aside all other considerations, it is fair to say that by mid-April, when tension between America and Russia began to mount, Secretary Stimson believed it wise to yield to considerable Soviet political influence in Poland in the interest of a solution to European economic problems. To attempt to press the Polish issue to a showdown he believed both futile and dangerous; the Russians would not yield, and a break would destroy the possibility of cooperation. On the other hand, Stimson felt that the record of military cooperation offered reason for hope of a successful postwar relationship. While other advisers urged a showdown with Russia, Stimson tried to "hang onto" the fact that Russia and the United States had "always gotten along for a hundred and fifty years' history, with Russia friendly and helpful." "Our respective orbits do not clash geographically and I think that on the whole we can probably keep out of clashes in the future," he noted.[66] But he reminded himself that this would "require the greatest care and the greatest patience and the greatest thoughtfulness."[67]

In this spirit the Secretary of War also opposed the tough approach to German problems. He advised against pressing the attempt to use the German troop positions to achieve political objectives in Austria.[68] Instead, he urged a policy of cooperation with Russia which would treat Germany "as an economic unit."[69] More generally, he urged that the United States dissociate its policy from British diplomacy. He believed that "Churchill, now that Mr. Roosevelt was dead, was seeking to take a more active part in the direction of matters of grand policy in Central Europe." At the end of April he suggested to Marshall that they "ought to be alert now that a new man was at the helm in the Presidency to see that he was advised as to the background of the past differences between Britain and America on these matters."[70]

Thus, on the specific diplomatic issues in question, and on the general issue of American collaboration with Britain, Stimson was opposed to the advisers who urged an immediate showdown with Russia. His policy, however, was not so simple and straightforward as the above analysis at first suggests. On May 14, Stimson told Assistant Secretary McCloy that "the time now and the method now to deal with Russia was to keep our mouths shut."[71] The word "now" must be carefully noted, for it is essential to remember that Stimson's recommendations were forged in the heat of an intense policy-making debate and were designed to counter the pressure for an immediate showdown with Russia. To understand his longer-term policy, it is necessary to consider the Secretary's thinking on matters of great strategic importance.*

THE STRATEGY OF A DELAYED SHOWDOWN

ON APRIL 24, the day after Truman's showdown with Molotov, Stimson wrote to the President: "I think it is very important that I should have a talk with you as soon as possible. . . . [The atomic bomb]† has such a bearing on our present foreign relations and such

---

* For a detailed exposition of Stimson's views on the need to treat the German and Continental economies as a unit, see *Conference of Berlin*, II, pp. 754–57, 808–9.

† Because of wartime security requirements, the weapon was usually referred to indirectly or by the code terms "Tube Alloys" and "S-1." Hereafter the words "the atomic bomb" will be used within brackets in place of all indirect references in quoted text.

an important effect upon all my thinking in this field that I think you should know about it without much further delay."[72]

The President agreed to see Stimson immediately, and on April 25 Truman was briefed at length on the nuclear development program. The Secretary presented a memorandum which began: "Within four months we shall in all probability have completed the most terrible weapon ever known in human history. . . ."[73] Stimson was extremely confident of success.*[74] He said that a "gun-type" bomb would be ready about August 1. For this weapon no test would be necessary. A second would be available before the end of the year. Early in July a test of an implosion weapon would be held in New Mexico. Another trial could be held before the first of August if necessary. Less than a month after the successful test a "Fat Man" weapon would be ready for combat.[75]

For three quarters of an hour Stimson discussed the atomic bomb with the President. It was *assumed*—not decided—that the bomb would be used.† Stimson told Truman that for some time Japan had been the target of the weapon development program. A special Twentieth Air Force group was about to leave for its overseas base. Stimson expressed confidence that the bomb would shorten the war.[76] However, the use of the bomb against Japan was not the main subject the Secretary wanted to discuss.

Although shortly after Roosevelt's death Stimson had casually mentioned to Truman that an "immense project . . . was under way—a project looking to the development of a new explosive of almost unbelievable destructive power," he had felt no compelling reason to discuss the matter fully with the new President at that time.[77] It was only after the showdown with Molotov that he asked for a special interview with the President. He was prompted to do so not because of the weapon's potential effect on the Japanese war, but primarily be-

---

* A diary entry notes "success is 99% assured." (Stimson Diary, April 11, 1945.) On April 23, British representatives reported to London that it was "as certain as such things can be" that the first bomb would be ready in late summer. (Ehrman, *Grand Strategy*, p. 275.)

† Stimson later noted, "*At no time* from 1941 to 1945 did I ever hear it suggested by the President or any other responsible member of the government that atomic energy should not be used in the war." (*On Active Service*, p. 613.) A few days after Stimson's talk with the President, Field Marshal Wilson, the British representative on the Combined Policy Committee (which discussed nuclear developments) informed Sir John Anderson that the Americans had *already* proposed "to drop a bomb sometime in August." (Ehrman, *Grand Strategy*, p. 276.) *See also* Gowing, *Britain and Atomic Energy*, p. 372.

cause it had "such a bearing on our present foreign relations and such an important effect upon all my thinking in this field."[78]

Although we do not have full information on Stimson's discussion with the President, it is important to understand the Secretary's conception of the atomic bomb's role in diplomacy. On April 25 he told Truman the bomb was "certain" to have a "decisive" influence on relations with other countries. Truman reports that the discussion centered "specifically" on "the effect the atomic bomb might likely have on our future foreign relations," but summarizes the forty-five-minute conversation in only three short paragraphs. Consequently, one must go beyond this information to understand the general line of strategy Stimson advocated.[79]

The key to the Secretary's view was a consistent judgment—held from at least mid-March 1945—that the atomic bomb would add great power to American diplomacy once it was developed.[80] He considered that no major issue could be realistically discussed without an estimate of the bomb's role.[81] He believed it "premature" for the United States to raise diplomatic issues in the Far East until the bomb had been tested.[82] Similarly, he believed it essential that the discussion of European issues be postponed; he told the President on May 16,"We shall probably hold more cards in our hands later than now."[83]

As Secretary of War, Stimson was the most important man in government with full information on the highly secret nuclear program. Urging his strategy of delay among the very small circle of advisers privy to the secret, he had to impress his colleagues with the incredible powers likely to be released by the still-untested weapon. The Secretaries of State and the Navy, and Ambassador Harriman, wanted not only an immediate showdown in Europe but also an immediate confrontation on certain Far Eastern diplomatic issues. Stimson records that he had "a pretty red-hot session" urging postponement of a meeting on the latter questions—"Over any such tangled weave of problems, [the atomic-bomb] secret would be dominant, and yet we will not know until after that time probably, until after that meeting, whether this is a weapon in our hands or not. We think it will be shortly afterward, but it seems a terrible thing to gamble with such big stakes in diplomacy without having your master card in your hand."[84]

Stimson urged that we take "time to think over these things a little bit harder."[85] He also took Harriman into his confidence and "talked over very confidentially our problem connected with [the atomic bomb]" and its relation to European matters.[86] At the same time, he discussed the role of the bomb and European diplomacy with British Foreign Secretary Anthony Eden, outlining "to him the progress which we have made and the timetable as it stood now, and . . . its bearing upon our present problems of an international character."[87] In general, the point the Secretary of War repeatedly emphasized was the need to postpone any confrontation with the Russians until the atomic bomb had been proved and demonstrated.

Despite his emphasis on the weapon's value for diplomacy, Stimson did not believe the new power could be used to *force* the Russians to accept American terms on diplomatic issues. He thought such a course would inevitably lead to an arms race.[88] Stimson knew, as he told Truman, that it was "practically certain" that the United States could not maintain a monopoly of the bomb for very long.[89] He explained that "the future may see a time when such a weapon may be constructed in secret and used suddenly and effectively with devastating power by a willful nation or group against an unsuspecting nation or group."[90] For these reasons, Stimson believed that some form of international control of the new development was absolutely essential. If control were not achieved, the results could be disastrous. "In other words," he told Truman, "modern civilization might be completely destroyed."[91]

Thus, Stimson's view that the atomic bomb would be "decisive" in diplomacy did not depend upon its use as a threat. Caught between the desire to use the bomb as an instrument of diplomacy and the knowledge that its use as a threat would lead to a "disaster to civilization," Stimson resolved his dilemma by urging that the secret of the weapon be offered as a bargaining counter in negotiations to establish a peace settlement.[92] As early as December 1944, the Secretary searched for diplomatic *"quid pro quos"* which might be asked of Russia in exchange for information on nuclear energy and participation in a system of international control.[93] Two months before Roosevelt's death, he raised the same question with subordinates.[94] Discussing the problem with Truman at the April 25 interview, he declared: "The question of sharing [the atomic bomb] . . . and . . . upon what terms, becomes a primary question of our foreign relations."[95]

Stimson suggested that the President appoint a special "Interim Committee" to advise him on the method to use the bomb against Japan and the political implications of the new force.[96] Following the April 25 interview, the Secretary and Truman discussed problems connected with the bomb on several occasions, at least on May 1, 2, 3, and 4.* Stimson suggested that the President have a close confidant and personal representative on the Interim Committee.[97] It was clear that the most important problems would relate to the role of the bomb in diplomacy, and the obvious choice in Stimson's view was James F. Byrnes, the man Truman had privately designated to become his new Secretary of State.[98]

Although the diplomatic implications of the atomic bomb dominated private discussions between Stimson and Truman during the last week of April and the first week of May, we do not have precise information on the exact date on which Stimson advised the President to postpone diplomatic confrontations with the Russians. From available information, there can be no doubt that the Secretary urged this general view during the last week of April, probably at the April 25 meeting.† But in the tense atmosphere of the showdown over Poland and the developing stalemate in Central Europe, Stimson's general point soon reduced to a more specific recommendation—the Secretary advised that a heads-of-government meeting be delayed until the atomic bomb had been tested early in July. He felt that "the greatest complication was what might happen at the meeting of the Big Three" if the tests had not been completed.[99]

In urging this line of advice, Stimson came into direct conflict with those policy makers who wanted to maintain the firm line. They feared that unless there was an immediate showdown—before American troops were substantially withdrawn from Europe—the Soviet Premier would not yield. Forced to acknowledge the crucial role of the troops—and, indeed, as aware of their importance as the other advisers and Churchill—Stimson offered specialized military information to support his strategy of delay. In company with General

---

* There probably were other discussions not recorded in the documents.

† See Appendix II for a detailed examination of the probable date.

Marshall, on May 14 he explained the role of the atomic bomb to Anthony Eden. He assured the Foreign Secretary that there was no reason to fear delay, since the actual figures for troop withdrawals for the rest of the summer would not reach 50,000 per month out of a total of three million.[100] Stimson explained to the President two days later: "The work of redeploying our forces from Europe to the Pacific will necessarily take so long that there will be more time for your necessary diplomacy with the other large allies than some of our hasty friends realize."[101]

With this reassurance, Stimson's strategy of a delayed showdown was fully developed. Though at first glance it appeared that Stimson was prepared to concede Soviet political domination in Poland, in fact, the Secretary had a far more subtle strategy in mind. He was opposed to an *immediate* showdown on the Polish issue, for he believed the Russians would not yield on a matter so vital to their security. This would be especially true if the atomic test failed and, as expected, American troops were eventually withdrawn from the Continent. But while he opposed a strong immediate stand on the Polish issue, he did not give up hope of influencing affairs in Poland and elsewhere in Eastern Europe. At the very least, the atomic bomb would seal whatever cooperative arrangements cautious diplomacy could negotiate, and it was likely to be much more effective; two months before the bomb was to be used, he looked to the future, confiding to his diary a brief sketch of the *"quid pro quos* which should be established in consideration for our taking [the Russians] into partnership" for control of the new force. Among the Soviet concessions he sought were a satisfactory "settlement of the Polish, Rumanian, Yugoslavian, and Manchurian problems."[102] Thus, though he was more restrained in approach, Stimson's ultimate aims were not substantially different from those of Truman's other advisers.

Nor, indeed, did he differ on the need for a showdown, for Stimson did not think the Russians would be brought into line without a show of American determination. "It is a case where we have got to regain the lead," he told McCloy, "and perhaps do it in a pretty rough and realistic way." There would probably have to be a forceful confrontation of some kind, and Stimson had few doubts about the ultimate outcome—it "was a place where we really held all of the cards." Success depended only upon prudence, subtlety, and delay. He told

McCloy that the American bargaining position was like "a royal straight flush and we mustn't be a fool about the way we play it. . . . We have coming into action a weapon which will be unique. Now the thing is not to get into unnecessary quarrels by talking too much and not to indicate any weakness by talking too much; let our actions speak for themselves."[103]

CHAPTER III

The Decision to Postpone a Confrontation with Stalin

*If we ever compromise with principle,
such compromise is only a temporary
measure in order the better to attain our
main objective in the end.*
—ACTING SECRETARY OF STATE
JOSEPH C. GREW
June 4, 1945

IMMEDIATELY AFTER his April 25 talk with Stimson, President Truman began to respond to the broad line of advice offered by his Secretary of War. Within a few days even British representatives knew a committee would be set up "to consider the whole range of political issues which will arise in connection" with the atomic bomb.[1] On May 2, Truman authorized arrangements for the Interim Committee and accepted Stimson's suggested list of members. On May 4, formal invitations for the first meeting of the Committee were issued.[2]

At the same time he approved this proposal, Truman also named a personal representative to the Committee. Evidently agreeing that the atomic bomb would have decisive implications for diplomacy, Truman followed the suggestion that the man designated to be Secretary of State represent the President. On May 3, James F. Byrnes's agreement to serve on the Interim Committee was secured.[3] Shortly thereafter the President also asked Byrnes to make an independent study of the bomb's potentialities.[4]

There is very little direct evidence available regarding Truman's personal view of the atomic bomb during April and May.* It may therefore be important to note that in choosing Byrnes, the President put his confidence in a man who took an extremely tough-minded view of the weapon's role in diplomacy. From the very first, Byrnes seems to have exaggerated the power of the development. It was Byrnes, not Stimson, who first told the President the key facts about the atomic project. When he did, on the day after Roosevelt's death, he declared "with great solemnity" that the United States was "perfecting an explosive great enough to destroy the whole world."[5] Byrnes believed that a nuclear monopoly could be maintained for seven to ten years.[6] Hence he did not fear an arms race as did Stimson. Nor did he search for diplomatic *quid pro quos* the Russians might offer for admittance to an international control scheme. Instead, Byrnes felt that during the monopoly period the Russians would be forced to agree to an American plan for lasting world peace. Once established, the new regime of peace would obviate possible conflicts in the postmonopoly period.† In mid-April, Byrnes told the President that in his belief the atomic bomb would "put us in a position to dictate our own terms at the end of the war."[7]

Truman's choice of Byrnes to become his Secretary of State and personal representative for atomic matters is only indirect evidence of the President's sympathy with Byrnes's general approach.‡ As we shall see, in the following months, as each crucial decision regarding the atomic bomb and diplomatic strategy arose, when there was a choice between the views offered by Stimson and by Byrnes, the President almost invariably followed the advice of his Secretary of State. However, in April and May, when the atomic bomb was still only an expectation, the President did not often have to choose between the two men. In fact, from his point of view the only important question

---

* There is a great deal known about the President's view for each of the following months of 1945. This will be discussed in due course.

† See Hewlett and Anderson, *The New World*, pp. 354–57. Also below, pp. 196–198.

‡ Byrnes, who had taken his own shorthand notes at Yalta, also briefed Truman on the meaning of the agreements. Byrnes was deeply concerned about Eastern Europe and, in fact, was personally responsible for bringing a reluctant Roosevelt to propose those sections of the Yalta protocol which later committed the United States to a direct interest in the area. It may, therefore, be extremely significant that at the time Truman decided upon a firm showdown approach over Poland, the only person to have advised him on the role of the atomic bomb in diplomacy, problems of Eastern Europe, and the relationship between the two questions, was the tough-minded man he had chosen to become his Secretary of State. (Truman, *Year of Decisions*, pp. 11, 22, 87; Byrnes, *Speaking Frankly*, pp. 32–33.)

Truman had to decide at this time was whether or not to postpone diplomatic issues until the bomb was tested. Decisions as to methods of utilizing the new power could be made after it had been proved.

As we have seen, by the last week of April the President was committed to the immediate showdown strategy on the Polish issue, and he had adopted a correspondingly tough attitude toward American troop positions in the Soviet zone of Germany. Early in May he had cut Lend-Lease shipments to emphasize American determination. However, the President's general line of policy had achieved very little success. In fact, the immediate showdown strategy had reached an impasse; the Russians had not yielded on the problem of Poland and there was no sign that an Allied Control Council would be established in Germany. With Stalin failing to respond to increased pressure, American policy makers had to consider their course of action.

The deadlock over the symbolic Polish issue was a direct personal challenge to those who had urged a firm line. To retreat not only would involve a loss of face, but would defeat the fundamental purpose of a showdown designed to structure Soviet-American relations on a new basis. Hence, only three months after Yalta, there seemed no suitable course but another heads-of-government meeting and an immediate confrontation with the Soviet Premier. At such a meeting all matters in dispute could be discussed and the full range of American bargaining counters could be brought into play. Churchill argued the same point to Eden: "The Polish problem may be easier to settle when set in relation to the now numerous outstanding questions of the utmost gravity which require urgent settlement with the Russians. . . ."[8]

At precisely the same time these views were being pressed, Secretary Stimson began intensive policy discussions in preparation for the coming atomic test. In fact, the Polish issue and the atomic bomb now became inextricably bound together as Stimson discussed the implications of the weapon with the President almost every day of the tense first week of May. Stimson had already urged Truman to avoid a break over the Polish problem.[9] After the showdown with Molotov, he had urgently sought an interview because of the atomic bomb's bearing on the current crisis.[10] He told Truman that, once tested, the weapon would be decisive in all matters of foreign relations.[11] And it is undoubtedly at this time that he first introduced the idea that a basic confrontation should be delayed until the new power had been demonstrated.

Thus, Truman found himself at the focal point of two contradictory streams of policy advice. It was now impossible to continue the existing course without a new show of determination or a radical change; by the end of the first week of May Stalin had shown he would not yield unless something more was done. Indeed, the Soviet Premier had already taken unilateral action by recognizing the Warsaw government, by concluding with them a bilateral treaty, by transferring German territories to Polish administration, and by announcing the arrest of Western-oriented Polish underground leaders. If Truman failed to act, it was obvious that new *faits accomplis* would eliminate all hope of Western influence and democracy in Poland. The President's policy had to go forward; it could not stand still.

Truman sympathized with the arguments of his "firm" advisers, and he shared Churchill's general conception of the Polish dispute.[12] Temperamentally suited to straightforward actions, he had initially adopted the showdown strategy not only with little hesitation but with much enthusiasm. His convictions and the commitment of his prestige argued powerfully for a continuation of the strategy to its logical conclusion and an early meeting with Stalin. Standing firmly in the path of these considerations, however, was new information of what Truman termed "the almost incredible developments that were under way and the awful power that might soon be placed in our hands."[13] Could a delay be endured? The President now had to choose between the strategy of an immediate showdown and the only other alternative offered—the strategy of a delayed showdown.

Truman's crucial decision came in an early-May response to a cable from Churchill. The President stated that he agreed a tripartite meeting was necessary, but that he could not leave Washington for another two months![14] Truman's enthusiasm for an immediate showdown had disappeared. He would not be able to come to a meeting until early July, the time when the first atomic test would be held.* A

---

* The atomic test was later delayed for technical reasons and, accordingly, Truman later delayed the meeting again. (See below, pp. 100–101.) Available records establish that Truman postponed the Potsdam meeting because he wished to wait for the atomic test. Unfortunately, however, they do not disclose the precise date of discussions leading to this decision. See Appendix II for a review of available information bearing on the matter.

few days later he discussed the matter in great secrecy with Secretary Stimson. The full records of this conversation are not available, but there is no question about the main point at issue. Truman told Stimson his strategy concerning the timing of the tripartite meeting. Stimson left the meeting completely satisfied, and in a "skeleton outline" circumspectly summarizing the discussion, he commented that he agreed with the President that there was much to gain and little to lose by delay. Then, writing the same phrases he habitually used to refer to the secret project, Stimson added: "Therefore I believe that good and not harm would be done by the policy toward your coming meeting which you mentioned to me. We shall probably hold more cards in our hands later than now."[15]

Thus, by the second week of May, Truman had accepted the fundamental point of Stimson's strategy—a confrontation with Stalin would be delayed. Truman's decision came as a shock to most of the advisers who felt that a meeting with Stalin had to be held at the earliest possible time. If the meeting was delayed, the showdown might take place after large numbers of troops had been redeployed to the Pacific. Doubts would be cast upon America's determination. Besides, what could be gained by waiting?* Grew, Harriman, and Leahy found Truman's decision all but incomprehensible; until this time the President had not only accepted each logical step in the firm line of policy, but had taken the lead in establishing the American position. His advisers begged him to reconsider his decision. Ambassador Harriman warned the President he "would be confronted with a much more difficult situation two months from now than he would if the meeting could be arranged within the next few weeks."[16]

Similarly, Churchill expressed great disappointment at the late date—"every minute counts." He proposed that the two heads of government take the initiative by inviting Stalin to a meeting, and pleaded that American troop positions be held.[17] At the same time, the Prime Minister urgently instructed Ismay: "All reduction of Bomber Command is to be stopped."[18] And he asked Eisenhower not to destroy

---

* Outside the inner circles of the atomic-development project very few had Stimson's faith in the power of the new weapon. As Stimson has written, that the atomic bomb might "be a lemon" was an "opinion common among those not fully informed." Admiral Leahy was certain the atomic bomb would not work. Although Harriman knew of the project, he conceived of it only as a possibility pending actual test. (Stimson, *On Active Service*, p. 615; Leahy, *I Was There*, pp. 265, 440; Truman, *Year of Decisions*, p. 11; Feis, *Between War and Peace*, p. 97*fn*.)

captured German aircraft—"We may have great need of these some day."[19] On May 12 he cabled Truman again: "I am profoundly concerned about the European situation. . . . Anyone can see that in a very short space of time our armed power on the Continent will have vanished. . . . This issue of a settlement with Russia before our strength has gone seems to me to dwarf all others."[20]

But Truman would yield neither to the pleas of his advisers nor to the logic of Churchill.* Responding to Harriman, Grew, and Bohlen, he was firm: he could not leave Washington because he had to prepare a "budget message."[21] On May 14 he told Churchill that while he agreed that an early tripartite meeting was essential, he could not yet suggest a date for the meeting.[22]

In reality, of course, Truman's mention of a "budget message" was an impossibly weak excuse and was evidently given only to those (like Bohlen) who were not privy to the atomic secret. Everyone agreed upon the overriding importance of the issues in dispute, and there was overwhelming logic in maintaining the diplomatic pressure by an immediate meeting. Once troop withdrawals began Stalin would understand, as Churchill pointed out, "time is on his side if he digs in while we melt away."[23] A "budget message" could not explain Truman's rejection of such considerations and it appears that on May 10 and May 14 Stimson confidentially delineated the more sophisticated strategy to Harriman and Eden.[24]

In delaying a confrontation with Stalin, Truman relaxed pressure on the Russians and thereby cast doubt upon America's determination to force matters to a showdown. However, he did not give up all diplomatic leverage; the main objection to delay was fear that American troops would actually be withdrawn. Churchill consistently stressed the inevitable weakening effect upon the Western negotiating position, Eden raised the matter with Stimson on May 14, and Harriman urged it upon the President on May 15.[25] Truman fully agreed on the importance of the troops[26] and, in fact, spent the first week of May studying the redeployment timing.[27] As we have seen, when he

---

* Eden was informed of the atomic bomb's role in diplomatic strategy on May 14, 1945. It is probable that Churchill received a briefing on the matter from Harriman when they dined together privately on May 22. Thus, it appears that Churchill, like the American advisers, pressed for an early meeting despite his awareness of the strategy. It is probable that he was simply unwilling to gamble such important European diplomatic stakes on the outcome of the atomic test. (Stimson Diary, May 14, 1945; *Conference of Berlin*, I, p. 20.)

decided to delay a meeting with Stalin, he did so on Stimson's specific assurance that "the work of redeploying our forces from Europe to the Pacific will necessarily take so long that there will be more time for your necessary diplomacy with the other large allies than some of our hasty friends realize."[28]

TRUMAN'S SYMBOLIC REVERSAL

TRUMAN'S POSTPONEMENT of a confrontation with Stalin was the crucial decision of the spring of 1945. Once he made up his mind, Truman was forced to consider his course on all major issues in dispute with Russia. He knew it was futile to continue his firm line without an immediate face-to-face meeting. On the other hand, the President did not want to yield the points at issue. In this situation, necessity was the mother of invention; the President had to devise a method which would reduce tensions, forestall a unilateral Soviet solution to the Polish problem, and keep the door open to Western influence.* In short, he needed to gain time. These points, of course, followed the general logic of Stimson's delayed showdown strategy, but Truman's method—an ingenious one—was apparently his own creation; he decided upon symbolic missions to Moscow and London which would dramatize America's desire to break with the firm Churchillian policy and would explore ways to re-establish—at least temporarily—the Rooseveltian policy of cooperation.

Information on the decisions of early May is extremely sketchy. Although Truman made no change in his public stand until late in May, it appears that he began to prepare a conciliatory course even before his cable telling Churchill that a meeting had to be delayed. On May 4 Truman asked Roosevelt's old aide Harry Hopkins, who was at that time terribly ill, if he would be able to serve as his personal representative to Stalin.[29] When Truman finally committed himself to the Hopkins mission two weeks later—at the height of the tense atmosphere emanating from the deadlock over Poland and Central Europe—his decision had powerful overtones. As Halifax pointed out, Hopkins was "the most eminent living repository of Mr. Roose-

---

* Compare also Admiral Leahy's early view that the Polish matter should "be put to the Russians in such a way as not to close the door to subsequent accommodation." (Forrestal, *Diaries*, p. 50.)

velt's policy."[30] The mission, according to Secretary Stettinius, was designed to "assure Stalin that the death of Mr. Roosevelt would not alter the United States' policy of co-operating with the Soviet Union."[31] But this is an understatement, for the mission signaled a fundamental break with the firm line—the decision to send a negotiator to Moscow blatantly reversed the British-American declaration that the Polish question could not even be discussed until satisfactory information had been given about the arrests of the Polish underground leaders.*

Although the Secretary of the Navy was told that Hopkins was going to Moscow only to get "an evaluation" of the Russian attitude on questions "on which at the present time there seems a danger of a sharp and substantial division," it was clear that a special representative would not be going to Moscow unless Truman had decided to make some concessions.[32] For this reason, when the State Department was consulted—at the last minute—it strongly opposed the trip.[33] So did Byrnes, who had personally briefed Truman on the Yalta argeements.[34] Arthur Bliss Lane, the man who would go to Warsaw as American ambassador, was "filled with misgivings" and threatened to resign.[35]

Truman's decision to break with the firm line of policy was underscored by a second aspect of the Hopkins mission: the President did not tell Churchill of his plans until after the mission was publicly disclosed.[36] He also refused to agree to Churchill's urgent request that Hopkins visit London as well as Moscow.[37] Instead, Truman asked Joseph E. Davies to visit Churchill.[38] This move was dramatic and ironic notice of Truman's new line of action, for Davies, a former ambassador to the Soviet Union, was personally opposed to the tough Churchillian approach and was a well-known advocate of Soviet-American cooperation.[39] The purpose of the Davies mission was equally symbolic: the Ambassador was to tell Churchill that Truman wished to meet with Stalin *alone* before the Big Three Conference.†[40]

There could be no better way to emphasize America's desire to dissociate policy from Churchill's influence. The mission was a com-

---

* See above, p. 35.

† Truman later tried to minimize this point, but there is no doubt about his intentions at the time. See Truman, *Year of De-* cisions, p. 260; Churchill, *Triumph and Tragedy*, p. 577; Feis, *Churchill, Roosevelt, Stalin*, p. 650; *Between War and Peace*, pp. 124–25; *Conference of Berlin*, I, pp. 67–85; Woodward, *British Foreign Policy*, p. 521*fn.*

plete reversal of attitude. From the very first days of his administration Truman had indicated a strong desire to work closely with Churchill and to meet with him at the earliest possible time.[41] The President had suggested a Washington meeting at the time of Roosevelt's funeral[42] and, on April 22, had urged Churchill to come to the United States during the San Francisco United Nations Conference.[43] Plans had been set for a visit by Churchill at the end of May.[44] A visit by Truman to Churchill had also been discussed and the President had been more than willing to go to London.[45] But with the Davies mission all these plans were abruptly abandoned. Truman now told his advisers that a meeting with Churchill might "give the Russians the impression we were ganging up on them," he cabled the same point to the Prime Minister, and he asked Davies to convey the message directly.[46] Thus, instead of a symbolic meeting with Churchill, there was to be a somewhat ostentatious change of plans: a private presidential meeting with Stalin!

Although the Davies and Hopkins missions were not announced until the end of May, as we have seen, Truman had begun to consider this course of action even before he announced the decision to delay a confrontation with Stalin. Stimson spoke with Truman about the atomic bomb on April 25, two days after the showdown with Molotov. Almost immediately Truman contacted Davies and Hopkins. He held his first meetings with them on April 30 and May 4 respectively.[47] Thus, he had begun to prepare his alternative policy even as he continued to adhere publicly to the firm line. Evidently sustaining the hope, as late as May 12, that Stalin might yield, Truman took his first irrevocable steps away from the immediate-showdown strategy almost a month after summoning the two men.[48] Only on May 19 and May 22—after it was unquestionably clear that Stalin would not back down—did Truman dispatch short messages to Moscow and London suggesting the trips.*[49]

Truman was extremely secretive about preparations for the two missions. He did not consult the Secretary of State, the Acting Secretary of State, the Polish experts in the Department of State, or Admiral Leahy, until the very eve of the trips, a month after he had

---

* The origin of the Hopkins mission is one of the most closely guarded government secrets. Despite repeated attempts, the State Department has refused my requests for further information. A report on additional details must await the opening of the presently closed archives.

initially contacted Davies and Hopkins.[50] The Secretary of the Navy did not learn of the trips until May 20.[51] As Arthur Bliss Lane, the designated ambassador to Poland, has written, all that was known in the Department of State was that "suddenly and secretly, in the last days of May, Harry Hopkins" left for Moscow.[52] Thus, almost all of the advisers who wanted an "immediate showdown" were unaware of the alternative approach the President was preparing.* Moreover, the President ordered that Hopkins's cables be shown only to a limited few of the senior advisers who customarily had access to such information.[53] This unusual secrecy is further indirect evidence of the relationship of the trips to the secret atomic project; it would have been inconceivable, except in extraordinary circumstances, for Truman to send Hopkins to discuss the most important outstanding diplomatic questions without consulting, or at least notifying, the Secretary of State.†

FORESTALLING A SOVIET SOLUTION IN POLAND

THUS, HAVING DECIDED to postpone a confrontation with Stalin, Truman dispatched his special envoys to repair damage done during the showdown crisis.[54] The general problem was to reduce tensions, but Hopkins had more specific tasks; he sought to forestall a unilateral Soviet solution of the Polish problem, to get consultations for reorganization of the Warsaw government started, and to keep the way open to as much Western influence in the country as possible.

Hopkins's first meeting with Stalin took place on May 26. Immediately he declared his purpose: "He wished to tell the Marshal of the real reason why the President had asked him to come, and that was the question of the fundamental relationship between the United States and the Soviet Union."[55] He said he "wished to state as frankly and forcibly as he knew how to Marshal Stalin the importance that he,

---

* It is true that in mid-April, Harriman suggested Hopkins might be a good man for a mission to Moscow. However, it is not clear from the available evidence whether Harriman made this suggestion in a general sense or in connection with Stimson's strategy. It appears that the former was the case, for Harriman disagreed with the strategy even after he learned of it on May 10. (Truman, *Year of Decisions*, pp. 257–58; Stimson Diary, May 10.) As is obvious, Sherwood's report that Harriman suggested the trip in mid-May is simply in error. (*Roosevelt and Hopkins*, pp. 885–87.)

† See Appendix II for a critique of other interpretations of the Hopkins mission.

personally, attached to the present trend of events and that he felt that the situation would get rapidly worse unless we could clear up the Polish matter."[56]

It had been clear from the beginning—and had been a chief policy consideration—that the Polish question would have implications for basic Soviet-American relations. On a number of occasions in his discussions with Stalin, Hopkins underscored this point, emphasizing that the problem "had become a symbol."[57] He said that although there were a number of other matters he wished to discuss, the Polish impasse was the primary problem.*[58] He told Stalin the President had decided upon a special mission because he felt great anxiety over the situation and because he wished to find some way out of the difficulty so as to continue Roosevelt's policy of cooperation.[59]

Harriman, who accompanied Hopkins, also stressed the importance of the point. He observed that in selecting Mr. Hopkins the President "had chosen a man who, as the Marshal knew, not only had been very close to President Roosevelt, but personally was one of the leading proponents of the policy of cooperation with the Soviet Union." He noted that the United States had "very intimate relations with Great Britain," but nevertheless felt it "desirable that the United States and the Soviet Union should talk alone on matters of special interest to them and that that was also one of the reasons for Mr. Hopkins's visit."[60]

At first these gestures of conciliation must have seemed a suspicious change from the firm line American policy had taken until this time. Stalin commented only that "the reason for the failure on the Polish question was that the Soviet Union desired to have a friendly Poland, but that Great Britain wanted to revive the system of *cordon sanitaire* on the Soviet borders."[61] When Hopkins replied that the United States did not have such intentions, Stalin said "if that be so we can easily come to terms in regard to Poland."[62]

The next day, May 27, Hopkins asked Stalin for comments on questions worrying him. The Soviet Premier immediately listed a number of issues where "recent moves on the part of the United States Government" had caused "a certain alarm." He said Soviet government circles had the "impression that the American attitude toward

---

* See below, pp. 80, 101–102.

the Soviet Union had perceptibly cooled once it became obvious that Germany was defeated, and that it was as though the Americans were saying that the Russians were no longer needed."[63] Of the issues Stalin raised, the two most important touched directly on the strategy of an immediate showdown. He was bitter over the American position on the Polish question, and he disliked the methods used by American diplomacy.

"At Yalta it had been agreed that the existing government was to be reconstructed and . . . anyone with common sense could see that this meant that the present government was to form the basis of the new," Stalin declared. "No other understanding of the Yalta Agreement was possible. Despite the fact that they were simple people, the Russians should not be regarded as fools . . . nor were they blind and they could quite well see what was going on before their eyes."[64]

Stalin then criticized the manner in which Lend-Lease had been curtailed: "If the refusal to continue Lend-Lease was designed as pressure on the Russians in order to soften them up, then it was a fundamental mistake. He said he must tell Mr. Hopkins frankly that if the Russians were approached frankly on a friendly basis much could be done but that reprisals in any form would bring about the exact opposite effect."[65]

This brought the main problems out into the open and a good deal of the second meeting was devoted to Hopkins's attempt to explain the American position on all of the points at issue.[66] After considerable discussion, Hopkins reverted to the fundamental problem—the United States wished to find a way to end the Polish stalemate and begin consultations for the government reorganization. While he hoped a way to begin could be found, "he had no thought or indeed any right to attempt to settle the Polish problem during his visit."[67] Later, focusing on specifics, Hopkins stressed the substantive requirements of American policy for Poland; there would have to be assurances that early elections would be held and that they would take place in a free atmosphere. There must be freedom of speech, right of assembly, right of movement. All political parties except the fascist should be permitted free use of press, radio, meetings, and other facilities of political expression. All citizens should have the right of public trial, defense by their own counsel, and the right of habeas corpus. "If we could find a meeting of minds in regard to these general principles which would be the basis for future free elections then he was sure we could find ways and means to agree on procedures. . . ."[68]

Stalin replied that "these principles of democracy are well known and would find no objection on the part of the Soviet Government." He assured Hopkins the Polish government would welcome the principles. He had reservations on only two points: in time of war the freedoms could not be enjoyed to the full extent; and they could not be applied fully to fascist parties trying to overthrow the government.[69]

Having reached agreement on the requirements for free elections, the two men took up the points at issue in the deadlock. Early in the talks Stalin had emphasized the need to recognize the Warsaw government as the "basis" of the new government. He had again urged the Yugoslav precedent be followed: one Polish leader should be admitted to the government for each four existing Cabinet members. This would provide four new posts out of a total of eighteen or twenty, and was precisely the same view Stalin had urged throughout the spring.[70]

Until this time the United States had rejected the Soviet position, and the stalemate had begun with Stalin's subsequent refusal to summon the Polish leaders for consultations to reorganize the government.[71] However, at the time he decided to send Hopkins, it appears that Truman also decided to concede the major point at issue; now, on May 30, Hopkins declared the President "anticipated that the members of the present Warsaw regime would constitute a majority of the new Polish Provisional Government."[72] This broke the log jam, for it committed American policy to the existing government as the "basis" of the new government. Hopkins cabled the President: "The conference tonight was encouraging. It looks as though Stalin is prepared to . . . permit a representative group of Poles to come to Moscow to consult with the Commission."[73]

The precise discussion of how great a majority the Warsaw government would have in the reorganized government is not available, but the American commitment went beyond Hopkins's general statement. Stalin proposed a list of candidates for inclusion in the government and after discussion Hopkins cabled that the United States would have to accept the Soviet view if any progress was to be made. Truman approved this recommendation.[74] It appears that after considerable haggling, Stalin and Hopkins split the difference between the original American view that Warsaw should have about half the seats in the new Cabinet and the Russian view that they should have about four fifths: when the Polish political leaders finally reached Moscow for discussions, they met a united stand of the three powers and were told that the Warsaw government would have the main part of the government.[75] Thereafter two thirds of the Cabinet was assumed to be Warsaw's share.*[76]

Once Warsaw's role as the "basis" of the new government had been recognized, Stalin was quite willing to invite the Poles to Moscow for consultations. In fact, as Hopkins noted in another context, Stalin seemed inclined "to make it easy for Churchill to get out of a bad situation."[77] Originally, Truman and Churchill had suggested that eight Poles be invited to Moscow for the reorganization talks. They had suggested four from the Warsaw government, one independent from Poland, and three from the London Polish groups.[78] (This would give Warsaw half of the delegation and accorded with the idea that the Warsaw government might have half the seats in the new Cabinet.) However, after Stalin and Hopkins had completed their discussions, it was agreed that a total of twelve Poles would be invited to Moscow: only four from the Warsaw government, five indepen-

---

* The available documents on the Hopkins-Stalin talks omit the key paragraphs on this point, and my requests for further information have been refused. However, there is enough other evidence to leave little doubt about the commitment: Feis reports Hopkins agreed to a "dominant" role for the Warsaw government. (*Between War and Peace*, p. 107.) That this probably meant the two-thirds figure seems clear since (1) Stettinius and Harriman broached this figure to Eden early in May; (2) on his way to Moscow, Harriman raised the power ratio with Mikolajczyk; (3) the Polish talks began on the two-thirds basis with no American objection; (4) after the completion of the talks Harriman again reported his opinion that two thirds was the best figure possible. (Woodward, *British Foreign Policy*, p. 510; Rozek, *Allied Wartime Diplomacy*, pp. 379–80, 395–98; Mikolajczyk, *The Pattern of Soviet Domination*, p. 143; *Conference of Berlin*, I, p. 727.) The American Ambassador to Poland, Arthur Bliss Lane, reports that Hopkins agreed to a ratio which would deprive the independent Poles of majority control. For this reason he believed the reorganization talks would fail, asked to see the Presi-

dent to protest the "Yugoslav precedent," and considered resignation. (*I Saw Freedom Betrayed*, pp. 70–71, 73, 75.) Supplementary evidence comes from the British side. Churchill vaguely indicated to Mikolajczyk that the British and American ambassadors were instructed to agree *both* to the Yugoslav precedent and a 50–50 ratio! (Rozek, *Allied Wartime Diplomacy*, p. 390.) Churchill actually instructed Clark Kerr, in part, that "the settlement will inevitably be 'based upon' the present Warsaw Government." He warned that "so far as public appearances are concerned" it had to look like the Poles reached this conclusion themselves. (Feis, *Between War and Peace*, p. 204.) The American position is also indirectly indicated by Harriman's complaint that Clark Kerr's instructions did not allow him to make the British commitment sufficiently clear. Also note Molotov's unchallenged remark at the first Commission meeting that there was no need to direct the Poles since the powers were already agreed that the Warsaw government would be the "basis" or "nucleus" of the new government. (Feis, *Between War and Peace*, p. 207.)

dents from Poland, and three from London.[79] Thus, from the point of view of public appearances, Stalin accorded the Warsaw government a far smaller role in the consultations than had originally been proposed by Truman and Churchill.*

With this successful compromise, the chief purpose of Hopkins's mission to Moscow had been accomplished. A unilateral Soviet solution to the Polish problem had been avoided, the negotiations to reorganize the government would soon be resumed, and the door had been kept open to Western influence in the country. With the deadlock broken, there remained only two tasks. First, the actual reorganization of the government would have to take place. Second, the pledge of free elections would have to be fulfilled. Both of these problems would be taken up later, but before leaving Moscow, Hopkins attempted to clear up one final aspect of the Polish dispute. He asked that the sixteen arrested Polish underground leaders be released "so that we could clear the atmosphere."[80] Stalin refused this request, but promised lenient treatment.†[81]

On June 15, a week after Hopkins completed his work, the various Polish leaders arrived in Moscow for consultations to reorganize the provisional government.[82] There were no divisions within the three-power Commission, and by June 22 agreement had been reached granting fourteen of twenty-one seats in the new Cabinet to the Warsaw government.‡[83] Harriman gave his government's approval to the understanding, and on July 5 Truman accorded the government diplomatic recognition.[84] The President also reported: "The new Polish Provisional Government of National Unity has informed me in a written communication that it has recognized in their entirety the

---

* It is interesting to note that Admiral Leahy, who believed the Yalta language sustained Stalin's interpretation, had predicted this result from the very first: "I did not believe that the dominating Soviet influence could be excluded from Poland, but I did think it was possible to give to the reorganized Polish Government an external appearance of independence." (*I Was There,* p. 352.) Much later Mikolajczyk claimed that "three or four" of the five Poles chosen from within Poland were biased in favor of the Warsaw government. However, at the time he was highly pleased with the list. He noted that Stalin had agreed to name three honorable but nonparty people from within

Poland. The remaining two had been named not by Stalin but by Truman. (*The Pattern of Soviet Domination,* p. 128; Rozek, *Allied Wartime Diplomacy,* pp. 384–86; *Stalin's Correspondence,* II, p. 216.)

† He made good on this promise. Four of the sixteen were not tried, the remainder received light prison sentences, and all were released in 1946. (Lane, *I Saw Freedom Betrayed,* p. 75*fn.*)

‡ After the agreement the figure was changed to sixteen of twenty-one. (*Conference of Berlin,* pp. 716–17, 727.) Unaccountably Woodward gives fourteen of twenty. (*British Foreign Policy,* p. 514.)

decisions of the Crimea Conference. . . . The new Government has thereby confirmed its intention to carry out the provisions of the Crimea decision with respect to the holding of elections. . . ."[85]

RE-ESTABLISHING COOPERATION IN CENTRAL EUROPE

WITH THIS DECLARATION, Stimson's original point—that a tension-reducing compromise would have to be found in Poland—was implemented as policy. As will be shown, the President had reason to believe that early free elections would establish a democratic Poland organized along Western lines.* Truman's mid-May objectives were not restricted to the negative goal of preventing a Polish *fait accompli*, however. Once the heads-of-government meeting had been delayed, the President was confronted with the immediate need to establish at least temporary working arrangements to prevent a breakdown of the European economy.

Each day in the spring of 1945 dramatized the importance of a cooperative relationship with the Russians. From all sides came reports of danger. As early as April 13—the first full day of his Presidency—Truman received an urgent State Department memorandum declaring: "Political stability and the maintenance of democratic governments which can withstand the pressures of extremist groups depend on the restoration of a minimum of economic stability."[86] Two days later the same point was made personally by the Secretary of State—the success of the United Nations would "be seriously jeopardized, if not defeated, by internal chaos in the liberated countries."[87]

On April 20 Secretary Stimson told the Cabinet that Assistant Secretary of War McCloy had "found conditions of chaos and in some cases of near anarchy in Germany."[88] On April 26, McCloy reported directly to the President: "There is complete economic, social and political collapse in Central Europe . . ." The Assistant Secretary emphasized the imperative need for food, fuel, and transportation in Germany. He advised: "We are going to have to work out a practical relationship with the Russians. It will require the highest talents, tolerance and wisdom to accomplish our aims."[89]

---

* See below, pp. 87–90.

On April 27, Oliver Lyttelton, British Minister of Production, informed the President that not only the liberated countries but Britain faced a serious shortage of food and other materials.[90] Truman's assistant, Judge Samuel I. Rosenman, returned from an extensive inspection of economic and food problems in Western Europe reporting a "critical" food situation and "desperate" conditions requiring American help.[91] A week after the collapse of German resistance, Secretary Stimson warned of the "strong probability of pestilence and famine in Central Europe."[92]

Although the President had initially differed with Stimson on the Polish question, he had always shared the Secretary's fundamental concern about general European problems; both men believed European stability absolutely essential to world peace. Truman regarded the chaotic economic situation in liberated Europe as "one of the most urgent" crises he had to resolve.[93] He saw a "grave danger of such political and economic chaos as to . . . jeopardize . . . economic stability which is the necessary basis for a firm and just peace."[94]

Like Stimson, the President viewed European problems with an eye to American national interest. Truman also saw that two European wars had inevitably drawn the United States into conflict. From this experience Stimson had generalized that peace was "indivisible." Similarly, Truman held that "a breach of peace anywhere in the world threatens the peace of the entire world."[95] He later wrote that "the one purpose that dominated me in everything I thought and did was to prevent a third world war."[96] Because he wanted "a peace settlement that would be lasting," the President believed it necessary to organize European economic conditions so as to prevent "another Hitler['s] rise to power."[97] To Truman it was the "literal truth" that "if we let Europe go cold and hungry," the United States would lose "the foundations of order on which the hope for world-wide peace must rest."[*][98]

Having defined world peace as dependent upon European stability, and American security as dependent upon world peace, Truman concluded: "The reconstruction of Europe was a matter that directly

---

* The British ambassador, sensing this deep concern, cabled Churchill: "I should also expect the Americans in dealing with us to be more responsive to arguments based upon the danger of economic chaos in European countries than to the balder pleas about the risks of extreme Left Governments or of the spread of Communism." (Churchill, *Triumph and Tragedy*, p. 611.)

concerned us, and we could not turn our back on it without jeopardizing our own national interests."[99] In the first week of June 1945—two full years before the Marshall Plan—Truman told his advisers: "We were committed to the rehabilitation of Europe, and there was to be no abandonment this time."[100]

In general, Truman also agreed with Stimson that it was vital to bring together the Eastern and Western halves of the European economic unit. Food was the critical problem, and supplies from Eastern Europe were essential. Even before taking over the Presidency, Truman had given the problem considerable thought. In a May 16 discussion with the Secretary of War, he recalled at great length talks he used to have with his friend Senator Elbert Thomas of Utah—"I would point to a map of Europe and trace its breadbasket, with Hungary a cattle country and Rumania and the Ukraine as the wheat area. Up to the northwest lay Western Germany, Northern France, Belgium and Britain with their coal, iron, and big industries. The problem . . . was to help unify Europe by linking up the breadbasket with the industrial centers."*[101]

Truman also shared Stimson's conviction that a strong German economy was essential to European stability. Unlike Roosevelt, "at no time" did Truman believe Germany should be dismembered.[102] As a Senator, he had opposed the Morgenthau plan, and as President he felt even more strongly about the issue.[103] On May 10, Truman approved a new directive for the administration of Germany—JCS 1067/8—which considerably modified the tough economic terms Roosevelt's earlier directive had imposed.[104] Moreover, although he endorsed almost all of Roosevelt's other appointments, Truman replaced Roosevelt's reparations representative with his own man.[105] Roosevelt had named a Jew, Dr. Isador Lubin, who could be expected to show little sympathy to the Germans. Truman chose Edwin W. Pauley precisely because he did not wish to weaken the German economy and he knew Pauley would be "tough" in the reparations talks with Molotov.[106] Indeed, Truman was completely in accord with Stimson's basic recommendations on Germany. The Secretary of War

---

* Truman seems to have taken an especially deep interest in this problem. Other visitors also found he would pull out a map of Europe to explain his profound conviction that a way had to be found to link the trade of Eastern and Western Europe. (See Smith, *My Three Years in Moscow*, p. 27.)

confided to his diary: "The President . . . has been very receptive to all my efforts in these directions."[107]

Thus, in all essential respects Truman understood the problems of European stability in much the same way as his Secretary of War. It was necessary both to strengthen the European economy and to work out a way to link the food-producing areas with the industrial zones. From such premises, it was immediately evident that the crucial problem was administration in the heart of Central Europe, primarily in Germany. But Red Army occupation of the eastern part of that country presented the same problem, on a smaller scale, which persisted in the larger unit of the Continent: there could be no economic stability without Soviet cooperation. "There was danger of complete economic and social collapse," Truman reasoned. "Therefore, it was imperative that there be established at the earliest possible moment a council to make policy for Germany as a whole."[108]

It is important to recognize that, despite appearances, Truman's April 23 showdown with Molotov was in complete accord with the fundamental objective of achieving Soviet cooperation. Indeed, it was a means to that end. Truman had initially judged that a symbolic showdown and strong language would force the Russians to cooperate not only in Eastern Europe but in their general relations with the United States. He had not envisioned a tense stalemate, but a blunt clarification of attitudes which would clear the way for cooperation on a self-consciously realistic basis. In initially rejecting Stimson's conciliatory advice, he had differed primarily on tactics, not on objectives. Similarly, in maintaining American troops in the Soviet zone of Germany he had expected not Soviet intransigence, but a realistic trading of advantage which would secure American political objectives in Austria.

But by mid-May, in Germany, as in Poland, there was no sign that Stalin would yield to the firm approach. As we have seen, one group of advisers felt that an immediate meeting with Stalin was the only possible course of action; Churchill continued to urge that American armies hold their positions in the Soviet zone. However, the implications of Truman's decision to postpone a meeting with Stalin were as clear for his German policy as for his Polish policy. The moment the President decided to delay a Big Three meeting until the atomic bomb was tested, he was forced to devise a new course of action. The Secretaries of State, War, and the Navy all advised that a declaration of principles for Allied administration of Germany be issued and that the Allied Control Council be promptly activated.[109] As in the Polish case, Truman had to find a formula which would elicit Soviet cooperation and yield as little advantage as possible.

Establishing an administrative council was the heart of the matter, and although the Polish impasse was the primary cause of the Hopkins mission, Truman set his representative an important secondary task: he was to try to secure Stalin's agreement to the German Control Council.[110] Following the President's instructions, Hopkins raised the issue early in his talks with the Soviet Premier. He noted that Eisenhower had already been named American representative for the Council and asked that Marshal Zhukov be designated Soviet representative.[111]

Initially, Stalin replied that he had not heard of Eisenhower's appointment, but would designate Zhukov in the near future.[112] A day passed, and Hopkins pressed the point again: "It would be most desirable if Marshal Stalin could announce publicly as soon as possible the appointment of Marshal Zhukov . . . so that that body could start its work as soon as possible."[113] At the same time Hopkins raised the matter in Moscow, instructions were sent to the American representative at the European Advisory Commission in London; he was to propose that an Allied declaration of principles for the administration of Germany be signed and issued by June 1.[114]

Hopkins reported that Stalin seemed quite willing to designate Zhukov and that he agreed "on the necessity of having a unified policy towards Germany . . . ; otherwise he said the Germans would attempt to play one off against the other."[115] This confirmed reports from London and Frankfurt of a strong Soviet desire for joint administration of the country.[116] From the Soviet point of view, cooperative administration would provide badly needed industrial materials from the western zones in exchange for food from the eastern zones.[117] It also appeared that cooperative control of Germany was a key point in Soviet plans for postwar security. Stalin told Hopkins: "Not only this war but the previous war had shown that without United States intervention Germany could not have been defeated and that all the events and developments of the last thirty years had confirmed this."[118]

Despite Soviet interest in cooperative administration, it was doubtful that the Control Council could be established so long as Truman maintained American troops in the Soviet zone of occupation. Eisenhower sensed this clearly, and at the same time Hopkins was discussing the appointment of Zhukov, the American Commander asked the Combined Chiefs of Staff for instructions on the troop positions. He said he anticipated one question the Russians would raise when the declaration of principles was signed would be the date on which American forces would withdraw from the Russian zone. "It is possible that Russians may establish such withdrawal as a corollary to the establishment of Control Council on a functioning basis," he noted. "Any cause for delay in . . . withdrawal would be attributed to us and might well develop strong public reaction."[119]

A week before Hopkins left for Moscow Truman had told Churchill he preferred to wait to see what happened before deciding either to withdraw the troops or hold them in place until a Big Three meeting.[120] For the next three weeks—throughout the period of the Hopkins mission—Truman maintained this position. On the President's instructions, the Joint Chiefs of Staff refused Eisenhower permission to withdraw the troops as a condition of the establishment of the Control Council.[121]

But this decision was very soon challenged. Hopkins secured Stalin's agreement to designate Zhukov as Eisenhower's counterpart.[122] When the two military leaders met in Berlin on June 5 to sign the Four Power Declaration for Germany, American troops were still deep in the Soviet zone of occupation. It was now a month after the German surrender, and Zhukov immediately made it clear that the agreement to establish the Control Council would not be implemented until American troops were withdrawn to the agreed occupation zones.[123]

Initially, Truman had linked the troop withdrawals with the unresolved Austrian zonal problems. By the first week of June, however, these issues (which, in any case, had never been of great importance) were all but resolved. The only question in dispute concerned the disposition of airports in Vienna.[124] Thus, Truman had to decide whether to maintain the American troop positions despite the all but completed accord in Austria.

Churchill cabled that he viewed "with profound misgivings the retreat of the American army to our line of occupation in the Central Sector, thus bringing Soviet power into the heart of Western Europe."[125] He said he hoped "that this retreat, if it has to be made, would be accompanied by the settlement of many great things."[126] Privately he told the Foreign Office: "I am still hoping that the retreat of the American centre to the occupation line can be staved off till 'the Three' meet . . ."[127]

However, from Germany three separate and dissenting appreciations were sent to Washington. Eisenhower again advised that the troops should be withdrawn.[128] Robert Murphy, Eisenhower's political adviser, cabled a similar view, adding that he saw no grounds for discouragement about the prospects of Soviet cooperation—"On the contrary I find that definite progress has been made. I am convinced that the Russians believe the Control Council necessary. . . ."[129] Finally, Harry Hopkins, returning from Moscow via Germany, cabled that the "present indeterminate status of the date for withdrawal of Allied Troops from area assigned to the Russians is certain to be misunderstood by Russians as well as at home."[130]

Truman's decision came in the second week of June. Hopkins's successful resolution of the Polish issue undoubtedly helped convince the President he could deal with Stalin. With the Potsdam Conference more than a month away, he decided that the price of Soviet cooperation in Germany was withdrawal of American troops.[131] On June 12, he cabled Churchill: "In consideration of the tripartite agreement . . . I am unable to delay the withdrawal of American troops from the Soviet zone in order to use pressure in the settlement of other problems . . . I am advised that it would be highly disadvantageous to our relations with the Soviet to postpone action in this matter. . . ."[132] After incorporating a modification suggested by Churchill, on June 14 Truman proposed to Stalin that orders be given for simultaneous troop withdrawals in Germany and Austria.[133]

This settled the matter in all essential respects. The firm line taken at the end of April was repealed. Although there was a slight delay connected with the final determination of zones in Vienna and Berlin, the American troop withdrawal took place in the first days of July.[134] At about the same time, final agreement on the Austrian zonal problem was reached.[135] Soviet troops were withdrawn from the western zones in Austria on July 22,[136] and by the end of the month the

Allied Control Council was functioning in Germany.[137] As in Poland, Truman's new diplomacy achieved its basic aims. The crisis in Allied relations had been resolved and the way was clear for cooperative administration in the heart of Germany. A second major point of Stimson's recommendation had been implemented.

THE HOPE OF THE STRATEGY OF DELAY

ON JUNE 6, 1945, Acting Secretary of State Grew sent a short but emphatic cable to Hopkins, who was preparing to leave Moscow: "The President, the Secretary and I send you heartiest congratulations and appreciation."[138] At about the same time, Assistant Secretary of War McCloy commented to the Secretary of the Navy that "Harry's visit had largely dispelled the growing suspicion of Stalin and Molotov."[139] To a Cabinet meeting, Acting Secretary Grew proudly reported: "I don't believe as a rule in crowing before the sun is really up, but I may say that the international scene is a great deal brighter. . . . "[140] And Admiral Leahy noted in his diary that both he and the President "felt that Hopkins had been very successful in allaying some of the suspicions that the Russians had about our motives."[141]

To the many who have interpreted the Hopkins mission as a victory for Stalin's policy in Poland and Germany, it is very difficult to explain why official Washington considered the mission a great success.* After all, the President had yielded basic points of a policy he had adamantly pressed only a few weeks earlier. The key to understanding, of course, is not difficult to find when one looks beyond the views of the Polish exiles and Churchill—who regarded any compromise as a defeat—to the views of the President *after* he had agreed to Secretary Stimson's strategy. Once the President had decided to wait for the atomic bomb, his main objectives were to avoid a Soviet *fait accompli* in Poland, and to establish a practical cooperative relationship in Germany. Both objectives required, as Leahy neatly summed it up, that the suspicions of Stalin be allayed.

In fact, Hopkins's mission perfectly implemented the strategy of a delayed showdown offered by Secretary Stimson. As we have seen, the

---

* See, for example, Churchill's comment that the Russians "had gained their object by delay." (*Triumph and Tragedy*, p. 583.)

Secretary had defined a number of actions necessary to establish proper relationships in Europe. First, he recommended that a confrontation on major issues be postponed until the atomic test. Second, he counseled that much of the Russian position on Poland would have to be accepted—at least temporarily. Third, he argued that United States policy had to be dissociated from the principles and person of Churchill. Finally, he urged that some way be devised to "persuade Russia to play ball" in Central Europe.

In every respect, Truman's use of the Hopkins mission fulfilled these objectives. In fact, Hopkins did even better than hoped, for on the spur of the moment he was able to resolve a major conflict over voting procedure for the Security Council of the United Nations.[142] Joseph Davies's mission to Churchill simultaneously underscored America's intention to break symbolically with Churchill. In this, its major objective was accomplished, and despite the fact that Churchill refused to agree to a preliminary private meeting of Truman and Stalin, the Prime Minister could do little about the President's refusal to meet privately with him in Britain.[143] As Truman had promised, there was to be no "ganging up."

In the spirit of this broad strategy, Truman also reversed himself on other points. His original blunt cutoff of Lend-Lease was now modified in two respects: on the day Hopkins left for Moscow, Truman told a press conference all materials provided for in existing Lend-Lease agreements would be delivered. He explained that the original cutoff order was not so much a cancellation of shipments as a gradual readjustment to conditions following the collapse of Germany.[144] Four days later, in Moscow, Ambassador Harriman amiably offered to review the whole Lend-Lease situation with Molotov.[145] In succeeding discussions, American aid was once more provided on the basis of usefulness to the prosecution of the war, rather than as a diplomatic weapon of pressure in the Polish conflict.[146]

Similarly, the firm line yielded on a second economic point. At Yalta it had been agreed that a commission made up of the three powers would meet to determine German reparations. However, after the Yalta Conference, the United States and Britain had urged that France be added to the commission. The Soviet Union refused to go beyond the Yalta agreement, and the Western powers, quite aware of the intense Soviet desire for industrial reparations, refused to allow the commission to meet unless the French were accepted.[147] The Western effort followed the same logic of economic pressure which figured in the initial Polish showdown. As late as the first week of May the United States had refused Soviet requests to begin the commission talks,[148] but when Hopkins arrived in Moscow he informed Stalin that the American reparations representative would come to Moscow—without the French.[149]

A similar change occurred in regard to the captured German fleet. On May 23 Stalin cabled Truman noting that the German Navy had refused to surrender to the Soviet Union.[150] In this message, and three days later in a talk with Hopkins, Stalin recalled the agreement that the Allies would require German forces to surrender to the forces they had fought. He pointed out that when German troops who fought Russia tried to surrender to the West, Eisenhower had promptly turned them over to the Soviet commander. He asked that, as in Italy, a fair share (one third) of the German fleet be turned over to the Soviet Union.[151] Again Truman's reply was conciliatory. Hopkins was allowed to say that the United States had no objections to such sharing.[152] Eisenhower proposed that a naval commission be established to arrange for the dispositions.[153] And the President cabled he was sure a solution could be reached which would be "fully acceptable to all of us."[154]

Despite Truman's relaxation of pressure in connection with these three issues, in reality, the President yielded very little. The Lend-Lease talks were restricted to deliveries for a six-month period, and subsequently less than half of the new Soviet requests were granted.[155] The Moscow Reparations Commission met for the first time on June 21 (four months after it had been authorized at Yalta), failed to resolve basic reparations issues, and merely delayed the problem until the Big Three met in mid-July.[156] Similarly, although Truman's response on the German fleet question was sympathetic, there was no action on the Soviet request after May 30 and the matter was also held over for the Big Three.[157]

It is not surprising that Truman chose to maintain control over final disposition of these economically important matters. From the beginning, the President had recognized the huge requirements of the war-ravaged Soviet economy and had sought to capitalize on this weakness by using American economic resources to achieve diplomatic objectives. There is no evidence that Truman ever abandoned this basic approach.* Indeed, as he prepared for his coming meeting with Stalin, he asked Congress for authority to increase the Export-Import Bank's lending capacity to $3,500,000,000. This would make an additional $2,800,000,000 available for loans during the coming year.[158] Of this amount, approximately one billion dollars was to be earmarked for a Soviet loan.[159] Accordingly, the first item on the suggested agenda for the talks with Stalin was: "Credits to the U.S.-S.R."[160]

Thus, Truman looked to the future expecting American economic power would still be of great value in dealing with Russia. His satisfaction with Hopkins's mission reflected this confidence, for he felt the door had been kept open to the future exercise of that power. He was not thinking only of the Soviet Union, however. The President believed American economic assistance would be effective in persuading the newly organized Polish provisional government to hold early elections. Such elections, he believed, would produce a democratic Poland governed along Western lines and amenable to American influence.

It will be recalled that Truman had directed Hopkins to obtain guarantees for a number of specific democratic principles for the new Poland. On recognizing the new provisional government, the President had underscored its pledge of support for all aspects of the Yalta agreement, including the provisions for early free elections. To the President, the pledge for free elections was not merely a slogan of idealistic intent; shortly after Hopkins finished his talks with Stalin, Harriman began to discuss the conditions of American economic aid to the ravaged country. He made it clear that free elections, and nondiscriminatory treatment of American investments and trade, would insure a friendly American attitude.[161]

Within policy-making circles there was no attempt to disguise this strategy. As final negotiations on the composition of the Polish government neared completion, Harriman cabled that it was "of inestimable importance from a political standpoint to begin negotiations

---

* As late as a December 1946 Cabinet discussion, "the President mentioned the reports in the morning's newspapers of the deficiencies in the grain crop in Russia. . . . He said he believed . . . that it must have become clear to them by now that they, as well as others, would have to look to the United States as the sole source of relief on the question of food." (Forrestal, *Diaries*, p. 234.)

at once with a view of granting promptly a small credit," and that this "will have a far-reaching and permanent effect on the influence of the U.S. in the political scene in Poland and particularly on our influence in connection with the carrying out of the final step in the Crimea decision, namely, the holding of truly free elections."[162] Harriman also reported the new government had agreed to allow American representatives to travel freely in the country and to admit American news correspondents.[163] He had great hopes that the elections, when held, would be fully observed.

Harriman's recommendation for an immediate small loan was well received in Washington. Although legal restrictions prohibited a credit, the American ambassador was authorized to promise economic assistance from a number of other available sources.[164] As the State Department looked to the future, it delineated its plans in explicit terms: "In order to implement our policy of establishing a truly independent democratic Polish state, we should be prepared . . . to assist through credits or otherwise in the reconstruction of Polish agriculture and industry."[165] Furthermore, in assisting "through credits and otherwise . . . we should insist on the acceptance by Poland of a policy of equal opportunity for us in trade, investments, and access to sources of information."[166]

In reality, a strategy based on the vigorous use of American economic aid to obtain political objectives in Eastern Europe was nothing more than a continuation of the broad line of policy laid down in the April showdown with Molotov. However, by late May, Truman and his advisers had come to believe that economic aid was only one weapon—and perhaps the least effective—in the American diplomatic arsenal. The belief that the atomic bomb would add great power to American diplomacy now dominated the thinking of the most important American policy makers. On May 28—the day Hopkins held his third talk with Stalin—designated Secretary of State Byrnes told one of the nuclear scientists that America, by possessing and demonstrating the atomic bomb, would make Russia more manageable in Eastern Europe.[167] On June 4, Byrnes expressed great confidence in the atomic bomb to Admiral Leahy.[168] On June 6—the last day of the Hopkins-Stalin talks—Secretary Stimson confided to his diary his belief that a satisfactory solution for the Polish problem would be arranged in exchange for allowing the Russians to participate in a system of international control of atomic energy.[169] On the same day—before Stimson could express these thoughts—President Truman told the Secretary of War that the bomb would be the crucial factor in achieving a favorable resolution of not only the Polish issue, but of problems in Rumania, Yugoslavia, and Manchuria.[170] Thus, while Hopkins negotiated an agreement which kept the door open to future American influence, Byrnes, Stimson, and Truman all waited expectantly for the atomic bomb. They were confident that once it was available it would strengthen the American hand; it would provide sanctions for the pledge of free elections and would be useful in securing other objectives in Poland and elsewhere in Eastern Europe.

For all these reasons Truman looked to the future with immense confidence. He did not regard Hopkins's negotiation as a defeat, but as a subtle success which kept the way clear for further diplomacy; he viewed the Polish agreement as "only a beginning."[171] The new American ambassador to Poland, Arthur Bliss Lane, not knowing of the atomic bomb, could not understand why Truman had postponed a meeting and had apparently yielded so much to Stalin. At the time Hopkins was completing his talks with Stalin, Lane complained to the President that "our attitude toward Soviet Russia in connection with the Polish issue should be integrated with the many other issues in Central Europe, particularly the Soviet blackouts in the Balkan states and the states of Central Europe." Truman told Lane there was nothing to fear. He said "that he had precisely the same opinion and that this would be the fundamental subject which he intended to discuss at the Big Three meeting." However, he would not force the issue to a showdown now. The President explained that while Hopkins was negotiating "it would be desirable not to exert too much pressure." Nonetheless, as Acting Secretary of State Grew minuted, the President left *no doubt as to his intention to insist on the eventual removal of the Soviet blackout in the countries mentioned. . . .*"[172]

In sum, the President and his advisers regarded Hopkins's diplomacy as a delaying action, not a defeat. It matters little that the strategy eventually failed. What is important is that in the thinking of American policy makers final determination of the Polish issue and of other problems in Eastern and Central Europe depended upon the results of the atomic test. An early showdown had failed, but a later one—if necessary—would probably succeed. In this spirit, Ambassador Harriman cabled his feeling that "the stage is set as well as can be done at the present time."[173] And, confidently writing to a friend, Acting Secretary of State Grew declared: "If we ever compromise with principle, such compromise is only a temporary measure in order the better to attain our main objectives in the end."[174]

The Far East and Two Faces of the Strategy of Delay

> It may be necessary to have it out with Russia on her relations to Manchuria and Port Arthur and various other parts of North China, and also the relations of China to us. Over any such tangled weave of problems [the atomic-bomb] secret would be dominant . . .
>
> —SECRETARY OF WAR
> HENRY L. STIMSON
> May 15, 1945

ALTHOUGH THE POLISH PROBLEM and the rumblings of dispute in Central Europe dominated official Soviet-American relations during the spring of 1945, within policy-making circles the urge to alter America's approach to Russia had not been limited to European matters. At the same time the President's advisers recommended a showdown on Poland, they also advocated that Truman reconsider American policy toward the Far East.

At Yalta, when Soviet help had been thought essential to the invasion of Japan, Roosevelt had pledged American support for certain Soviet Asian objectives, primarily in Manchuria and North China. In exchange he had received Stalin's promise to enter the war two to three months after Germany's collapse and his pledge to support Chiang Kai-shek's Nationalist Government in China. The Red Army would enter the war on condition that "the former rights of Russia violated by the treacherous attack of Japan in 1904" were restored. Specifically, the southern half of Sakhalin Island would be returned to the Soviet Union; the Manchurian port of Dairen would be internationalized ("the pre-eminent interests of the Soviet Union in this port being safeguarded"); Port Arthur would be leased to the Soviet Union as a naval base; and the Chinese Eastern and the South Manchurian railroads, "which provide an outlet to Dairen," would be operated by a Soviet-Chinese company ("it being understood that the pre-eminent interests of the Soviet Union shall be safeguarded . . ."). Additionally, Roosevelt promised American support to preserve the *status quo* in Outer Mongolia. Finally, the Kurile Islands would be handed over to the Soviet Union.[1]

The Manchurian railroads and ports were of considerable importance to the Russians because they provided a warm-water outlet for the Trans-Siberian Railroad.[2] Since it was understood that the agreement concerning these matters (and Outer Mongolia) would require the concurrence of Chiang Kai-shek, Roosevelt agreed to "take measures" on "advice from Marshal Stalin" to obtain Chiang's approval so that the claims of the Soviet Union would be "unquestionably fulfilled" after the defeat of Japan.[3]

Roosevelt's endorsement of this accord was given with little hesitation. He regarded the concessions as extremely reasonable—they constituted little more than the restoration of Russia's pre-1905 rights in the area.[4] Ambassador Harriman felt that the Yalta agreement usefully defined and limited Soviet claims: "It would have been a simple matter for the Soviets to give expression to popular demand by establishing People's Republics of Manchuria and Inner Mongolia."[5] Since the area had not been controlled by Chiang Kai-shek for many years Admiral Leahy believed that in exchange for Soviet support in the war, Stalin had received only "misnamed" concessions.[6]

Indeed, the agreement seemed quite advantageous to the United States. Besides the then vital promise of an early Soviet declaration of war, Stalin's support for Chiang Kai-shek was regarded as extremely important. China was in many ways a mirror image of Poland; in both countries if the great powers chose to support their own dissident political groups, the result was likely to be civil strife and international tension. Stalin needed Western support for the Soviet-oriented Warsaw government and Roosevelt needed Stalin's support for Chiang's Nationalist regime. After Yalta, American policy makers felt there was a good chance that—as in 1927—the Soviet Union would support Chiang Kai-shek in his struggle against the Communists.[7] The American ambassador to China, convinced that the Soviet Union controlled the Chinese Communists,[8] was delighted when they agreed to take a subordinate role in Chiang's official delegation to the San Francisco United Nations Conference.[9] Stalin made no effort to raise the status of the Communists, although at precisely the same time he was trying (unsuccessfully) to get Western recognition of the Warsaw government's right to represent Poland at San Francisco.[10]

Stalin also showed every sign of following through on the pledge to enter the Japanese war. On April 5 the Soviet Union publicly declared its intention to denounce the Soviet-Japanese nonaggression pact.[11] Even the most casual observers recognized, as the *New York Herald Tribune* commented, "Russia is preparing to enter the war in the Far East."[12] Ten days later Stalin reaffirmed the Soviet commitment to become a belligerent in a conversation with General Patrick J. Hurley, the American Special Representative and Ambassador to China. The Soviet Premier underscored both his intention to support Chiang and his plan to enter the war two to three months after the defeat of Germany. (This was the length of time it would take to transport sufficient supplies and troops from Europe across the Trans-Siberian Railroad.)[13] Although it was necessary to maintain secrecy to prevent Japanese intelligence from learning of the Soviet plan, Stalin and Hurley delineated a specific understanding to implement the accord. It was agreed that the President would arrange to have the Chinese Foreign Minister, T. V. Soong, come to Moscow by June 15. At that time treaties embodying Stalin's pledge of support for Chiang, and Chiang's approval of the Yalta arrangements for Outer Mongolia and Manchuria would be negotiated. Then Stalin would declare war.[14]

In the first days of his Presidency, Truman did nothing to alter Roosevelt's commitments. On April 19, a week after taking office, he told T. V. Soong that he should go to Moscow "as soon as he could, so that relations between China and Russia could be established on a firmer basis."[15] Three days later the President reaffirmed Roosevelt's Far Eastern pledges in a discussion with Molotov. He "intended to carry out all the agreements made by President Roosevelt."[16]

Even as Truman was making these pledges, however, American specialists on Soviet affairs began to argue the need for a "reconsideration" of Roosevelt's agreement. On April 19, Harriman told the State

Department he believed Hurley's judgment of Stalin was "too optimistic." Harriman believed Stalin would eventually support the Communists against Chiang.[17] Similarly, General Deane persuaded the Joint Chiefs of Staff that Russian aid for an invasion of Japan was no longer needed and that it would involve political problems.* By April 24 the Joint Staff Planners had gone so far as to advise: "If Russia enters the war her forces will probably be the first into Manchuria. This will raise the question of introducing at least token U.S. forces into Asia."[18] Finally, George F. Kennan, the chargé d'affaires in Moscow, and a good friend of Harriman and Deane, cabled a powerful argument in support of a new firm approach. His position was delineated in a State Department summary presented to the President on April 24:

> Kennan . . . calls attention to the fact that words have a different meaning to the Russians. Stalin is prepared to accept the principle of unification of Chinese armed forces and the principle of a united China, since he knows that these conditions are feasible only on terms acceptable to the Chinese Communists. Stalin is also prepared to accept the idea of a free and democratic China, since a free China means to him a China in which there is a minimum of foreign influence other than Russian. Kennan is convinced that Soviet policy will remain a policy aimed at the achievement of maximum power with minimum responsibility and will involve the exertion of pressure in various areas. He recommends that we study with clinical objectivity the real character and implications of Russian Far Eastern aims. . . .

The chargé's final argument dovetailed with the advice of Harriman and Deane: "It would be tragic if our anxiety for Russian support in the Far East were to lead us into an undue reliance on Russian aid."[19]

These views reached the President at precisely the same time he chose to force a showdown on the Polish issue. He was warned of the politically disadvantageous consequences of Soviet military operations on the China mainland at the same time that he was told that Soviet entry into the war was no longer essential for an invasion. Immediately the President was faced with a twofold question: Should the United States encourage Russia to declare war, or would it be better to procrasti-

---

* See above, p. 31.

nate, refusing to fulfill the Yalta understanding? Such a course might discourage Soviet entry indefinitely—or at least until Stalin had given specific assurances that he would respect Nationalist sovereignty in Manchuria and North China.

A May 10 cable from General Hurley precipitated a major discussion of the issue. Hurley reported that he had discussed the general Far Eastern situation with Chiang Kai-shek. He believed Chiang knew most of the terms of the Yalta accord and was certain that the Chinese leader would agree in substance to all of its provisions. There might only be problems about the use of words such as "pre-eminent" and "lease," which had especially unfavorable connotations in China. Hurley said that Chiang had already received reports of large-scale Soviet troop movements across the Trans-Siberian Railroad. With speculation rife in Chungking, he advised that it was time for Truman to allow him to reveal the Yalta agreement.[20]

Hurley's cable required a decision as to whether the Soviet Union should be encouraged to enter the war. Harriman, about to return to Moscow, argued that the United States should not fulfill the Yalta agreement—or at least not until new Russian pledges had been obtained. On May 11 he told a meeting in the Secretary of the Navy's office that "it was time to come to a conclusion about the necessity for the early entrance of Russia into the Japanese war." Deeply pessimistic in his view of Soviet intentions, he told Forrestal that once the Red Army entered the war "Russian influence would move in quickly and toward ultimate domination . . . There could be no illusion about anything such as a 'free China' once the Russians got in . . . The two or three hundred millions in that country would march when the Kremlin ordered."[21] Later the same day, Harriman told Admiral Leahy that Russia would enter the war "and will in the end exercise control over whatever government may be established in Manchuria and Outer Mongolia."[22]

The next day Harriman argued his case at the State Department. Before going back to Moscow he wished to have a precise definition of the American view of Soviet entry into the war. He posed these questions: "(1) The Yalta Agreement: Should it be re-examined? . . . (2) How urgent is the necessity for quick Russian participation in the war? . . ." Harriman also wanted to know whether Soviet occupation of Japan would be accepted, what arrangements would be made for a trusteeship in Korea, and how the United States wished to handle a number of other minor Far Eastern questions.[23]

The meeting agreed that Harriman's points should be formulated precisely "for discussion with the President."[24] Working in great haste to prepare for Harriman's return to Moscow, on the same day Acting Secretary of State Grew produced a formal exposition of the problem. In parallel letters to the Secretaries of War and the Navy, Grew stated that before fulfilling the Yalta agreement, the State Department thought it "desirable" to obtain additional commitments and clarifications from Stalin; the Soviet government should agree not only to support Chiang Kai-shek, but also to influence the Chinese Communists to yield to the Nationalist government; the Soviet government should reaffirm support for Chinese sovereignty in Manchuria and for a four-power trusteeship for Korea; the Soviet government should also agree to grant emergency landing rights for commercial planes in the Kurile Islands.

Grew declared that the State Department wished to withhold fulfillment of the existing Yalta accord as a bargaining tactic to obtain the new commitments. Aware that this would be breaking Roosevelt's agreement, Grew wanted to know whether there were military objections to such an approach: "Is the entry of the Soviet Union . . . of such vital interest to the United States as to preclude any attempt . . . to obtain Soviet agreement to certain desirable political objectives? . . . Should the Yalta decision in regard to Soviet political desires in the Far East be reconsidered, or carried into effect in whole, or in part?" Finally, should a Soviet demand for participation in the Japanese occupation be granted?*[25]

Truman did not wait for a judgment as to the military value of Soviet entry into the war. Sympathetic to Harriman and others who predicted the consequences of Soviet military operations on the China mainland, Truman did not wish to encourage Soviet entry if he could help it.†[26] On May 12 he cabled Hurley that it was not "appropriate at the present time" to fulfill the agreement.[27] On May 14, in a talk with

---

* On May 19, 1945, Acting Secretary Grew passed a sleepless night and, mulling over the international situation, confided his private fears to paper: "Once Russia is in the war against Japan, then Mongolia, Manchuria, and Korea will gradually slip into Russia's orbit, to be followed in due course by China and eventually Japan. . . ." (Grew, *Turbulent Era*, II, pp. 1445–46.)

† Later his view changed slightly. See below, p. 120.

T. V. Soong, the President held back information on the Yalta accord and refused to respond to questions regarding the role of the Soviet Union in the Far East. Soong, anxious for Stalin's help against the Communists, told the President he thought it very important that he should "proceed to Moscow to discuss this situation with the Soviet authorities . . ." But now Truman's earlier advice that Soong should leave "as soon as he could" had been revised. At the suggestion of Grew, it was decided to postpone consideration of his trip. As the Acting Secretary summarized the discussion, "this matter was left open."[28]

Thus, Harriman had achieved his primary objective: he had blocked immediate fulfillment of the Yalta agreement. While senior officials debated a further course, the United States would not give up the bargaining counters it held by virtue of its influential position with the Chinese government. Moreover, the President's decision, like his decision in favor of a showdown over Poland, certainly showed that he was not anxious to encourage Soviet participation in the war. There was a good chance that he might be persuaded to continue to refuse instructions to complete America's half of the Yalta bargain.

Inevitably, Truman's May 14 decision to postpone fulfillment of the Far Eastern agreement also opened the way for the Secretary of War's strategy of delay. When Stimson received the State Department inquiry, his response was instantaneous: "The questions cut very deep. . . . In my opinion [they] are powerfully connected with our success with [the atomic bomb]."[29] His reasoning followed his earlier advice on the Polish question: It would be wise to delay all negotiations until the atomic bomb added its power to the American bargaining position. Now it was time, as he told McCloy on May 14, "to keep our mouths shut."[30] The next day, discussing the "questions which Grew had propounded to us in relation to the Yalta Conference and our relations with Russia," Stimson tried desperately to convince Harriman, McCloy, Forrestal, and Grew of the need for delay. He summarized his argument in a long diary entry:

> I tried to point out the difficulties which existed and I thought it was premature to ask those questions; at least we were not yet in a position to answer them. The trouble is that the President has now promised apparently to meet Stalin and Churchill on the first of July and at that

time these questions will become burning and it may be necessary to have it out with Russia on her relations to Manchuria and Port Arthur and various other parts of North China, and also the relations of China to us. Over any such tangled weave of problems [the atomic-bomb] secret would be dominant and yet we will not know until after that time probably, until after that meeting, whether this is a weapon in our hands or not. We think it will be, shortly afterwards, but it seems a terrible thing to gamble with such big stakes in diplomacy without having your master card in your hand. The best we could do today was to persuade Harriman not to go back until we had had time to think over these things a little bit harder.[31]

POSTPONING A RECONSIDERATION OF FAR EASTERN ISSUES

ONCE MORE the same question had been posed: Should the United States raise delicate political problems for negotiation now, or later? Although the still-untested weapon might add great power to the American bargaining position, the State Department felt the only absolutely certain bargaining counters derived from American influence with Chiang Kai-shek. Negotiations should take place before Russia entered the war. The War Department, on the other hand, argued the wisdom of waiting until the "master card" was available before attempting to "have it out with Russia."

Contrary to a commonly held opinion,* the War Department did not object to raising the political questions because it feared this might jeopardize Soviet assistance in the war against Japan. Although some military leaders still wished for an early Russian declaration of war, at the end of April Truman's handling of the Polish issue had established a new principle: American political objectives were worth more than Soviet help for the invasion strategy. This judgment was reaffirmed when the Secretary of War answered Grew's questions with the declaration: "Military considerations . . . do not preclude an attempt by the United States Government to obtain Soviet agreement to desirable political objectives in the Far East."[32] Stimson's official War Department assessment was supported by General Marshall, Secretary Forrestal, and Assistant Secretary of War McCloy.[33]

---

* See Feis, *Churchill, Roosevelt, Stalin,* p. 637.

For this reason, Stimson bolstered his argument for delay not with dire warnings about the consequences of losing Soviet help in the war, but with the argument that America was in a relatively weak diplomatic bargaining position at the present juncture. He made it clear that without the strength of the new weapon, the power relationships in the Far East were much more favorable to Russia than to the United States: "The concessions . . . are generally matters which are within the military power of Russia to obtain regardless of U.S. military action short of war." His official conclusion was a study in understatement: "It is not believed that much good will come of a rediscussion at this time."[34]

Although a "rediscussion" raising the threat of a refusal to fulfill the Yalta agreement seemed futile, Stimson had no objection to beginning an exploration of the Soviet position. He concurred in the desirability of obtaining the commitments and clarifications, but argued against pressing the American position too far. Finally, of course, Stimson pointed out that it was much too early to raise the question of Soviet occupation of Japan.[35]

With the State Department urging an immediate reconsideration and the War Deparment counseling delay, the decision was now brought directly to the President. Each side pressed its case once again; Harriman, about to leave for Moscow, told Truman on May 15 that he felt it important to have an understanding of the American position before he met with the Russians. Truman agreed in general terms, but took no stand on the matters in dispute.[36] The next day Stimson met with the President to discuss diplomatic timing.[37] There is little doubt that it was also at this meeting that he expressed the deep concern of his previous night's diary entry—his awareness that a heads-of-government meeting in the first week of July would occur a few weeks too early to know the atomic-test results.[38]

Presently available records do not show to what extent the Secretary of War voiced his view that it would be "a terrible thing to gamble with such big stakes in diplomacy without having your master card in your hand"[39]—that is, to what extent he urged not only the general principle of delay, but specifically that the meeting be postponed beyond the end of June. They do show, however, that by the end of his conversation with the President, all of the Secretary of War's fears had been dispelled.[40] When he left Truman, he was satisfied that the President fully agreed with him as to strategy, and in a memorandum written later the same day he expressed his approval of Truman's approach.[41] Truman's subsequent actions show both that, as in the Polish case, the President chose Stimson's advice over Harriman's, and that Truman agreed to an additional postponement.*

There was very little Truman had to do to implement the strategy of delay in the Far East; the essence of Stimson's view was to do nothing until after the atomic test. Earlier, when Truman had agreed to reverse his initial decision on Poland, it had been necessary to send a mission of conciliation to allay the suspicions caused by the premature showdown. Now, however, Stimson asked only that "we keep our mouths shut"—that is, that the President stall. Thus, on the one hand, Truman had only to continue to withhold instructions to fulfill the Yalta conditions of Soviet entry into the war, and on the other, he had only to continue to refuse the State Department's suggestion that the threat of a "rediscussion" be used to obtain new Soviet concessions.

Following Stimson's advice with great precision, the President did absolutely nothing. Hurley received no instructions to inform Chiang Kai-shek of the Yalta agreement, and the State Department was not allowed to initiate a new *démarche*. Two and a half weeks after Truman began to procrastinate, he once more reviewed strategy with the Secretary of War. Meeting with Stimson on June 6, the President reaffirmed his agreement that the issues would not be settled until after the atomic bomb had been demonstrated, saying he hoped that at that time the Russians would offer cooperation in Manchuria as one of a number of diplomatic *quid pro quos* for taking them into partnership to control the new atomic force.[42]

During the weeks Truman was holding off Ambassador Hurley and the State Department, Stimson tried to speed up the tempo of work on the atomic bomb at the Los Alamos Laboratories.[43] "We were under

---

* From Stimson's May 15, 1945, diary entry (quoted on p. 97) it is clear that he was under the impression that Truman had definitely committed himself to a meeting on July 1. As has been shown, the President had only suggested an indefinite date after June 30. In the previous chapter I have described some of the conversation between Stimson and Truman reviewed in this paragraph, to show how the President pleased the Secretary of War by accepting his general strategy toward the meeting. Here, I wish to stress that in the same conversation Stimson's specific worry about whether the meeting was definitely fixed for July 1 was also dispelled.

incredible pressure to get it done before the Potsdam meeting," J. Robert Oppenheimer, director of the Laboratory, has testified.[44] For his part, the President tried to postpone his meeting with Stalin once again. Altering his earlier suggestion that the heads of government might meet any time after June 30, he cabled Churchill in the third week of May to state that he could not yet name a date for the meeting but that "I may, within the next two weeks, have more information bearing on a date."[45] The contractors supplying firing circuits and molds for casting the nuclear explosive had fallen two weeks behind in deliveries; thus, the test would take place two weeks later than originally expected.[46] With the latest information available, on May 28 Truman instructed Hopkins to suggest that the Big Three meet on July 15.[47] Thus, when a week later Stimson warned of the "greatest complication" if the bomb had not been "laid on" Japan by the time of the meeting, Truman reassured him that he "had postponed that until the 15th of July on purpose to give us more time."[48]

This new delay of the Potsdam meeting enraged Churchill. The Prime Minister had never understood why the President wished to hold off so long and now—still wishing to maintain pressure on the Russians—he was furious. Churchill cabled both Truman and Stalin, urging that the meeting be held "in the very near future . . . about the middle of June."[49] On May 30, Stalin replied that it was Truman, not he, who had suggested the July 15 date. Churchill's reply was filled with urgency: "I consider that July 15th, repeat July, the month after June, is much too late. . . . I have proposed June 15th, repeat June, the month before July, but if that is not possible, why not July 1st, July 2nd, or July 3rd?" Stalin's response was brief: "I should like to tell you again that July 15 was suggested by President Truman . . ." It was only when faced with the united stand of Truman and Stalin that Churchill yielded to the frustrating and seemingly inexplicable dictates of the strategy of delay.[50]

A WAY TO PREVENT RED ARMY CONTROL OF MANCHURIA

ALTHOUGH STIMSON had opposed a "rediscussion" based on a threat to withhold completion of the Yalta understanding, he had raised no objection to an *exploration* of the Soviet position vis-à-vis the Far

East. With no fundamental disagreement between the State and War Departments on this narrow point, Truman instructed Hopkins to undertake a third task while in Moscow—on May 28 he and Harriman sought a clarification of the Soviet attitude on the future treatment of China, Manchuria, and Korea.[51] Hopkins's report to the President summarized the favorable results of the discussion:

> Stalin made categorical statement that he would do everything he could to promote unification of China under the leadership of Chiang Kai-shek. . . . He specifically stated no Communist leader was strong enough to unify China. . . . He repeated all his statements made at Yalta, that he wanted a unified and stable China . . . to control all of Manchuria. . . . He stated categorically that he had no territorial claims against China and mentioned specifically Manchuria and Sinkiang and that he would respect Chinese sovereignty in all the areas his troops entered. . . . Stalin stated that he would *welcome representatives of the Generalissimo to be with his troops entering Manchuria* in order to facilitate the organization of Chinese administration in Manchuria. . . . Stalin agreed with America's "open door" policy and went out of his way to indicate that the United States was the only power with the resources to aid China economically after the war. He observed that Russia would have all it could do to provide for the internal economy of the Soviet Union. . . . Stalin agreed that there should be a trusteeship for Korea. . . .* [52]

These assurances were all that could be asked. The exploratory talks had obtained the objectives sought and even from the State Department's point of view had rendered an immediate "rediscussion" of the Yalta agreement unnecessary. On purely diplomatic grounds there was now far less reason to consider withholding fulfillment of the Yalta accord.† Although it was impossible to know whether Stalin would honor his pledges, both Hopkins and Harriman were optimistic. "We were very encouraged by conference on the Far East," Hopkins cabled; and Harriman added, "The talks . . . were of real value, particularly Stalin's agreement to take up . . . the political matters

---

* The emphasized sentence was thought to be the most important point, for it would mean a dominant role for the Nationalist Government rather than the Communist Chinese. (*Conference of Berlin*, I, p. 62.)

† For this reason it is not possible to know for certain whether Truman might have changed his position and permitted the State Department to threaten a breach of the Yalta agreement. Even while Hopkins and Harriman were in Moscow, the State and War Departments struggled over the issue. (Feis, *China Tangle*, p. 308*fn.*) More light may be shed on this point when access to all the relevant documents is allowed.

affecting China . . . and also his agreement to allow the Generalissimo's representatives to go into Manchuria with the Russian troops. . . ."[53]

Even though he felt the ultimate settlement of the Manchurian issues could not be completed until the atomic bomb had been demonstrated, Truman was delighted with these reports. In a diary entry at this time Stimson records: "[The President] asked me if I had heard of the accomplishment which Harry Hopkins had made in Moscow and when I said I had not he told me there was a promise in writing . . . that Manchuria should remain fully Chinese except for a ninety-nine-year lease of Port Arthur and the settlement of Dairen which we had hold of. . . ."*[54]

At the same time Hopkins pleased the President with his report on the Far East he also cabled that Stalin had repeated the pledge that the Red Army would be prepared to march by August 8, but that no troops would be committed until agreement on the basis of the Yalta accord had been reached with China. Stalin suggested that T. V. Soong come to Moscow as soon as possible. Hopkins advised: "This procedure seems most desirable from our point of view. . . . He left no doubt in our mind that he intends to attack during August. It is therefore important that Soong come here not later than July 1st."[55]

Truman agreed to send Soong to Moscow to begin discussions with Stalin before the beginning of July.[56] Despite this decision, however, *he did not decide to fulfill Roosevelt's Yalta pledges.*† On June 4 he informed Hurley in general terms that a number of problems relating to the maintenance of a democratic government in China would be dealt with *when the heads of government met.*[57] And, as we shall see, he continued to follow the strategy of delay, refusing to settle the final negotiations until the atomic bomb had been shown.‡ Although this decision initially followed the rather simple logic that the new weapon would be a "master card" in the ultimate diplomacy, there was now a second reason for wishing to delay the negotiations. If a Soviet declaration of war could be postponed, it now became obvious that the atomic

---

* This is apparently an exaggeration. No record of a written agreement has been found, nor does such an agreement reappear in later negotiations on these points.

† I have emphasized this point because some have thought that because Truman agreed to send Soong, he also agreed to fulfill the Yalta accord. As will be shown, the deduction does not follow from the fact. (See Feis's error, *Between War and Peace,* pp. 113–14.)

‡ See below, pp. 192–194.

bomb might end the war before the Red Army crossed the Manchurian border. Thus, not only would the bomb influence the negotiations, but—far more important—it might provide a way to prevent Soviet military control of the area.

In fact, the Soong mission now became intimately bound up with the use of the atomic bomb and the desire to prevent the Red Army from entering Manchuria. This subtle and complex question will be taken up in due course. But, for a proper understanding of American strategy, it must first be understood that, contrary to the opinion of some writers,* the President's seemingly conciliatory decision to send Soong to Moscow (and his subsequent attitude toward the mission) did not derive primarily from a feeling that great care had to be taken for fear that Stalin might delay his entry into the war. On the contrary, by mid-May this fear (which had indeed troubled Washington at an earlier date) had all but disappeared. In its place there was now almost unanimous agreement that the Red Army would attack in mid-August.

Ironically, Truman's showdown over Poland had provided the best test of Soviet intentions in the Far East: although General Marshall had warned that a tough approach might jeopardize an early declaration of war against Japan, in fact, his judgment had been proven wrong.† Even at the height of the tensions over Poland, there was every sign that Russia would enter the war as soon as sufficient numbers of troops had been transported across the Trans-Siberian Railroad. Before Hopkins left for Moscow, and before there was any break in the tense atmosphere, Stimson noted in his diary (on May 15) that there was no longer much doubt about Stalin's plan to enter the war at an early date.[58]

---

* Feis consistently presents the unsupported opinion that "the surviving wish to have Russian cooperation in the war continued to constrain American officials in their differences with the Soviet Union over various European situations." This is a vital point in one accepted interpretation of this period; those who have not taken proper account of the atomic bomb's role in the diplomacy of delay must explain why Truman adopted a conciliatory attitude during May and June. The easiest, but incorrect, explanation is the one offered by Feis: Truman did not want to lose Russian help in the war against Japan. As will be shown, however, not only was there no longer a fear that Russian help would be lost by political action, but Truman hoped to *delay* Russian entry. Thus, as explained, the Hopkins mission and Truman's conciliatory approach derived not from military considerations, but from the desire to delay a diplomatic confrontation with Stalin until the atomic bomb had been shown. (Feis, *Churchill, Roosevelt, Stalin*, pp. 599–600; *Japan Subdued*, p. 14; Ehrman, *Grand Strategy*, p. 294. See also my Appendix II.)

† See above, p. 51.

Indeed, for some time Marshall seems to have been almost alone in his cautious estimate of Stalin's intentions; his was the conservative Army view (as Admiral Leahy has observed), which carefully and skeptically examined every form of assistance which could be added to the invasion strategy.[59] But both before and after the showdown, the fear that Stalin might delay his entry into the war does not seem to have dominated the thinking of other senior policy makers. Throughout the last half of the war, at Teheran, at Moscow, at Yalta, Stalin had promised to join the fight against Japan two to three months after the defeat of Germany.[60] After October 1944 Churchill had "no doubt whatever" that Stalin would declare war as soon as Germany was beaten.[61] And Roosevelt told Harriman, "I have at no time entertained any doubts whatever" as to Stalin's intentions.[62]

Even those who did have doubts were greatly reassured by the April Soviet notice of intention to denounce the nonaggression pact with Japan.[63] As we have seen, in mid-April Stalin explicitly reaffirmed his plan to declare war two to three months after German surrender.[64] On April 22 Molotov made it clear to Truman that Russia had lost no interest in the Yalta understanding.[65] The two American representatives in Moscow, Ambassador Harriman and General Deane, repeatedly counseled that Russia would enter the war at an early date because of its own interests in the Far East.[66] Secretary Forrestal, Acting Secretary of State Grew, Secretary Stimson, all agreed with this estimate.[67] There were continuous reports of Soviet troop movements to the Far East and by mid-May even Marshall seems to have been won over. After a talk with the cautious General, Stimson recorded that "we" now think Russia will enter the war at an early date.[68] A week later Marshall endorsed Stimson's assurance that there was no danger that raising the political issues would jeopardize a Russian declaration of war.[69] Hence, Hopkins's May 28 report that Stalin "left no doubt in our mind that he intends to attack during August" only confirmed the existing consensus.*[70]

Thus, it is clear that after mid-June the American approach to the question of Soviet entry into the Japanese war was no longer domi-

---

* Note also the phrasing of Grew's May 12 letter: " . . . In connection with the political effects of the *expected Soviet entry* . . . " (Department of Defense, "Entry of the Soviet Union into the War against Japan," p. 69.) Compare Churchill's May 14 message to Halifax: "Having regard to their [Russia's] own great interests in the Far East, they will not need to be begged . . . " (Churchill, *Triumph and Tragedy*, p. 576.)

nated by a fear that Stalin might delay until all of the "dirty work" had been done, as Marshall had once feared. Secretary of the Navy Forrestal was probably closer to the truth when he later commented that "fifty divisions could not have kept them *out*."[71] The real question was whether the war could be ended before the Red Army—and, inevitably, Soviet influence—flowed from Siberia across the Manchurian border. As they pondered this question, American policy makers had to consider Japan's capacity to sustain the hostilities and to decide whether or not the United States could afford to dispense with a Soviet declaration of war.

From any rational military point of view, Japan was already defeated. By early summer the better part of the Imperial Navy had been sunk and the Imperial Air Force had been reduced to the impotence of sporadic kamikaze attacks.[72] B-29 bombers met only limited resistance as they struck at targets of choice. Between March 9 and June 15 almost seven thousand bomber missions were dispatched for urban incendiary attacks; losses amounted to only 136 planes, an average of a mere 1.9 per cent of the sorties.[73] Japanese morale slumped after repeated poundings, in the course of which the greatest single man-made disaster in history was recorded: the March 10 raid on Tokyo resulted in 124,000 casualties.[74] General Curtis E. LeMay's grisly boast was only a slight exaggeration: the bombing raids were "driving them back to the stone age . . ."[75] But this was only the beginning. With the capitulation of Germany, it was clear that the full force of American and British power would be focused on only one target.[76] Now Japan, with a productive capacity only 10 per cent as large as America's, would bear the brunt of the best military resources accumulated during the European war.[77] Clearly, defeat was inevitable. In fact, Japanese leaders had already reached this conclusion; their main reason for continuing the struggle was a desire to try to modify the rigid unconditional-surrender formula. They hoped that by purchasing the good offices of the Soviet Union with Japanese-controlled concessions on the China mainland they might improve the surrender terms.[78] But here too there were ominous signs; Soviet denunciation of the nonaggression pact raised grave doubts that this frail hope could be fulfilled.[79]

In this situation American policy makers recognized the crucial role a declaration of war by Russia would play. It would close the one remaining loophole which allowed Japanese leaders to find hope in a continuation of the war. Indeed, with Japanese power and morale crumbling, the continued though fading Soviet neutrality was the proverbial straw to the drowning man; *both* Japanese military *and* political leaders, for different reasons, rested their hopes and their strategies on the next move of the Soviet Union. The military thought possibly that Russia might be persuaded to join with Japan, but, more realistically, they hoped for Soviet neutrality. The political leaders thought possibly that Russian neutrality might be maintained, and hoped that Russian mediation might end the war with less stringent surrender terms.[80]

Although Japanese peace feelers had been sent out as early as September 1944[81] (and Chiang Kai-shek had been approached regarding surrender possibilities in December 1944),[82] the real effort to end the war began in the spring of 1945. This effort stressed the role of the Soviet Union. In April a new Japanese government headed by the moderate Admiral Suzuki was formed. The man chosen to be foreign minister—Shigenori Togo—was carefully selected; he was well known for his opposition to the war and his friendliness toward the Soviet Union (he was a former ambassador to Moscow). Togo accepted the post on the understanding that he would be free to try to end the war,[83] and immediately the new government initiated a major diplomatic *démarche* which, subtly straddling the narrow agreement between the various Japanese political and military groups, delicately carried Japan's last hope forward in exploratory talks with Russia.[84]

It is not the purpose of this essay to analyze the various Japanese maneuvers based on the hope of Russian help.* These continued from April until the end of the war,[85] and since the United States had broken the Japanese codes much earlier in the war, they were known to the highest American authorities.[86] The important point for our purposes is that the increasing dependence of Japan upon the attitude of the Soviet Union had major implications for American policy. Although the April 24 report that Soviet help was no longer needed *for*

---

* For more information on these matters, see Butow, *Japan's Decision to Surrender;* Kase, *Journey to the Missouri;* Togo, *The Cause of Japan;* F. C. Jones, *et. al., The Far East 1942–46;* Zacharias, *Secret Mis-* sions. Note especially Butow, pp. 60, 61, 65, 66, 67, 71, 72, 78–80, 83–91, 110, 123; Kase p. 84; Jones, pp. 126–32; Zacharias, pp. 359–60.

an invasion was endorsed by the Joint Chiefs on May 10,[87] it now appeared that a Soviet declaration in and of itself might shock Japan into surrender long *before* an invasion would have to be launched.

The political and psychological value—as distinct from the purely military value—of Russian entry into the war had long been acknowledged by Churchill. As early as September 1944 the Prime Minister had argued that Japan would surrender once faced by the combined strength of the three powers.*[88] However, American policy makers had been reluctant to rely upon the shock value of Russian entry. For months, as they cautiously plotted an invasion, they had refrained from overly optimistic assessments of the possibility of surrender.[89] But by the late spring of 1945, it was impossible to overlook this opportunity to end the war without an invasion.

In mid-April the Joint Intelligence Committee reported that Japanese leaders were looking for a way to modify the surrender terms to end the war.[90] The State Department was convinced the Emperor was actively seeking a way to stop the fighting.[91] By April 24 the Joint Staff Planners cautiously suggested that an invasion *"threat* in itself" might bring *unconditional* surrender.[92] The War Department too was impressed by the changed Japanese attitude.[93] In late April the chief United States Army planners initiated studies on "what we do if Japan decides to surrender on V-E Day."[94] Admiral Leahy was convinced the war could be ended long before an invasion would have to be launched.[95] Secretary Forrestal and Acting Secretary Grew believed that a statement reassuring the Japanese that "unconditional surrender" did not mean dethronement of the Emperor would probably bring an end to the war.[96] Secretary Stimson thought that even a powerful *warning* by itself might bring capitulation. He added that guarantees for the Emperor would make the prospect for quick surrender much better.[97]

Within Japan, the destruction of the last of Japanese naval power and the loss of Okinawa—the first major island of the home chain—strengthened the hand of the moderates urging peace.[98] By mid-June six members of the Supreme War Council had secretly entrusted For-

---

* The judgment was held consistently for almost a year; on July 17, 1945, General Ismay reported a Combined Intelligence Staff estimate to Churchill that "when Russia came into the war against Japan, the Japa-nese would probably wish to get out on almost any terms short of the dethronement of the Emperor." (Quoted in Ehrman, *Grand Strategy*, p. 291.)

eign Minister Togo with the task of approaching the Soviet Union "with a view to terminating the war if possible by September."[99] By early July the United States had intercepted messages from Togo to the Japanese ambassador in Moscow which showed that the Emperor himself had now taken a personal hand in the matter and had directed that the Soviet Union be asked to help end the war.[*][100] The Emperor's intervention confirmed earlier intelligence estimates, and it unquestionably signaled Japan's willingness to surrender. Forrestal termed the telegrams "real evidence of a Japanese desire to get out of the war."[101] Grew has confirmed the importance of the Emperor's intervention; for American leaders, as Leahy put it, "were certain that the Mikado could stop the war with a royal word."[102]

As the Japanese position deteriorated, on May 21, Secretary Stimson advised that a Russian declaration of war would have a "profound military effect." He ordered further studies of the problem. As these were being prepared, Stalin reported to Hopkins that there were renewed Japanese feelers aimed at securing Soviet help to end the war.[103] In early June, Stimson received a report from the War Department's Operations Division which concluded:

> Like [that of] the Germans, [Japanese] protracted resistance is based upon the hope of achieving a conditional surrender. . . . Probably it will take Russian entry into the war, coupled with a landing, *or imminent threat* of landing . . . to convince them of the hopelessness of their position.[104]

By mid-June even the extremely cautious General Marshall advised the President that "the impact of Russian entry on the already hopeless Japanese may well be the decisive action levering them into capitulation at that time or shortly thereafter if we land in Japan."[105] In early July the Combined Intelligence Committee was even more definite—"An entry of the Soviet Union into the war would finally convince the Japanese of the inevitability of complete defeat."[†][106]

---

* Truman's recent declaration that he knew of these approaches removes former doubts as to whether the intelligence information reached the highest officials. (*Conference of Berlin*, I, p. 873.)

† The complicated and continuously changing military picture has been misunderstood by almost every important observer. Ehrman's analysis, which recognizes that American policy makers were not overly anxious for Russian help, is the best. However, Ehrman misses the two radical shifts in American military thinking; he fails to give proper weight to the April 24 judgment that Russia (*Continued on next page*)

The various assessments of the shock value of a Russian declaration of war were based, of course, upon the assumption that the Japanese would be forced to accept "unconditional surrender." However, by the end of May, every important senior American policy maker, including the President, had decided that, if necessary, the rigid surrender formula would be substantially modified to assure the Japanese that the Emperor would retain his throne.[107] As Acting Secretary of State Grew noted on May 29, it was only "the question of timing [that] was the nub of the whole matter."[108] As early as April 18 the Joint Planners had reported that a clarification of the surrender terms in itself might be all that was needed to achieve surrender.[109] Throughout May this judgment was continuously reinforced so that by June it was clear to American leaders that either a Russian declaration of war or a change in the surrender terms was likely to bring capitulation.[110] Almost certainly a combination of the two measures would stop the fighting immediately.

(It is not my purpose to argue whether either or both of these measures would, in fact, have ended the war. What I wish to show is that American leaders *believed* such a result was likely. Hence, their decision to use the atomic bomb was made at a time when the best intelligence and military advice indicated there were other ways to end the war without an invasion. As will be shown, the bomb was used not because there were no alternatives, but precisely because American policy makers wished to avoid the political consequences of these alternatives.)

Thus, as each day of the spring passed, it became more and more doubtful that an invasion would be needed to force Japanese capitulation. To be sure, it was important to go forward with planning for an invasion, especially since General Marshall did not wish to weaken morale by raising possibly false hopes, but such planning now took on a contingency aspect; it was necessary to be prepared, but actual

---

(*Continued from preceding page*)
was no longer needed *for an invasion,* and he misses the mid-June judgment that a Russian declaration of war could make an invasion unnecessary. (Ehrman, *Grand Strategy,* pp. 292–95.) Feis's failure to distinguish results is the other possible error; he thinks American policy makers always wanted Russian help. He mentions, but does not realize the importance of the April 24 judgment

and completely misses the mid-June assessment. Typically he fogs the argument by mixing up early-April judgments with late-April opinions and with general comments from different periods throughout the summer. (Feis, *Japan Subdued,* p. 13.) Hewlett and Anderson make the same mistakes, confusing different assessments made at different times throughout the summer. (*The New World,* p. 349.)

operations would be launched only if all other methods to end the war failed.[111] Thus, as Admiral Leahy has stressed, *"The invasion itself was never authorized."*[112] Prudence, not necessity, dictated military thinking. Advance preparations for an invasion which would not in any event begin until November 1 (three months after Russia was expected to declare war) followed the logic of Admiral Ernest J. King's advice to the President:

> So far as preparation was concerned, we must aim now for Tokyo Plain; otherwise we will never be able to accomplish it. If preparations do not go forward now, they cannot be arranged for later. Once started, however, they can always be stopped if desired.[113]

In this spirit, when Truman approved the plans outlined by the Joint Chiefs on June 18, he made it absolutely clear that he would "decide as to the final action later."[114] As Assistant Secretary of War McCloy has emphasized, the President let it be known that he would withhold his final decision until the time "beyond which there would not be further opportunity for a free choice."*[115]

While American military planners outlined alternatives for all eventualities, the President and his senior civilian advisers focused their attention on more immediate matters; every important American policy maker, including the President, had grave reservations about Russian military operations in Manchuria. Some, of course, like Admiral Leahy (who took a "jaundiced view" of Russian domination of the area) had never believed a Russian declaration of war should be encouraged.[116] But if it could be arranged, Harriman, McCloy, Grew, Forrestal, Stimson, Byrnes, and Truman, all preferred to end the war without Russia, or at least before the Red Army had gotten very far into Manchuria.†[117] Thus, they no longer directed their efforts to forcing capitulation before the November 1 target date for an invasion, but before the August 8 target date for Soviet entry. "I

---

* This point is often overlooked. For instance, R. C. Batchelder's recent *The Irreversible Decision* (p. 119) still argues that an invasion was taken for granted.

† Even Leahy's published memoirs hint at this purpose. Note his discreet understatement: "Some of us indulged in a hope that Japan might get out of the war before the Soviet Government came in." (Leahy, *I Was There*, p. 419.) See also Eisenhower's report of a discussion with Truman in mid-July: "I told him that since reports indicated the imminence of Japan's collapse I deprecated the Red Army's engaging in that war." (Eisenhower, *Crusade in Europe*, pp. 441–42; Forrestal, *Diaries*, pp. 78–79.)

must frankly admit . . . I would have been satisfied had the Russians determined not to enter the war," Secretary of State Byrnes cautiously hinted in 1947. "I believed the atomic bomb would be successful and would force the Japanese to accept surrender on our terms."[118]

But the fact that all eyes were on the August 8 target date, rather than the November 1 invasion date, has been affirmed and reaffirmed in much more explicit terms: "Though there was an understanding that the Soviets would enter the war three months after Germany surrendered," Byrnes has more recently testified, "the President and I hoped that Japan would surrender before *then*."[119] And still more explicitly: "We wanted to get through with the Japanese phase of the war before the Russians came in."*[120]

A War Department report made to Stimson at the time stated the crucial consideration in more general terms:

> [An early] Japanese surrender would be advantageous to the U.S., both because of the enormous reduction in the cost of the war and because it would give us a better chance to settle the affairs of the Western Pacific *before too many of our allies are committed there and have made substantial contributions to the defeat of Japan. . . .*[121]

Byrnes has also stated specifically that he wished to end the war before Russia entered, because "I feared what would happen when the Red Army entered Manchuria."[122] This statement deserves close attention, because it underscores the important point that Japan was so weakened and Russia had so little capacity to undertake an amphibious invasion that there was never any danger of Soviet operations in the Japanese home islands.† Thus, the desire to end the war before Russia entered was not based primarily, as is sometimes thought, on a

---

* This fact also undoubtedly accounts for Byrnes's use of the conjunction "and" instead of the preposition "to" in a key statement in his memoirs; he writes that it was "essential to end the war as soon as possible *and* avoid the invasion." The two goals, of course, were not the same. Elsewhere Byrnes has admitted that from among the alternative ways to end the Japanese war before an invasion the atomic bomb was chosen so as to avoid Russian entry. (Byrnes, *All in One Lifetime,* pp. 286, 300, 308.)

† Max Beloff has noted this point, but misunderstood its significance. Attempting to confute P. M. S. Blackett's argument that the atomic bomb was used to end the war before the Russians reached Japan, he rightly notes that there was never any chance that the Russians would get that far. However, he overlooks the more fundamental point that American policy makers saw the bomb as a way to keep the Russians out of Manchuria. Thus Blackett's argument, though wrong in detail, is right in substance. (Beloff, *Soviet Policy,* p. 106; Blackett, *Military and Political Consequences,* pp. 116–30. See also U.S. Senate, *Hearings: Military Situation in the Far East,* p. 6.)

wish to prevent Soviet occupation of Japan.* Rather, American policy makers, aware that Russia could conquer the Japanese armies on the China mainland in less than two months,[123] desperately hoped to end the hostilities before Soviet military operations paved the way for Soviet domination of Manchuria and North China.

It was with this diplomatic objective in mind that American policy makers once again considered the political value of the atomic bomb. Despite their subsequent assertions, they were no longer primarily worried about having to undertake a costly invasion of Japan.[124] They believed a Russian declaration of war in itself would probably end the war quickly if necessary. They were also prepared to moderate the surrender terms to end the war before an invasion.† Consequently, the fundamental objective was no longer military, but political—could the war be ended before August 8?

Truman had already decided (or assumed) that the bomb would be used in Japan. Even in his April 24 discussion with Stimson, there had never been any question about whether the new weapon would be employed when it was ready.‡ At the end of April, General Marshall gave Field Marshal Wilson information on the operational use of the new bomb and told him it would be used sometime in August.[125] Indeed, the President has emphasized: "Let there be no mistake about it. I regarded the bomb as a military weapon and never had any doubt that it should be used."[126]

Thus the only question was how, not whether, the atomic bomb would be employed. Originally, at about the time of the Yalta Conference, the bomb had been regarded as a new tactical weapon of unusual force; Marshall planned to use it *in conjunction with an invasion*.[127] A total of nine bombs were to have been dropped as three

---

* Later, Stimson argued that an end to the war before Russian operations had begun in Manchuria would also obviate Soviet claims to help occupy Japan. See below, p. 190.

† This fact also allows us to delineate American priorities with some precision. The most important objective was to end the war without an invasion. Since there seemed little problem about this, the dominant questions were: Could the war be ended before Russia entered? And could the unconditional-surrender formula be maintained? It is easy to show that if forced to choose between Russian entry and modifications of the surrender formula, American leaders preferred to relax the surrender terms offered to the Emperor. But, as Byrnes has written, a further political value of the bomb was that it seemed to obviate such a choice—"I believed the atomic bomb would . . . force the Japanese to accept surrender *on our terms*." (Knebel and Bailey, *No High Ground*, p. 36; Stimson, *On Active Service*, p. 621; Grew, *Turbulent Era*, II, p. 1450; Byrnes, *Speaking Frankly*, p. 208.)

‡ See above, p. 56.

armies assaulted the island of Kyushu from different directions. Two bombs would have supported each attack, and in each case a third would have been brought into operation against Japanese reserves.[128] From this point of view, the idea that the few available bombs might be squandered on civilian or quasi-military targets would have seemed a waste of irreplaceable resources needed for the invasion. However, the deterioration of Japanese power and morale permitted a reconsideration of these plans.

In fact, American policy makers now saw a Russian declaration of war and the atomic bomb as military and psychological equivalents. Originally, they had regarded Russian entry as important mainly because of its value to the invasion strategy. Shortly after they revised this assessment, however, they saw that a Russian declaration of war in and of itself might be enough to shock Japan into surrender. Similarly, although they had first regarded the atomic bomb as a supporting weapon, to be used tactically in the actual invasion, they now came to see that it might be powerful enough in and of itself to shock Japan into surrender. Thus, by the end of May the President's special representative, Byrnes, "was confident that, when developed, it would bring a speedy end to the war in the Pacific."[129]

It was for this reason that the Interim Committee seriously considered neither whether to use the atomic bomb, nor whether to use it in support of an invasion. Japan was in such dire straits that American leaders felt it wise to approach the bomb as a weapon of terror. Hence, when the Interim Committee met on May 31 to consider the problem, the only important question was how the bomb could be used to end the war quickly, that is, how it could be used with the greatest psychological effect.[130] As Stimson was later to write, to edge the faltering Japanese into capitulation, all that was needed was "a tremendous shock,"[131] or, in General Marshall's words, "a terrific shock."[132]

The Interim Committee considered the matter first in a joint meeting with its scientific panel. As Arthur H. Compton, a member of the panel, has written, "It seemed a foregone conclusion that the bomb would be used. It was regarding only the details of strategy and tactics that different views were expressed."[133] In fact, the Committee was not given much information about the relationship of the bomb to the war. There was little discussion of alternative methods to end the war.

Although Hopkins had just reported that there was "no doubt" Stalin would enter the war in August, apparently nothing was said about awaiting the results of the Russian declaration of war or about using the bomb in conjunction with the Russian declaration.[134] J. Robert Oppenheimer has testified: "We didn't know beans about the military situation in Japan. We didn't know whether they could be caused to surrender by other means . . ."[135] The only question was the best way to use the bomb so as to create a dramatic and shocking effect.*[136]

First, the President's special representative asked one scientist about a suggestion that the Japanese be given some striking but harmless demonstration of the bomb's power before using it in a manner that would cause great loss of life. For about ten minutes the proposition was the subject of general discussion. Oppenheimer could think of no demonstration sufficiently dramatic to convince the Japanese that further resistance was futile. Others objected that the bomb might not explode, or that the Japanese might shoot down the delivery plane or bring American prisoners into the test area. If the demonstration failed to bring surrender, the chance of administering the maximum surprise shock would be lost.[137]

After some discussion, Stimson offered a conclusion which commanded general agreement: there would be greater shock value if the bomb was dropped without advance warning. While it would be unwise to aim only for a civilian area, it would be best to make as profound a psychological impression on as many of the inhabitants as possible. James B. Conant suggested, and Stimson agreed, that the best target would be a vital war plant employing a large number of workers closely surrounded by workers' houses. The next day, when the Interim Committee met in executive session, Byrnes formally proposed the Committee recommend that the bomb be used as soon as possible and without warning against a Japanese war plant surrounded by workers' homes. The Committee adopted the suggestion.†

---

* I have seen no evidence for Ehrman's assumption that "the Interim Committee made its recommendations with full knowledge of the strategy for the Pacific." (*Grand Strategy*, p. 279.)

† The preceding paragraphs rely heavily upon Hewlett and Anderson, *The New World*, pp. 358–60.

I have not dealt with the important story of the attempt by a group of scientists to prevent use of the atomic bomb against a civilian target. On June 16 the Scientific Panel, reviewing suggestions made by a number of scientists, reported to the Interim Committee that they could propose no (*Continued on next page*)

At the same time the Interim Committee was reaching this conclusion Secretary Stimson and General Marshall discussed the best method to employ the new weapon.[138] Of course, the Secretary of War bore ultimate responsibility for recommendations as to the use of the weapon, but there was little difference between his view and that of the Committee. The objective was the most dramatic and shocking disclosure of the new force, and Stimson and the Committee agreed that an unannounced strike upon a large city was the best approach[139]—"Any other course . . . involved serious danger to the major objective of obtaining a *prompt* surrender from the Japanese."[140]

Stimson took every precaution to ensure that the attack would make the greatest impression. Fearing that the B-29 raids might bomb out Japan so thoroughly that the atomic weapon would not have a fair background against which to show its strength, Stimson spoke to both the President and Army Air Forces Chief, General Henry H. Arnold, about the matter. It was agreed that orders would be issued not to bomb a number of cities, so that unblemished targets would be available when the bomb was ready.[141]

On June 1 Byrnes reported the recommendation of the Interim Committee to the President.[142] Since Truman had already assumed use of the weapon, and since he already saw it primarily as a way to end the war before Russia entered, the only real point he had to approve was whether the Committee's approach would produce the greatest shock effect. He told Byrnes that, regrettable as it might be, so far as he could see, the only reasonable conclusion was to use the bomb.[143] He told Stimson the bomb "should be dropped as nearly as possible upon a war production center."[144] He approved the Committee's recommendation,[145] and early in June the commander of the special B-29 group stationed in the Pacific was informed that one atomic bomb would be available for use against the enemy on August 6, 1945.[146]

(*Continued from preceding page*)
technical demonstration likely to bring an end to the war. This recommendation was based on two assumptions: (1) that the bomb was needed to avoid an invasion; (2) that the war had to be ended very quickly. Since neither the panel nor the Committee discussed alternative ways to end the war without an invasion, it is not surprising that this recommendation was produced. Note that even this evaluation came two weeks *after* the Interim Committee had reported the best method to use the bomb to the President, and two months after Truman had assumed its use in the war. The views of the scientists never reached the President. (Feis, *Japan Subdued*, p. 43; Hewlett and Anderson, *The New World*, pp. 369–70;

A SUBTLE PROBLEM OF THE STRATEGY OF DELAY

THUS STIMSON'S JUDGMENT that the atomic bomb would be dominant over the "tangled weave" of political problems in the Far East became a major feature of American policy. When Stimson first offered his strategy of delay, he had stressed mainly that the bomb would eventually strengthen the American diplomatic hand. However, now a second aspect of the policy had emerged: the atomic bomb could pay political dividends by ending the Japanese war before Russia entered. Obviously, this would preclude Russian domination of Manchuria, but there were also important implications for European political problems: a quick end to the war would allow the President to maintain large concentrations of troops in Europe during the initial postwar negotiations.

Indeed, Truman felt it politically so important to have a major force in Europe that on June 6 (a month *after* German surrender) he told his staff he "would withdraw only the troops we could *spare from Europe* for our war in the Pacific."[147] In reality, however, by now he hoped the bomb would allow him to end the war not only before an invasion had begun, but many months before—that is, before massive troop transfers, which could take from four to six months to complete, had progressed very far.[148] The thought "uppermost" in his mind was "how soon we could wind up the war."[149] Thus, in a talk with Stimson concerning the atomic bomb, he "stressed the need for speed in the Pacific" at the same time he argued the necessity of maintaining troops in Europe for political purposes.[150]

Although Stimson had successfully urged the political value of the atomic bomb's capacity to end the war quickly, there was a major

---

Knebel and Bailey, "The Fight over the A-Bomb"; see also Alice K. Smith, "Behind the Decision to Use the Atomic Bomb.")

One member of the Interim Committee, Under Secretary of the Navy Ralph A. Bard, later changed his mind. His June 27 dissent stressed a combination of three alternative ways to end the war without the use of the bomb: "Emissaries from this country could contact representatives from Japan . . . and make representations with regard to *Russia's position* and at the same time give them some *information* regarding the proposed use of *atomic power,* together with whatever *assurances* the President might care to make *with regard to the Emperor* of Japan. . . . It seems quite possible to me that this presents the opportunity which the Japanese are looking for. I don't see that we have anything in particular to lose . . . The only way to find out is to try. . . ." (Quoted in Knebel and Bailey, *No High Ground,* pp. 109–10.) Emphasis supplied.

problem which prevented straightforward execution of the strategy of delay. As Stimson had noted on May 15, one of the "great uncertainties" was "when and how the [atomic bomb] will resolve itself."[151] This point was also raised at Truman's June 18 discussion of military strategy. Until this time all conventional military planning by the Joint Chiefs had been kept quite separate from discussions of the atomic bomb.[152] At this meeting, however, Assistant Secretary of War McCloy found the invasion plan fantastic; he was sure the bomb would end the war. As he later told Secretary Forrestal, he argued that the bomb "was pertinent not merely to the question of the invasion of the Japanese mainland but also to the question of whether we needed to get Russia in to help us defeat Japan."[153] Although the President welcomed McCloy's arguments, the meeting went forward with its plans because it was agreed that no one could be absolutely sure the bomb would work. The President would make his final decision later.[154]

Despite the great confidence of Stimson and the others, American policy makers were still dealing with an untested weapon; simple prudence required that they not rely entirely upon the unknown quantity. It was undoubtedly for this reason that, as we shall see, despite his desire to end the war before the Red Army crossed into Manchuria, Truman did not yet wish to abandon a Russian declaration of war as an alternative way to prevent an invasion. In fact, Truman told his military advisers that firmly securing the declaration was a major objective of his trip to Potsdam.[155]

Indeed, if the bomb should fail, he would lose nothing by encouraging early Russian entry, for without the new force the United States would hardly be in a position to oppose Stalin's political objectives in Asia. As Stimson had pointed out, the Russians could choose to "await the time when U.S. efforts will have practically completed the destruction of Japanese military power and can then seize the objectives they desire at a cost to them relatively much less than would be occasioned by their entry into the war at an early date."[156]

Since an early declaration might still be useful, there was every reason to hold on to the option of a Russian shock ending to the war. Yet Truman's problem was extremely subtle; for, if the bomb should work as expected, he did not want, as we have seen, to encourage Stalin to launch his Manchurian offensive. Truman's late-May decision to send Soong to Moscow forced him to consider his course with some care. When Soong arrived at the end of June, he would be asked to affirm the Yalta accord as a condition for Russian entry into the war. Should the United States fulfill Roosevelt's pledge to "take measures" to ensure that Russia's claims would "unquestionably" be met?

Weighing all considerations, on June 13, the Joint Chiefs of Staff recommended that a Soviet declaration of war was just valuable enough to warrant fulfillment of the Yalta accord.[157] Now that the shock value of Soviet entry had replaced the minimal value of the Red Army's usefulness to an invasion, the Joint Chiefs reversed the April 24 decision that no Pacific supply route would be cleared "until the Soviets on their own initiative so request."[*][158] They now also discarded the judgment that "only such contributing operations as are essential to establish conditions prerequisite to invasion" should be conducted.[159] Instead, on June 29 they directed that new plans be prepared for keeping open a sea route to Russian Pacific ports.[160] General Deane was instructed to tell the Russian military that the Joint Chiefs would like to discuss coordination of efforts for the war, and *for the first time* the scope of the Potsdam Conference was broadened to include a discussion of military cooperation in the Japanese war.[†][161] Nevertheless, the Joint Chiefs (with the exception of Marshall) were restrained in their enthusiasm for Soviet help. At the military discussion of June 18 the President was left with this statement of the military position:

> Admiral King said he wished to emphasize the point that, regardless of the desirability of the Russians entering the war, they were not indispensable, and he did not think we should go so far as to beg them to come in. While the cost of defeating Japan would be greater, there was no question in his mind but that we could handle it alone. He thought that the realization of this fact should greatly strengthen the President's hand in the forthcoming conference.[‡] [162]

---

* See above, p. 31.

† I have not been able to find the precise date of the decision to broaden the Conference agenda. Available evidence shows that it was after Stalin agreed to the Potsdam meeting at the end of May. The decision probably was taken on June 13, together with the recommendation that Russia be encouraged to declare war. (Department of Defense, "Entry of the Soviet Union into the War against Japan," p. 72.)

‡ In fact, of the professional military leaders Marshall, still taking the Army view that Russian help would be valuable, was the only positive force in favor of encouraging Russia. King's view is given above, Leahy had never wanted the Russians to enter the war, and the following day General Arnold presented the view that the Air Force could finish the war alone. (Craven *(Continued on next page)*

Despite its qualifications, the mild recommendation that the Yalta conditions for Soviet entry be met was at odds with Stimson's argument that the Far Eastern negotiations should be delayed. Truman's decision was once again in favor of the Secretary of War. Although he had to send Soong to Moscow or risk revealing that he might not fulfill Roosevelt's Yalta pledge, Truman now decided that the Chinese Foreign Minister would not be allowed to complete his negotiations with Stalin.[163] As Byrnes has subsequently revealed, the President's execution of the strategy of delay was extremely subtle:

> Our purpose was . . . to encourage the Chinese to continue negotiations. . . . If Stalin and Chiang were still negotiating, it might delay Soviet entrance and the Japanese might surrender. The President was in accord with that view.* [164]

Thus, Truman continued to straddle two policies at once. He continued to attempt to delay a Soviet attack, hoping that the war could be ended quickly by the atomic bomb;[165] and on the other hand, until he was sure of his course, he avoided any action which might lose the insurance of a Russian declaration of war should the atomic test fail.[166]

Probably because of the notorious inability of the Chinese to maintain secrecy, Truman did not reveal his strategy to Soong. Instead, he let it be known in various indirect ways that he wished the Sino-Soviet negotiations to drag out at least until mid-July and probably longer. Meeting with T. V. Soong on June 9, Truman revealed the Yalta agreement and indicated generally that he would continue Roosevelt's commitment.[167] However, when Soong met with Grew two days later to discuss details, the Acting Secretary of State refused to give a precise definition of the American position. Soong wanted to know what was meant by the pledge to support the *"status quo"* in Outer Mongolia, and the "pre-eminent interests" of Russia in Dairen and the

---

(*Continued from preceding page*) and Cate, *Air Forces in World War II*, V, pp. 711, 741.)

Compare General Ismay's comment that Soviet help was "worthless from the military point of view." Also Churchill's remark: "We are in a good position there. We don't care if [Stalin] comes into the war against the Japanese or not. We don't need him now." (Ismay, *Memoirs*, p. 403;

Mikolajczyk, *The Pattern of Soviet Domination*, pp. 133–35.)

* Although this statement was made with respect to a specific cable sent to Soong after his arrival at Moscow, I have placed it here at the outset of the argument as it is my purpose to show that this course was followed from the end of June, with slight variations, until the middle of August.

Manchurian Railroad.[168] Grew's vague responses brought Soong at one point to ask just what the United States had supported. Grew would give no definite answers. Instead, he said he assumed no final agreement could be reached until the Big Three considered the problem at Potsdam.[169]

Such a statement from the Acting Secretary of State spoke volumes; the United States had no interest in an early conclusion of the Sino-Soviet negotiations. However, Soong still wished for more details, and unable to get them from Grew, he asked to see the President again.[170] On June 14 he probed Truman's stand, trying to get a more definite assessment, but he found that the President would not be pinned down.[171] He stated only that he wanted to get early Russian help in the war, but that he "wished to assure Dr. Soong that he would do nothing which would harm the interests of China, since China was a friend of the United States in the Far East."[172] Two days later, on June 16, Grew and Truman privately agreed that certain portions of the Yalta accord could not be settled until the Big Three met.[173] Shortly thereafter Grew included Far Eastern problems on the recommended agenda for Potsdam.[174]

At the same time that the President met with Soong he instructed General Hurley to inform Chiang Kai-shek of the Yalta commitment.[175] Hurley found that Chiang had already been told of the understanding by the Soviet ambassador.[176] He reported that the Chinese leader was pleased with Soviet assurances of support for Chinese territorial integrity and political independence under Nationalist sovereignty.[177] Since Chiang counted heavily upon Stalin's help against the Communists, and since China had no control over the areas in which Russia sought concessions, Hurley was certain there would be no difficulty in fulfilling the Yalta accord—"I am convinced that the Soviet Union and China will be able to reach an agreement quickly."*[178]

Thus, when Soong reached Moscow in an American Army plane at the end of June a curious reversal of roles had occurred.[179] The United States, which had originally agreed to press Chiang to accept

---

* General Wedemeyer later attempted to argue that Chiang was disappointed at the Yalta terms, and General Hurley later contended that he was trying to modify the Yalta terms, but these claims are not borne out by the 1945 documents. (See U.S. Senate, *Military Situation Far East*, pp. 2417, 2432, 2885–89.)

the Yalta terms, had now lost interest in completing the Sino-Soviet negotiations. In fact, Truman clearly wished to delay a settlement and was in no hurry to fulfill the conditions of Soviet entry into the war. On the other hand, Chiang Kai-shek greatly valued an agreement with Stalin which would redound to his benefit in the struggle against the Chinese Communists. He was only too happy to pay the Yalta price in an area where Chinese authority had not been exercised for years.[180] He had nothing to lose, for once the Red Army crossed the Manchurian border there would be little he could do to eliminate Soviet influence. Consequently, as Harriman has testified, when Soong reached Moscow, the Chinese Foreign Minister "made it clear to me that his Government was anxious to reach an agreement with the Soviet Union, and to this end he was prepared to make concessions which *we* considered went beyond the Yalta understanding."[181] Indeed, as soon as the negotiations began, the American ambassador found that instead of having to "take measures" to see that the Chinese agreed to Stalin's claims, he had to hold Soong back at a number of steps along the way.[182]

Stalin offered a four-piece package: a treaty of friendship and alliance which explicitly and publicly conveyed Soviet support to Chiang instead of the Communists; an agreement to recognize the independence of Outer Mongolia; an agreement regarding the Manchurian ports of Dairen and Port Arthur; and an agreement covering the Manchurian railroads.[183] The points where differences might arise were not of great importance. They inevitably involved the interpretation of the Yalta pledge to preserve the *status quo* in Outer Mongolia and to safeguard the "pre-eminent interests" of the Soviet Union in the Manchurian ports and railroads.[184]

China had not exercised control over Outer Mongolia since 1911, and Stalin interpreted the phrases to require *de jure* Chinese recognition of the country's acknowledged *de facto* independence.* He also argued that Soviet "pre-eminent interests" required Soviet administrative control over an internationalized regime in the port of Dairen; and joint Sino-Soviet ownership of railroads, with Soviet manage-

---

* The situation was anomalous in that both the Soviet Union and China paid lip service to Chinese sovereignty in the area, while the Mongolian government entered into independent relations with foreign powers. (*Conference of Berlin,* I, pp. 865–67.)

ment.*[185] These claims were far less than the pre-1905 rights Roosevelt had promised to support, and Chiang had no important objections to the substance of the Yalta accord.[186] Initially, however, he wished to avoid the politically difficult recognition of Outer Mongolian independence.[187] He also preferred Chinese administration over Dairen, and Chinese ownership of the railroads, with joint Sino-Soviet control and mixed management.[188]

As can be seen, none of these were important points of disagreement. The differences were trivial compared with Stalin's pledge to support Chiang materially and morally against the Communists, to withdraw Soviet troops from Manchuria after the fighting and, above all, to take Chiang's administrators with the Red Army into the Soviet zone of combat.[189] As Stalin and Soong began to bring their initial negotiating positions closer together, however, the United States intervened decisively. Despite the State Department's recommendation that Chiang "would be well advised" to recognize the independence of Outer Mongolia,[190] on July 4 Truman instructed Harriman to "informally" tell Soong that he did not believe the Yalta agreement necessitated recognition of the Mongolian government.[191] Byrnes, who had just taken office as Secretary of State, "was afraid Soong would . . . make additional concessions if he were in doubt about our attitude."[192] Hence, a further message was sent to Chungking urging Chiang not to go beyond the American interpretation of Yalta.[193]

Truman later characterized these efforts as "strong diplomatic support to China while T. V. Soong negotiated . . . in Moscow," but this description is misleading.[194] In fact, Truman attempted not to support Chiang, but to *restrain* him.† By now it was clear that the talks could be stretched out until the atomic test and the Potsdam Conference.[195] Thus, on July 6—the day Truman sailed for Potsdam—Harriman received a further instruction: he was now to tell the Rus-

---

* Later it was claimed that Stalin's demands went "substantially beyond the Yalta understanding." At the time, however, the State Department advised that Stalin's claims were "clearly more advantageous to China" than the terms calling for the complete restoration of the rights possessed by Russia prior to the Russo-Japanese War to which Roosevelt had agreed. (*Congressional Record*, Aug. 27, 1951, p. A5415; *Conference of Berlin*, I, pp. 864–72.) The State Department has also advanced the dubious argument that the general agreement to recognize Chinese sovereignty in Manchuria should have taken precedence over the specific terms regarding the restoration of previous rights. (*Ibid.*, p. 870.)

† This is sometimes obscured, because despite *Chiang's* desire for agreement, *Soong* did not wish to be personally responsible for yielding on the politically touchy issues. (*Conference of Berlin*, II, pp. 1245–46.)

sians and Chinese that the United States wanted no final agreement to be concluded until the American government had been fully consulted. At an "appropriate time" the United States would also like to make certain that the treaties provided for nondiscriminatory treatment against third parties in the operation of the ports, railroads, and trading arrangements in the area.[196] This would ensure that America's traditional "Open Door" policy would be protected. Finally, Harriman was told that the United States could not accept Stalin's interpretation of the "pre-eminent" Soviet interests in the ports and railroads.[197] Following these instructions, the American ambassador secured Soong's promise that no agreement would be concluded until Truman had been consulted.[198] Harriman then advised Soong to break off his negotiations with Stalin.[199]

As these diplomatic efforts went forward, military planning placed less and less reliance on the Soviet Union. On July 3, the Joint Chiefs instructed General Arnold to reserve four cities for attack by the atomic bomb.[200] On July 4 the British formally approved the use of the new weapon against Japan.[201] On July 11, the Joint Chiefs recommended that only after other competing demands had been met should Russia be sent Lend-Lease equipment for possible use in the Japanese war.[202] And on the eve of the Potsdam Conference Admiral Leahy rejected the suggestion that he "take up with the President as soon as possible the question of Lend-Lease to Russia." He felt the matter "was involved with the date that Russia might enter the war against Japan and that the date might not be determined at this conference, since it might depend upon agreement between Russia and China."[203]

While the American government laid its plans on the assumption that Sino-Soviet agreement would not be reached, however, Chiang Kai-shek and T. V. Soong made renewed efforts to conclude the negotiations. "The fact is that in spite of the position I took Soong gave in on several points to achieve his objectives," Harriman later testified.[204] Chiang sent Soong new instructions: he was now to yield to the Soviet position regarding Outer Mongolia. Soong was instructed to suggest that a plebiscite be held and to promise that China would accord *de jure* recognition to a new independent status at the war's end. In exchange for this concession, Chiang asked for specific pledges of Soviet help against the Communists.[205]

Stalin too was anxious to complete the negotiations. On July 10 he accepted Chiang's offer. He "stated categorically that he would support only the National government in China and that all the military forces in China must come under the control of the government."[206] Now the only points in dispute concerned the minor questions of control and management for Dairen and the Manchurian railroads.[207]

At this juncture, Harriman and T. V. Soong considered their next step. The Chinese Foreign Minister had already agreed not to complete the negotiations until Truman had been consulted.[208] With the Big Three Conference (and the atomic test) less than a week off, Harriman reported that if the United States held to its interpretation of the Yalta agreement, the negotiations would be delayed at least that long.[209] Truman and Byrnes, now in mid-Atlantic aboard the cruiser *Augusta,* radioed back instructing Harriman to say that although the United States did not want to act as interpreter, they believed the Chinese should not meet the Russian position regarding the port of Dairen and the railroads. Harriman was also told to reaffirm the American demand that no final agreement be concluded until the United States had been consulted.[210] This message, together with Soong's previous assurances, precluded final agreement. The Chinese Foreign Minister now followed Harriman's advice and, despite Stalin's protests, broke off the talks and left for Chungking on July 14.[211] Harriman reported that Soong was willing to leave the final negotiations in Truman's hands.*[212]

Thus, the strategy of delay had been fully implemented. Truman looked forward with great optimism as he considered the leverage the July 16 atomic test might give to two faces of his diplomacy[213]—now the Manchurian negotiations would be completed only after the "master card" had been demonstrated; and, with luck, the war might be dramatically ended with the Red Army still stalled on the far side of the Manchurian border.†

---

* For more information on these discussions see Feis, *China Tangle,* pp. 315–21; *Japan Subdued,* pp. 60–61; *Between War and Peace,* pp. 113–14; Truman, *Year of Decisions,* pp. 315–21; Byrnes, *Speaking Frankly,* p. 205; *All in One Lifetime,* pp. 290–91; U.S. Dept. of State, *Relations with China,* pp. 114–25; *Congressional Record,* Aug. 27, 1951, pp. A5410–16.

† Ehrman, misunderstanding this subtle point, thinks the United States "did not intend to seek actively to prevent Russia from declaring war. . . . " (*Grand Strategy,* p. 292.)

Under the influence of the new strategy, American military policy had gone through radical reversals in the few months of Truman's Presidency. From the early judgment that Russian entry was "a prerequisite to a landing in the Japanese homeland," it had shifted to the late-April decision that "early Russian entry . . . is no longer necessary." Finally, Truman's ultimate conclusion had been reached: *"If the test should fail, then it would be even more important to us to bring about a surrender before we had to make a physical conquest. . . ."*[214]

American diplomacy had followed suit. At Yalta, Roosevelt had promised to "take measures" on "advice from Marshal Stalin" to arrange Chiang Kai-shek's concurrence in the conditions for Soviet entry into the war. The American ambassador had received a stern directive: "We should not permit the Chinese Government to gain the impression that we are prepared to assume responsibility as 'adviser' to it in its relations with the U.S.S.R."[215] Truman, however, had reconsidered Roosevelt's arrangements and in the middle of May had decided to postpone fulfillment of his predecessor's pledges. By mid-June his policy had come full circle; the American ambassador now coached the Chinese Foreign Minister in his every move. And the Soong mission, originally designed to induce an early Soviet declaration of war, now served quite another purpose. Contesting minor railroad and port issues, American diplomacy utilized the mission to execute a carefully articulated stalling action; as the President and his advisers waited for the atomic bomb, the Soong negotiations were carefully set in the path of the Red Army poised for its assault across the Manchurian border.

The Tactics of the Potsdam Conference (I)*

The President was tremendously pepped up by [the report of the successful atomic test] and spoke to me of it again and again when I saw him. He said it gave him an entirely new feeling of confidence and he thanked me for having come to the Conference and being present to help him in this way.

—SECRETARY OF WAR
HENRY L. STIMSON
July 21, 1945

A FACE-TO-FACE MEETING with Stalin had originally played no part in President Truman's approach to Manchuria and the intimately related question of Soviet participation in the Japanese war. Despite the President's June comment that it was important to meet with the Soviet Premier in order to insure an early Russian declaration of war, the decision to hold a heads-of-government meeting so soon after Yalta had initially derived from entirely different considerations. The original motivation had been a desire to maintain the pressure of the immediate showdown approach; and the chief concern had been to

*I have chosen the word "tactics" for the title of this and the next chapter to emphasize that in no way can the essay be considered a history of the Potsdam negotiations. Many complicated and important questions are treated only briefly. Other questions are not dealt with at all. I have, however, taken up the substantive issues Truman and Byrnes felt to be most important (Byrnes, *Speaking Frankly*, pp. 67–68), and the reader is referred to *Conference of Berlin*, I and II, for a detailed record of the meeting.

reduce or eliminate Soviet influence in Eastern and Central Europe.*

The President's decision to delay a confrontation with Stalin implied no abandonment of this fundamental approach. Although Truman's conciliatory attitude during May and June has led many observers to believe that Truman was determined to follow Roosevelt's broadly cooperative approach, in fact, the firm line of policy initiated in April had been set aside only as a temporary tactical maneuver as the President awaited the outcome of the atomic test. Hopkins's resolution of the Polish issue only removed the chosen symbol of the President's policy; but there was no change in the fundamental objective. The Polish issue had taken on special significance mainly because it had seemed to afford an opportunity to establish precedents for all of the liberated countries† and now the basic question once more came to the fore.

Thus, even as Hopkins negotiated in Moscow, the President and his advisers laid plans to renew the firm approach to political and economic problems in Eastern and Central Europe. Truman told Grew this would be the "fundamental subject" of his meeting with Stalin.[1] And on June 15, the President directed Admiral Leahy to prepare an agenda for the Conference. The restrained approach could now be abandoned. It was time, he stated, "to take the offensive."[2]

Originally, three powerful considerations had given Truman confidence that his firm approach to the Soviet Union might succeed. Not only had it been decided that Soviet help was no longer needed *for an invasion* of Japan, but the American Army had been at its greatest strength in Europe; and the leverage of American economic power had seemed irresistible at a time when the Soviet government was beginning to consider its vast postwar reconstruction requirements.‡ These fundamental considerations did not change during the two summer months of conciliation and delay.

Despite Churchill's earlier fears, Stimson's promise that redeployment would not materially weaken American strength on the Conti-

---

* See above, pp. 39–40. This of course, continued to be the primary motivation. See, for example, Byrnes's statement: "We anticipated little discussion at Potsdam about the Japanese phase of the war. . . . [In preparation] we concentrated on the sub-jects incident to winding up the European conflict. . . . " (Strauss, *Men and Decisions,* p. 437.)

† See above, pp. 22–23.

‡ See Chapter I.

nent was fulfilled; as Potsdam approached there were still more than three million American and British troops in Europe.* Prospects for the future also looked bright; the Joint Chiefs of Staff reported there would be excess troops on the Continent well into 1946.[3] And on July 5, the day before Truman embarked for the Conference, the House Select Committee on Post-War Military Policy gave approval to proposals for a peacetime military conscription and training program, an action which stimulated hope that American conventional power would not be dissipated immediately after hostilities.[4] Secretary of State Byrnes—acting less than twenty-four hours after taking office on July 3—reminded the President that American troops in Europe would be of primary importance "from the political aspect."[5] Byrnes thereby officially affirmed his support for the consensus that, as Grew put it, without adequate power "our diplomacy becomes weak and ineffective."[6]

Similarly, as Potsdam approached, there was no diminution in American economic bargaining strength, and, indeed, the President's advantage in this respect had considerably increased. Truman intended to offer economic aid to Stalin, and as we have seen, the first item on his agenda was "Credits to the U.S.S.R."[7] But whereas in April the President had only been able to speak of his hope that Congress would make this source of negotiating power available to his administration, now he was in a far stronger position. As the President left for his meeting with Stalin, both the Senate and House committees considering postwar financing gave an extremely friendly reception to Lend-Lease Administrator Leo T. Crowley as he presented the administration's official proposals. Crowley encountered few objections to legislation to increase the lending authority of the Export-Import Bank from $700 million to a full $3.5 billion in the first year of peace. Even the eminently conservative Senator Robert A. Taft agreed with Crowley's suggestion that Russia could receive a first-year credit of approximately one billion dollars.[8] Taft thought this a "fair amount."[9]

Such support undoubtedly added to Truman's confidence that he would be able to dispose of large-scale credits in his bargaining with

---

* Information provided by the U.S. Department of Defense. Estimated world-wide strength of American (excluding British) forces on August 31, 1945: 11,913,639; estimated total for USSR on the same date: 10,600,000. See also Eisenhower, *Crusade in Europe*, p. 429.

Stalin. Additionally, however, the President knew he would have control over other resources certain to be of great importance to the Soviet government. Stalin had already pressed his strong interest in German industrial reparations and in a division of the German fleet—and control over both of these was largely in Western hands. Moreover, there were other bargaining counters available, for it was known that Stalin would seek Anglo-American agreement to a revision of the Montreux Convention governing the Dardanelles, to Soviet participation in a trusteeship over former Italian colonies, and to recognition of the governments established under Soviet auspices in the Balkans.[10]

But more important than any of these considerations, of course, was Truman's belief that the atomic bomb would almost certainly lend great power to his diplomacy. Indeed, the need to wait until the new force had been tested and demonstrated before discussing diplomatic issues with Stalin had been a controlling factor throughout the summer. The Potsdam meeting itself had been twice postponed for this reason. Now, in early July, as Truman has written, "Preparations were being rushed for the test atomic explosion in Alamogordo, New Mexico, at the time I had to leave for Europe, and on the voyage over I had been anxiously awaiting word on the results."[11] On the eve of his first meeting with the Soviet delegation, the President confidently told an associate: "If it explodes, as I think it will, I'll certainly have a hammer on those boys!"[12]

With such an array of diplomatic power at his disposal the President was evidently quite hopeful that although his initial showdown had been frustrated, a new "offensive" might succeed. The primary objective remained the promotion of economic and political stability throughout Europe—a goal regarded as the *sine qua non* both of world peace and of American security.* For one thing, this meant a commitment to a strong Continental economy which had powerful implications for the American approach to Germany.† But in Eastern Europe, "if the political situation . . . could be adjusted so that Hungary, Yugoslavia, Rumania, and Bulgaria, as well as Poland and Aus-

---

* See above, pp. 52–55, 77–80.   † See below, pp. 161–173.

tria, could all have governments of their own people's choosing," Truman believed, "this would help us in our plans for peace."[13]

Thus, as in Poland, although American diplomats were concerned with possible restrictions on free trading arrangements,[14] the first objective was to secure reasonably representative and Western-oriented governments which would promote democracy through free elections.[15] As in Poland, as Crowley told Congress, economic leverage would provide one source of strength in the attempt to achieve this objective in each country.[16] But, first it would be necessary to reduce or eliminate dominant Soviet influence. It was the hope of American diplomacy that the Soviet Union would agree to establish representative governments throughout its zone of military control. And it was the belief of American diplomats that early free elections would dissipate whatever remained of the substantial Soviet wartime authority in the area.[17] (1965)

At this late date in the Cold War it is extremely difficult to recapture the assumptions and conceptions of American diplomacy in 1945. It must therefore be emphasized that at the time the optimistic American appraisal was not simply wishful thinking. Stalin's December 1944 abandonment of the Greek Communists seemed very real evidence of his willingness to cooperate. In France, Italy, and Belgium, the Communist parties, at the height of their influence because of their predominance in the resistance movements, meekly yielded much authority to Western-oriented governments.[18] In Finland, where Soviet influence was great, free elections had already taken place (in March).[19] In Austria, the Renner government established with Soviet support met the State Department's criterion as "representative."[20] In Czechoslovakia, President Eduard Benes reported no Soviet interference in political matters, American reporters were given free rein and the United States maintained satisfactory diplomatic relations.[21]

Even in Poland, the hope that early free elections would be held as pledged was strengthened when visiting Western correspondents were permitted unrestricted freedom and when wartime political controls restraining the Western-oriented groups were relaxed.*[22] To be sure,

---

* The political situation in Poland presented a mixed picture. However, American hopes were reinforced by reports, such as the one from the Western-oriented former premier, Mikolajczyk, that he was "hopeful that through the strength of the Peasant party a reasonable degree of freedom and (*Continued on next page*)

there were disturbing events at this time,[23] and at a later date the entire atmosphere was to change, but one cannot understand American strategy without recognizing that in the late summer of 1945 there seemed reasons to believe that Stalin might be prepared to work with the West: The actions of the Communist parties in France, Greece, and Italy, and Soviet support for democratic governments in Finland, Czechoslovakia, and Austria were of very real political significance: They yielded power to anti-Communist groups in the crucial formative period of postwar politics. For the Communists to attempt later to regain the lead would not be easy.*

Thus, though their hopes were later to be disappointed, as American diplomats surveyed the problems of Europe in the late summer of 1945, they were not deeply worried about problems in the West,[24] and they had considerable confidence that their plans for democratic governments might be implemented almost everywhere on the Continent.† Their confidence, however, did not easily extend to Southeastern Europe. For here, despite the fact that Communist armies found themselves supporting monarchies,[25] Stalin did not show the same attitude he exhibited elsewhere. And for this reason, the real focus of American attention was in the Balkans.‡

The immediate issues arose because the conduct of the war had given the Soviet Union predominant political power in Hungary, Bulgaria, and Rumania. American policy makers acknowledged, as the Acting Secretary of State advised the President on June 28, that "spheres of influence do in fact exist, and will probably continue to do so for some time to come."[26] Grew went on to comment: "In view of the actual Eastern European sphere and the Western Hemisphere bloc

---

(*Continued from preceding page*)
independence can be preserved now and that in time, after conditions in Europe become more stable and Russia turns her attention to her internal development, controls will be relaxed and Poland will be able to gain for herself her independence of life as a nation. . . . " (*Conference of Berlin*, I, p. 728.)

* For an illuminating account of how this policy appeared from the point of view of the more militant and independent Communists, see Djilas, *Conversations with Stalin*, especially pp. 12–13. Regarding the Soviet abandonment of the Greek Communists, see below, p. 134.

† Byrnes did not lose this confidence for

a very long time. In July 1947—exactly two years after Potsdam—he was still convinced that there was no immediate danger of Communist revolution in Western Europe and his interest was still focused on Eastern Europe. If the other powers would "hold firm," he was certain that the Soviets would "retire in a very decent manner." (*Speaking Frankly*, pp. 294–95.)

‡ The term "the Balkans" does not properly include Hungary. However, the State Department regarded the problems of Hungary, Bulgaria, and Rumania as the same, and it is therefore convenient to use "the Balkans" in the loose sense common in many documents. This is also Churchill's usage. (*Triumph and Tragedy*, p. 227.)

. . . we are hardly in a position to frown upon the establishment of measures designed to strengthen the security of nations in other areas of the world . . ."[27] Despite this judgment, however, Grew and others did not hesitate to urge an active initiative to promote American policy objectives throughout the Soviet-controlled areas.[28]

The problems of implementing a policy designed to establish a new political and economic order within the Soviet area were considerable. American awareness that spheres of influence existed reflected not only the obvious fact that the Red Army occupied the entire region; equally important was the fact that the Soviet political position in each country had been acknowledged—and indeed, endorsed—by the United States and Britain in three separate agreements negotiated during the last months of the war.

The first was the famous arrangement initiated by Churchill and concluded between the Soviet Union and Britain after discussions lasting from May to October 1944. "Let us settle our affairs in the Balkans," Churchill had proposed to Stalin, and the two had agreed to acknowledge "90 per cent" Soviet influence in Rumania in exchange for "90 per cent" British influence in Greece. Additionally, Soviet influence was defined as "80 per cent" in Bulgaria, "80 per cent" in Hungary, and "50 per cent" in Yugoslavia.* Churchill had thus recognized varying degrees of Soviet predominance in three Balkan countries in exchange for a free hand in Greece and joint responsibility in Yugoslavia. In his report to the Cabinet on this accord, Churchill stressed the need to respect Soviet security requirements: "Thus it is seen that quite naturally Soviet Russia has vital interests in the countries bordering on the Black Sea, by one of whom, Rumania, she has been most wantonly attacked with twenty-six divisions, and with the other of whom, Bulgaria, she has ancient ties."[29]

Roosevelt had initially accepted the Churchill-Stalin arrangement for only a three-month trial period.[30] There is no doubt that the President had qualms about the idea of a division of responsibilities, but there was little he could do about it.[31] He allowed his ambassador to "observe" the negotiations between Churchill and Stalin, and although Harriman could not commit the President, neither did Roose-

---

* These final agreed percentages are taken from Woodward, *British Foreign Policy*, p. 308. Churchill's report (*Triumph and Trag-* *edy*, p. 227) gives only the initial British bid and neglects to discuss subsequent negotiation between Molotov and Eden.

velt instruct him to raise any objections.[32] Indeed, by mid-October Roosevelt had cabled Churchill and Stalin: "I am most pleased that you are reaching a meeting of your two minds. . . ."[33] More important than this general message of approval, however, was the fact that by early 1945 Roosevelt, fully aware of the meaning of his action,[34] had explicitly endorsed the general understanding when it was "translated"[35] into the terms of the armistice agreements for Hungary, Bulgaria, and Rumania.[36]

These second Balkan agreements granted the Soviet commander (who was also chairman of the Allied Control Commission in each instance) the same almost unlimited authority which the earlier Italian armistice had granted to the West.[37] In Rumania, Soviet authority was to continue without diminution until a peace treaty had been signed.[38] Reflecting the reduced percentages (as was explicitly understood),[39] the Bulgarian and Hungarian armistice terms vaguely allowed that Western representation on the Allied Control Commissions in the two countries might be increased in the "second phase" beginning after German capitulation and extending until the peace treaties had been signed.*

The Churchill-Stalin arrangements were tested in December 1944, when British troops were used to establish order in Greece.[40] "Stalin . . . adhered strictly and faithfully to our agreement of October," Churchill has written, "and during all the long weeks of fighting the Communists in the streets of Athens, not one word of reproach came from *Pravda* or *Izvestia*."[41] As Churchill was to point out, Stalin's respect for British predominance in Greece, "in spite of the fact that all this was most disagreeable to him . . ."[42] reaffirmed the validity of the basic accord and underscored the reciprocal obligations toward the Soviet sphere undertaken by the West.[43]

The Churchill-Stalin arrangement, the armistice agreements, and the Greek incident established the framework for the early 1945 discussions at Yalta. Here the third agreement covering the Balkans was negotiated. Before the Conference, the State Department—which had

---

* It is quite surprising that scholars have paid so little attention to the only detailed agreements relating to Southeastern Europe. The armistice texts are readily available. (See Senate Committee on Foreign Relations, *A Decade of American Foreign Policy*, 1941–49, pp. 455, 482, 487, 494.)

objected to Roosevelt's acknowledgment of the first informal Churchill-Stalin accord and his endorsement of the armistices[44]—tried to convince the President that his position had to be reconsidered.[45] On the eve of the Conference, the State Department argued that Western influence in the area could be re-established only if democratic governments were promoted and free elections were held. In addition to a general "Declaration" of intent, the Department urged the President to propose a new consultative agency with real power to assist the countries "in setting up governmental authorities broadly representative of all democratic elements in the population."[46]

Roosevelt, however, was not prepared to challenge the Soviet prerogatives he had so recently endorsed. Byrnes reports that he "did not like" the State Department's proposal.[47] And shortly before the Conference, Stettinius told Eden of Roosevelt's "misgivings."[48] Under considerable pressure from his own delegation (among them Byrnes, who was "greatly impressed" with the proposal), during the Yalta meeting Roosevelt reluctantly agreed to propose a considerably modified version of the Declaration.[49] This pledged the powers to consult "where in their judgment conditions require" assistance to establish democratic governments.[50] The requirement of unanimity even before consultations could begin, of course, acknowledged Soviet authority and veto rights in the area. But Roosevelt gave further and more specific definition to his understanding of the spheres-of-influence arrangement. Without hesitation, the President rejected the heart of the State Department proposal, excising the provisions which would have established an agency with power to implement the broad ideals. Moreover, Secretary of State Stettinius was authorized to remove even the few phrases of the general Declaration which pledged the powers to "establish appropriate machinery for the carrying out of the joint responsibility set forth in this Declaration."*[51]

Similarly, at Yalta Roosevelt made no attempt to reconsider the specific conditions of the armistice agreements he had signed, and it is apparent from discussions before and during the Conference that the President regarded the broadly phrased Declaration primarily as a device to offset domestic criticism of the *de facto* spheres-of-influence

---

* It is difficult to understand how Feis can characterize these as "some minor changes of language." (*Churchill, Roosevelt, Stalin*, p. 550.)

understanding.* Truman's special representative for the Balkans later commented: "The facile use without any definition of such controversial terms [as 'democratic elements,' 'free elections,' et cetera] would alone be sufficient reason to doubt the soundness of the document as a basis for joint action."[52]

Indeed, two weeks after Yalta, when the Soviet government exercised its prerogatives under the armistice agreement by intervening in Rumania to establish a new government under Petru Groza, Roosevelt (like Churchill), refusing to make more than a mild gesture on the basis of the Declaration, suggested only that consultations might be in order.[53] When the Soviet government rejected this suggestion by pointing out that their actions were within the terms of the armistice agreement,[54] much to the dismay of the State Department, Roosevelt refused to pursue the matter.† American representatives remained at their posts in Rumania, and the President told associates that the situation could not be considered a "test case" of relations with Russia.‡[55]

---

* The Secretary of State's special assistant supported the Declaration as "the most powerful antidote that we can devise for the rapidly crystallizing opposition in this country" to the United Nations idea. Stettinius himself offered it to Roosevelt because something was needed "to reassure public opinion in the United States and elsewhere." (*Conferences at Malta and Yalta,* pp. 98, 101.)

† Molotov's rejection argued that even the mild American *démarche* "envisaged a broader interpretation of the Crimea decisions . . . than corresponds with the facts. The declaration in question . . . is based upon the presence . . . of Allied Control Commissions." (See *Conference of Berlin,* I, p. 398.)

‡ Churchill later wrote: "If I pressed [Stalin] too much he might say, 'I did not interfere with your action in Greece; why do you not give me the same latitude in Rumania?' . . . I was sure it would be a mistake to embark on such an argument." (*Triumph and Tragedy,* p. 420–21.)

It is often claimed that the Churchill-Stalin deal was meant to last only until the end of the war, and that Soviet unilateral actions in the liberated countries violated the Yalta agreement. (Churchill, *Triumph and Tragedy,* p. 227; Byrnes, *Speaking Frankly,* p. 73.) Neither claim stands up to careful examination.

Although Churchill initially tried to secure Roosevelt's and the Cabinet's agreement to his arrangements with the argument that they would last only for the duration of the war, and although in 1953 he was to make the same claim, there is no evidence that Churchill ever reached such an understanding *with Stalin.* On the contrary, it was only too obvious that the agreement would have lasting influence, and it was precisely for this reason—to protect the British position in Greece—that Churchill promoted it. Furthermore, *after* German capitulation, in correspondence and talks with Stalin, Churchill explicitly acknowledged the continuing obligations of the arrangement. (*Triumph and Tragedy,* pp. 74, 75, 77–78, 227, 560, 636; Woodward, *British Foreign Policy,* pp. 307–08.)

More important, however, is the fact that the agreement was directly translated into the armistice terms, which specifically endorsed Soviet predominant influence. Again, though the West hoped to improve its status after the war, the agreements make no provision for this. As Lord Strang has stated, the result of even the more moderate Bulgarian armistice terms "was to open the way for exclusive Soviet influence." (Strang, *At Home and Abroad,* p. 225.) And indeed, before Roosevelt agreed to the terms of the armistices, Harriman carefully and explicitly warned him that they acknowledged Soviet control over internal politics. (Feis, *Churchill, Roosevelt, Stalin,* pp. 415–16, 448–57.)

Finally, besides the fact that the broadly

A REVERSAL OF VIEWPOINT

WITH THE DEATH of Roosevelt, however, the State Department found itself with a second opportunity to press the case for an active American interest in the Soviet sphere of influence. It now seemed possible that actions to implement the broad ideals of the Yalta Declaration might be taken. By May 10, Secretary Stimson, sensing a State Department campaign to commit the new President, and fearing the consequences of a new initiative, noted that it was "time to take precautions against a stampede into a dangerous reversal of our viewpoint . . . namely, not to get mixed up in a Balkan row."[56] On the same day, he advised Truman: "We have made up our minds on the broad policy that it was wise not to get into the Balkan mess even if the thing seemed to be disruptive of policies which the State Department thought were wise." He reminded the new President that "we have taken that policy right from the beginning, Mr. Roosevelt having done it himself or having been a party to it himself."[57]

At first, Truman seemed briefly to accept Stimson's advice.[58] But during the period immediately preceding Hopkins's mission, true to his basic view that the United States had a vital interest in the problems of the entire Continent, the President accepted the strong views of the State Department by committing himself to an active policy of intervention in an area controlled by Yugoslavia.[59] By the end of May, Truman had moved five divisions to the Brenner Pass and had shifted part of the Adriatic fleet north in a show of power which forced Tito to accept Western control of the important port of Trieste.*[60]

---

phrased Yalta Declaration in no way affected the armistice terms, as has been shown, Roosevelt quickly agreed to strike all of the operative clauses from the State Department's proposal. The Declaration does indeed proclaim the ideal of "concerting the policies of the three Powers," but after Roosevelt's alterations, what was left was an agreement to consult *only* "when, in the opinion of the three governments, conditions . . . make such action necessary." (*Conferences at Malta and Yalta*, p. 972.) Hence, the Russians were accorded full power to veto even the suggestion of consultations. Though the Secretary of State based much of his rhetoric on the Yalta Declaration,

Byrnes was only too aware that its specific terms justified Soviet rejection of American approaches. (*Speaking Frankly*, p. 34.)

For other information on the rights of the various powers under the Churchill-Stalin deal, the armistice arrangements, and the Yalta Declaration, see *Conference of Berlin*, I, pp. 211–17; Hull, *Memoirs*, II, p. 1458; Kennan, *Russia and the West*, p. 366; Roberts, *Rumania*, p. 266; Dennett and Johnson, *Negotiating with the Russians*, pp. 176–77.

* For more information on this question, see Grew Papers, May 12–June 12, 1945; Stimson Diary, same dates; Feis, *Between* (*Continued on next page*)

This firm action, however, was taken in an area of the Balkans which—despite the Churchill-Stalin agreement to share responsibility—was not directly related to vital Soviet interests. As Grew noted after a meeting with the President on May 14, "It was generally agreed that Tito was not very sure of himself and it was not believed that Stalin would give him unlimited support."*[61] In areas of the Balkans more intimately related to Soviet interests, Truman initially showed similar enthusiasm for a firm American approach, but soon his actions became more subtly involved in the broader strategy of delay.

In the first days of May, at a time when Truman was still committed to the immediate showdown approach in Poland, he suggested to Acting Secretary Grew that it would be wise for the United States to demonstrate its interest by calling home American representatives in protest over the situation in Rumania and Bulgaria.[62] Although the President quickly changed his mind and withdrew this proposal, he did not lose interest in Balkan affairs.[63] Even as he planned Hopkins's conciliatory mission to Moscow, the President ordered new State Department studies of the problem of the Balkans.[64] And despite the fact that Churchill personally informed Truman of his arrangement with Stalin, and despite the President's understanding that "Russian dominance in these countries had thus been recognized,"†[65] Truman now accepted the State Department's view that

---

(Continued from preceding page)
War and Peace, pp. 40–46; Feis, Churchill, Roosevelt, Stalin, pp. 627–30; Clark, Calculated Risk, pp. 443–45; Truman, Truman Speaks, pp. 70–71; Truman, Year of Decisions, pp. 244–45; Churchill, Triumph and Tragedy, pp. 552–55; Bryant, Triumph in the West 1943–46, p. 468.

* Truman's attitude is illuminated by Stimson's diary entry: "The Yugoslavs under Tito are retiring . . . and it has had such an inspiring effect upon our chief, the President, that he had given Grew instructions . . . to give them force if they sought to break back on the agreements. McCloy and I both thought that was a little overzealous . . ." (Diary, June 12, 1945.)

This is another case which shows how Truman gave priority to establishing American influence in Eastern Europe and the Balkans. General Marshall's advice that a strong stand on the Polish question might jeopardize the Japanese war effort had been rejected in late April. Marshall advanced the same argument in mid-May against a show of force regarding Trieste. Leahy noted that Marshall told the President that "every effort at any cost should be made to avoid a clash." (Leahy Diary, May 11, 1945, p. 81.) But Truman once more rejected his advice.

The point is of considerable importance for it is sometimes asserted that Truman's conciliatory diplomacy vis-à-vis Europe in late May and June derived from agreement with Marshall that the war effort might be jeopardized. As has been argued before, and as the Trieste incident shows again, Truman was not in agreement with Marshall on this point. (For another interpretation, see Feis, Churchill, Roosevelt, Stalin, pp. 599–600.)

† See also Byrnes's statement that "we knew they had reached the informal understanding that, if the British found it necessary to take military action to quell internal disorders in Greece, the Soviets would not interfere. In return, the British would recognize the right of the Soviets to take the lead in maintaining order in Rumania." (Speaking Frankly, p. 53.)

the Yalta Declaration provided a basis for American action in the liberated areas. Consequently, Truman devoted much time during the period from early May to early July to the study of ways in which he might reverse Roosevelt's decision and implement the broad ideals of the Declaration once the temporary period of conciliation had come to an end.[66]

In each country the situation facing the President was slightly different. Nowhere had the Russians installed Communist premiers. The State Department reported that in Hungary ("80 per cent" Soviet influence) power was exercised by "a coalition government headed by a conservative general [which] includes representatives of the five principal parties of the center and the left. . . . There has been no attempt . . . to substitute a purely leftist regime for the present coalition government." However, the State Department believed that Communist political strength was increasing due to the presence of the Red Army. There were also minor complaints that the American members of the Control Commission suffered from restrictions under the Soviet interpretation of the accepted rules of procedure.[67]

In Bulgaria ("80 per cent" Soviet influence), the situation appeared to be slightly less favorable to the West. Four days after the armistice had been signed in October 1944 a popularly supported coup d'état had installed a "Fatherland Front" government under Colonel Kimon Georgiev.[68] The new premier (whom the State Department's representative described as "a true conservative")[69] and four other Cabinet ministers were members of the moderately conservative Zveno party. Four other Cabinet posts were controlled by Agrarians, four by Communists, and three by Social Democrats.[70] Although the Fatherland Front enjoyed considerable popularity in the country, the State Department considered it to be Communist-dominated.[71] Fearing that an early election controlled by the government might give endorsement to the existing power distribution, the State Department had proposed tripartite observation to ensure free elections even while the war was in progress, but when this suggestion was rejected the matter had been taken no further.[72]

In Rumania ("90 per cent" Soviet influence), the Groza government installed by the Soviets shortly after Yalta had now consolidated its position. Although the government was responsive to the Soviet occupation authorities, the political situation was not clearly defined. Molotov had publicly proclaimed that the Soviet Union had no intention of "changing the existing social order";[73] Groza himself, a prosperous landowner and industrialist, had established a long anti-Communist record;*[74] and the Russians permitted widespread publicity for speeches by Cabinet members attacking Communist directives.[75] As in Bulgaria, however, the State Department believed the Groza government to be Communist-dominated.[76] In both Bulgaria and Rumania, the State Department was also disturbed because the Soviet Union had already concluded bilateral trading agreements which paid little heed to the Department's desire for more open, multilateral trading arrangements.[77]

During the conciliatory months of May and June, Truman made no major effort to intervene directly in Balkan affairs. The only manifestation of his interest was an attempt to take advantage of the provisions of the Hungarian and Bulgarian armistice agreements which hinted at increased American representation on the Control Commissions after German capitulation. The President attempted to make the most of these slight loopholes in the agreements which authorized Soviet predominance in the area: Although the degree of representation had not been defined for the "second phase," and although there was no basis for such a modification in the Rumanian armistice, Truman instructed Ambassador Harriman to propose that the United States and Britain be accorded veto power over the actions of the Soviet commander in all three countries.†[78]

This initial attempt to undo the Churchill-Stalin understanding and the armistice agreements was greeted skeptically in London. Many months earlier, the Foreign Office had concluded that to press the Russians in Southeastern Europe would endanger the hope of postwar cooperation. It was believed that since the area had never experienced Western democracy, and since the war had "proletarianized" the population, there was likely to be far greater internal demand for stability than for Western political institutions. Opposition to the Soviet Union in an area vital to its security would be of little service to British policy.[79] Indeed, until the death of Roosevelt, none of the Big Three had acted upon the assumption that Soviet predominance could

---

* Byrnes's later reference to Groza as "the Communist leader" is mistaken. (*Speaking Frankly*, p. 51.)

† Harriman made his approach regarding Hungary on June 1, Rumania on June 12, and Bulgaria on June 14. (*Conference of Berlin*, I, pp. 368, 399, 372–73, 364.)

be directly challenged. Now, of the Big Three, Truman alone wished to act. The American ambassador in London reported that the Foreign Office believed it "useless" to make an approach to the Russians —"Moscow would never allow itself to be maneuvered into position where Brit[ish] and Am[erican] Rep[resentatives] would be able to outvote Soviets. . . ."[80]

Truman disregarded this judgment and went ahead with his approach to Moscow. Undoubtedly to the surprise of the Foreign Office, the American initiative met with a favorable response. Stalin replied to Harriman's request with a major concession in the Balkans —he would agree to modify the armistice terms so as to permit a Western veto on the Hungarian Control Commission, and he proposed that American and British representatives be accorded the privilege of prior consultation in Bulgaria and Rumania.[81] Stalin's offer was made shortly after Hopkins had yielded on the Polish question— at a time when General Deane found a generally friendly atmosphere in Moscow[82]—but within a few weeks (during the Potsdam Conference) the Soviet Premier went even further: He accepted the full American proposal, agreeing that Western representatives in Bulgaria and Rumania would be accorded the same powerful veto position as in Hungary.[83]

Truman's successful attempt to increase the status of his representatives in the Balkan countries was only an interim measure. A far more important policy objective was the promotion of democratic, Western-oriented governments pledged to early free elections. Although the President had no doubts about the desirability of reorganizing the governments in Rumania and Bulgaria, he did not present this demand to Moscow during May and June. In Poland, the President had been forced to abandon a hastily conceived showdown over the same issue once Stimson's more subtle strategy had been accepted, and he did not make the mistake of attempting a premature confrontation on the Balkans. Instead, as in his handling of Far Eastern matters, Truman simply stalled.

Although the President made no official moves, he lost no interest in the problem. When, for example, on May 10 Grew brought him a long cable from George Kennan, the chargé d'affaires in Moscow, warning of the deeper implications of Soviet Balkan policy, Truman, much interested in the report, told the Acting Secretary he was already "fully alive" to the danger.[84] Similarly, although in early June he had told Grew and Ambassador Lane it would be desirable not to exercise too much pressure while Hopkins negotiated, the President made it absolutely clear that in due course he would act decisively to remove "the Soviet blackout" from the Balkans as well as the rest of Central and Eastern Europe.[85]

Although the President's summer strategy of delay in the Balkans dictated patience and the postponement of an American initiative, there were strong indications, even to those not privy to his private calculations, that Truman was not prepared to accept the *status quo*. The decision not to accept the Georgiev and Groza governments was carried forward by Truman's determined refusal to recognize either government after the collapse of Germany. Since opposition political leaders throughout the Balkans had already approached American representatives, searching for some sign that the United States might champion their cause against the Soviet Union, the negative act of refusing to accord diplomatic recognition took on ever-increasing importance in the domestic politics of each country. It now became possible to hope that the United States would not accept the established governments.* Because Truman's inaction was a powerful source of instability during the immediate postwar jockeying for political position, as the President's Balkan representative Mark Ethridge has written, "the withholding of its accord" became an "important American instrument of pressure."[86]

Fully aware that the absence of American recognition was a destabilizing force in the Soviet sphere, Stalin raised the matter directly with Truman three weeks after German capitulation: "More than eight months have passed since Rumania and Bulgaria broke off relations with Hitler Germany, signed an armistice with the Allied countries, and entered the war on the Allied side. . . . The Soviet Government deems it proper and timely right away to resume diplomatic relations."[87] But the strategy of delay in the Balkans, as elsewhere, was characterized by studied inaction. Although Truman did not judge it timely to press his own demands, neither would he yield anything of importance. His response to Stalin's plea arrived in Moscow on June 2, while Hopkins was still negotiating, but the Presiden-

---

* See below, pp. 208–210, 218–219.

tial representative, fearing that the cable might upset his conciliatory diplomacy, recommended that it be delivered only after he had left the Soviet Union.[88] Hence it was only on June 7 that Stalin received Truman's complaint that the governments were "neither representative of nor responsive to the will of the people." Truman did not reveal his demand that the governments be changed, however. Vaguely promising "it is my sincere hope that the time may soon come when I can accredit formal diplomatic representatives," Truman only suggested that it might be well to have discussions "in order to concert more effectively our policies and actions in this area."[89]

Stalin's response implicitly directed attention to the absence of free elections and the subservience to American and British forces of the governments in the West: "The opportunities for the democratic elements in Rumania and Bulgaria are not less than, say, in Italy, with which the Governments of the United States and the Soviet Union have already resumed diplomatic relations." The Soviet Premier once more demanded immediate diplomatic recognition,[90] but on June 19 Truman replied: "I am giving this matter further study. . . . I therefore propose that we discuss it at our forthcoming meeting."[91] Stalin's final pre-Potsdam communication was abrupt: "I maintain as heretofore that there is no justification for further delay in resuming diplomatic relations with Rumania and Bulgaria."[92]

Truman's basic attitude disturbed the Foreign Office. Just before Potsdam, in a conversation with Assistant Secretary of State James C. Dunn, Sir Alexander Cadogan "expressed disagreement with our reluctance to conclude peace with Bulgaria, Rumania and Hungary and reiterated UK view that treaties of peace would solve our difficulties in those countries. . . ."[93] Despite the British objections, however, as before, Truman simply ignored the advice. Thus, until the eve of the Potsdam meeting, on the one hand, the President refused to recognize the governments and, on the other, he held back his demand that they be changed. As in the Far East, he postponed action on the fundamental issue.

As has been shown, in general, Truman's strategy of delay was conceived in terms of the power the atomic bomb would eventually add to American diplomacy. From the very first, his decision to postpone a confrontation with Stalin had derived from the belief that the atomic bomb would relate not only to the Far East, but to European issues as well. Both Secretary Stimson and Secretary Byrnes had urged this view, and Byrnes, having stressed that the weapon might allow the United States to dictate her own terms, had specifically argued that it would make Russia more manageable in Eastern Europe. It is not surprising, therefore, to find that the President's own view of the Balkan issue followed the logic of this approach.

Indeed, on June 6, Truman had been specific in stating to Stimson that once the new weapon was demonstrated it would be useful in achieving a satisfactory solution to the Balkan as well as to the Polish and Manchurian problems. He said that in this area, too, he believed a settlement would be reached when the Russians granted *quid pro quos* in exchange for admitting them to partnership for international control of the new atomic force.[94]

At the same time that he offered this view, the President and his Secretary of War had discussed the best tactics to employ in approaching the broad problem. As we have seen, Stimson had advised Truman that "the greatest complication" would arise if the bomb had not been conclusively demonstrated before the meeting with Stalin. Although Truman had postponed the Potsdam Conference in order to give the physicists more time, Stimson had "pointed out that there might still be delay." He had also told the President the Interim Committee recommended "that there should be no revelation to Russia or anyone else of our work in [the atomic bomb] until the first bomb had been successfully laid on Japan." If, as Stimson thought possible, this had not occurred by the time of the meeting, and if "the Russians should bring up the subject and ask us to take them in as partners," the Secretary had urged that "our attitude was to . . . make the simple statement that as yet we were not quite ready to do it."[95]

In this discussion Stimson had underscored a new and important point. Although in mid-May he had urged only that Truman should not "have it out with Russia" until he *knew* for certain "whether this [was] a weapon in our hands or not," during the Interim Committee discussions the strategy of delay had become much more specific. In the first week of June, Stimson advised that mere knowledge of the success of the atomic test would not be enough to influence the power realities; it would first be necessary to publicly demonstrate the weapon by "laying it on Japan" before Stalin could be expected to be greatly impressed. If the heads-of-government meeting took place before the battle demonstration there would be "the greatest complication."

Truman's agreement with this new recommendation had profoundly ironic implications. Throughout the month preceding the Truman-Stalin meeting, Stimson's fear that the bomb might not be publicly demonstrated before the negotiations proved to be only too correct. Although, as J. Robert Oppenheimer has testified, "I don't think there was a time where we worked harder at the speed-up than in the period *after* the German surrender,"[96] by the end of June it was certain that the bomb would not be "laid on Japan" until early August.[97] Thus, Truman's twice-postponed meeting still would occur a few weeks too early for the atomic bomb to strengthen his diplomatic hand. In fact, as Stimson advised, the President should not even reveal the weapon to Stalin until it was shown in a dramatic battle demonstration.

The President now had no alternative but to go ahead with the arrangements for a mid-July heads-of-government conference. But it was clear that he could not yet press his diplomatic demands to a showdown. Ironically, the logic of his position ensured that the much heralded confrontation with Stalin could only be a modified continuation of the strategy of delay! Undoubtedly the hobbles the technological timetable now placed upon the President's diplomacy must have been extremely frustrating, for he was committed to a meeting which would take place a scant two weeks too early to be decisive. In a letter to his family written on July 3, Truman made no attempt to hide his feelings: "I am getting ready to go see Stalin and Churchill, and it is a chore. . . . Wish I didn't have to go, but I do, and it can't be stopped now."[98] On the voyage to Europe he wrote to complain again: "I wish this trip was over. I hate it. But it has to be done."[99]

POTSDAM

DESPITE THE DEEP IRONY that inevitably Truman would not be able to force matters to a showdown in his talks with Stalin, there was now no longer any reason why the President could not state the full American position. By the time the two heads of government had met, Truman would know the results of the atomic test, and the battle demonstration in Japan would be only a few weeks off. There would be no reason why the President should forego the opportunity to personally present the United States proposals. Thus, Truman carried with him a bluntly worded paper aimed at reversing the Churchill-Stalin arrangement, the armistice agreement, and Roosevelt's Yalta decisions.[100] The day Truman sailed from Norfolk, Virginia, Acting Secretary of State Grew revealed to the American ambassador in London that the previously rejected State Department position had now become official policy. Although Roosevelt had excised the operative clauses of the Yalta Declaration, Grew now cabled: "You may . . . tell Fo[reign] Off[ice] that . . . at forthcoming highest-level discussions we intend to press strongly proposals for implementation. . . ."[101]

The decision to state the full American case at Potsdam—at a time when a final showdown could not be expected to occur—produced a curious combination of firm demands, unyielding rejections of Soviet proposals, and most of all, continued willingness to postpone all questions in dispute. As is apparent, the subtleties involved in such a negotiating posture cannot easily be understood without reference to the atomic bomb. Nor can they be explained without recognizing that there had as yet been no reason to modify the existing strategy of delay. At the time, British diplomats found the American approach quite confusing—until they learned more of the atomic bomb.* It is not surprising that students of the problem who have not had access to previously classified information have also been confused. Undoubtedly, the scarcity of material (and the fact that the American approach ultimately failed) accounts for the poverty of scholarship in this matter,† and that, so far as I know, the American approach to Eastern Europe and the Balkans at Truman's only meeting with Stalin has not been adequately described.

Secretary of State Byrnes has written that both he and the President felt the attempt to reduce or eliminate Soviet influence in Southeastern Europe to be one of the most important objectives of American diplomacy at Potsdam.[102] As a matter of fact, once the Conference began, American proposals regarding this area precipitated the first prolonged discussions of the meeting.[103] Truman later described as the

---

* See below, pp. 152–154.
† See for example, Woodward, *British Foreign Policy*, pp. 552–53, 555–57. Note especially his mistaken view that the United States "gave up hope" of influencing the politics of the Balkans (p. 557).

"bitterest debate" of the entire meeting his arguments with Stalin over the issue.[104] And Admiral Leahy never qualified his statement that "Stalin suffered his greatest defeat" in connection with the Balkan discussions at Potsdam.[105]

Thus, unquestionably the American delegation ascribed great importance to its proposals involving the Soviet sphere of influence. Because *they* felt them to be far more important than have latter-day students of the problem, and because Truman's characteristic yet subtle approach to the Balkan issues provides a perfect illustration of the continued strategy of delay in action, it is useful to isolate, day by day, the attitudes and maneuvers of the President and his advisers and to relate them to the reports of the atomic bomb which flowed continuously from New Mexico and Washington to Berlin.

Truman arrived at Potsdam during the late afternoon of Sunday, July 15.[106] As Stimson had promised, on Monday, July 16, at 5:30 A.M. (local time) the first successful atomic test took place at the Alamogordo site, in New Mexico.[107] A cryptic report reached the Secretary of War early the evening of the same day: "Operated on this morning. Diagnosis not yet complete but results seem satisfactory and already exceed expectations. . . ."[108] This message was immediately brought to the attention of the President and the Secretary of State. "Truman and Byrnes . . . were of course greatly interested," Stimson noted, "although the information was still in very general terms."[109]

The following day, after Stalin had suggested that Truman take the chair at the opening plenary session of the Conference, the President wasted no time in stating his full position. "Seizing this hoped-for opportunity to take the offensive," Admiral Leahy confided to his diary, Truman "presented at once, without permitting any interruption, the . . . proposals for the agenda which we had prepared. . . ."[110] In striking contrast to Roosevelt, who had habitually allowed Stalin and Churchill to take the lead,[111] Truman confidently produced detailed American proposals for the broad range of issues he intended to discuss during the Conference.* Taking up Eastern Europe, the President bluntly asserted that the obligations of the three governments undertaken in accord with the Yalta Declaration had not

---

* Compare Roosevelt's letter to Stalin before Yalta: "We understand each other's problems and as you know, I like to keep these discussions informal, and I have no reason for formal agenda." (Feis, *Churchill, Roosevelt, Stalin,* p. 497.)

been fulfilled. He quoted the State Department's prepared statement of steps required to implement the Declaration, demanding:

1. ". . . the immediate reorganization of the present governments in Rumania and Bulgaria . . ."
2. ". . . immediate consultations to . . . include representatives of all significant democratic elements . . ."
3. three power assistance ". . . in the holding of free and unfettered elections."[112]

In essence, the demands were precisely those which Truman had pressed in the first showdown over Poland: a reorganization of the government and immediate free elections.

The first plenary session, of course, was devoted only to listing items for the agenda.[113] The three foreign ministers were instructed to review the proposed items and to suggest specific questions for the heads of government.[114] Before discussion of the President's proposals by the foreign ministers, however, further word of the atomic test was received from New Mexico. Again the coded message was written in general terms, but it indicated far greater power than had been expected. It implied that the blast could be heard at a distance of fifty miles and seen at a distance of 250 miles.[115] "I at once took [the message] to the President, who was highly delighted, . . ." Stimson records. "The President was evidently very greatly re-enforced . . . and said he was very glad I had come to the meeting. . . ."[116]

The following day (July 19) at the foreign ministers' meeting, Byrnes requested that the President's paper on the implementation of the Yalta agreement be put on the agenda for the Big Three.[117] This was agreed to, but at the plenary session Stalin asked that the subject be put off because the Soviet delegation had a proposal of its own to make regarding this set of issues.[118] Consequently, discussion of the problem was once more briefly delayed. However, in private conversation with Churchill on the previous day, Stalin had already indicated his general reaction to the American proposal. As the Prime Minister reported it, Stalin was clearly affirming his continued adherence to the spheres-of-influence arrangement: The Soviet Premier ". . . said that he had been hurt by the American demand for a change in Government in Rumania and Bulgaria. He was not meddling in Greek affairs, and it was unjust of them."[119]

When Molotov took up the issue now referred to the July 20 foreign ministers' meeting, he gave a more detailed presentation of this basic response. Molotov introduced a new Soviet statement, which combined a rejection of the American proposal with a strong attack on the situation in Greece. The Soviet paper called attention to the fact that the governments in both Bulgaria and Rumania were fulfilling the armistice agreements. Rejecting the American suggestion for a reorganization of the governments, it stated that the Soviet government saw no reason for the powers to become involved in the domestic affairs of Bulgaria and Rumania. Molotov went on to urge restoration of diplomatic ties "in the nearest days." Then, switching to the offensive, he stated: "There is one country—Greece—in which no due order still exists, where law is not respected, where terrorism rages directed against democratic elements . . ." Molotov concluded that it was necessary to take action to establish democratic government in Greece.[120]

Despite this use of the Greek issue to underscore the abrogation of the spheres-of-influence agreement,* the primary focus of attention of the meeting was the status of the established Bulgarian and Rumanian governments. In fact, the general debate over recognition begun during May and June by Truman and Stalin was now brought to a climax by the foreign ministers. Molotov demanded immediate recognition of the Georgiev and Groza governments. Byrnes stated that the United States "could not recognize them at this time."[121] The Secretary of State repeated Truman's demand for reorganization of the governments and supervision of elections. He also urged that American press representatives be allowed to observe freely and to report on conditions in the countries.[122] Molotov steadily refused to alter the *status quo* or to accept supervision of the elections. However, he said he had "no objection to" improving the position of American press representatives, and he offered to consider written suggestions regarding both the elections and freedom of the press.[123]

While these were being drafted,[124] a third report on the atomic test arrived by special courier. This presented a detailed, full-length de-

---

* Another instance of this occurred after Attlee replaced Churchill. Stalin presented another series of charges against Greece in retaliation for a British paper on Yugoslavia. Bevin suggested they drop both issues, and Stalin immediately replied: "Yes, welcome." (Byrnes, *Speaking Frankly*, p. 75.)

scription of the test by General Leslie R. Groves, the project director. A brief excerpt offers a sense of the statement:

> . . . in a remote section of the Alamogordo Air Base, New Mexico, the first full scale test was made of the implosion type atomic fission bomb. For the first time in history there was a nuclear explosion. . . . The test was successful beyond the most optimistic expectations of anyone . . . I estimate the energy generated to be in excess of the equivalent of 15,000 to 20,000 tons of TNT; and this is a conservative estimate. . . .
>
> The feeling of the entire assembly was . . . profound awe. . . .*

The arrival of this report on July 21 was the psychological turning point of the Conference. "It was an immensely powerful document, clearly and well written and with supporting documents of the highest importance," Stimson noted. "It gave a pretty full and eloquent report of the tremendous success of the test and revealed far greater destructive power than we expected. . . ." Stimson's diary entry continues:

> I then went over to the "Little White House" and saw President Truman. I asked him to call in Secretary Byrnes and then I read the report in its entirety and we then discussed it. They were immensely pleased. The President was tremendously pepped up by it and spoke to me of it again and again when I saw him.

The Secretary of War concludes: *"He said it gave him an entirely new feeling of confidence and he thanked me for having come to the Conference and being present to help him in this way."*[125]

That the atomic report did help by producing a new sense of confidence in the President's power to secure his diplomatic objectives is evidenced by Truman's attitude at the plenary session which took place almost immediately after his meeting with Stimson. In the course of the discussion, Stalin decided to raise the Balkan issue directly with the President. He proposed an amendment to the American proposal, asking immediate recognition of the governments of the liberated countries.[126] Truman's confidence—and, indeed, his bluntness—is apparent even from the official third-person report of the discussion:

---

* For the entire report see *Conference of Berlin*, II, pp. 1361–71.

The President stated that the American Government was unable to recognize the governments of the other satellite countries. When these countries were established on a proper basis, the United States would recognize them and not before. The President stated that the meeting would proceed and that this question would be passed over.[127]

This declaration precisely stated Truman's basic view at Potsdam. He would not agree to the Soviet position; he had stated his own demand; and he was quite prepared to pass over the matter at this time.* Churchill was struck by Truman's new confidence, and the next day, after Stimson had read the full-length report to the Prime Minister, he reflected on the President's attitude. Stimson recorded:

> [Churchill] told me that he had noticed at the meeting of the Three yesterday that Truman was evidently much fortified by something that had happened and that he stood up to the Russians in a most emphatic and decisive manner, telling them as to certain demands that they absolutely could not have and that the United States was entirely against them. He said "Now I know what happened to Truman yesterday. I couldn't understand it. When he got to the meeting after having read this report he was a changed man. He told the Russians just where they got on and off and generally bossed the whole meeting." Churchill said he now understood how this pepping up had taken place and that he felt the same way. His own attitude confirmed this admission. . . .[128]

Thus, the first effect of the atomic bomb was a simple, yet profoundly important one—it confirmed the President's belief that he would have enough power to reverse Roosevelt's policy and attempt actively to influence events in the Soviet sphere of influence. It would, however, still be a few weeks before the battle demonstration of the new weapon. Hence, the full impact of the new weapon upon the diplomatic and power balance could not yet be tested. From Truman's point of view, therefore, after the July 21 meeting of the heads of government there was no reason to press matters any further. And, indeed, since Stalin and Truman both held their ground, no further

---

* See also the President's stand on July 24:

TRUMAN. We are asking reorganization of these governments along democratic lines . . .

TRUMAN. I have made clear we will not recognize these governments until they are reorganized . . .

TRUMAN. May I suggest that we again refer the matter to the Foreign Ministers?
—*Conference of Berlin*, II, pp. 371–72.

substantive progress was made on the Balkan issues. The final protocol recorded the agreement for improved Control Commission procedures discussed earlier and accepted in final form at the meeting. It stated that "the Three Governments have no doubt" that representatives of the Allied press would now enjoy full freedom to report; and it diplomatically papered over the stalemate on the fundamental issue: "The Three Governments agree to examine each separately in the near future, in the light of conditions then prevailing, the establishment of diplomatic relations . . ."*[129]

The American delegation was quite pleased with this outcome; the final issue had been successfully delayed and, as Admiral Leahy noted, although Stalin "tried every trick in the book, [he] did not succeed in getting the diplomatic recognition he sought."†[130] Truman, who had not really wanted to come to the inevitably premature Conference in the first place, was now convinced that nothing more could be accomplished at this time. "The United States was standing firm," he told Stimson on July 23. (The Secretary noted that "he was apparently relying greatly upon the information as to [the atomic bomb].")[131] And, the following day, "The President was frank about his desire to close the Conference and get away. . . ."[132]

A PROBLEM OF FRANKNESS

DESPITE THEIR OBJECTIONS, before the Potsdam meeting began, the Foreign Office had informed the State Department that "British officials at Potsdam would support the American view [of the Balkan issues] even though they had little hope that the Soviet Government would agree to it."[133] However, the First Secretary of the Embassy in Washington had told an American official "it was his understanding that if the Soviet Government does not agree to the U.S. position the British officials will then endeavor to persuade the U.S. to agree to the

---

* Note that early in the Conference Truman agreed that "observation" of the elections was as good as "supervision." (*Conference of Berlin*, II, p. 166; Truman, *Year of Decisions*, p. 362.)

For a detailed discussion of how these agreements were reached, see references provided under "Yalta Declaration," *Conference of Berlin*, II, p. 1643.

† His basic "trick" was to refuse to accept the American proposals for Italy unless his proposals for the Balkans were accepted. In the end, as might be expected, agreement was reached to postpone both issues. (See *Conference of Berlin*, II, pp. 168–69, 207, 1492.)

early recognition of the two governments."[134] This view, of course, reflected Churchill's appraisal (made in mid-1944 and held consistently until Potsdam) that the West would not be able substantially to influence Soviet policy in the Balkans.

The State Department's successful attempt to convince the Foreign Office to adopt an initially parallel position on Balkan and other questions, of course, marked the end of Truman's temporary effort to avoid "ganging up" against the Russians during the short period of conciliation.* However, Churchill was still nervous about breaking the spheres-of-influence arrangements he had promoted. On July 18, after the vague first report of the atomic test, the Prime Minister dined alone with Stalin and noncommittally replied to the Soviet Premier's protests by stating he had not yet seen the American proposals.[135] But when the full report of the successful test arrived, his reservations disappeared. "From that moment our outlook on the future was transformed," Churchill has testified. "We were in the presence of a new factor in human affairs, and possessed of powers which were irresistible."[136] The Foreign Office never made the projected effort to convince the United States to recognize the Bulgarian and Rumanian governments. Instead, they gave active and powerful support to the American Balkan demands.[137]

Churchill's unhesitating breach of the agreements he himself had originally proposed confirms the impact of the atomic bomb upon his estimate of the power realities. The Balkans, which had once seemed beyond the reach of Western diplomacy, now again seemed accessible.† Lord Alanbrooke's diary entry for July 22 offers a glimpse of Churchill's state of mind and an indirect reflection of American attitudes:

> [The Prime Minister] . . . had absorbed all the minor American exaggerations and, as a result, was completely carried away. . . . We

---

* See above, pp. 69–70.

† Churchill's action illuminates the difficult question of what Truman might have done had the atomic test failed. It is probable that Truman himself could not have answered this question in advance, for, unlike Churchill, Truman made his calculations on the basis of the extremely confident predictions of the Secretary of War. Nevertheless, Grew records that on May 31 Truman did ask for studies "of what points we should stand out for and on what points we could compromise or yield." (*Conference of Berlin*, I, p. 158*fn.*) Although Truman would probably have begun with the same proposals, it is difficult to judge which points he might have yielded at Potsdam—or subsequently—had the atomic test failed and the American Army been withdrawn from Europe. Churchill's preatomic view that the Balkans were the first place to yield, and his postatomic change, are probably the best guide to the Anglo-American judgment of the power realities at the time.

now had something in our hands which would redress the balance with the Russians. The secret of this explosive and the power to use it would completely alter the diplomatic equilibrium which was adrift since the defeat of Germany. Now we had a new value which redressed our position (pushing out his chin and scowling); now we could say, "If you insist on doing this or that, well . . ." And then where are the Russians![138]

Alanbrooke subsequently commented that Churchill

> was already seeing himself capable of eliminating all the Russian centres of industry and population. . . . He had at once painted a wonderful picture of himself as the sole possessor of these bombs and capable of dumping them where he wished, thus all-powerful and capable of dictating to Stalin![139]

One result of Churchill's new confidence was, as Stimson noted, that the Prime Minister "not only was not worried about giving the Russians information of the matter but was rather inclined to use it as an argument in our favor in the negotiations."[140] It was only after he read the full report of the test that Churchill reached the conclusion that Stalin ought to be informed; but American officials had come to this view a few weeks earlier. In fact, the Interim Committee's initial recommendation that nothing should be said of the new weapon until it had been "laid on Japan" had been slightly modified on the eve of the Potsdam meeting.

Under pressure from nuclear scientists working at the University of Chicago, the scientific panel had reconsidered the initial recommendation at a meeting held on June 16.[141] The basic proposal of the scientists was presented in a report drafted by Dr. James Franck. The report argued that it was futile to hope the secret of the new weapon could be maintained. It stressed that an attempt to do so was bound to stimulate a desperate arms race, and that the United States, with its large centers of population and industry, would eventually be at a great disadvantage. It urged that the only hope lay in international control of the new force and concluded, therefore, that it would be unwise to use the weapon in a manner which might prejudice international cooperation. Suggesting a technical demonstration of the bombs, it strongly recommended against a surprise attack upon Japan: "Russia and even allied countries which bear less mistrust of our ways and intentions . . . may be deeply shocked by this step."*

Although the scientific panel rejected the basic proposal of the Franck report, it did agree that circumstances of the wartime use of the weapon might affect prospects for international cooperation.[142] It therefore recommended that the Soviet government be informed of the new weapon's existence before it was used.[143] This recommendation was unanimously approved by the Interim Committee on June 21.[144] On July 3, Stimson carried the final recommendation to the President:

> He should look sharp and, if he found that he thought that Stalin was on good enough terms with him, he should shoot off at him what we had arranged . . . simply telling him that we were busy with this thing working like the dickens and we knew he was busy with this thing and working like the dickens and that we were pretty nearly ready and we intended to use it against the enemy, Japan; that if it was satisfactory we proposed to then talk it over with Stalin afterwards, with the purpose of having it make the world peaceful and safe rather than to destroy civilization. If he pressed for details and facts, Truman was simply to tell him that we were not yet prepared to give them. The President listened attentively and then said that he understood and he thought that was the best way to do it.[145]

The following day, July 4, Stimson mentioned this conclusion to the British members of the Combined Policy Committee: "If nothing was said . . . its subsequent early use might have a serious effect on the relations of frankness between the three great Allies. . . ."[146] The Secretary of War also took it up with Churchill at Potsdam on July 17—after the first cryptic report, but before the full-length report. At this point Churchill took a strong stand against mentioning the weapon to Stalin.[147] The next day Truman discussed it with the Prime Minister. Churchill reports: "On behalf of His Majesty's Government I did not resist his proposed disclosure of the simple fact that we have this weapon. He reiterated his resolve at all costs to refuse to divulge

---

* See *Bulletin of the Atomic Scientists,* May 1946, for full report. Also Hewlett and Anderson, *The New World,* p. 366; Feis, *Japan Subdued,* pp. 40–43; Smith, "Behind the Decision to Use the Atomic Bomb," *Bulletin of the Atomic Scientists,* XIV (October 1958).

Former President Eisenhower has recently disclosed that at Potsdam he too advised Stimson that Japan was "already defeated," that the atomic bomb should not be used, and that the United States should "avoid shocking world opinion." (See Eisenhower, *Mandate for Change,* pp. 312–13.)

any particulars. . . ."[148] As we have seen, once the full report came in, Churchill's attitude switched from opposition and passive acquiescence to strong approval of the idea.

Thus, it was with Churchill's agreement that on July 24—the day after he decided it was time to close the Conference as soon as possible—Truman casually mentioned to Stalin that a new weapon of unusual force had been developed.[149] However, he used neither the word "nuclear" nor the word "atomic," and Churchill, who was watching the encounter with intense interest, "was sure that [Stalin] had no idea of what he was being told."[150] Indeed, immediately after his conversation Truman boasted to the Prime Minister: "He never asked a question!"[151] Both Byrnes and Leahy confirm that, despite the recommendation of the Interim Committee and the Secretary of War, when the actual discussion took place Truman did not tell Stalin that an atomic weapon had been developed.*[152] Instead, apparently hoping that his action might allow him to rebut future charges that he had been less than frank with the Soviet ally, Truman offered only the vaguest hint of the weapon. As we shall see, for reasons intimately related to the fundamental logic of his strategy, the President had decided that the actual disclosure of the new force would also be delayed.†

---

* This is often misunderstood. See, for example, the erroneous statement that "Stalin was told of the new weapon . . ." (Craven and Cate, *Air Forces in World War II*, Vol. V, p. 712.)

† See below, p. 183.

The Tactics of the Potsdam Conference (II)*

> [*The atomic bomb*] *is tying in with what*
> *we are doing in all fields* . . .
> —SECRETARY OF WAR
> HENRY L. STIMSON
> July 23, 1945

AS EARLY AS the first week of June it had been assumed that the atomic bomb would strengthen American diplomacy only after it was demonstrated in combat. This view was inevitably reinforced by the Potsdam decision to keep the atomic test secret from Stalin. From Truman's point of view, therefore, there was now even less reason to begin serious negotiations; the President was extremely impatient with the discussions, and he did not conceal his belief that there was little point to continuing the diplomatic sparring at Potsdam.† His desire to end the Conference as soon as possible was indicated to Stalin on July 24 (although as yet no major agreements had been reached) when Truman declared that "when there was nothing more upon which they could agree, he was returning home."[1] On the same day, Byrnes told Molotov that "the United States delegation wants to dispose of pending matters so that the Conference can end."[2]

Truman's attitude had important tactical implications. As one ob-

---

* The word "tactics" must be emphasized here even more than in the preceding chapter. The German reparations issue here considered involved extremely complicated negotiations which I have only attempted to summarize. If one bears in mind the limitations discussed in footnote on p. 171, it may be helpful to consult the more detailed summary in *Conference of Berlin,* II (pp. 940–49).

† Truman later recalled: "I was becoming very impatient, and on a number of occasions I felt like blowing the roof off the palace." (*Year of Decisions,* p. 369.)

server has noted, much of the remainder of the Conference was "conducted under the threat of imminent American departure, with or without agreement."[3] The President's desire to leave, of course, did not derive from a feeling of despair. On the contrary, as Stimson remarked at the time, the American delegation was in the best of spirits.[4] Ambassador Harriman also "commented on the increasing cheerfulness evidently caused by the news from us [of the atomic test]."[5] On July 24, Stimson recorded: "[The President] told me about the events of yesterday's meeting with which he seemed to be very satisfied."[6] And on July 28, Secretary of the Navy Forrestal noted: "[The President] said he was being very realistic with the Russians and found Stalin not difficult to do business with."[7] Later, Byrnes was to recall that even the difficult debate and the stalemate over Bulgaria and Rumania "perhaps should have stifled my optimism, but it didn't."*[8]

The American delegation's sense of satisfaction and confidence, apparent to all firsthand observers, also marked its approach to what Byrnes termed "the most difficult issue before us—Germany."[9] Considering that most writers have agreed with Byrnes's view that Germany was the most significant problem discussed at Potsdam, it is vital to recognize that Truman's July 23 decision to end the Conference quickly was taken *before* the heads of government or the foreign ministers had even begun serious consideration of the main issues in dispute. And, as both Truman and Byrnes were to make clear during the remainder of the Conference, if the Russians did not find the American proposals for Germany acceptable, the United States delegation was quite prepared to leave with no agreement; the matter could be taken up at a later date. Thus, the tactics followed in dealing with the Balkan issues were to be followed in the treatment of Germany as well.

The American approach to Germany was a logical extension of the basic desire to establish a stable Europe. Together with the Balkan demands, the proposals for Germany constituted the core of the policies Truman and Byrnes thought it important to urge at Potsdam.[10]

---

* It is true that some Americans were disturbed by Soviet suggestions for a base in the Dardanelles and for Soviet participation in a trusteeship for one of the Italian colonies. However, the President does not seem to have been greatly worried. After a discussion with Truman on July 23, Stimson recorded: "He evidently thinks a good deal of the new claims of the Russians are bluff . . ." (Diary, July 23, 1945.)

The combination offered the hope of a democratic, economically and politically stable Continental system.*

Truman found that there was not much disagreement with his suggested political principles for postwar Germany; with little dispute, the Conference endorsed the American proposal on July 18.[11] However, at the time Truman began to search for a way to close the Conference, the subcommittee considering the crucial economic issues reached a deadlock.[12] This caused some worry, for as Stimson had urged throughout the summer, and as American economic experts stressed, there was need for a cooperative settlement: "The Russian zone [is] the 'bread basket' of Germany, while the [Western] zones together constitute a deficit food area."[13] Accordingly, although Truman was prepared to leave Potsdam without an understanding,† he and Byrnes went to considerable lengths to attempt to force agreement on American terms.

Again, there was not much difficulty in the negotiations over general principles for the economic administration of Germany. The real controversy arose over the basic question of the scale and power to be permitted the postwar German economy. The level of reparation withdrawals was the heart of the matter, for a decision on this issue would determine what was to be left in Germany and would control a host of other subsidiary questions. At Yalta, Roosevelt had agreed to establish a Reparations Commission charged with responsibility for creating a detailed plan and for "the fixing of the total sum" of reparation payments to be made by Germany. It was agreed that the Commission would

> take in its initial studies as a basis for discussion the suggestion of the Soviet Government that the total sum of the reparation . . . should be 20 billion dollars and that 50% of it should go to the U.S.S.R.[14]

Roosevelt's commitment to twenty billion dollars as a basis for discussion was not a definitive statement of policy. Nevertheless, it established the order of magnitude for reparation withdrawals. Indeed, because the British Cabinet would not agree to such a commitment,

---

* For American views on the need to treat Europe as an integrated unit, see *Conference of Berlin*, I, pp. 257–61; II, pp. 754–57, 808–9.

† See below, p. 170.

Churchill refused to endorse this aspect of the agreement. (This is the one provision of the Yalta protocol which bears the signatures of Roosevelt and Stalin, but not of Churchill.)[15] More important than the precise figure, however, was Roosevelt's endorsement of the principle that a firm target for reparations would be established in advance. His agreement that "Germany must pay in kind for losses caused by her"[16] also endorsed the principle of "compensation"[17]—rather than the principle of "capacity to pay"—as the basic criterion to guide reparations negotiations. Since there was no question that Soviet damages had been much greater than one half of twenty billion dollars,[18] Roosevelt's agreement to very large-scale reparations was thus doubly confirmed.

This understanding gave first priority to establishing a target figure for reparation withdrawals. The accord treated only as a residual item the question of what industrial resources were to be left in Germany after the reparations had been paid, and it gave only secondary importance to the inevitable debilitating effect such withdrawals would have upon the German standard of living. Thus, it accepted Stalin's argument that the Germans should pay for some of the tremendous devastation their armies had caused in the Soviet Union.[19]

Even before Yalta, this approach had been severely criticized by Stimson and others who feared that weakening the German economy would seriously endanger European stability.[20] Roosevelt was fully aware of this difficulty and was also reluctant to agree to excessive withdrawals from the German economy.[21] But ultimately the President's decision had been taken with regard to other than purely economic considerations.

Throughout the last year of the war American policy makers had been faced with the difficult but unavoidable task of creating a viable plan for postwar European security. To most American leaders, the necessary condition of such a plan was a system of specific guarantees against the revival of German power. Unable to hope that the American public would permit retention of occupation forces in Europe for more than two years after the war's end,[22] Roosevelt had been forced to find a nonmilitary solution to the security problem. The President evolved two complementary approaches. The first was an attempt to work out a cooperative relationship with the Soviet Union. In Europe, this involved a coordinated effort to control Germany and was first expressed in the plans for a German Allied Control Council. "It is by now a commonplace," one State Department official characteristically noted, "that Germany cannot commit another aggression so long as the Big Three remain united."[23]

Roosevelt's second policy was based upon a calculated decision to weaken the industrial basis of German military power. Although Roosevelt disclaimed the "Morgenthau Plan" to remove 80 per cent of German industry,[24] in fact, the Yalta decision followed the fundamental logic of this approach. Massive reparations and what was termed the "industrial disarmament"[25] of Germany were two sides of the same coin. It may be true that Roosevelt underestimated the difficulties such a policy would create,[26] but as Byrnes knew, he had very little sympathy for those who urged a "soft" peace for the Germans.[27] On the eve of the Yalta meeting, the President somewhat overenthusiastically told his Cabinet that as far as he was concerned, the Germans "could live happily . . . on soup from soup kitchens."[28]

Roosevelt also felt that international control of the Ruhr industrial area would be a useful guarantee against a German military revival.[29] But the heart of his approach to the security problem was a melding of his two basic policies. Since Stalin desperately wanted industrial reparations to compensate for destruction wrought by Hitler's armies, at Yalta the agreement to extract large-scale reparations met Soviet requirements—thereby consolidating a cooperative relationship—at the same time that it reduced the industrial basis of German power.*[30]

This approach to the European security problem had obvious implications for the stability of the German economy. The hardened Russian answer to those who protested that there were not enough resources to meet Europe's needs, reparations, and German requirements, was: "Let the German standard of living be reduced."[31] In America, however, when Truman took office, those who feared the effects of such a policy urged the new President to reconsider Roosevelt's approach.[32] As we have seen, Truman was completely in accord

---

* Note how Roosevelt broke with Churchill over the question after being prompted by Hopkins that "the Russians have given in so much at this conference that I don't think we should let them down." (*Conferences at Malta and Yalta*, pp. 902, 920.)

Much of the information contained in the preceding analysis is taken from Paul Y. Hammond's excellent study, *Directives for the Occupation of Germany: The Washington Story*. This is presently available in mimeograph form from the author or from the Twentieth Century Fund, but is soon to be published.

with Stimson's advice that the German economic contribution to Europe should not be reduced.* Morgenthau's views were rejected, and by June 8 Grew was able to write: "There is no longer disagreement concerning the need for assuring such essential economic rehabilitation in Germany as is necessary to the fulfillment of the purposes of occupation."[33] One result of this change was that the United States continued to procrastinate on the reparations issue and, as we have seen, the American reparations representative began negotiating on the matter some three and a half months later than had been envisioned at Yalta.†

Even more significant, however, was the fact that only a short time after taking office, Truman asked for the resignation of Secretary of the Treasury Morgenthau—the primary architect of Roosevelt's policy.‡[34] On June 1, the new President also gave instructions to increase the production of German coal.[35] More specifically, the President felt that the Russian desire for large-scale reparations from Germany— "although morally she should have been made to pay"—could not be met.[36] "America was not interested in reparations for anybody,"[37] he later wrote. And, fearing that massive withdrawals from Germany would necessitate American assistance, on May 18, he instructed his "tough" reparations negotiator, Edwin Pauley, to oppose "any reparation plan based upon the assumption that the United States . . . will finance directly or indirectly any reconstruction in Germany or reparation by Germany."[38] Despite this attitude, however, before the Potsdam Conference, Truman refused to attempt openly to reverse Roosevelt's Yalta decision.

Instead, Pauley was instructed to try to secure Soviet agreement to a set of concepts to guide reparation withdrawals, which shifted emphasis away from the basic principles of Roosevelt's commitment but still paid lip service to the Yalta decision. Thus, Pauley was told: "It is and has been fundamental United States policy that Germany's war potential be destroyed, and its resurgence as far as possible prevented, by removal or destruction of German plants, equipment, and other

---

* See above, pp. 79–80.
† See above, pp. 85–86.
‡ Morgenthau had wanted to come to the Potsdam meeting because of his deep interest in the German economic issue. According to Truman, he threatened resignation over the matter. Truman recalls: " 'All right,' I replied, 'if that is the way you feel, I'll accept your resignation right now.' And I did. That was the end of the conversation and the end of the Morgenthau Plan." (*Year of Decisions*, p. 327.)

property."[39] At the same time, however, he was to urge a new approach to the determination of actual withdrawals: Experts should establish the amount of industry required to produce a German standard of living approximately equal to that of the surrounding nations; industrial resources in excess of the amount needed to produce this standard would then be distributed as reparations. Receipts from goods produced for export each year would be used, in the first instance, to pay for German imports; what was left after these claims had been met would be used to satisfy reparations requirements.[40] In this fashion the American interest in a reasonably strong German economy would be given first priority, while reparations would be treated as a residual. The Yalta principle of compensation would be replaced by the principle of "capacity to pay." Hence, in any conflict over the distribution of limited German resources, although the Yalta principle would have given preference to the claims of the invaded countries, the new approach would have favored the German standard of living.

When Pauley first brought forward this set of principles in the Moscow discussions during June, the new American approach was bitterly opposed by the Russians.[41] A debate first arose over the suggestion that yearly exports be used in the first instance to pay for imports rather than reparations.[42] The Russians argued that reparations could not be considered a mere residual.[43] Backed by Truman's firm decision that the United States would not pay for German reconstruction* and aided by the determination of the State and War Departments to avoid paying for German imports,[44] Pauley held his ground; the negotiations on the issue ended in stalemate.[45] While these discussions were going on, Pauley also asked the State Department to permit him to make a direct assault on the fixed-figure requirement, the heart of the Yalta agreement.[46] The Russian representative "keeps coming back to the 20 billion dollar sum," Pauley complained on June 19.[47] American policy, he argued, "should not fix any total figure in advance." Instead, "a formula [should] be adopted which will emphasize percentages, rather than dollars."[48]

Although Pauley's suggestion would have directly contradicted the

---

* Truman felt the United States had indirectly financed German reparations after World War I and he vowed not to allow this to happen again. (Truman, *Year of Decisions*, p. 307; Byrnes, *Speaking Frankly*, p. 82.)

Yalta decision, it was only a logical extension of Truman's instructions; if the level of German industry and the standard of living were to be established as fixed targets, reparations would automatically become a residual. Before Potsdam, however, Truman was not prepared so directly to countervene his predecessor's agreement. On July 2, Pauley was sent a somewhat ambivalent instruction: "The interest of this Government in questions of the total amount of reparations . . . is subservient to its interest in the firm application of those principles and procedures . . ." Despite this statement, however, Pauley was told that the United States would not take a stand against establishing a firm target figure. He was instructed that although the twenty-billion-dollar mark was too high, there was no objection to discussion of a figure in the twelve-to-fourteen-billion-dollar range.[49]

Interpreting these somewhat contradictory instructions along lines favoring his own approach, on his own initiative a few days before Potsdam, Pauley boldly told the Soviet reparations representative that he was no longer prepared to establish a fixed reparations target![50] This, of course, produced a deadlock. As Pauley reported on July 7, although some progress had been made, no agreement had been reached on "fundamental problems."[51] Hence, the reparations issue, which had taken up much of the Yalta Conference, and which, it had seemed, would be disposed of shortly thereafter, was now transferred to Potsdam.[52]

THE FIRM APPROACH TO REPARATIONS AND A NEW SOLUTION TO THE SECURITY PROBLEM

FROM ONE POINT OF VIEW, the discussion of the reparations issue in Berlin was bound to strengthen the basic American viewpoint. When American policy makers arrived in Germany they were appalled at both the destruction of the country and at what Stimson termed the "rather oriental" policies of the Russians.[53] At every turning they came across workers feverishly dismantling German industrial installations for immediate shipment to the Soviet Union.[54] But, although they were shocked by the scale and pace of these activities, during the first days of the Potsdam meeting, Truman and Byrnes made no alteration in their approach to reparations.

It was only after the full report of the atomic test arrived that they changed tactics. The confidence evidenced in the handling of the Balkan issues now appeared in the treatment of Germany as well. The need for Soviet cooperation, which had followed from the same considerations important to Roosevelt, and which had been expressed in Truman's troop withdrawal during the summer,* now ceased to be a decisive influence upon policy. A tremendous new assertiveness characterized the American attitude as Truman and Byrnes abandoned the ambivalence of the summer instructions. Although only four days before the American delegation had sailed for Potsdam they had told Pauley that a figure of twelve to fourteen billion dollars would be acceptable, now, the reparations negotiator was directed to refuse to adhere to the agreement that a fixed reparations figure be established.[55]

This direct assault upon the Yalta principles was in line with Pauley's earlier recommendation. However, the President also received powerful advice on the matter from other quarters. Significantly, the German problem was the one issue, besides the atomic bomb, which directly concerned Secretary Stimson.[56] Throughout the previous year he had argued against the destruction of German industry,† and now, during the first days of the Potsdam meeting he stressed the vital importance of a healthy German economy.[57] Using language which strikingly contrasted with his usual moderate style, he argued that "it would be foolish, dangerous and provocative of future wars to adopt a program calling for the major destruction of Germany's industry and resources."[58]

That responsibilities for policy regarding both the atomic bomb and the German issue were united in the person of the Secretary of War emphasizes (and symbolizes) the fact that it is extremely artificial to ignore the relationship between the new weapon and the Americans' confidence in their power to achieve solutions to diplomatic problems.‡ Stimson's July 23 comment that the atomic bomb "is tying in with what we are doing in all fields"[59] suggests the connection, and the fact is that the development was both psychologically and conceptually§ related to the American attitude toward Germany. The most obvious

---

* See above, p. 83.
† See above, p. 53.
‡ Although the State Department was also deeply involved, the War Department had a major share of the responsibility because of the military role in the occupation. (*Conference of Berlin*, II, p. 754.)
§ See below, pp. 172–173.

point, of course, was the sense of independence the new weapon gave the American negotiators; Stimson's basic approach and Pauley's specific policy now became the essence of an unyielding set of American proposals.

Secretary Byrnes made the position clear at a foreign ministers' session on July 23, two days after the full report of the test arrived. Objecting to the broad definitions the Russians wished to apply to "war booty," worried about the economic effects of Polish control of part of eastern Germany,* and, as always, fearing the effects of large-scale withdrawals, Byrnes stated unequivocally: "There will be no reparations until imports in the American zone are paid for. There can be no discussion of this matter."[60] True to his word, Byrnes refused to consider Molotov's suggestion that if German consumption were reduced, reparations and imports could both be paid for.[61] Nor would he consider the proposal that consumption, reparations, and imports, each be accorded an equal claim on export receipts so that a reduction in exports would affect all in the same proportion.[62] Moreover, he asked that the discussion of the fundamental target-figure question be postponed for a short while.[63]

Since the Russians held to the same views they had taken during the Moscow talks, it is not surprising that the July 23 negotiations ended in a stalemate. The Secretary of State was undoubtedly aware of the futility of the effort, for even before announcing his firm stand in the tripartite foreign ministers' meeting, he had come to the conclusion that quite a different handling of the dispute was necessary. His request that the target-figure question be postponed was directly related to his new appraisal, for, with the approval of the President, an hour earlier on the same day he had already approached Molotov privately

---

* Truman and Byrnes were disturbed that by turning over former German territories east of the Oder-Neisse line to Poland the Russians had seriously reduced Germany's economic resources and also her capacity to pay reparations. This matter took up considerable time at Potsdam and subsequently. However, the importance of the issue has probably been unduly emphasized, for (1) the entire area comprised only approximately (by American estimate) 5.9 per cent of Germany's movable assets, 6 per cent (or 9.7 per cent) of total manufacturing assets, 7.1 per cent of mining and manufacturing production; (2) the Yalta agreement provided that in any event much of the area would be given over to Poland after the peace treaty; and (3) most important, Stalin told Truman he was not committed to Polish administration of the area and seems at one point to have been willing to negotiate a compromise settlement. (See Conference of Berlin, I, p. 635; Ibid., II, pp. 861–62, 879–81, 943, 1572.) Finally, of course, the facts of the Oder-Neisse dispute were well known throughout the summer and had not affected the State Department's willingness to discuss a twelve-to-fourteen-billion-dollar target before Potsdam.

with an alternative suggestion: "The Secretary said that under the circumstances he wondered whether it would not be better to give consideration to the possibility of each country taking reparations from its own zone." If the Russians wished industrial reparations from the West, they might pay for them with food and coal.[64]

For the remainder of the conference Byrnes directed his primary effort toward securing agreement to this zonal plan. Although he was prepared to continue discussion of the Yalta understanding that Germany would be treated as an economic unit for reparations purposes, he would do so only on the assumption that no fixed target would be established and that reparations would have last claim on export receipts.[65] Molotov was therefore faced with the choice of accepting the new zonal approach, or having to agree to an alteration of the Yalta agreement which eliminated the crucial target figure and which treated all reparations as residuals.

Byrnes was fully aware of the meaning of his negotiating stance: the Russians, who desperately wanted heavy industrial reparations, occupied a zone primarily devoted to raw-material production, agriculture, and light industry.[66] The Ruhr, in Western hands, was the key to the reparations issue; and the proposal that each side satisfy its claims from its own zone was an open threat to the understanding that the Russians would be allocated half of all reparations selected from the whole of Germany.*

Molotov soon bitterly "pointed out that if they failed to agree . . . the result would be the same as under Mr. Byrnes's plan. Each side would draw reparations from their respective zones. . . ."[67] And even United States Assistant Secretary of State William L. Clayton cautioned Byrnes: "Any decision to exclude them from any participation in the distribution of the heavy equipment in the Ruhr as reparations, would be considered by the Russians as a reversal of the Yalta and Moscow position, since no Allied understanding would be necessary to enable them to get reparations from their own zone."[68]

Indeed, taken together, the refusal to fix a target and the proposal that each side take reparations from its own zone all but eliminated the expectation that the Soviet Union would receive industrial repara-

---

* Byrnes also supported the zonal proposal with the argument that separate administration would avoid quarrels over actual reparation determinations. (*Conference of Berlin*, II, p. 274; *Speaking Frankly*, p. 83.)

tions from the Western zones.[69] Molotov strongly opposed the zonal proposal. He told Byrnes he was quite prepared to reduce the amount of Soviet claims, but that a fixed figure for the entire economy was absolutely essential.[70] With Byrnes still refusing to discuss such a figure, on July 27 Molotov asked point-blank "if the decision with regard to reparations which was taken at the Crimea Conference remained in force."[71]

Byrnes replied that Pauley had "considered the proposal and that in view of the circumstances now existing he regarded it as impractical." At Yalta, he added, "all that was done was to accept the proposal [regarding twenty billion dollars] as the basis for discussion. If he were asked for a million dollars and he said he would discuss it, this did not mean that he would write a check for it."[72] Molotov responded stressing the importance of establishing some fixed target, rather than the twenty-billion-dollar estimate itself; he would like "to know what remained from the Crimea decision as a basis for discussion. Mr. Byrnes knew that the Soviet delegation was willing to consider reducing the amount of reparations."[73] But Byrnes refused to adhere to the fixed-target principle. After careful consideration, he said, "he had determined that it was now in his opinion impractical."[74]

Byrnes's refusal to establish a fixed figure did not derive, of course, from technical considerations. Although it was difficult to obtain accurate statistics on Germany, even six months earlier Roosevelt had been prepared to agree to a rough estimate of twenty billion dollars for reparations, the State Department had already established twelve to fourteen billion as a reasonable target, and during the Potsdam meeting Pauley himself produced a slightly more conservative estimate of ten to twelve billion.* Byrnes's basic opposition to large-scale reparations was the underlying factor.[75] But his reluctance to negotiate, his refusal to consider any of Molotov's proposals to reduce the target figure (which at one point brought the Russian request within one billion dollars of the State Department estimate),† and his refusal

---

* On the rough assumption that half of the reparations would come from capital goods and half from current production, I have derived this figure by doubling Pauley's estimate that five to six billion dollars would be available from capital goods alone. (*Conference of Berlin*, II, p. 892.)

† At one point Molotov offered to reduce the Soviet claim to eight billion dollars. (*Conference of Berlin*, II, p. 297.) It seems likely that had Byrnes been prepared to bargain, Molotov might have reduced this unilateral offer further and, perhaps, might have accepted the State Department's seven-billion-dollar estimate (i.e., 50 per cent of fourteen billion).

to put forward his own estimates derived from tactical, not statistical, considerations—and from Pauley's suggestion that there was wisdom in delay.[76]

Consequently, with Molotov stubbornly insisting on the Yalta terms, and Byrnes completely unwilling to establish a firm target, on the substantive issue there was very little progress.[77] On more limited aspects of the problem, however, there was some forward movement. After a series of complicated negotiations, Molotov finally agreed in principle to Byrnes's proposal that each side satisfy its claims from its own zone.[78] However, he did so on condition that a certain percentage of industrial-capital reparations from the Western zone would be partly given, partly sold to the Soviet Union.*[79]

This understanding altered the form but not the substance of the fundamental issue. Since the Soviet zone comprised approximately 40 per cent of German industrial resources, supplemental payments from the Western zone would have to be made to meet the Yalta require-ment that 50 per cent of German reparations be paid to the Soviet Union.[80] The question now was: Precisely how much would the Rus-sians be given from the Western zone? Although certain percentages had been agreed, as Molotov stressed, a percentage "of an undeter-mined figure meant very little."[81] Thus, the debate over a fixed figure for the entire economy narrowed to a struggle over the more limited question of whether or not to establish a target for industrial repara-tions from the Western zone.[82]

Once again Byrnes refused to be pinned down; and once again it was not for technical or statistical reasons.[83] The Secretary of State had available to him expert estimates of the potential reparations available from the Western zone.[84] These were presented with Pauley's advice that the prudent sum for withdrawals from the Western zone "differs so widely from the figure which the Russians have in mind that I believe the mere mention of this figure at this time would pre-clude any agreement being made at all."[85] In fact, Pauley told Byrnes,

---

* During the Potsdam bargaining the pre-cise percentages, and the zones to which they were applied, were constantly changed. In order to save space by avoiding a lengthy description of this process I have chosen to use the summary term "a certain percentage" throughout this essay. The in-terested reader will find the details of this aspect of the negotiations well summarized in *Conference of Berlin,* II, pp. 944–47.

he believed the West should pay only about 10 per cent of the reparations the Russians believed justifiable under the Yalta agreement.*

The Secretary of State received additional strong support for his refusal to return to the Yalta principle from the War Department when Assistant Secretary McCloy agreed that it would be a "great risk . . . if the amount of reparations . . . [were] absolutely fixed now."[86] But more important, as the controversy with Molotov reached a climax, the underlying fact that the American delegation was prepared to postpone final determination of the issue gave Byrnes a tremendous advantage.

In conversations with Admiral Leahy on July 26 and July 27, the President reaffirmed his decision to "depart for home at the earliest practicable date" and to "terminate" the Conference.[87] Although Stalin's illness and the British elections[88] caused some delay, the day after the British delegation returned to Potsdam, Truman and Byrnes decided to state the American case privately to Molotov.[89] On July 30, Byrnes made the position abundantly clear to the Soviet Foreign Minister: It was time to wind up all of the negotiations. Now the proposal that each side satisfy its reparations requirements from its own zone (with a certain percentage to be transferred to the Soviet zone from the West) was to be "conditional upon agreement on two other proposals." Byrnes brought forward previously discussed papers on lesser issues relating to the treatment of Italy and the satellite nations and the Polish western border. All three would have to be accepted as a package. If Molotov did not agree, Byrnes "was willing to report to the Big Three and they could decide whether to continue the discussion or refer the matter to some future conference."[90] The following day Byrnes was more explicit: "I told him we would agree to all three or none, and that the President and I would leave for the United States the next day."[91]

Thus, the American tactics on the German issue paralleled the approach they had taken to the Balkans. Roosevelt's previous understanding was abandoned, and the Russians were told that the position would have to be accepted or no agreement would be possible; Truman and Byrnes were more than willing to postpone a final settle-

---

* The figure was 214 *million* dollars in capital removals from the Western zone— i.e., about one tenth of the Russian estimate of 2 *billion*. (*Conference of Berlin*, II, pp. 297, 892.)

ment. Moreover, the basic conception of the April showdown now once again came to the fore; aware that the Russians desperately needed economic aid—from American credits or from Western-controlled German reparations—Byrnes now attempted to bargain industrial withdrawals for Soviet concessions on other diplomatic issues.

Although Stalin had rejected the demand that the governments of Bulgaria and Rumania be changed, he apparently reasoned that the promise of a percentage of Western industrial reparations (even though it was a percentage of an undetermined figure) was better than no reparations agreement at all. Hence, after bitterly criticizing Byrnes's tactics,[92] on July 31, agreeing to abandon the Yalta principle, he accepted the American reparations plan.[93] The tough-minded negotiator Pauley found "keen satisfaction" in the result.*[94] Admiral Leahy believed it one of the "major achievements" of the Conference.[95] And Secretary Byrnes was subsequently to boast that the United States "finally succeeded in eliminating from the agreed declaration any mention of a total amount."†[96]

The firm tactics and the decision to reverse Roosevelt's agreement undoubtedly were related to the "entirely new sense of confidence" which Truman told Stimson the atomic test had given him. There is no

---

* Truman's recollection is illuminating: "If Pauley had not been as tough as he is, we could never have got any reparations policy. . . . He is a tough, mean so-and-so. . . ." (Daniels, *Man of Independence,* p. 305.)

† It was also agreed that reparations from the Eastern zone would be used to meet not only Soviet but also Polish claims and that the Soviet Union would renounce its interest in German external assets in Western Europe, German gold captured by the Allied armies, and a share in corporate assets of German enterprises (such as railroads) which would necessarily be left in the country. (See *Conference of Berlin,* II, pp. 944–46, 1485–87.)

The reparations negotiations, as seen from the American viewpoint, are usefully summarized in *Conference of Berlin,* II, pp. 940–49. In using this State Department document, however, it is important to remember (1) that it was written two months after Potsdam; (2) that the State Department, of course, has no wish to emphasize Truman's break with Roosevelt's agreement; and (3) that the report incorporates a radically new interpretation of the zonal reparations agreement. The last point is of con-

siderable importance, for shortly after Potsdam both American and British policy makers were to hold that "the zone plan . . . did not contemplate separate reparations plans." (*Ibid.,* p. 944.) Specifically, it was later claimed that the agreement to treat the German economy as a unit precluded Soviet reparations extractions so long as there was a deficit in the import-export balance of the western zones. (Byrnes, *Speaking Frankly,* pp. 167, 189.) The publication of the Potsdam papers shows this claim to be false. At the time, Ernest Bevin was only too aware that the plan "cut across the agreement to treat Germany as a whole economy," but his objections were expressly overruled. As Byrnes told Molotov, "If the Soviets agreed to his plan they would have no interest in exports and imports from our zone . . ." (*Conference of Berlin,* II, pp. 490–91, 520–21.) Despite Byrnes's subsequent decision to break the agreement, he himself emphasized the meaning of his plan on numerous occasions at Potsdam, both to Bevin and to Molotov, and he proposed various modifications of the final protocol to clarify the point. (*Ibid.;* see especially pp. 291, 572, 827, 932; also pp. 450, 475, 487, 490, 491, 520, 822, 822*fn.*)

way, of course, to know if Truman and Byrnes would have taken such an unyielding line had they not been "greatly re-enforced" by the news. But it is vital to recognize that the new approach was adopted only after the atomic report was received. Moreover, in a more fundamental sense, the relationship between Truman's decision and the atomic bomb is greatly illuminated by considering that Truman inherited not only the Yalta agreement from his predecessor, but the basic problem of European security.

For both Roosevelt and Truman, the need to establish specific guarantees against the possibility of another German military revival was a fundamental condition of policy. Although he very much wished to maintain American troops in Europe,* Truman, like Roosevelt, was unable to count on Congressional authority for such action. Hence, he too had had to search for nonmilitary guarantees against a rebirth of German power. And despite his desire to maintain a strong German contribution to Continental economic stability, he had been forced to rely upon "industrial disarmament" and Soviet cooperation on the Control Council as the foundations of his policy.[97]

For this reason, during May and June, Hopkins had been authorized to tell Stalin that Truman, like Roosevelt, was prepared to agree to international controls for the Ruhr industry, and Pauley had also been allowed to discuss the matter.[98] Similarly, Pauley's first reparations plan emphasized (albeit to a lesser extent than Roosevelt's had) the destruction of selected German arms industries.[99] And, as we have seen, until the very eve of the Potsdam Conference, Truman continued to hold on to the major premise of Roosevelt's policy. Although the twenty-billion-dollar reparations figure was to be reduced to twelve to fourteen billion, until the atomic-test report Truman did not abandon the substance of Roosevelt's Yalta decision—a decision which had established the conditions of Soviet-American cooperation in Europe and of the industrial disarmament of Germany.

"The problem which presents itself . . ." Stimson advised Truman before details of the atomic test arrived, "is how to render Germany harmless as a potential aggressor, and at the same time enable her to play her part in the necessary rehabilitation of Europe."[100] The Secretary of War stated in precise terms the question which had confronted

---

* See below, p. 224.

both Roosevelt and Truman, but within hours of his statement the dilemma inherent in the problem had been resolved in a radical and dramatic way. As Truman explained to General de Gaulle shortly after Potsdam, there was no longer any need for international control of the Ruhr, nor for other specific and material guarantees against renewed aggression—"The German menace should not be exaggerated," for "the United States possessed a new weapon, the atomic bomb, which would defeat any aggressor."[101]

Thus, although Truman continued to endorse "industrial disarmament" as a way to achieve European security, he knew that the United States would never again greatly fear the threat of German military power.[102] Truman no longer required Soviet cooperation or massive reductions in German industry to achieve his primary objective. Acting in accord with his view of the undeniable merits of the American plan for European stability, the President could afford to ignore the German devastation of Russia and the Yalta agreement. There was no need to compromise; the reparations issue now took on a distinctly secondary importance. In the last analysis, therefore, the atomic bomb influenced the fundamental problem Truman faced to an even greater extent than it did his tactics; by revolutionizing the problem of European security the new weapon rendered trivial the considerations which had dominated Roosevelt's approach until his death.

DEADLOCK, CONFIDENCE AND DELAY

As has been shown, Truman's tactics on major issues at Potsdam were much the same: the President unveiled the full extent of the American demands, he refused to make important concessions, and he made it clear that if no agreement was reached, he was quite prepared to postpone consideration of the issue until a later date. "That was his position yesterday, that was his position today, and that would be his position tomorrow"—Truman's statement in the course of one of the debates provides a fitting summary of his approach.[103] Such an attitude combined the confidence derived from the new atomic weapon with the basic strategy postulate that it would be wise to delay final negotiations until after the atomic weapon had been demonstrated. That Stalin accepted the substance of the American proposal for Germany should not obscure the fact that Truman followed the same tactics on this issue as on others. Even the German settlement contained a considerable element of delay, for although the Russians were promised a percentage of industrial reparations from the western zone, the total to which this percentage would apply—and consequently the central issue of the agreement—would not be decided for many months.[104]

It had been clear even before the American delegation left Washington that the President had little real desire to begin serious negotiations at this time. Once at the Conference, neither Truman nor his Secretary of State attempted to wield the powerful bargaining leverage which had played such a crucial role in the first showdown over Poland; instead of following the plan to negotiate a large credit in exchange for Soviet diplomatic concessions, this effort had also been suspended for a few more weeks.* A Council of Foreign Ministers, established by the heads of government at Byrnes's suggestion, would meet to take up the diplomatic negotiations in less than a month.†[105] And, as Churchill has written, it would have much to do, for "a formidable body of questions on which there was disagreement was . . . piled upon the shelves."[106]

Thus, the only real agreements reached at Potsdam were on those questions over which there was little dispute (such as political principles for postwar Germany). On proposals concerning the American-controlled areas (such as Italy) to which Stalin would not agree, there was little progress;[107] on proposals concerning the Soviet-controlled area (such as the Balkans) there was postponement; on proposals concerning jointly controlled areas (such as Germany) there was either delay or an agreement along the broad lines of the American proposals written in vague and sometimes contradictory terms which, as it turned out, could be interpreted in a different way by each side.‡

---

* See below, pp. 223–224.

† It is probable that the American proposal to establish machinery for post-Potsdam negotiations was directly related to the expectation that there would be little likelihood of a settlement during the heads-of-government meeting. In the presently available material I have found no evidence on this point, and the American argument for the new Council of Foreign Ministers was put forward—and accepted—as the most efficient way to speed the peace settlement. Yet it is impossible to ignore the fact that the American delegation was extremely interested in establishing a council to take up all the postponed issues immediately after the atomic bomb was to be demonstrated and only three weeks after the President was to return to America.

‡ The reparations and economic agreements are universally regarded as confused and were later the source of considerable dispute. (See McNeill, *America, Britain, and Russia, 1941–46*, p. 625; Ratchford and Ross, *Berlin Reparations Assignment*, pp. 44, 187; Penrose, *Economic Planning for the Peace*, p. 284.

Inevitably, the main result of the Conference was a series of decisions to disagree until the next meeting.[108] As Admiral Leahy has conveniently summarized the outcome, in addition to the Balkan issue, these were some of the "problems on which no agreement could be reached":

(1) internationalization of major waterways (American proposal); (2) trusteeships of colonial possessions, principally Italy's holdings in Africa (Soviet proposal); (3) Macedonian-Greek frontier (British proposal); (4) settlement of Soviet claims for Turkish territory and control of the Dardanelles; (5) Russian seizure of British and American industrial property in Rumania; (6) Italian reparations; (7) naming of "high war criminals," although it was agreed that a special commission would make its "nominations" within a month; (8) Russian attempt to force Britain and America to sever diplomatic relations with Spain (the best Stalin got on that one was language in the communiqué which stated that Spain should not belong to the United Nations); (9) Stalin's effort to open up the question of control of Tangier and the Levant; and (10) Russian attempt to have the *status quo* in Yugoslavia accepted by the other two Allies.[109]

Reviewing the communiqué produced by the Potsdam Conference, General de Gaulle commented: " . . . We learned that it had concluded in a kind of uproar."*[110] His judgment of the result would have been correct, of course—*if* the American government had hoped to achieve a major negotiated settlement at this juncture. But, the whole point of strategy throughout the summer and throughout the Potsdam meeting, was to delay the settlement of controversial issues until the atomic bomb had been demonstrated. It is for this reason that the American delegation was not at all depressed with the seeming stalemate recorded in the Potsdam protocol. At the end of the Conference the President told Eisenhower he had achieved his objectives,[111] and as Byrnes has written, from the American point of view, the Conference could only be considered a success.[112] Byrnes believed that a few discussions at the foreign ministers' meeting, scheduled to meet only

---

* The British also felt this way. After reading the minutes of the Big Three on July 23, Alanbrooke confided to his diary: "One fact that stands out more clearly than any other is that nothing is ever settled!" (Bryant, *Triumph in the West 1943–46*, p. 478.) See also Churchill's comment: ". . . Frustration was the fate of this final Conference . . ." (*Triumph and Tragedy*, p. 668.)

three weeks after his return to Washington, would clear the way for a settlement in Eastern Europe.[113] The Potsdam protocol, in his view, provided a "basis" for the "early restoration of stability in Europe."[114] Attempts to erect a lasting structure upon this foundation and to settle all outstanding issues would only begin when the strategy of delay had reached its climax.*

CODA: CULMINATING TACTICS OF DELAY IN THE FAR EAST

THROUGHOUT JUNE AND JULY, Truman's approach to the Manchurian and Chinese diplomatic issues had followed a delaying strategy roughly similar to his approach to European issues. However, at Potsdam, once again the related issue of Soviet entry into the Japanese war complicated the tactical problem facing the President. There was no reason for Truman to conceal his views on European issues, for his ultimate goal was prompt agreement along the lines of American proposals. But despite his earlier plans to complete the Soviet-Chinese negotiations at Potsdam,† with the public demonstration of the new weapon still a few weeks off, Truman had no wish to reach a settlement which would also be the cue for an immediate Soviet declaration of war. Consequently, his approach to Far Eastern problems was far less candid than was his blunt assault upon the European issues.

As we have seen, in the weeks preceding Potsdam, Chinese Foreign Minister T. V. Soong had been carefully advised at each step of his negotiations with Stalin so as to maintain the insurance of Soviet participation in the war at the same time that final agreement and an actual declaration of war were delayed until the atomic test.‡ As this approach was followed it became increasingly evident that the Japanese were seeking an early end to the hostilities. American intercepts of cables between Tokyo and the Japanese ambassador in Moscow confirmed the "real evidence"§ that the Emperor—the one person all agreed could end the war—had now taken an active hand in the

---

* See below, pp. 200–204, 226.   ‡ See above, pp. 120–126.
† See above, p. 121.   § See above, p. 109.

matter.* In the week before Potsdam, formal decisions of the Imperial Conference to stop the fighting were revealed in the cables, and the Japanese ambassador begged for an interview with Molotov to discuss a special mission to be headed by Prince Konoye "carrying with him the personal letter of His Majesty stating the Imperial wish to end the war."[115] Molotov, however, refused an interview, and the ambassador was forced to carry his message to a subordinate official. He was then told that a response would undoubtedly be delayed because of the impending Big Three meeting.[116]

On July 17, the day of the first plenary session, another intercepted Japanese message showed that although the government felt that the unconditional-surrender formula involved too great a dishonor, it was convinced that "the demands of the times" made Soviet mediation to terminate the war absolutely essential.[117] Further cables indicated that the one condition the Japanese asked was preservation of "our form of government."[118] A message of July 25 revealed instructions to the ambassador in Moscow to go anywhere to meet with Molotov during the recess of the Potsdam meeting (caused by the British elections) so as to "impress them with the sincerity of our desire" to terminate the war.[119] He was told to make it clear that "we should like to communicate to the other party through appropriate channels that we have no objection to a peace based on the Atlantic Charter." The only "difficult point is the . . . formality of unconditional surrender."[120]

With the interception of these messages there could no longer be any real doubt as to Japanese intentions; the maneuvers were overt and explicit and, most of all, official acts. As Eisenhower told Stimson, "Japan was, at that very moment, seeking some way to surrender with a minimum loss of face!"[121] Even the covert, devious, and unofficial maneuvers made in Germany a few months earlier had been recognized as important opportunities to secure a surrender and had been

---

* It is impossible to determine whether the President saw every one of the intercepted cables. That he surely was familiar with the contents of the most important ones cannot be doubted, and he has confirmed that he saw the two crucial cables (July 12 and July 25). (*Conference of Berlin*, I, p. 873.) Moreover, both Stimson and Forrestal had full information regarding the intercepts. (*Conference of Berlin*, II, p. 1266; Stimson, *On Active Service*, p. 617; Forrestal, *Diaries*, pp. 20, 74–76.) Forrestal also made a special effort to bring a number of the texts to the attention of Byrnes at Potsdam. (Strauss, *Men and Decisions*, p. 188; Byrnes, *All in One Lifetime*, p. 297.)

rapidly exploited by American officials.* To be sure, the Japanese proposals had not yet been made in detail, and the unconditional-surrender formula would require some modification, but Truman had already determined that, if necessary, he would be quite prepared to modify the formula so as to allow the Japanese to maintain their Imperial institutions, and he reaffirmed this intention during the Potsdam Conference.[122]

Thus, the cables showed not only the Japanese desire to end the war, but the fact that the Japanese and American governments were not very far apart in their conception of final surrender terms. Most important, however, the cables also confirmed that the last frail hopes of the Japanese were now unmistakably focused upon the as yet indeterminate position of the Soviet Union. The insistent attempts to see Molotov were such obvious evidence of Japanese anxiety that at one point the ambassador in Moscow had to caution the foreign minister in Tokyo against moves "which would only result in exposing our uneasy emotion and would be of no benefit to us."[123]

Despite this advice and the continual reports that there was little reason for optimism concerning Russian intentions,[124] the Japanese government continued to cling to the belief that so long as Stalin remained uncommitted it might be possible to hope for Soviet mediation, or at least Soviet neutrality.[125] Undoubtedly, the Soviet enigma gave pause to even the most ardent Japanese peace advocates. The combination of uncertainty and hope precluded open peace maneuvers within governing circles, for as long as Soviet mediation was a possibility, no government could assume the dishonor and disadvantage of suing for peace on unconditional terms.†

Throughout the summer, the American government had recognized how this situation greatly enhanced the shock value of a Soviet declaration of war—it would eliminate the last hope and was likely to force capitulation.‡ Now the point was even more obvious. On July 16, Stimson advised the President that "the impending threat of Russia's participation" and "the recent news of attempted approaches on the part of Japan to Russia" had produced "the psychological moment" to attempt to warn Japan into surrender.[126] On July 18, Secretary Byrnes

---

* See McNeill, *America, Britain, and Russia, 1941–46*, pp. 569–70. Also my Appendix I, pp. 256–260.

† See Butow, *Japan's Decision*, pp. 112–41.

‡ See above, pp. 106–110.

also noted the dependence of the Japanese on Soviet actions, commenting that the recent Japanese maneuvers were quite evidently inspired by a fear of what Russia might do.[127]

This confirmation of earlier estimates of the crucial psychological and political role played by the Soviet Union was matched, at Potsdam, by renewed proof of Stalin's intentions. Since mid-May, American policy makers had been convinced that the Soviet Premier would enter the war, as pledged, as soon as the Soong negotiations were completed. Now, on July 17, Stalin once more reaffirmed his plans in a private talk with Truman and Byrnes; the Red Army would be prepared to cross the Manchurian border by mid-August and would do so as soon as the Chinese treaty was initialed.[128] On July 21, the Joint Chiefs of Staff informed the American commanders in the Pacific that they could expect a Russian declaration of war on or about August 15.[129]

Thus the alternatives which had emerged during the summer of delay were confirmed at the Potsdam Conference; if all that appeared necessary to force Japanese capitulation was a "tremendous shock," the United States could choose to accomplish the objective with either a Soviet declaration of war or the atomic bomb. Additionally, there was the possibility of a negotiated settlement involving guarantees for the Emperor.[130]

Truman did not hesitate. He had no wish to test the judgment that a Soviet declaration of war would probably force capitulation. Nor was he interested in attempts to negotiate. Instead, he simply followed through on earlier plans to use the atomic weapons as soon as possible. "The atomic bomb was no 'great decision,' " he later recalled, ". . . not any decision that you had to worry about";[131] and he has confirmed on numerous occasions that he "never had any doubt that it should be used."[132] Once the cables announcing the tremendous success of the New Mexico test began to flow into Potsdam, Truman was concerned only with operational details.* Formal British agreement to use the weapon had already been recorded on July 4,[133] and Chur-

---

* Since the story of the use of the atomic bomb against Japan has been described in detail elsewhere, I have eliminated interesting but well-known information relating to the various presidential and other decisions involved in the actual operations. For a good account, see Hewlett and Anderson, *The New World;* and Craven and Cate, *Air Forces in World War II,* Vol. V.

chill confirms: "The historic fact remains, and must be judged in the after-time, that the decision whether or not to use the atomic bomb . . . was never even an issue."[134]

Secretary of War Stimson records only that on July 22 the President "was intensely pleased" with word that the weapons might be delivered somewhat earlier than had been expected.[135] When more detailed information arrived stating "operation may be possible any time from August 1,"[136] Truman "said that was just what he wanted, that he was highly delighted."[137] And on July 25, the formal order to use the weapon in combat was issued by the Secretary of War.[138] As the President later recalled, "I . . . instructed Stimson that the order would stand unless I notified him that the Japanese reply to our ultimatum was acceptable."[139]

Having reaffirmed the decision—or assumption—which had guided policy since April, Truman turned to the problem of Soviet entry into the war. Again, he continued to follow the earlier tactics of delay. When on July 18 Stalin had personally brought copies of the latest Japanese messages to the President's attention,[140] Truman had made no attempt to follow up the Japanese overtures. Instead, he had simply agreed with Stalin's suggestion that "it might be desirable to lull the Japanese to sleep . . . [through an] unspecific answer."[141] When the full report of the unexpected power of the test reached the President, however, he went beyond the vagaries and ambivalence of his initial position.

As early as July 18, having heard from the President that "the war might come to a speedy end," Prime Minister Churchill was quite aware of a new confidence in Truman's approach to military problems in the Pacific.[142] When the full report of the test arrived, there could no longer be any question. On July 23, Alanbrooke noted one of the "American exaggerations" Churchill had absorbed and taken as his own: "It was now no longer necessary for the Russians to come into the Japanese war; the new explosive alone was sufficient to settle the matter."[143] Later the same day, reporting to the Cabinet on a conversation with Byrnes, Churchill cabled: "It is quite clear that the United States do not at the present time desire Russian participation in the war against Japan."[144]

Churchill's observation was completely accurate. As Byrnes has written, "The reports made it clear that the bomb had met our highest hopes and that the shock of its use would very likely knock our already wavering enemy out of the war."[145] On July 23, Stimson recorded that even the cautious General Marshall "felt, as I felt sure he would, that now with our new weapon we would not need the assistance of the Russians to conquer Japan."[146] This confirming view was reported to the President the next day,[147] and now there was unanimity; the ambivalent strategy of delay had paid off; it was no longer even necessary to attempt to maintain the insurance of a Soviet declaration of war. Thus, there was a double irony in the Potsdam meeting, for not only was it too early to settle European matters, but the only other reason for coming to the Conference—to insure a Soviet declaration of war—had now also disappeared.[148]

During June and early July American officials had agreed that a proclamation attempting to "warn Japan into surrender" would be issued from the Potsdam meeting. The warning had been conceived partly in the hope that if it were accepted the atomic bombing would be forestalled; but its primary objective had been to reinforce the impact of the bombing—for then, as Stimson had emphasized, although the atomic bomb would not be specifically mentioned in the declaration, the new weapon would be related to a demand for surrender, and it would serve as a "sanction" to the warning.[149] Thus, the primary aim of the proclamation was to encourage a prompt Japanese surrender, and the War Department, for its part, had supported the measure not only to end the war before an invasion, but more precisely, "before too many of our allies are committed there."[150]

Nevertheless, it was realized, as Stimson and Stettinius had specifically advised (and as was apparent to all concerned), that if the warning was endorsed by the Soviet Union its effectiveness would be multiplied manifold.[151] Before Potsdam, optional phrases including the Soviet Union as one of the signatory powers had been written into the warning at various points. These would be used if it was decided to invite Stalin to join in issuing the proclamation.[152] Similarly, before Potsdam, General Marshall and former Secretary of State Hull had particularly emphasized the great value of the Soviet "sanction" to the warning.[153] And Stimson's memorandum of advice to the President, reflecting the pre-Potsdam ambivalence, was replete with conditional phrases regarding the possibility of utilizing "the ominous threat of Russia" in conjunction with the proclamation.[154]

Now, however, greatly bolstered by the atomic test, Truman decided to strike out the tentative phrases and issue the proclamation without asking Stalin's participation.[155] During June, American leaders, aware that the Soviet Premier might not like to give the enemy advance indications of his intentions, had hesitated before suggesting that the United States Chiefs of Staff come to Potsdam; after the German defeat, military discussions could only be concerned with the Far East, and, "having in mind the possible Japanese reaction" to such a powerful hint of Russian plans, they were quite aware that Stalin might avoid military consultations.[156] Now, however, there was no fear of embarrassing the Soviet leadership or of prejudicing the military situation in Manchuria; much to the surprise and apparent anger of the Russians, the warning proclamation was issued from the site of the tripartite meeting even before the Russians were informed of its existence.[157]

Similarly, when on July 29 Molotov requested that the President provide a formal letter inviting Soviet participation in the war, Truman attempted to avoid the issue.[158] The Secretary of State and his assistant Benjamin Cohen spent the better part of the afternoon trying to devise a response to the Soviet request.[159] "We had, of course, begun to hope that a Japanese surrender might be imminent and we did not want to urge the Russians to enter the war," Byrnes has testified.[160] After considerable thought, finally the President sent Stalin a legalistic letter stating that he felt the new United Nations Charter (although not yet ratified) made it proper for the Russians to join in the war against an aggressor.[161] Undoubtedly aware of the limitations of this document, in a covering note Truman told Stalin: "If you decide to use it, it will be all right. However, if you decide to issue a statement basing your action on other grounds or for any other reason prefer not to use this letter, it will be satisfactory to me."[162] As General Deane has noted, " . . . Soviet participation was no longer an essential ingredient . . . we were in a position to be tough and indifferent."[163]

But avoiding the issue was only the most passive aspect of the American approach at Potsdam. By this time American leaders not only had little desire to maintain the possibility of a Russian declaration of war, but they were deeply concerned that the Red Army might cross the Manchurian border before the Japanese surrender. Secretary of the Navy Forrestal discussed the problem with the Secretary of State on July 28. His diary entry records: " . . . Byrnes said he was most anxious to get the Japanese affair over with before the Russians got in, with particular reference to [the Manchurian ports of] Dairen and Port Arthur. Once in there, he felt it would not be easy to get them out. . . ."[164] Moreover, as Byrnes has recently revealed, it was primarily for this reason that the earlier decision to inform Stalin of the successful atomic test had been rejected in practice; the vague statement that a powerful new weapon was available had been made because Truman and Byrnes feared that if Stalin were aware of the full power of the atomic test—and the possibility that the atomic bomb would end the war before Russia entered—the Soviet Premier might immediately order the Red Army to attack.*

And it was also for this reason that American policy makers—for the third time—shifted the emphasis of their approach to the Soong mission. No longer interested in preserving the possibility of an early declaration of war, Truman and Byrnes now hoped to use the negotiations only as a way to hold off the Red Army attack while the atomic bombs were brought into action. As General Deane has written, "It was a foregone conclusion that a satisfactory adjustment would be reached,"[165] but with the full report of the New Mexico test in hand, on July 23, the President and the Secretary of State, carefully trying to avoid the appearance of disregarding Roosevelt's pledges, cabled Chiang Kai-shek that they did not want him to make any concessions. They also declared that it was important for the Chinese to resume negotiations with Stalin.[166] "I had some fear," Byrnes later reported, "that if they did not, Stalin might immediately enter the war."[167]

Thus the strategy of delay continued. Despite the American interest in Sino-Soviet agreement on the complicated Chinese and Manchu-

---

* This information comes from Byrnes. Asked about the question many years later, Truman did not deny this intent, but stated that he did not remember such a consideration. (Feis, *Japan Subdued*, p. 89; also see above, p. 156.)

This fear may also partly account for the fact that despite Truman's desire to leave the Conference after July 23, he stayed on until August 2. Truman and Byrnes may well have wished to keep Stalin negotiating until the atomic bomb was used. At one point, it seemed the first attack could have taken place any time after August 1. Similarly, brief military conversations took place at Potsdam. Undoubtedly these were held though they were no longer needed, because cancellation of the talks would have aroused Soviet suspicions.

rian issues, the President had no wish to complete the negotiations until after the atomic bomb had been used and, as hoped, the Japanese war had ended. Although on July 17 the President informally discussed with Stalin the American desire to maintain the "Open Door" in Manchuria, and specifically, to treat Dairen as a free port, he did not pursue these matters during the remainder of the conference.[168] Similarly, although Stimson, Byrnes, and Harriman greatly feared that Russian control of the ports and railways of Manchuria might affect American commercial interests in the area, and although Stimson pressed his fears repeatedly in discussions with the President, Truman had no desire to attempt to secure new guarantees from Stalin at this juncture.[169] Finally, Truman rejected a proposal by State Department experts that Soong be summoned to Potsdam to conclude negotiations on the few remaining points in dispute.[170]

Even more obviously than in his handling of the European matters, the President made it clear that he had no wish to negotiate. His summer plans to complete the treaties in his talk with Stalin were suspended. The agenda items on the Far East were not taken up, and Truman did not press his earlier demand to be consulted before the Soviet Chinese treaty was signed. The "appropriate time"* had not yet arrived; first there would be an attempt to end the war. Then, with the Red Army stalled on the far side of the Manchurian border and—as Stimson had urged two months earlier—with the "master card" in hand, it would be time to "have it out with Russia on her relations to Manchuria and Port Arthur and various other parts of North China, and also the relations of China to us."†

During the last days of the Potsdam meeting, Stalin brought a further Japanese message to the attention of the President. Replying to the Soviet request for more definite information regarding the proposed Prince Konoye mission, the Japanese ambassador stated:

> The mission . . . was to ask the Soviet Government to take part in mediation to end the present war and to transmit the complete Japanese case in this respect. . . . Simultaneously, he wished to repeat that Prince Konoe (*sic*) was especially charged by His Majesty the Emperor to convey to the Soviet Government that it was exclusively

---

* See above, p. 124. † See above, p. 98.

the desire of His Majesty to avoid more bloodshed by the parties engaged in the war. . . .*[171]

Though the message was still lacking in detail, there could be now no doubt that the Japanese government was seriously looking for a way to end the war. But again, the President had little interest in attempting to investigate the possibilities the Japanese approach offered. He simply agreed to the suggestion that the Russians should give a definite negative answer to the request that Prince Konoye be received, and he moved on to other business.†[172]

On the same day that Truman and Stalin discussed this matter (July 28), the Japanese Premier told a press conference that his government would *"mokusatsu"* the Potsdam warning.[173] Truman interpreted this as a rejection of the proclamation, taking the Japanese term to mean "ignore" or "regard as unworthy of public notice."[174] For this reason, earlier instructions to utilize the new weapons as soon as possible were not countermanded.

Truman permitted the bombing despite new cable intercepts which strongly indicated that the Japanese decision to *"mokusatsu"* did not mean an abandonment of the attempt to end the war. In fact, the cables suggested that the Premier had wished to convey by his ambiguous word the equally possible meaning, "withhold comment at this time."[175] A cable intercepted on the same day of the press conference showed that in the two days since the proclamation had been received the Japanese government had not yet reached a decision on how to treat the important question it raised. Truman's earlier decision to issue the warning proclamation without Soviet endorsement had been responsible to a considerable degree for the prolongation of Japanese indecision; despite the fact that the Soviet Union was not a belligerent, a proclamation from the Big Three Conference but signed only by Truman and Churchill (and Chiang Kai-shek) had increased the confusion with which the Japanese appraised the Soviet attitude. The cable to the Japanese ambassador stated: "The position taken by the Soviet Union in connection with the Potsdam joint declaration . . . will henceforth have a bearing on our planning and will be a

---

* Truman had already seen an intercepted copy of this message. (*Conference of Berlin*, I, p. 873; II, pp. 1262–63.)

† As can be seen the Russians for their own reasons were little interested in negotiations to end the war.

very important problem." It stressed that the Soviet attitude raised a number of questions which could not be immediately answered. "For the time being, countermeasures against the joint declaration will be decided after we receive and study the Soviet reply to our" latest message.*[176]

This intercepted cable was followed by another, on August 2, which stated: "The battle situation has become acute. There are only a few days left in which to make arrangements to end the war. . . . Since the loss of one day relative to this matter may result in a thousand years of regret, it is requested that you immediately have a talk with Molotov . . ."[177] But the President evidently had no interest in these cables, nor in potentially time-consuming attempts to explore the opportunity to bring the hostilities to an end.†

On the contrary, as T. V. Soong reached Moscow, the first days of August took on the air of a frenzied race for time. Although under the previously delivered orders the bombing could take place anytime after August 3, weather conditions in Japan frustrated the desire for an immediate strike.[178] Now, apparently worried that Stalin might become impatient with the continued stalling of the Chinese negotiators, or that Soong might yield, on August 5, Truman sent a final instruction to Ambassador Harriman asking him to tell Stalin that the United States believed the Chinese could be expected to go no further toward meeting the Soviet demands.[179]

Thus, as the President and his entourage aboard the cruiser *Augusta* reached mid-Atlantic on the return voyage from Potsdam, the strategy of delay entered its final phase. Truman and Byrnes (and

---

* There can be no doubt that the President and the Secretary of State were as well informed on this and subsequent cables as they were on the previous ones. Byrnes reports that on July 28, for example, "Secretary Forrestal arrived and told me in detail of the intercepted messages from the Japanese government to Ambassador Sato in Moscow, indicating Japan's willingness to surrender." (*All in One Lifetime*, p. 297.)

† It is sometimes argued that Truman had to use the atomic bomb because the Japanese would not accept "unconditional" surrender. (Byrnes, *Speaking Frankly*, pp. 211, 262.) This argument neglects the fact that early in the summer Truman had decided if necessary to permit a conditional surrender allowing the Japanese to maintain

the Imperial institutions. (See above, p. 110.) Hence, his use of the atomic bomb must be explained in other terms. See also Stimson's diary entry of July 24: "I then spoke [to Truman] of the importance which I attributed to the reassurance of the Japanese on the continuance of their dynasty . . . I hoped that the President would watch carefully so that the Japanese might be reassured verbally through diplomatic channels if it was found that they were hanging fire on that one point. He said he had that in mind, and that he would take care of it. . . ." (*Conference of Berlin*, II, p. 1272.) See Lord Alanbrooke's similar conclusions, and his suggestion that "an opportune moment to make it clear to the Japanese might be shortly after a Russian entry into the war." (*Ibid.*, p. 36.)

Stimson, already in America) fixed their attention on the much awaited battle test of the revolutionary new weapon.[180] Hopefully, it would end the war before the Red Army entered Manchuria. By its dramatic blast it would herald a new and unprecedented advance in American power and—if the logic followed throughout the summer of delay continued to hold true—its force would permit a new American initiative in European and Far Eastern diplomacy.

American Diplomacy Takes the Offensive

Byrnes had already told me . . . that in his belief the bomb might well put us in a position to dictate our own terms at the end of the war.
—PRESIDENT HARRY S. TRUMAN on a conversation with James F. Byrnes in April 1945

THERE IS NO WAY to recapture the shock of the bombing of Hiroshima and Nagasaki. It requires an extraordinary feat of historical imagination to recreate the surprise and drama and horror of the day the world first learned of the atomic bomb. And it is all but impossible to recall the instant change in American thinking, the new sense of confidence and power the first atomic explosions engendered. To understand the impact of the new weapon upon diplomacy, one must go beyond the simple assertion that the added military power could be useful in war and in diplomatic maneuvering. In the first instance, its influence was psychological.

Truman's exuberance and Churchill's excitement at Potsdam show some of the emotional force of the new development. Though he had expected the bomb to be a success for many months, and despite the fact that at Potsdam he learned how greatly the test had exceeded expectations, when the President was informed of the successful bombing of Hiroshima, the effect was remarkable. Aboard the cruiser *Augusta,* Truman hurried back and forth telling officers and crew alike the news.[1] "I was greatly moved," the President has told us; and his sentiment was not remorse, but satisfaction. His first remark to those with him at the time was the unqualified assertion, "This is the greatest thing in history!"[2]

To the average American, as well as to most senior government officials, news of the atomic bomb came first from the newspapers. Here too the weapon's power was disclosed in a way which produced great emotion and optimism about its usefulness as an instrument of high policy. On August 7, newspapers were filled with banner headlines announcing the devastation of Hiroshima.[3] Not only was the development an unprecedented and amazing—indeed, at the time, fantastic*—scientific feat, but at once the bomb's seemingly incredible power for war and peace was dramatically disclosed. In less time than it took to read a newspaper, the American public learned that the bomb might reduce the Japanese war from a publicly estimated year and a half to a few short weeks or even days. Immediately, news of Nagasaki convinced those who might have doubted the extent of the new power. In less than a week, the war—which until then had been a long series of costly island-to-island battles against an enemy who fought to the death—was suddenly over. Not only was the atomic bomb spectacular in itself, but it immediately demonstrated its apparent capacity to force surrender upon a powerful enemy.†[4]

While the public at large was treated to the dramatic news of the weapon, the President and his senior advisers worked feverishly to end the Japanese war quickly. Ironically, the atomic bomb had not fulfilled one hope of the strategy of delay; with the Soong negotiations still stalled, on August 8—three months, to the day, after German capitulation—the Soviet Union declared war on Japan, and early the

---

* The *New York Herald Tribune* (Aug. 7, 1945) commented that the new force was "weird, incredible and somehow disturbing; one forgets the effect on Japan or on the course of the war as one senses the foundations of one's own universe trembling . . ."

† In recalling the effect of the bombing upon the American public I wish only to point out that most Americans did not doubt (and do not doubt) that the atomic bomb ended the war. (See, for example, Truman, *Year of Decisions*, p. 426; Byrnes, *Speaking Frankly*, p. 264; *All in One Lifetime*, p. 308.) Though a good case can probably be made that the Soviet declaration of war actually provided the *coup de grâce*, there is no need to argue the point,

nor can a final answer to this question ever be given. However, note that the Japanese Cabinet did not decide to surrender after the first atomic bomb, that the Cabinet fixed its hopes on the undetermined Soviet attitude until the very moment Stalin declared war, that the Russian entry hit where it counted (ending the hope of *the military leaders*), and that American propaganda directed at Japan after Hiroshima stressed the importance of the Russian attack. (Ehrman, *Grand Strategy*, pp. 283, 306–7; Hewlett and Anderson, *The New World*, p. 403; Craven and Cate, *Air Forces in World War II*, Vol. V, pp. 730–32; S. E. Morison, "Why Japan Surrendered," *The Atlantic*, October 1960, p. 47.)

next morning the Red Army crossed the Manchurian border.[5] In the few days between the Soviet declaration and the formal surrender of Japan, Stimson, Byrnes, and Truman continued to follow the basic line of strategy they had adopted during the summer. Stimson urged the President that "the thing to do was to get this surrender through as quickly as we can before Russia . . . should get down in reach of the Japanese homeland . . . It was of great importance to get the homeland into our hands before the Russians could put in any substantial claim to occupy and help rule it."[6]

Byrnes, of course, emphatically agreed.[7] But an August 10 Japanese message accepting the Potsdam Proclamation was conditional; it asked guarantees that the Emperor's position be respected.[8] Stimson urged that American assurances for the Emperor would produce a quick surrender.[9] Byrnes, agreeing with the objective, disagreed on tactics—such assurances might appear as a sign of weakness and could "cause much delay."[10] Finally, Truman accepted a suggestion by Forrestal that a message which implicitly recognized the Emperor's position but which was explicitly "unconditional" would be the best way to secure a prompt response.[11] In the meantime, "the President observed that we would keep up the war at its present intensity."*

Byrnes now attempted to arrange quick approval for this approach from the other Allies.[12] When Molotov asked for a day to consider the

---

* The tremendous desire to end the war quickly was expressed in many ways. Since the bomb dropped on Hiroshima accomplished the shock effect, the use of the second bomb against Nagasaki may well be explained by noting that Truman and Byrnes wished to leave absolutely no doubt about their resources or their intentions, and were anxious to avoid any time-consuming delays. Byrnes has testified they knew "the Japanese were patently anxious to surrender," but after the first Japanese acceptance message came in, Truman ordered conventional military operations to continue full force. At the Cabinet meeting on August 10, Stimson "suggested . . . that it would be a humane thing . . . that might affect the settlement if we stopped the bombing. . . ." However, his view was "rejected on the ground that it couldn't be done at once because we had not yet received in official form the Japanese surrender. . . ." Stimson's diary entry continues: "This of course was a correct but narrow reason, for the Japanese had broadcast their offer of surrender through every country in the world." (Stimson Diary, Aug. 10, 1945.) Forrestal's diary shows that Stimson also "cited the growing feeling of apprehension and misgiving as to the effect of the atomic bomb even in our own country," and that the Secretary of the Navy supported the advice that conventional bombing should cease. (Forrestal, *Diaries*, p. 83.) Truman refused to let up the pace even after the Japanese accepted the final American message, which implicitly acknowledged the position of the Emperor. Long after Radio Tokyo had broadcast acceptance of these terms (on August 14), but before the message had reached Washington through official channels, General Arnold (who wished to stage as big a *finale* as possible) was permitted to send 1,014 aircraft (approximately 800 B-29's and 200 fighters) to drop six thousand tons of conventional explosives on Honshu. (Byrnes, *All in One Lifetime*, p. 305; Truman, *Year of Decisions*, p. 423; Leahy, *I Was There*, pp. 434–36; Craven and Cate, *Air Forces in World War II*, Vol. V, pp. 699, 732–33; *New York Times*, Aug. 15, 1945.)

American message, Byrnes made it clear through Harriman that the United States was quite prepared to accept the surrender without the Soviet Union unless approval for the American message was immediately given.[13] Stalin quickly yielded to the American demand,[14] and the message was sent to the Japanese on August 11.[15] Now there was nothing to do except wait for the response.

Aware that each hour meant a further advance of the Soviet armies, and also some loss of life, American leaders now became extremely impatient.[16] "Never have I known time to pass so slowly!" Byrnes recalls.[17] When Japanese acceptance of the American message arrived, Byrnes abandoned all diplomatic requirements. Although the three powers had attempted to coordinate the acceptance and announcement of the German surrender,[18] Byrnes now cut consultations short and, giving the other Allies less than three hours' notice, he declared that the President would announce acceptance of the Japanese surrender at 7 P.M., August 14; the others could join in at that time if they wished.[19]

Thus, the war was ended five days after the Red Army entered Manchuria. Despite the fact that the atomic bomb did not prevent the attack, however, it did fulfill the other hope of the strategy of delay. Truman has characterized the result: "Our dropping of the atomic bomb on Japan . . . forced Russia to reconsider her position in the Far East."[20] Indeed, as Stimson had predicted, after the bombing the relative positions of the United States and the Soviet Union were radically altered. A new firmness immediately appeared in American diplomacy and, correspondingly a new willingness to yield appeared in the Soviet stance.

After the New Mexico test, Truman had decided to exclude the Soviet Union from a significant role in the occupation and control of Japan.[21] For this reason the August 11 message, as Stimson noted, "asserted that the action of the Emperor must be dominated by the Allied commander, using the singular to exclude any condominium."[22] When Harriman had demanded immediate Soviet agreement to the message, Molotov had asked for time to consider just this point.[23] But Moscow was in no position to dispute American prerogatives and by endorsing the American message the Soviet government formally paved the way for unilateral American control of Japan.[24]

Similarly, Stalin could do very little when Truman simply refused his request that the Red Army be allowed to take a token surrender in the Japanese homeland (on the northern half of the island of Hokkaido).[25] And Stalin's readiness to accept American conditions after Hiroshima was underscored a week after surrender when an American proposal for a Far Eastern Advisory Commission was accepted.[26] This body, unlike the Control Commissions governing the other ex-enemy states, was to be virtually powerless. Its location—in Washington—stressed the fact that it would have little control over the operating decisions of the Supreme Commander, General Douglas MacArthur, in Tokyo.[27] Thus, it was with the general approval of the Russians that Truman told the press on August 16 that Japan would not be divided into occupation zones, and declared in the first week of September that as far as Japan was concerned, "in the event of any differences of opinion [among the Allied powers] the policies of the United States will govern."*[28]

That the atomic bomb had strengthened the American hand was even more clearly demonstrated when the "tangled weave" of Manchurian issues was taken up. Japan, of course, was beyond the reach of the landlocked Red Army. But even in the area of Soviet military operations, Truman now found Stalin prepared to accept most American terms. The President had delayed the Manchurian negotiations all summer, and he had rejected the State Department's suggestion that they be concluded at Potsdam. However, as soon as the news of Hiroshima was made public, on August 7, 9, and 10, following his instructions, Harriman told Stalin and Soong that the United States believed the Chinese should make no further concessions.[29] With only a short debate, Stalin now conceded almost all of the points he had pressed so diligently during the past month of talks with Soong:† Dairen was to become a free port under Chinese administration

---

* Later, during the London Conference, Stalin reversed his attitude, demanding a greater role in Japan. As Walter Lippmann, James Reston, the London Times, the Christian Science Monitor, and others noted at the time, his reversal was probably in retaliation to the pressure Byrnes put on the Soviet position in the Balkans. (New York Herald Tribune, Sept. 25; New York Times, Oct. 14; London Times, Oct. 2; Christian Science Monitor, Oct. 3, 1945.)

† See above, pp. 122–125.

(except in time of war),[30] and the jointly owned Manchurian railways were to be governed by a ten-man board of directors (five from each country) whose President was to be a Chinese Nationalist with decisive power to cast two votes.[31] A treaty was initialed on August 14 which "generally satisfied" Chiang Kai-shek,[32] and Ambassador Harriman cabled that T. V. Soong "was very grateful for our support and is convinced that unless we had taken an active part in the negotiations he would have had to accede to all Stalin's demands."*[33]

In Chungking, Ambassador Hurley was enthusiastic about the value of the treaties to internal Chinese politics. As in 1927, the Russians took a stand against the Chinese Communists:† "The publication . . . has demonstrated conclusively that the Soviet Government supports the National Government of China and also that the two governments are in agreement regarding Manchuria."[34] In America, most commentators expressed great satisfaction with the settlement in an area not administered by China for many years and under the direct military control of the Soviet Union.[35] On August 29, Madame Chiang visited Truman to thank him for his support. The President told his press conference: "She was very happy over the Russian-Chinese treaty, just as all of us are."[36]

To be sure, at a later date the hopes these successful negotiations produced were to be dissipated. But at the time—and for a very considerable period—Stalin respected the treaties.[37] Chiang Kai-shek's administrators were permitted to take over civilian control in the Red Army zone of operations[38] and the American Air Force and Navy ferried thousands of Nationalist troops (who had no independent way to reach the area)[39] to Manchuria to take over responsibilities from the Russians.[40] Although Stalin took advantage of his position to remove a number of Manchurian industries as "war booty,"‡[41] the Red Army withdrew in April 1946.[42] As the State Department later summarized the situation: "It was considered that Russia had accepted

---

* For the texts of the agreements, see Department of State, *Relations with China*, Annexes 51–59, pp. 585–96.

† And in 1959–1965?

‡ As I have noted, in the late autumn of 1945 a new Soviet *démarche* in the Far East seemed to be a direct response to the American effort in the Balkans. (See above, p. 192*fn*.) It may well be that the Soviet interest in industrial reparations and "war booty" from Manchuria was also a response to the West's reluctance to adhere to the Yalta reparations formula and the subsequent breakdown of German administrative arrangements.

definite limitations on its activities in China and was committed to withhold all aid from the Chinese Communists. . . ."*[43]

Thus the primary American objectives in the Far East were achieved. Moreover, as had been expected throughout the summer, now Truman and Byrnes began to take the initiative to secure further political and commercial concessions in Manchuria. At Stimson's suggestion, Truman had also deferred an approach to the Russians on these additional matters during the summer.† At Potsdam he had rejected the suggestion that negotiations begin while Stalin and he were together. However, now the "appropriate time"‡ had arrived. In his first approach to Molotov after Hiroshima, Harriman was instructed to attempt to secure a new public statement affirming Soviet support for America's traditional "Open Door" policy in the area.[44] Molotov initially responded that such a statement was superfluous, since Stalin had repeatedly confirmed his support for this policy.[45] But Truman and Byrnes persisted, on August 22 instructing Harriman to press the matter with Stalin himself.[46] This effort succeeded. On August 27 the Soviet Premier overruled his foreign minister and said he was prepared to issue the declaration sought by Washington.[47]

THE SECRET CLOSE-IN APPROACH

IN THE WHIRLWIND DAYS immediately after Hiroshima and Nagasaki, American diplomacy changed so swiftly that few observers have caught the sweep of all the policy decisions unveiled in a few short weeks. Secretary Byrnes, however, has emphasized the importance of this brief period. Underscoring the breadth and scope of new diplomatic departures, he has recalled: "Those . . . days . . . were full of action."[48] In fact, the sheer volume of work caused the Secretary of

---

* Although it is still a matter of dispute to what extent Stalin aided the Chinese Communists in the first postwar years, there is substantial agreement that his assistance, if of any importance at all, was extremely limited. (Beloff, *Soviet Policy*, pp. 42–43; Department of State, *Relations with China*, p. 121.) The Red Army withdrew from Manchuria in April 1946. (*Ibid.*, p. 147; McNeill, *America, Britain and Russia, 1941–46*, p. 709.) As late as June 1947, Byrnes made no complaints that Stalin was supporting the Chinese Communists. At that time

Byrnes was still able to write: "Whether Stalin will continue to resist the temptation . . . is a question which . . . remains in the balance." (Byrnes, *Speaking Frankly*, pp. 227–29, 293.) Similarly, as late as September 1947 the Chinese Foreign Minister wished to do nothing which might cause Stalin to reconsider his obligations under the Sino-Soviet treaty. (Department of State, *Relations with China*, p. 121.)

† See above, pp. 98, 101–103.

‡ See above, p. 124.

State to ask that the London foreign ministers' meeting set for September 1 be postponed until September 10.[49]

Amongst all the activities, however, unquestionably the most important concerned atomic energy. At precisely the same time American Far Eastern diplomacy was achieving its objectives, Truman and Byrnes also made it clear that the United States intended to maintain its atomic monopoly.

Truman's August 6 statement—released with the news of Hiroshima—revealed that "it is not intended to divulge the technical processes of production or all the military applications."[50] In his August 9 report to the nation, the President declared: "The atomic bomb is too dangerous to be loose in a lawless world . . . We must constitute ourselves trustees of this new force."[51] Within a week of the presidential statement, the War Department released a long report on atomic energy with the notice: "The best interests of the United States require the utmost cooperation by all concerned in keeping secret now and for all time in the future all scientific and technical information. . . ."[52] In another week Truman directed that no information on the nuclear development project be released without the specific approval of the President.*[53]

Thus, Truman made public his resolve to maintain the production secrets of the new weapon. His declarations revealed that Stimson's early idea of exchanging information on nuclear energy (and simultaneously establishing international controls) had been rejected. Instead of the theory that the new development might be used as a bargaining counter with which to obtain diplomatic *quid pro quos* from the Russians, there was to be what Stimson had once described as "the secret close-in attempted control of the project by those who control it now."[54] Although initially Truman had had to decide only that diplomacy would be delayed until the atomic weapons were demonstrated, by the end of July he had also resolved the nascent dispute between Stimson and Byrnes; the President had adopted the Secretary of State's more narrow view that a temporary monopoly of nuclear weapons, in itself, would be valuable to diplomacy.†

---

* Churchill praised this decision in the House of Commons. (5th Series, *Hansard*, Vol. 413, Commons, 76–86.) Shortly thereafter Stimson's successor, Robert Patterson, reassured Congress that "the President has already said that he would not reveal the atomic bomb itself at all . . ." (U.S. House of Representatives, *Hearings: Atomic Energy Act*, Oct. 9, 18, 1945, p. 66.)

† See above, pp. 62–64.

Indeed, although the policy decision was taken in late July and made public only on August 6, the crucial assumptions of the narrow view had been adopted as early as the first week of June; for, despite Stimson's hopeful discussion of diplomatic *quid pro quos,* the Interim Committee had been strongly influenced by the Secretary of State–designate. In the May 31 meeting of the Committee, the director of the Los Alamos laboratories, J. Robert Oppenheimer, had argued that under a system of controls the United States should offer the world free interchange of nuclear information, with special emphasis on peacetime uses. He had felt the nation would strengthen its moral position if it acted before using the bomb.[55] General Marshall and Assistant Secretary of State Clayton, however, had argued against putting faith in a system of inspection safeguards for international control.[56] General Marshall had added his opinion that it would be best to build up a combination of like-minded powers that would bring Russia into line by the very force of the coalition.[57] As the discussion progressed, Byrnes had intervened decisively; he argued against giving information to the Russians, even in general terms. He concluded that the best policy was to push production and research and make certain that the United States stayed ahead.[58]

Byrnes's prestige—and his status as personal representative of the President—had not been ignored. The Interim Committee unanimously concurred in his judgment: It would be best to push research and production, to maintain secrecy, and to establish a combination of democratic powers for cooperation in atomic energy.[59] Byrnes and the Committee also expressed hope that some form of cooperation with Russia could be worked out so that under a control system each country would make public whatever work was being done on the subject.[60] However, in reality the Committee's recommendations all but excluded the possibility of international control of atomic energy: The Russians were unlikely to accept continued American production and research without attempting to secure nuclear weapons for themselves, and the Committee had no specific control proposals to make. Aware of the limitations of this approach, even as Stimson had discussed *quid pro quos* with the President on June 6, he had acknowledged that the Committee's ideas were "imperfect" and that they "might not be assented to by Russia." But he had told the President that "we were far enough ahead of the game to be able to accumulate enough material to serve as insurance."[61]

Thus, in the end, even Stimson, who knew that a nuclear monopoly could not be maintained, and who was deeply concerned by the prospect of an arms race, had given priority to continued weapons production and research instead of an attempt to establish international controls. Stimson briefly took great interest in a proposal that further production of atomic weapons should be halted temporarily as evidence of good faith, so that an approach to Russia could be attempted, but he did not pursue the idea.[62] On June 21 the Interim Committee, preparing a statement to be issued by the President, struck out a proposed sentence which would have committed the United States to attempt to achieve international control of atomic energy.[63] Stimson accepted the draft,[64] but although he continued to be troubled that, as he had once expressed it, "modern civilization might be completely destroyed,"[65] apparently few other members of the Interim Committee shared his fears.*

Most important, the President's personal representative, Secretary Byrnes, had few doubts about the wisdom of the "close-in" approach.[66] He believed the temporary atomic monopoly would be a great advantage to American diplomacy.[67] In his view, the primary task was to establish a "lasting structure of peace."[68] A stable Europe, essential to world peace and American security alike, was the number-one goal.[69] Byrnes also believed that the nuclear monopoly could be maintained for at least seven years.[70] He appears to have been convinced that within this period, with the support of the revolutionary new weapon, his diplomacy could easily achieve its idealistic objectives. Thus, the weapon seemed a crucial factor in forcing agreement to an American plan for permanent peace—a plan which, *ipso facto*, would prevent another world war. Since this vision promised an end to all war it implicitly obviated the danger of an arms race. There seemed plenty of time to accomplish the task before the Russians might break the American monopoly.† In any case, as Byrnes has written, "no one

---

* Oppenheimer is an exception. See Atomic Energy Commission, *Oppenheimer Hearings* for repeated references to his personal depression during this period and his fear for the future.

† "Permanent peace," or "lasting peace," or "durable peace," seems to have been a universal objective of American policy makers. (See above, pp. 53, 78.) In retro- (*Continued on next page*)

seemed too alarmed at the prospect, because it appeared that in seven years we should be far ahead of the Soviets in this field."[71]

Byrnes's arguments for secrecy and continued production of weapons convinced not only the Interim Committee but also the President. Although during June Truman also spoke optimistically of diplomatic *quid pro quos,* he accepted the recommendations presented to him. In mid-July, at Potsdam, the President told Churchill he would "at all costs . . . refuse to divulge any particulars."[72] He later wrote: "I had decided that the secret of the manufacture of the weapon would remain a secret with us."[73]

Indeed, during the Potsdam Conference both the President and Stimson lost the trace of interest in international controls each had evidenced earlier in the summer. Depressed by the omnipresent Soviet secret police in Berlin, both came to the conclusion that a control scheme could hope to succeed only if Russia were to become an open, democratic society.[74] As Harriman pointed out (and as Stimson soon realized),[75] to attempt to force the Soviet Union to change its national system would be to demand something no great power could consider.[76] However, once accepted, the idea that controls could be established only if Russia became a democracy inevitably destroyed even the meager remaining hope of international cooperation. Stimson's diary shows that this realization "troubled me a great deal,"[77] but as Truman has testified, the Secretary of War no longer urged the exchange of important information on the weapon.[78] And Stimson returned from Potsdam strongly opposed to the release of any atomic information.*[79]

The President later (in September) expressed some interest in meth-

---

(Continued from preceding page)
spect it is not surprising that leading officials, having personally experienced two world wars in one lifetime, should have aimed so consistently for a proper basis—as they defined it—which would eliminate a third world war. Nor, indeed, is it surprising that once given the unexpected power of the atomic bomb that they should have regarded the weapon as a means to achieve their goal. In this early period, Byrnes's view was the most straightforward, but compare Churchill's statement to the House of Commons, August 16, 1945: "The United States stand at this moment at the summit of the world . . . Let them act up to the level of their power . . . So far as we know, there are at least three and per-

haps four years before the concrete progress made in the United States can be overtaken. *In these three years we must remould the relationships of all men, wherever they dwell, in all the nations. . . ."* (5th Series, *Hansard,* Vol. 413, Commons, 80.) The newly available information on Byrnes's view also illuminates a previously enigmatic statement in his memoirs. Recalling discussions of the bomb with Churchill at Potsdam, Byrnes states: "In addition to his tremendous interest in the effect of the bomb on the war with Japan [Churchill] foresaw more clearly than many others the possibilities presented by the release of atomic energy." (*Speaking Frankly,* p. 262.)

For more information on Byrnes's view, see Hewlett and Anderson, *The New World,* ods for "controlling bomb warfare"[80] but the idea of sharing important information under a control scheme was dropped—"As far as I was concerned, this was not a matter for discussion."[81] Having accepted Byrnes's basic recommendations and having agreed that no control would be possible until the Soviet Union changed its system, Truman automatically—and apparently quite confidently—ended up strongly supporting the narrow view of his Secretary of State. Even before Potsdam there is little evidence that Truman showed much personal interest in promoting attempts to establish international controls. During the Conference he rejected the idea that frank relations and international cooperation required that he tell Stalin of the new weapon before using it.† After the Conference the President followed Byrnes's recommendations that no approach to the Russians be made. He told de Gaulle that because the United States had the only atomic bombs, "the peace problem . . . was therefore largely economic."[82] Stimson's Potsdam advice, which made control seem impossible, had bolstered Byrnes's conception of the role of the bomb in diplomacy; Truman concluded that so long as no "foolproof" method of control existed, "it was important to retain the advantage which the possession of the bomb had given us."‡[83]

---

pp. 354–60, 417, 418, 456, 458–59, 461, 469, 532; Atomic Energy Commission, *Oppenheimer Hearings*, p. 33; *The New York Times*, Sept. 6, 1945; Byrnes, *Speaking Frankly*, pp. 87, 179, 203, 261; *All in One Lifetime*, pp. 284, 303; Stimson Diary, Aug. 12–Sept. 3, Sept. 5, Sept. 11, 1945. The reader will note that I have not mentioned as one of the reasons for Byrnes's opposition to control schemes his belief that they were technically impossible. From all the evidence I have seen, it is quite clear that Byrnes *began* with the idea of basing his diplomacy on the atomic bomb (as his early April discussions with Truman show). Though he certainly distrusted the Russians, there is little evidence that at this time he opposed international control schemes because of doubts about their feasibility. Rather, he simply had no interest in any of the various schemes suggested which might have deprived him of the key factor in his diplomacy.

In 1947 Byrnes came to the conclusion that when the Russians caught up there would be little likelihood of war. Recalling that neither party used poison gas or germ warfare during the Second World War, he argued that a parallel situation would eventually be reached: "No nation dared use

these terrible weapons because they knew the same weapons would be used against them." (*Speaking Frankly*, p. 276.) Though Byrnes failed to achieve his diplomatic objectives, if the present delicate balance of terror can be maintained, ironically Byrnes's prediction may be borne out.

* Stimson later reconsidered his entire viewpoint. See Appendix III.

† See above, pp. 156, 183.

‡ The last sentence is Truman's 1955 recollection. From the evidence I have seen, however, it appears that between April and August 1945 Truman never had more than a passing interest in the idea of international control. Despite his comments about *quid pro quos*, in practice he seems to have consistently agreed with Byrnes that the implied threat of the weapon could not be given up to an international control scheme. Available evidence does not permit a final determination of how Truman saw the problem at the time, but as I have shown, even taking Truman's recollection at its face value, by the time of Potsdam he had defined the control problem in a way which could not be resolved. Thus, on his own terms the "advantage which the possession of the bomb had given us" could only be the advantage urged by Byrnes.

In this way the ideas Byrnes had urged during the summer became American policy: When it came, the much delayed showdown would not be based upon exchanging an international control system for diplomatic *quid pro quos*. Instead the "advantage" of the weapon could only be its value as an "implied threat."* The consolidation of this viewpoint was confirmed privately at the same time the President offered his public pledges to guard the secrecy of the new development. In early August, immediately after Hiroshima and Nagasaki, Assistant Secretary of War McCloy found Byrnes resolutely against any negotiations looking toward the international control of atomic energy.[84] The Secretary of State reiterated that "in his opinion we should continue the Manhattan Project with full force."[85] Similarly, Byrnes, representing the President, transmitted a direction through General Groves to J. Robert Oppenheimer that the work at Los Alamos was not to let up.[86] Expenditures of the Manhattan Project rose during the first months of peace from 43 million dollars in August to 51 million in September to 59 million in October.[87]

Byrnes's dominant position in policy making was evidenced in other ways immediately after Potsdam. The scientific panel of the Interim Committee now reported that thermonuclear weapons might be developed, and that their power would greatly exceed the power of the fission weapons used in Japan. It was the panel's "unanimous and urgent recommendation" that such developments be controlled by international agreement. Again, however, the President's personal representative took a negative view of any attempt to approach the Russians. Oppenheimer, who had helped draft the report and had carried the panel's recommendation to Byrnes, was told that the "proposal about an international agreement was not practical and that he and the rest of the gang should pursue their work [on the hydrogen weapon] full force."[88]

REMOVING THE SOVIET BLACKOUT
FROM THE BALKANS

TRUMAN'S STATEMENT that the United States would act as "trustees" of the new force came in his August 9 report to the nation on

---

* The term is taken from Stimson's diary report of Byrnes's privately expressed view of the bomb. (See below, p. 255.) Within a month the Secretary of War came to oppose the Byrnes view. On September 11, he also argued against "a succession of express or implied threats or near threats in our peace negotiations." (Stimson, *On Active Service*, p. 645.)

the Potsdam Conference. Thus, just as the atomic bomb had been intimately related to his European policy throughout the summer, the disclosure of the President's approach to the new weapon was implicitly linked to his first postwar discussion of European issues. Once again, however, it is necessary to recall that American departures in European diplomacy, in Far Eastern diplomacy, and in atomic-energy policy were revealed simultaneously, and in a great rush in the crowded second, third, and fourth weeks of August.

Truman's August 9 report on Potsdam emphasized his sense of confidence and optimism about the future; the Allies would "continue to march together to a lasting peace and a happy world."[89] Although he was not yet able to report that all his European objectives had been achieved, the President offered a convincing argument that the ultimate goal, a politically and economically stable Europe, would be achieved. In the main, the American proposals for Germany had been accepted. Agreement on political principles had been reached and, most important, the economic issue, which was dominated by the reparations question, had been settled along the lines of American proposals: The "idea of attempting to fix a dollar value . . . was dropped."[90] The President looked forward to early agreement on various other proposals when the foreign ministers held their first peacetime meeting in London. Soon most of the issues postponed at Potsdam might be settled.[91]

At the time Truman was making these remarks cooperative relations with the Russians began on a hopeful note almost everywhere on the Continent. In Germany, Eisenhower and Zhukov quickly established a warm friendship and close working relations.[92] Plans for free interzonal politics and trade were laid (and soon implemented).*[93] In Austria, General Mark Clark was less successful in his personal relationships, but he too found a considerable degree of Soviet coopera-

---

* The moderate Soviet approach in Eastern Germany and elsewhere during the early autumn of 1945 has been noted by many observers; and the radical changes which took place later have yet to be adequately explained. In addition to the fact that free enterprise, free trade, free travel, and free politics were promoted by the Russians in East Germany during this period, in October the Red Army ripped up vital rail communications extending from the Soviet Union through Poland to Germany. For more information on this fascinating but unexplored period, see Slusser, *Soviet Economic Policy in Postwar Germany*, pp. 16, 19, 20, 42, 55; Nettl, *The Eastern Zone and Soviet Policy in Germany, 1945–50*, pp. 80, 81, 281, 292; Leonhard, *Child of Revolution*, pp. 352, 379, 391, 411, 413–15, 427; Eisenhower, *Crusade in Europe*, p. 444. Similarly, at this time the Red Army, which controlled the greater part of Czechoslovakia and Hungary, withdrew. (McNeill, *America, Britain and Russia, 1941–46*, p. 734; Betts, *Central and South East Europe*, p. 126.)

tion immediately after Potsdam.[94] In Poland—the original symbol of Truman's policy—there also seemed to be signs of hope. At Potsdam, Truman had again secured Stalin's support for an early free election and for unrestricted reporting by Western correspondents.[95] Assistant Secretary of State Clayton and Ambassador Harriman had carried forward talks regarding economic aid with the Polish government.[96] Immediately after Potsdam, American correspondents requested permission to enter the country. (The Polish government agreed on August 24, and the reporters soon enjoyed unrestricted freedom.)[97] Ambassador Lane laid plans to bring to a culmination the summer strategy of attempting to bargain American credits for early elections and unrestricted trade. And, just as Truman had been confident the approach would work in April, Lane seemed to find every reason to believe the approach would now succeed.*

Thus, there seemed a reasonable basis for Truman's hopeful review of most European questions. But in his Potsdam report to the nation the President also discussed Southeastern Europe. And here, as had been clear before and during the Potsdam meeting, the Russians were not so amenable to American plans. Consequently, once again from Truman's point of view Southeastern Europe presented the most immediate challenge to American European policy. Truman's Potsdam demand that the governments of Bulgaria and Rumania be changed had been refused, but the President had made it quite clear that he was willing to postpone, not withdraw, his demand. Now, immediately after Hiroshima and Nagasaki, he publicly declared: "These nations are not to be spheres of influence of any one power."[98]

This statement of American opposition to Soviet domination of the Balkans was of major political significance. Here was the first open and public break in the wartime alliance. And immediately the President and his Secretary of State demonstrated that the declaration meant what it said: The United States demanded that the governments subservient to Soviet influence be removed. From the American point of view, forcing agreement on this issue was important not only in

---

* Lane held his first explicit talks with the Poles on September 3. Hoping to secure early free elections and the elimination of disciminatory trading agreements, he carried forward the April strategy in discussions throughout the autumn. "With complete candor," he stated that economic aid would be forthcoming only if the American proposals were accepted; "I determined to take advantage of the eagerness of the Polish Government for economic assistance and to use it as a lever. . . ." (Lane, *I Saw Poland Betrayed*, p. 145.)

itself, but also because the issue, like the Polish question in April, now came to symbolize American opposition to a Soviet sphere of influence throughout Eastern Europe. The crucial decision of the summer had been to delay a confrontation on this fundamental question until the atomic bomb had been demonstrated, and although the Potsdam meeting had unavoidably come a few weeks too soon, now there was no longer any reason to wait.

As early as mid-April, Byrnes had told the President that in his belief the bomb might well put America in a position to dictate terms at the end of the war.[99] He had told one of the nuclear scientists that the demonstration and possession of the new weapon would make Russia more manageable in Eastern Europe, specifically mentioning Poland, Rumania, and Hungary.* Now Secretary Byrnes set about the task of implementing his own basic view. In Byrnes's approach to the Balkans, and in Truman's support for this approach—more than in any other single diplomatic effort—American leaders demonstrated that the strategy of delay had reached its long-awaited climax. Together with British leaders, American policy makers now attempted to fulfill the President's summer pledge to "insist on the eventual removal of the Soviet blackout."[100]

Truman's declaration of opposition to spheres of influence was what one observer termed "the first gun" in an "Anglo-American diplomatic offensive."[101] In a series of powerful statements other American and British leaders drove home the President's point. Prime Minister Clement Attlee told Parliament he "looked forward with hope to the emergence of democratic governments based on free elections" in the Balkans.[102] Foreign Minister Bevin, revealing the Potsdam change in the British approach, declared that he would refuse to recognize the governments of Hungary, Bulgaria, and Rumania until free elections were held.[103] He added that under Soviet control, in his opinion, "one kind of totalitarianism [was] being replaced by another."[104] Winston Churchill publicly introduced the term "the iron

---

* Before his death, Dr. Leo Szilard offered a few more details of his May 28 conversation with the Secretary of State-designate: "Byrnes was concerned about Russia's having taken over Poland, Rumania, and Hungary, and so was I. Byrnes thought that the possession of the bomb by America would render the Russians more manageable in Europe. I failed to see how. . . ." (*U.S. News & World Report*, Aug. 15, 1960, p. 69.)

curtain"* and demanded an end to the "police governments," in the area.[105] At the same time he told the Commons his belief that the atomic bomb gave the West "irresistible" powers.[106]

In these speeches the privately expressed confidence so apparent at Potsdam was publicly manifested. Churchill's speech in the Commons made no attempt to hide the relationship between the new weapon and his judgment that the West now had the power to force Soviet acceptance of their approach in the Balkans. Although American spokesmen were not so explicit in public, a number of commentators noted the direct relationship between the "entirely new sense of confidence" in diplomacy and the atomic explosions. Indeed, it was all but impossible to miss the connection, for Truman's disclosure of the confrontation in the Balkans was heralded by the commanding news of the two atomic bombings; and the destruction of Nagasaki and the President's attack upon spheres of influence were made public on precisely the same day, August 9.†

The Anglo-American assault upon Soviet predominance in the Balkans was made despite the Churchill-Stalin arrangement, the armistice agreements, and the Yalta decisions. In fact, Truman's public declaration was a unilateral act which contravened the assumptions of an understanding the President had signed only a week earlier.[107] At Potsdam, Truman had acknowledged the authority of the Allied Control Commissions in each country and had reaffirmed the

---

* It had been used in private cables earlier. (Churchill, *Triumph and Tragedy*, p. 573.) It is interesting to note that almost immediately after Churchill used the term in the Commons the original situation it was meant to describe changed. Churchill used the term specifically to mean that British officials were restricted in their movements in Poland and the Balkans ("an iron fence had come down around them"—*Conference of Berlin*, II, p. 362) and to mean that Western correspondents were not allowed free range. However, at Potsdam the Western representatives were given all the additional rights in the Soviet zone that they asked (*Conference of Berlin*, II, pp. 1494–95), and after Potsdam, Western correspondents were given free access to Poland, Rumania, and Bulgaria. (State Department *Bulletin*, Aug. 26, 1945, pp. 283–84; *New York Times*, Sept. 13, 1945.) Hungary, of course, never presented a major problem in this respect. Although Churchill introduced his term in the autumn of 1945, it was only

considerably later that a new "iron curtain" descended in the Soviet zone of Europe.

† C. L. Sulzberger, noting the "diplomatic offensive" in the Balkans, commented: "The disclosure of an effective atomic weapon, completely shifting the actual balance of military power . . . revised the entire over-all atmosphere and the realities of a situation in which two rival Allied pressures were operating against each other." (*New York Times*, Aug. 26, 1945.) James Reston also noted the new American confidence and related it to the atomic explosions, which disclosed "the actuality of preponderant military power." (*Ibid.*) The *New York Herald Tribune* (Aug. 29, 1945) commented on the widespread opinion "that it is the Truman firmness, backed by the atom bomb and the five-ocean navy, which has produced the very moderate Sino-Russian treaty, the about-face in Bulgaria, the non-interference . . . in the internal affairs of the new Polish state and similar manifestations."

principle of joint action through the Commissions. Indeed, he had emphasized his commitment by successfully urging that the status of American members of the Commissions be raised, and that they be given veto powers.[108] Now, simply bypassing the Commissions and the obligations of the armistice terms, Truman's statement made a unilateral appeal to public opinion in each country. And following the appeal, Secretary Byrnes began a campaign of direct intervention in the internal politics of Hungary, Bulgaria, and Rumania.

Hungary was the first problem, but the least difficult, for Churchill's understanding seemed to be operating fairly well. The Russians were working closely with a government headed by the conservative General Bela Miklos, a former supporter of the Horthy dictatorship.[109] The State Department believed "the present 'Provisional National Government' [to be] a coalition regime representing all important anti-Nazi parties."[110] However, Byrnes urged better facilities for free campaigning and demanded that the already scheduled elections be postponed until new arrangements could be made.[111] Even before Potsdam, the Russians had shown themselves willing to admit the Allies to equal power on the Hungarian Allied Control Commission, and new procedures, permitting a Western veto, had actually been put into operation by July 16.[112] Now the Russians quickly acceded to the American demand, postponing the election on August 29.[113] Budapest municipal elections were held on October 7. The Soviet pledge of free elections was strictly adhered to, and the Communist party suffered a resounding defeat. The Hungarian national election of November 4 produced a similar result.[114]

Thus, the Russians were apparently willing to yield to American demands in Hungary. In Bulgaria and Rumania, where Soviet interests were greater (80–20 and 90–10 respectively, in Churchill's calculations) Stalin had not yielded to Truman's main demands at Potsdam. Now, after Hiroshima, the President forced a test of the new power relationships. Bulgaria was first. Here domestic political conflicts had begun to take on international implications earlier in the year, but there had been little active maneuvering for position between the big powers and Soviet responsibility had not been directly challenged during the war. Nevertheless, it was already clear that politicians within the country had begun to look to one or another of the powers to back their various causes.[115]

When the Fatherland Front government was formed it originally had the support of the Agrarian and Social Democratic parties.[116] The most important political personality among these groups was Nikola Petkov, the Agrarian leader.[117] However, the alliance which had brought together the Agrarian and Zveno parties on the one hand, with the Social Democratic and Communist parties on the other, was extremely unstable.[118] During the winter of 1944–45 Petkov and his followers accused the Communists of attempting to use the joint Fatherland Front committees—which governed Bulgarian towns and cities—to increase their own political strength in the country.[119] The Communists denied the accusation and charged the conservative groups with working against the occupying Soviet troops, a contravention of the armistice agreement,[120] and a breach of faith which would undermine the Fatherland Front government.[121]

The tension caused by the political crisis was severe; it divided groups not only along party lines, but within the parties as well. The basic cleavage appeared over the general question of to what extent it was necessary to cooperate with the Soviet Union and the Communists.[122] The spokesman for those who believed cooperation essential was the Zveno party leader and prime minister, Kimon Georgiev. The American State Department representative, Maynard Barnes, found Georgiev "a true conservative in his views of the sacredness of private property (otherwise he could never have held highest political office in country) . . ."[123] However, the Prime Minister also felt it necessary to establish a working relationship with the Russians. On July 30, Barnes reported:

> [Georgiev] sees world as largely divided between three great powers and their respective spheres of influence. It is his belief Balkans fall squarely within Russian sphere. He considers himself too much of a realist to [accept] the view that spheres of influence are outmoded. . . .[124]

Georgiev and others believed cooperation with the Communists and the promotion of the Fatherland Front government the *sine qua non* of a viable Bulgarian political accommodation to the postwar power realities. However, others, like Petkov, disagreed. They distrusted the Communists and hoped that if an immediate "free" election could be held, their power among the conservative peasant groups would thrust them into a dominant political position. They hoped that the Western powers would take their side against the Soviet occupation forces and enable them to establish a new government which would implement their more conservative political program.[125] Nevertheless, Petkov was not the spokesman for a united group of conservative politicians. Like the Prime Minister Georgiev, many other conservatives within the Agrarian and Social Democratic parties believed the Fatherland Front the only possible course for Bulgaria.

In fact, throughout 1945 differences of opinion over this issue engendered violent debate and hostility, splitting the Agrarian party into "cooperation" and "anticooperation" factions.[126] A test of strength took place between the groups at the May 1945 congress of the party. Petkov denounced the congress and the "cooperative" line it espoused.[127] However, the congress elected the right-wing Alexander Obbov leader of the Agrarian party on a platform of cooperation with the Fatherland Front.[128] This split the Agrarians into an official Obbov wing promoting cooperation and the dissident Petkov wing urging a more and more critical view.[129]

Though still a member of the Cabinet, Petkov obviously needed all the political support he could find, for he faced the combined forces of the Russian occupation and the remainder of the Fatherland Front government. It was not surprising that he looked first to the American representative for help. In Maynard Barnes he found an extremely sympathetic ally. Almost from the first, Barnes took Petkov's side.[130] Because it also sympathized with Petkov's views, the State Department championed the opposition demand for immediate "free" elections.[131] The Russians exercised their power under the armistice to reject an American bid for supervision of the elections in mid-April while the war still continued, but they promised early free elections on the Finnish pattern soon after the war's end.[132] A few weeks after Germany collapsed, an election date—August 26—was set.[133]

From May to July the political struggle within Bulgaria focused on preparations for the coming election. The past history of democracy in the country was not very promising.[134] The opposition quite naturally feared that the Fatherland Front would manage the election so as to preclude a free campaign and they were extremely suspicious of the election plans.[135] Petkov and a small dissident faction of the Social Democratic party, with the support of Barnes, raised the Yalta pledge of free elections as their standard.[136] Together, Petkov's supporters and the American representative (who went to the limit—and perhaps beyond—of his instructions) urged that the election plans be liberalized.[137] Both the Agrarian leader and Barnes attempted to secure open American support for a vigorous campaign to promote three-power supervision—or at least observation—of the elections.

Barnes's strategy was to avoid any act which would increase the status of the Soviet-backed government. For this reason in June he vigorously opposed signing a peace treaty with the Georgiev government, and he disputed as "spurious" the British "contention that conclusion of peace with Bulgaria now would entail withdrawal of Soviet troops."[138] Instead, he argued that if a new government could be formed on the basis of a free election, American influence would be greatly increased: "In the event we raised the question with Russia of continued occupation of Bulgaria by its troops we could count not only upon having the mass of Bulgn people behind us, but also the Bulgn Govt."[139]

Searching for a political handhold, Barnes seized upon the conservative peasant vote: "As I see matters so far as Bulgaria is concerned, the hope of the democratic nations must be based on the wide mass of agrarian opinion in this country . . ."[140] Hence, he recommended a determined effort to promote free democratic elections as a means to support "this overwhelming mass of the Bulgn population in the only way that is left to us."[141] In sum, on the eve of Potsdam he argued: "There seems only one wise course, namely to do everything we can at present to assure the freest election possible with the widest democratic participation that pressure from U.S. at this time can effect."[142]

Barnes met "clandestinely" (to use his term) with Petkov and his followers even before Potsdam and encouraged them in their opposition to the Fatherland Front.[143] Though prevented from making a direct pledge of American support, Barnes discussed the election situation with high Bulgarian government officials, indicating the likelihood that the Allies might soon intervene to postpone the scheduled elections, and urging more rigorous safeguards for the opposition.[144] At the same time, Barnes begged his own government for an all-out effort to support Petkov and the other opposition politicians. Cabling home, he repeatedly reminded the State Department of its interpretation of the Yalta free election ideal:

> If democratic elements within and outside the [Fatherland] Front could be made aware of views to which I have referred and that such views will be re-iterated at Potsdam, they would be galvanized into a resistance against Communist designs, which in absence of public encouragement from US, could only appear futile and hazardous to them.[145]

As this appeal for a public declaration indicates, foreign intervention was the key to the Bulgarian political situation. Without an active American initiative, few politicians would attempt to oppose the Fatherland Front government. With it, there was a possibility that a political crisis could be promoted which would open the way to a new pattern of power within the country. Consequently, Barnes was almost frantic in his efforts to persuade Washington to come to his aid: "I am sorry to keep harping on this point . . ." he cabled on July 9.[146] And, again on July 30:

> I realize that this is a very long telegram on what may quite naturally appear to many in the Dept as a situation very remote from real and active American interests. I report at such length in the hope of still convincing the Dept of the desirability of some public statement. . . .[147]

The fact that the United States had not recognized the Fatherland Front government until Potsdam was enough to sustain hope of intervention. However, as the Big Three Conference drew to a close, politicians in Bulgaria began to despair of American support. In the midst of the Conference, Barnes reported:

> I found Petkov still full of courage but very fearful that if no sign is forthcoming from the US and UK and particularly from US, of favorable reaction to his resistance to the [Fatherland Front] rigged elections, the independents . . . will waver in their loyalty to his leadership in this matter.[148]

Petkov himself attempted to stimulate American intervention. On July 26 the Agrarian leader bypassed the established channels of authority under the armistice agreement and circulated an open letter to the Prime Minister requesting postponement of the election and Allied supervision.[149] At this point Petkov had two complementary objectives: to weaken the authority of the Soviet-dominated Control Commission, and to bring the Western Allies into support of his position. Quite aware of the significance of Petkov's audacious challenge to the Soviet occupation authority, the Fatherland Front government was deeply disturbed. Petkov's maneuver brought forth a response indicative of the tense political situation and the anxieties of the government. The Prime Minister accused the Agrarian leader of treason: "Petkov's sin had not been merely venial but had been a mortal sin, because he had distributed copies of his letter to members of the [Allied Control Commission], thus giving the British and Americans an opportunity to intervene."[150]

A few days later, on July 31, Petkov's resignation from the government was accepted.[151] Barnes, reporting just as the Potsdam Conference ended, said he had hoped that Petkov's resignation would provoke a government crisis. However, without American intervention, Barnes was extremely doubtful that Petkov's lead would be followed:

> I fear in absence of any encouraging signs from Washington, London and Potsdam of Anglo-American interest in Bulgarian election situation Petkov's "departure" may not be followed, as I had hoped it would be, by resignations of Stoyanov, Cheschmedjieff, Pavlov and Derzhanski. I feel very strongly that time has come when Dept must tell me what, if anything, the US Govt is really prepared to do about local political and election situation.[152]

As is evident from these cables, Barnes was deeply perplexed and frustrated by the ambivalence of the American position during the period of the long delay. With no way to know of the atomic bomb and the President's plans, he greatly feared that his own initiative would not be supported. In pleading for help for Petkov he thought he was urging something which might "quite naturally appear . . . very remote from real and active American interests."[153] In fact, as we have seen, Truman had pledged an active initiative in the Balkans months earlier and, at the very moment Barnes's despairing cables reached Potsdam, Truman had already gone beyond the representative's proposals: While Barnes asked only that elections procedures be improved, the President adamantly demanded of Stalin that the Georgiev government be changed.*

Thus, after Potsdam, Barnes found that his own views were not only sympathetically received, but that Washington was ready to intervene far more directly and actively than he could have hoped. The President's continued refusal to recognize the Georgiev government and his pointed declaration that the Balkans were not to be considered a sphere of influence for any one power (made against the background of mushroom clouds rising in the Pacific) were dramatic signals of American intentions. They transformed doubt into confidence; Bulgarian politicians who had been afraid to oppose the government without foreign support were now prepared to act.

Now all that was required was sufficient time to undertake a successful campaign against the government, and sufficient safeguards to insure that such a campaign would not be impeded. The first point involved the timing of the election. Since few politicians (except Petkov) had been prepared to criticize the government until after Truman's statement, as the August 26 election approached there had been virtually no political campaigning against Fatherland Front candidates.† As a result—with the election only three weeks off—even if conditions were absolutely free, there was little likelihood that the opposition could convey its message to the public in time to substantially affect the outcome of the poll. Only too aware of the need for prompt action, Barnes had begged for a public statement from Washington throughout July. However, Truman's need to wait for the atomic bomb had complicated the problems he faced in Bulgaria.[154]

To make up for his own delay, therefore, the President first had to attempt to postpone the Bulgarian election to allow time for serious campaigning. Secondly, he wished to improve the election statute. And thirdly, he wished to remove the existing government so that the election would be administered by men more independent and more favorable to the West. Four days after Nagasaki, Secretary Byrnes moved speedily to the task, forcefully unveiling the full extent of the American demands. Bypassing the recognized authority of the Soviet commander under the armistice terms, on August 13, Byrnes sent an

---

* See above, pp. 148, 151.

† Apparently a similar problem arose in Yugoslavia; see Betts, *Central and South East Europe*, pp. 58–59.

open letter to Prime Minister Georgiev. He demanded that the elections scheduled for August 26—now less than two weeks off—be postponed.[155] Byrnes also gave notice that the United States would not recognize the Bulgarian government until it had been radically reorganized:

> The information available to the United States Government has not satisfied it that the first Provisional Bulgarian Government is adequately representative of the important democratic elements, of democratic opinion, or that the existing government has arranged for the scheduled elections to take place under conditions which will allow and insure the participation therein, free from the fear of force and intimidation, of all democratic elements.[156]

Byrnes's letter (which was followed by a similar British protest),[157] even more than the President's statement, was an explicit attempt to influence the political situation within the country. (Truman's Balkan representative later characterized the actions as "a major diplomatic effort.")[158] By committing American prestige to the main demand of the opposition, the Secretary of State's maneuver threw the Fatherland Front government into a state of frenzy. Its first reaction was a futile attempt to urge the American government to stand by the commitments it had made in signing the armistice agreement. Under that agreement, the government—which, of course, had no diplomatic relations with the United States—took orders from the Soviet chairman of the Allied Control Commission.* On August 23, Georgiev's Finance Minister, Petko Stainov, publicly stated the government's position: "The British and the United States Governments should rather have submitted notes to Moscow, reached an agreement, and then advised the Bulgarian Government."[159]

Despite this statement, the government was obviously weakened and much on the defensive. The four government ministers who had been unwilling to act without foreign help,† now told the Prime Minister that unless the elections were postponed and changes made in the electoral law, they would leave the government.[160] Georgiev refused to agree and accused the four of working with Barnes.[161] On August 17, the four resigned in protest over the plans for the forthcoming elec-

---

* See above, pp. 134, 140–141.   † See above, p. 210.

tion.[162] Georgiev countered the resignations with a firm declaration that the election would be carried out as scheduled.[163] He publicly attacked the four ministers and others who "allow themselves to be influenced by foreign powers."[164] New Cabinet members replaced the opposition group, and the government prepared to ride out the crisis.[165]

With the American government and the Petkov group of opposition leaders now publicly committed, there remained only the question of what action the Soviet Union would take to uphold a government it had sponsored for more than a year. Although Stalin, hoping to persuade Truman to act with him, had not recognized Georgiev before Potsdam,[166] after the President's statement attacking spheres of influence, the Soviet Premier had moved quickly to give strong support to the Fatherland Front. On August 15, Radio Moscow announced that the Soviet Union would accord diplomatic recognition to Georgiev.[167] Two days later, Moscow announced that the famous Bulgarian Communist Georgi Dimitrov would return from the Soviet Union to participate in—and lend his prestige to—the Bulgarian elections.[168] The return of Dimitrov, who had become famous during the Reichstag trial, further affirmed Soviet support for the elections and the government. *Izvestia* commented that the election plans were "most democratic."[169]

Thus the opposing positions of the various parties crystallized. "What must chiefly be regretted," observed the diplomatic correspondent of the London *Times* in Sofia, "is that a new complication is added to Allied relations. The Soviet Government has already recognized the Bulgarian Government and has sent an Ambassador to Sofia . . . A peace treaty can be made only with a recognized Government—and London and Washington appear to be committed not to recognize the Bulgarian Government. A deadlock appears inevitable."[170]

The implications of the conflict were also noted in Britain, where preparations for the first peacetime foreign ministers' meeting were underway. "The Bulgarian situation, it is said in official circles here, is likely to produce an early deadlock in the work of the new Council of Foreign Ministers,"[171] one American observed. Indeed, the challenge to Soviet influence in the Balkans seemed too obvious and too fundamental to permit of an easy reconciliation. The Foreign Office and others had been certain the Russians would not yield to the American demands before Potsdam, and once Soviet support had been publicly conveyed to Georgiev's rejection of the American note, there seemed no possible way to avoid a head-on collision. The Americans were adamant and the Russians were not likely to back down. Although the Soviet commander agreed to consult Moscow again, the Allied Control Commission meeting of August 22 produced no positive results.[172]

It was both a shock and a surprise, therefore, when on August 26—the very day of the election—radio Sofia interrupted its eleventh-hour appeals to voters and its denunciation of "foreign interference" to announce that the election had been postponed![173]

Truman's Balkan representative, Mark Ethridge, later boasted that the West's "determined action" had produced "remarkable results."[174] At the time, British Foreign Office officials were jubilant at the sudden success, telling reporters that the Bulgarian decision eased "considerably the Anglo-Soviet-American diplomatic tension."[175] Russian acquiescence in the American demand was an ignominious defeat for Soviet power in the Balkans.[176]

The dramatic *volte-face* and Stalin's apparent willingness to cooperate also greatly heartened the opposition politicians and the American officials in Bulgaria who were confirmed not only in their judgment of the situation, but also in their estimate of their own power to affect events. The opposition now presented a list of further conditions for the election and demanded that both the Prime Minister and the Minister of Interior resign.[177] The United States pressed the demand that the government be reorganized, and Barnes met with government and opposition leaders to attempt to reach agreement on changes in the government and preparations for the new election.[178]

The Georgiev government, helpless in the face of Soviet acquiescence to the Americans, could do little to repair the damage of the August 26 embarrassment. Instead, it began wholesale acceptance of various opposition proposals. Meetings were held with the American military representative and with Barnes to discuss requirements for the new election.[179] Pardons were granted to 302 political prisoners; another 400 had their sentences drastically reduced.[180] As Stalin had promised at Potsdam, American newsmen were allowed to enter the country and to report freely.[181] All four opposition parties were legally recognized and allowed to publish newspapers.[182] (It was necessary to give standing to those parties which, fearing to act without American support, had previously banded together in the Fatherland Front.)[183] Mixed committees, made up mostly of schoolteachers, were designated to oversee the elections.[184] The government proclaimed a series of administrative steps to insure free campaigning.[185]

In an attempt to close ranks, the government also invited the dissident opposition groups to reunite with the party leaders who had supported the Fatherland Front.[186] The move aimed at healing the breach between the two factions of the Agrarian and Social Democratic parties. However, the now confident opposition groups refused to reunite with their former colleagues. Instead, they demanded the dismissal of those Agrarian and Social Democratic ministers who had remained in the Cabinet,[187] and they began to hold public demonstrations to create public support for their position.[188] Once more they reiterated the demand that the Prime Minister and the Minister of the Interior resign. They now declared that unless this was agreed to, they would boycott the election.[189]

At this point the Georgiev government balked. Moscow and Sofia had yielded to the demand that the election be postponed and had agreed to a number of reforms to insure a free campaign.* However, the proposal that the government be changed, which had been refused when Truman first raised it at Potsdam, was apparently still too much to ask. As the London Conference approached, once more the Bulgarian political situation became tense. The American-supported groups were once more more in a direct confrontation with the Soviet-backed government. "The situation, therefore, remains on dead center," one observer noted.[190] Indeed, the renewed stalemate seemed even more rigidly defined than the original one had been.

Moreover, as the London Conference opened, the situation began to take on threatening overtones. Earlier, when the American demand

---

* Later the opposition boycotted the election, and the State Department declared that the election had not been freely conducted. However, this claim must be carefully examined, for (1) Truman's Balkan representative, who studied the problem in Bulgaria at the time, later wrote "it was by no means clear that the electoral boycott of the opposition was the best means of resolving the problem . . ."; (2) the British Foreign Office did not support the State Department's protests over the election; (3) most Western correspondents found little or no interference in the election; (4) at almost exactly the same time the Soviet-sponsored election in Hungary (which was not boycotted by the Hungarian opposition) was conducted in a "free" manner which met the State Department's standards. (Dennett and Johnson, *Negotiating with the Russians,* p. 191; *Sunday Times,* Nov. 18, 1945; *Christian Science Monitor,* Nov. 20, 1945; *Ibid.,* Sept. 20, 24; Oct. 12, 16, 17, 18; Nov. 17, 1945; Seton-Watson, *The East European Revolution,* p. 193; Betts, *Central and South East Europe,* p. 105.)

for a postponement of the elections had been received only four days after Nagasaki, there were scattered comments about the role of the atomic bomb in America's new-found "firmness."* Now, as the United States pressed the demand that the government be changed, mass meetings filled the streets of Sofia with defiant, repeated chants of "We don't fear the atomic bomb!"[191]

Thus, the fact that the atomic bomb had imparted an entirely new sense of confidence to American diplomacy was quickly recognized and interpreted in the most unfavorable light; it appeared as a menacing force—in brief, a threat. There were now also doubts as to the actual power of American diplomacy. It appeared that the diplomatic successes could only be attributed to the atomic bomb, for once it had been demonstrated, points at issue in Manchuria, Hungary, and Bulgaria which had not been yielded at Potsdam had now been accepted by the Russians. But now the failure to change the Bulgarian government seemed a sign that the diplomatic offensive which had scored so brilliantly might be losing its force. It remained to be seen to what extent Soviet policy would yield in a country far more vital to it than Hungary or Bulgaria.

DEADLOCK IN RUMANIA

EVEN CHURCHILL HAD DISTINGUISHED between the three ex-satellite countries, allocating, in the first instance, Soviet influence of "50 per cent" in Hungary, "75 per cent" in Bulgaria, and a full "90 per cent" in Rumania.† Though these figures had been modified in the bargaining process, from the Soviet point of view Rumania was obviously the most important Balkan country. Rumania occupied a key strategic position athwart the southwestern invasion route to Russia. Bulgaria had been able to wage war against the Soviet Union for only twenty-four hours;[192] but Rumania, in alliance with Hitler, had sent twenty-six divisions against the Soviets, devastating Russian territory, and penetrating as far into the interior as Stalingrad.[193] Moreover, Rumanians harbored traditional anti-Russian sentiments and were therefore more likely to use their strategic geographic position against the Soviet Union in any future hostilities.[194]

---

* See above, p. 204.   † See above, p. 133.

American policy, however, recognized no distinctions in the Balkans.* In Rumania, too, American leaders had long planned to take the initiative to change the government. The demonstration of the atomic bomb and the end of the long wait meant that these plans could now be implemented. Here, as elsewhere, the first move in the diplomatic offensive was Truman's attack upon spheres of influence— a declaration which gave heart to conservative politicians in Rumania as it had in Bulgaria. Here there was even greater excitement for, unlike Bulgaria, in Rumania the deep tradition of anti-Russian feeling had been increased, not diminished, by war propaganda and the defeat suffered at Russian hands.[195]

Even during the spring, while the war was still on, among Peasant and Liberal leaders there was a constant hope that somehow the Western powers would come to their assistance. According to one American in the country at the time, "they were wholeheartedly anti-Russian, and a good many of their members continued to assume that the Western Allies would somehow intervene."[196] Although it seems that a number of conservatives had been offered posts in the Groza government, they had apparently refused to join the government after a dispute over estimates of their relative importance in the domestic political balance.[197] The leading politician in the conservative ranks, the seventy-year-old Juliu Maniu, leader of the Peasant party (a figure corresponding roughly to Petkov in Bulgaria), had retired from chairmanship of his party two weeks after Groza took office.[198]

However, Maniu, like Petkov in Bulgaria, did not retire from active participation in politics. As Potsdam approached and the powers continued to withhold recognition, Maniu and his associates also hoped

---

* As many observers have pointed out, Byrnes never seemed to understand a dilemma inherent in his policy. There is no reason to doubt his numerous assurances that in urging free elections and new governments he had no wish to support governments hostile to the Soviet Union; nevertheless, as Roberts has written, "a popularly elected Government [in Rumania] would in all probability be anti-Soviet." Thus, inevitably Byrnes's idealistic policy must have seemed a threat to the Russians. (Roberts, *Rumania*, p. 269.)

On the viability of democratic government in Rumania, see also the views cabled to the War Department by its representative in Bucharest shortly before Potsdam: "Even under normal peacetime conditions, a representative government in Rumania would find it difficult to maintain itself in power. Rumanians have had no experience in democracy for over ten years, and the ability of members of any coalition government to work in harmony for the common goal, regardless of personal or party problems must be open to question." (*Conference of Berlin*, I, p. 397. For additional views, see Wolff, *The Balkans in Our Time*, p. 286; McNeill, *America, Britain and Russia, 1941–46*, pp. 698–701; Allen, *Great Britain and the United States*, p. 872; Williams, *The Tragedy of American Diplomacy*, pp. 258–59.)

that the Soviet-sponsored government might be changed.[199] Because of the strength of anti-Russian sentiment in the country, they could go farther than Petkov in Slavophilic Bulgaria. The Peasant and Liberal parties decided to organize demonstrations to show that opposition to the National Democratic Front government was an effective force. They also hoped to forestall a Potsdam decision to recognize Groza or a slightly altered government.[200]

In open violation of the specific terms of the armistice, on July 18 Maniu boldly began his political offensive with a speech to university students demanding that the Groza government be dismissed: "The country must no longer tolerate dictatorial governments imposed from abroad."[201] The speech was followed by a brief demonstration in the Palace Square.[202] Two days later, Constantin Bratianu addressed about seven hundred members of his Liberal party's youth organization in the same vein.[203] Following his speech, a larger demonstration and parade took place.[204] This time the protesting demonstrators were met by Communists and others who supported the government. A brief struggle between the two groups took place and two people were injured and approximately thirty-two were arrested.[205]

The acting American representative in Bucharest, Roy Melbourne, reported that the Groza government was greatly disturbed by the demonstrations.[206] A hastily summoned conference between party leaders and the National Democratic Front evidenced increasing anxiety over the internal and the international situation. The hopes of the Peasants and Liberals, and the fears of the government, were directed toward Potsdam. The opposition apparently believed that the Big Three might eliminate the Groza government and open the way for new elections. Groups within the government too, according to Melbourne, were "expecting Cabinet changes and fearing shifts detriment[al]" to the National Democratic Front position.[207]

As in Bulgaria, the internal political situation was ruled not only by the relative strengths of the various political factions, but by the role the big powers played—or might be expected to play. In the midst of the Potsdam meeting, Maniu sought an interview with Melbourne in Bucharest to report that "he had counseled his party that U.S. and Great Britain . . . could secure Soviet acquiescence to a democratic interpretation of Yalta."[208] He said that in his belief the National

Peasants could confidently expect an overwhelming electoral majority if free elections were held.[209] He urged that Groza be removed from office so that a new government would supervise the elections.[210] He asked the War, Interior, and Propaganda ministries for his own party. The National Peasant party could be expected to be impartial, he explained, since "it would be to its interest to conduct the elections in an unbiased manner. . . . An inevitable large National Peasant majority" would emerge in any event.[211]

Having made his proposal, Maniu went on to hint at the possible consequences if he failed to achieve his aims. If the Groza government was retained, he stated, his party would organize energetic country-wide opposition, including demonstrations. According to Melbourne, "in measured words he said that for such . . . action he was certain of support from the dissatisfied Rumanian peasants who would unite with the townspeople. . . ."[212]

In view of earlier Rumanian riots and bloodshed (even during the war),* there were ominous overtones in this statement. In fact, it contained the distinct hint of a threat and offered the prospect of violent disturbances. The "measured words" meant that the opposition could, if it so chose, create an unstable and dangerous situation. Earlier, one reason Churchill had proposed his spheres-of-influence arrangement to Stalin was his knowledge that political feelings ran so high in Rumania and Greece that civil war was a very real possibility—especially if the powers began to support different factions.[213] In Greece, where anti-British feeling had already resulted in a short outburst of civil war in December 1944,† and in Rumania where riots and violence had been suppressed just before Groza's appointment in the spring of 1945, Churchill's judgment was apparently a fair assessment of realities. Maniu's statement did no more than recall and confirm this earlier estimate. Shortly thereafter, Molotov affirmed the same view, telling Byrnes that Rumanian politics could easily erupt into a civil war if the powers did not concert their policies.[214]

Maniu undoubtedly made his statement in the hope of forcing a

---

* These precipitated the Soviet intervention discussed on p. 136.
† See above, p. 134.

more explicit American commitment to his cause. However, during the summer of delay, and at the time of the Potsdam Conference, the American representative could give the Peasant leader very little direct encouragement. Like his colleague in Bulgaria, he did not know to what extent Truman was prepared to press the matter. Nor did he know of the atomic bomb. As soon as the Conference ended without recognition of the Groza government, however, the opposition had its signal.[215] And, as in Bulgaria, the series of speeches denouncing spheres of influence and "police governments" sparked tremendous political activity within the country.

In Rumania, the attack upon the Soviet-sponsored government centered around, and was led by, the young King Michael. The King had already secretly asked for American help before Potsdam.[216] Now, privately encouraged to act by American representatives,[217] Michael publicly demanded that Groza resign.[218] He then bypassed the Allied Control Commission and appealed directly to the three Allied powers to help him form a new government.[219] Adding emphasis to his demand, the King gave notice that until a new government was formed, he would refuse to sign government decrees.[220] Shortly thereafter, the Minister of Finance resigned. Michael seized the opportunity and, refusing to authorize the appointment of a replacement, made it impossible to pay the salaries of government employees.[221] Michael also refused to appear at important public celebrations, and, in a dramatic gesture of opposition, he left Bucharest to wait for the elimination of the Groza government.[222]

Melbourne let Michael know that if he persisted the United States would support him,[223] and Byrnes immediately responded to the King's appeal. On August 22, the Secretary of State met with representatives of the press, welcomed Michael's request for help to replace Groza, and pledged official American support for efforts to change the government. The United States would gladly lend "assistance with a view to the formation of a government, which, according to the report of the Conference of Berlin, might be recognized by the principal powers," Byrnes declared.[224] The Secretary of State's favorable response confirmed the American intention to bypass the Allied Control Commission and it publicly committed the United States to the demand that the Groza government be changed.

Some observers noted that the initial Soviet decision to yield to "the firmness of the Western Allies" in Bulgaria had given the American and British governments confidence in their approach to Rumania.[225] Though undoubtedly the first success in Bulgaria confirmed American leaders' estimates of their ability to force the Soviet hand in the Balkans, as we have seen, Truman and Byrnes had decided to intervene to remove the Soviet "blackout" many months earlier. During the period of the long wait, and at Potsdam, they had made their intentions quite clear and had also told Stalin that they would not yield on their demand that the Rumanian government be changed.

Thus, implementing their earlier plans, and now apparently quite confident of the wisdom of their course and their power to pursue it successfully, throughout August, American leaders pressed the attempt to remove Groza from office. As the London Conference of Foreign Ministers neared, however, no sign of Soviet willingness to yield appeared as it had in Bulgaria. Apparently the Russians felt that Rumania was different and, in fact, they had already indicated differences in attitudes toward the two countries.

Immediately after Potsdam (on August 4), Moscow had hastened to accord diplomatic recognition to Bucharest, although it was two weeks later—and only in the brief period before yielding to American demands—that Moscow had accorded the same recognition to Sofia.[226] Thus, even before the new American effort in Rumania, the Soviet Union had declared its commitment to Groza. After Michael's appeal and Byrnes's response to it, Moscow again promptly and dramatically demonstrated that it was not prepared to yield easily in Rumania. *Izvestia* criticized "some foreign newspapers" for their antagonism to Groza.[227] The Soviet-supported government announced a campaign against "hirelings of the former Premier Radescu." Twenty "terrorists" were arrested for attempting to overthrow the government. Those who were "trying to create discord among the United Nations and seeking foreign support for the realization of their personal political ambitions" were castigated by the government.[228]

On August 28, it was announced that the Soviet envoy in Rumania had been raised to the rank of full ambassador.[229] A week before the London Conference, Groza and his Deputy Prime Minister Tatarescu were invited to Moscow, where they were given celebrity treatment, including a state dinner by Stalin.[230] On September 4, the Soviet Union refused a proposal by Byrnes for consultations on the basis of

King Michael's appeal.[231] At the same time, Groza issued a bitter statement from Moscow attacking Maniu and Bratianu for their role in the crisis:

> Maniu and Bratianu have lost all contact with the realities of present-day political life in Rumania. They endeavor to provoke a Government crisis by artificial means and to sow discord between the Government and the people on the one hand, and the Head of State, King Michael, on the other, by recommending him to actions harmful to the national interest and to the crown.[232]

The following day, *Izvestia* accused Britain and America of trying to force Groza out of office, specifically identifying the local representatives of the two powers as prime movers in Michael's maneuver. Giving notice that the Soviet Union would hold to its support of Groza, *Izvestia* commented:

> American and British representatives began to insist on the resignation of the Rumanian Government without first placing the matter before the Allied Control Commission, thereby violating established procedure in the work of the Commission. If this is called implementation of a coordinated Allied policy, what might be called unilateral acts violating the coordination of Allied policy? . . . The viewpoint of Soviet public opinion is quite clear. It firmly maintains that interference . . . is inadmissible.[233]

Stalin now gave further evidence of his commitment to Groza, sending the Rumanian Premier back to his country with numerous politically useful concessions. Groza received promises of a Soviet loan of 150,000 tons of grain, the return of railroads to Rumanian direction, the return of a number of locomotives, railway freight cars, merchant ships, and even a few warships. Moreover, the Rumanian Premier was able to bring back from Moscow an agreement to reduce the reparations burden and a pledge to repatriate immediately all prisoners of war. Finally, Stalin agreed that Soviet troops stationed in Rumania would help reconstruct towns destroyed in the war.[234]

In this way, Moscow underscored its intention to stand by Groza on the eve of the London Conference. Now Britain and the United States on the one hand, and the Soviet Union on the other, were publicly committed to diametrically opposed positions in Rumania. Within the country, the opposition and the Groza government were similarly committed and, as London approached, Maniu and Bratianu burned their bridges behind them, openly attacking the Soviet Union in direct contravention of the armistice.[235]

TOWARD A TEST OF STRENGTH

THUS, ON THE EVE of the first peacetime meeting of the foreign ministers, the American offensive in the Balkans, which had been met by initial Soviet willingness to compromise, now had reached major obstacles in both Bulgaria and Rumania. The over-all question first posed in April and again at Potsdam was still the same: Did the United States have the power to force Soviet acquiescence to its demands deep within the Soviet area of influence? From the early summer American leaders had been convinced that, once demonstrated, the atomic bomb would permit them to demand major changes in the border areas of the Soviet Union. But now this conviction would be tested, and the relative power of the United States and the Soviet Union defined, when the foreign ministers met on September 10.

As Secretary Byrnes prepared to leave for London, the various instruments of diplomacy which had not been actively employed during the summer of delay were now again readied for use. Although neither the President nor the Secretary of State had discussed a large-scale credit with Soviet representatives since the late-April showdown, now, after the atomic bomb had been demonstrated, they were prepared to negotiate. At a meeting with the President and the Secretary of State shortly after the Japanese surrender, Leo Crowley urged that the Lend-Lease cutoff—first attempted, then repealed in May—should now be firmly implemented. Once again, though his recommendation was based upon the law's requirement that Lend-Lease cease at the end of hostilities, and though it would have implications for all the Allies, Crowley made it clear that the primary advantage of *immediate* action was that it would force the Soviet Union to look for other means to pay for American material assistance. Both the President and the Secretary of State agreed with Crowley, and Truman authorized him to act promptly.*[236] After Lend-Lease shipments were

---

* See Byrnes, *All in One Lifetime*, pp. 309–10, for a report which indicates that the primary reason for the *timing* of the August cutoff—like the May cutoff—was the desire to force the Soviet Union into a de-*(Continued on next page)*

halted on August 22, the Russians were informed that the Export-Import Bank would consider an application for a large credit. It was soon made clear that they would be expected to offer, as *quid pro quo*, concessions in Eastern and Southeastern Europe.[237]

Similarly, throughout the summer Truman and his advisers had regarded the presence of conventional troops as vital to their European diplomacy. The atomic bomb, as Stimson had expected, had helped stabilize the situation by ending the war long before redeployment had substantially weakened American strength on the Continent.* But now, looking to the future when demobilization would drain troops from Europe, Truman moved swiftly to attempt to preserve his position; on August 17—the third day of peace—he publicly declared his intention to ask Congressional approval for a universal-military-training program for all able-bodied young men.[238] On the eve of the London Conference he gave details of his proposals for peace, telling an August 31 Cabinet meeting "that the time had come to initiate a new military policy. If we were to maintain leadership among other nations, we must continue to be strong in a military way."†[239]

But, as before, economic aid and the presence of conventional troops were the least important elements in the American diplomatic posture. Throughout the summer the expectation of the atomic bomb had dominated diplomatic strategy. Now, in late August, as Byrnes prepared for his meeting in London, the Secretary of State made it clear that the bomb continued to play a predominant role in his calculations. In a long discussion with Byrnes, Assistant Secretary of War McCloy found him "quite radically opposed to any approach to Stalin whatever" to attempt to establish international control of

---

(*Continued from preceding page*)
pendent position in the next round of credit negotiations. And, as in May, the President apparently was not guided primarily by a belief that the legal provisions required immediate and unequivocal action, for he made a number of exceptions to the Lend-Lease cutoff. For a report of these, see Mc-Neill, *America, Britain and Russia, 1941–46*, p. 785.

    * See above, p. 117.

    † Congress rejected Truman's proposal. Harriman was later to argue that this was the primary reason American diplomacy failed to achieve its European objectives:

"Only by keeping our military forces in being after Germany and Japan surrendered could we have attempted to *compel* the Soviet Union to withdraw from the territory it controlled. . . ." (*Congressional Record*, Aug. 27, 1951, p. A5416; emphasis added.) Similarly, Truman has written: "I am morally certain that if Congress had gone into the [military training] program thoroughly in 1945, when I first recommended it, we would have had a pool of basically trained men which would have made the Soviets hesitate in their program of expansion in certain strategic parts of the world." (*Year of Decisions*, pp. 511–12.)

atomic energy—"He was on the point of departing for the Foreign Ministers' meeting and wished to have the implied threat of the bomb in his pocket during the conference. . . ."[240]

And two days before sailing for London, Byrnes discussed the central role of the atomic bomb in his diplomacy with Secretary Stimson:

> Jim Byrnes had not yet gone abroad and I had a very good talk with him afterwards sitting in the White House hall . . . I took up the question which I had been working at with McCloy up in St. Hubert's, namely how to handle Russia with the big bomb. I found that Byrnes was very much against any attempt to cooperate with Russia. His mind is full of his problems with the coming meeting of foreign ministers and he looks to having the presence of the bomb in his pocket, so to speak, as a great weapon to get through the thing. . . .[241]

In this frame of mind Secretary of State Byrnes sailed for his first peacetime encounter with a representative of the Soviet Union. Since early April, the President and his senior advisers had focused their attention on political and economic conditions in Eastern Europe; they had never lost their active interest in reducing or eliminating Soviet influence in the area. In April the President had been able to back his diplomacy only with large-scale credits and the presence of the American army in Europe. Advised that there was much to gain if he would wait for the atomic bomb, Truman had decided to postpone a showdown over Eastern Europe.

Now, as Admiral Leahy has written, "it was no longer a theory. We had the bombs."[242] The firm approach so long in suspense could be resumed with the backing of unprecedented military power. For the first time since April, Secretary Byrnes was ready for a meeting with Molotov to discuss affairs in the Soviet zone of Europe. His immediate objective which, like the April showdown over Poland, was to have symbolic implications for all of Eastern Europe, was to force a change in the Balkan governments. The Secretary of State was extremely confident of success.[243] His meeting was to be, as he later wrote, "in a very real sense, a test of strength."[244]

Conclusions

One factor that was to change a lot of ideas, including my own, was the atom bomb . . .

—ADMIRAL WILLIAM D. LEAHY
CHIEF OF STAFF
TO THE PRESIDENT

BYRNES FIRMLY PRESSED his demand that the Bulgarian and Rumanian governments be changed, but when Molotov refused to yield at London, the first peacetime meeting of foreign ministers broke down completely—it was impossible even to agree upon a joint protocol recording the failure.* The initial climax of the post-Hiroshima struggle was a continued and open deadlock. "We had come to the crossroads," Byrnes recalls.[1] In forcing a public break over the issue, the Secretary of State's action was intended to be symbolic. As in the Polish dispute in April, American policy aimed not only at a favorable resolution of the specific points at issue, but at a reconsideration of fundamental political and economic arrangements throughout the Soviet-controlled zone of Europe—"Only by refusing to bow to Soviet domination could we establish sound relations for the future."[2]

Byrnes has written that "our attitude was a shock to them," and it is certain, as both he and John Foster Dulles (who assisted the Secretary of State at London) have emphasized, that postwar Soviet-American tension must be dated from the London Conference.[3] It is also undoubtedly true that the atomic bomb not only influenced the attitude American policy makers took in their approach to the confrontation,

---

* Technically, the Conference broke down over a procedural issue, but as Byrnes has written, in reality, "the chief cause" was the dispute over the governments of Rumania and Bulgaria. (*Speaking Frankly,* pp. 104–8; see also, Senate Committee on Foreign Relations, *A Decade of American Foreign Policy, 1941–49,* p. 55; Leahy Diary, Sept. 23, 1945, p. 163.)

but also, as Prime Minister Attlee cabled to President Truman at the time, the weapon completely overshadowed the discussions.[4]

The political developments after August 1945, like the later (mid-1946), ill-fated attempts to control atomic energy, cannot here be analyzed.* And, unfortunately, Admiral Leahy's summary judgment that the Cold War began in the Balkans can only be tested with further research.[5] However, at this point the major conclusions to be drawn from a study of American policy during the first five months of the Truman administration can be briefly summarized. It is also possible to attempt to define certain other problems which, with presently available materials, can be stated but cannot be conclusively resolved.

The most important point is the most general: Contrary to a commonly held view, it is abundantly clear that the atomic bomb profoundly influenced the way American policy makers viewed political problems. Or, as Admiral Leahy has neatly summarized the point, "One factor that was to change a lot of ideas, including my own, was the atom bomb . . ."[6] The change caused by the new weapon was quite specific. It did not produce American opposition to Soviet policies in Eastern Europe and Manchuria. Rather, since a consensus had already been reached on the need to take a firm stand against the Soviet Union in both areas, the atomic bomb *confirmed* American leaders in their judgment that they had sufficient power to affect developments in the border regions of the Soviet Union. There is both truth and precision in Truman's statement to Stimson that the weapon "gave him an entirely new feeling of confidence."[7]

This effect was a profoundly important one. Before the atomic bomb was tested, despite their desire to oppose Soviet policies, Western policy makers harbored very grave doubts that Britain and America could challenge Soviet predominance in Eastern Europe. Neither Roosevelt nor Truman could have confidence that the American public would permit the retention of large numbers of conventional troops in Europe after the war. (And Congressional rejection of Truman's

---

* The official history of the Atomic Energy Commission demonstrates how Byrnes opposed later attempts to control atomic energy, and how he finally agreed to approach the Russians with a control plan only after being assured that the proposal would guarantee continued American production of atomic weapons for some years. (Hewlett and Anderson, *The New World*, pp. 417, 456, 459–60, and especially 461.)

military-training program later confirmed the pessimistic wartime predictions.) Thus, at the time of the Yalta Conference, as Assistant Secretary of State William L. Clayton advised Secretary Stettinius, "a large credit . . . appear[ed] to be the only concrete bargaining lever for use in connection with the many other political and economic problems which will arise between our two countries."[8]

That this lever of diplomacy was not sufficiently powerful to force Soviet acceptance of American proposals was amply demonstrated during the late-April and early-May crisis over Poland. Despite Truman's judgment that "the Russians needed us more than we needed them,"[9] Stalin did not yield to the firm approach. Hence, without the atomic bomb it seemed exceedingly doubtful that American policy makers would be able substantially to affect events within the Soviet-occupied zone of Europe. It may well be that, had there been no atomic bomb, Truman would have been forced to reconsider the basic direction of his policy as Churchill had done some months earlier.

Indeed, Churchill's 1944 estimate of the power realities usefully illuminates the problems faced by Western policy makers as they attempted to judge their relative strength vis-à-vis the Soviet Union. As soon as Roosevelt rejected Churchill's desperate pleas for an invasion through the Balkans, the Prime Minister understood that he would have little power in Southeastern Europe, and that, indeed, the British position in Greece was seriously threatened. As he told Roosevelt, "the only way I can prevent [utter anarchy] is by persuading the Russians to quit boosting [the Communist-oriented] E.A.M."[10] Again, there was overwhelming logic in his parallel 1944 argument: "It seems to me, considering the Russians are about to invade Rumania in great force . . . it would be a good thing to follow the Soviet leadership, considering that neither you nor we have any troops there at all and that they will probably do what they like anyhow."[11] As he later recalled, before the atomic test, "the arrangements made about the Balkans were, I was sure, the best possible."[12]

As I have attempted to show, by the time of the Yalta Conference, somewhat reluctantly, and against the wishes of the State Department, Roosevelt came to the same conclusion. Even the State Department was forced to adopt the official view that "this Government probably would not oppose predominant Soviet influence in [Poland and the Balkans]."[13] And one high-ranking official went beyond this judgment; substituting his concern for Western Europe for the Prime Minister's specific fears about Greece, he stated: "I am willing to sponsor and support the Soviet arguments if it will save . . . the rest of Europe from the diplomacy of the jungle which is almost certain to ensue otherwise."[14] As Truman's Balkan representative recalled the Yalta Conference, it was "fateful that these discussions should have been held at a time when Soviet bargaining power in eastern Europe was so much stronger than that of the western allies."[15] But it remained for Byrnes to summarize the early-1945 relative strengths of the powers: "It was not a question of what we would *let* the Russians do, but what we could *get* them to do."[16]

As I have shown, this appraisal was radically changed by the summer of 1945. Since Byrnes advised Truman on both the atomic bomb and the need for strong opposition to the Russians in Eastern Europe before the President's first confrontation with Molotov, the new weapon's first impact possibly can be seen as early as the April showdown.* However, no final judgment can be rendered on this point, using the evidence presently available. But there is no question that by the middle of July leading American policy makers were convinced that the atomic bomb would permit the United States to take a "firm" stand in subsequent negotiations. In fact, American leaders felt able to demand *more* at Potsdam than they had asked at Yalta. Again, Churchill's post-atomic appraisal is in striking contrast to his view of the pre-atomic realities: "We now had something in our hands which would redress the balance with the Russians."[17] And Byrnes's new advice to Truman was quite straightforward: "The bomb might well put us in a position to dictate our own terms. . . ."[18]

Once the profound impact of the atomic bomb upon American judgments is recognized, considerable light is cast upon the complicated events of the summer of 1945. The curious reversals in American Polish policy and the Hopkins mission both become understandable. The period is one in which two groups of officials debated strategy. Although there were differences of emphasis, since all agreed on the broad objective of attempting to force the Soviet Union into cooperative relationships in Eastern and Central Europe, the real struggle was over timing. Those outside the War Department who had little knowledge or little faith in the as yet untested atomic weapon argued that an immediate showdown was necessary. In this their views

---

* See above, p. 63*fn.*

paralleled Churchill's, who, having come to terms on the Balkans, feared a further weakening of Western determination, combined with a withdrawal of American troops, would convince Stalin time was on his side if he dug in while the West melted away.[19]

Secretary Stimson, however, was able to counter this argument in two ways: He was able to show that conventional strength on the Continent would not be substantially reduced during the two months' delay until the atomic test; and he was able to promise that if a confrontation could be postponed the United States would soon be possessed of "decisive" powers.[20] After forcing a premature showdown on the symbolic Polish issue, Truman reversed himself and accepted Stimson's broad strategy. The price he paid for delay was not high; he was forced to yield the substance of the point at issue in the Polish controversy, and he had to withdraw American troops to the agreed zonal positions in Germany. Significantly, he later characterized his first attempt to utilize economic bargaining strength through the Lend-Lease cutoff as a "mistake."[21] From Truman's point of view, not only was the first showdown badly timed, but the need to reverse his public position and to send Hopkins on a mission of conciliation must have been a great personal embarrassment.

However, it is vital to recognize that Truman's conciliatory actions during late May, June, and early July did not represent his basic policy. He had demonstrated in the April showdown and in the decision to maintain American troop positions in Germany that his view of how to treat with Russia was far different from Roosevelt's. His decision abruptly to cut off Lend-Lease, his show of force over the Trieste dispute, his reconsideration of Roosevelt's Far Eastern agreement, his breach of the Balkans understandings, his refusal to adhere to the Yalta reparations accord—all these acts testify to the great gulf between his view and the view of his predecessor.

Those who argue that "Mr. Truman intended to continue the policy laid down by President Roosevelt"[*][22] have focused attention on an extremely brief period when Truman did indeed adopt a more moder-

---

* Woodward, whose statement I have quoted, uncritically follows Truman's claim: "I stood squarely behind all commitments and agreements entered into by our late great President and . . . I would do every-thing I could to follow along that path." (*Year of Decisions*, pp. 75–76.) Feis makes the same mistake: "Truman felt faithful to the ideas and ideals of the war leader . . ." (*Churchill, Roosevelt, Stalin*, pp. 599–600.)

ate approach. But his actions during this period—symbolized by his attempt to avoid the appearance of "ganging up" with Britain against the Soviet Union—were only a manifestation of his tactical retreat. In a fundamental sense, even the conciliatory period can only be explained by recognizing that its primary purpose was not to continue Roosevelt's policy, but to facilitate a far different policy based upon the overwhelming power soon to be available. Truman replaced the symbolic April showdown over Poland with a parallel August and September effort in the Balkans. Both before and after the brief conciliatory period, the President's attitude is best summed up in the statement he made eight days after Roosevelt's death: He "intended to be firm with the Russians and make no concessions."[23] And both before and after the temporary period of no "ganging up," Truman's effort to coordinate policy with Britain was a hallmark of his approach. As Byrnes has written, Molotov's conclusion that American policy had changed after Roosevelt's death was "understandable."[24]

The Potsdam meeting clearly illustrates how the strategic decision to wait for the atomic bomb dominated American policy making from mid-May until early August. The primary reason most Western leaders began to call for another meeting with Stalin only three months after Yalta was their desire to have a confrontation on the important European questions then in tense dispute. But, as I have shown, Truman rejected the advice of his advisers and Churchill, and twice postponed a face-to-face meeting with Stalin because of his decision to wait for the atomic bomb. Ironically, however, in the end he committed himself to a meeting which was still a scant two weeks too early to be decisive. For this reason, to focus attention on the Potsdam meeting itself, as many writers have done,* is to completely misunderstand American policy. Indeed, the interesting question is not what happened at the meeting, but why very little happened at all.

Thus, the importance of the atomic bomb in American calculations is underscored by the negative result of the heads-of-government meeting; had the new weapon not played such a crucial role in American strategy, there would have been every reason for Truman to

---

* Note how both Woodward and Feis conclude their studies (*British Foreign Policy* and *Between War and Peace*) with the Potsdam Conference, rather than the immediate post-conference diplomacy.

attempt to achieve a negotiated settlement as quickly as possible after the defeat of Germany. Assuming, as Churchill did until mid-July, that it was unwise to gamble on the possibilities of the as yet untested weapon, the Prime Minister was undoubtedly correct to argue that "the decisive, practical points of strategy" involved *above all,* that a settlement must be reached on all major issues between the West and the East . . . *before the armies of democracy melted . . .*" As he told Eden, the "issue . . . seems to me to dwarf all others."[25] Without the atomic bomb, Churchill believed, the only hope lay in an "early and speedy showdown."[26]

Just as he had hurried to arrange an understanding in the Balkans before the Russian position became overwhelmingly powerful in late 1944, he now searched for ways "we may be able to please them . . . as part of a general settlement."[27] Churchill sought to establish a *modus vivendi* before American conventional strength disappeared from the Continent. He wished to give priority to the German question, to recognize the Balkan governments, to settle all frontier issues, to complete the peace treaties quickly and to give only secondary attention to establishing new machinery for post-Potsdam discussions.[28]

Until the atomic test report arrived, Churchill must have thought it incomprehensible that the Americans were not interested in a negotiated settlement. Though they wished to state their case on all issues in dispute, the American delegation was far more concerned with establishing a Council to take up unsettled questions than they were in serious negotiations while the heads of government were together.[29] Thus, significantly, London met with no success in a pre-Potsdam effort to convince Washington of the seemingly obvious point that the German issue was more important than the procedural matter of arranging for new meetings of the foreign ministers.[30]

As we have seen, once the detailed report of the atomic test arrived at Potsdam, Churchill reversed himself completely: "We were . . . possessed of powers which were irresistible."[31] But Churchill's pre-Potsdam appraisal of Stalin's position was probably correct; for, unless the West was prepared to negotiate a settlement, the Soviet Premier undoubtedly calculated there was everything to gain if he waited until the American troops were withdrawn from the Continent.* Since Truman did not tell Stalin of the atomic bomb, it could not yet be expected to play a major role in Soviet-American relations. And, indeed, with no apparent changes in the power relationships, on most issues discussed at the Conference, *both* Truman and Stalin held their ground. The Potsdam Conference took place at a unique moment in history, when each side undoubtedly believed time was on its side. The logic of the situation ensured—as the final protocol showed —that the Conference could only end in deadlock.

Undoubtedly Soviet intelligence knew generally of the work being done on the atomic bomb. However, it is probable that Stalin had no specific knowledge of the New Mexico test—or that if he knew of it, he did not know in detail how greatly it had exceeded expectations. His post-Hiroshima reversals in Manchuria, Hungary, and Bulgaria testify to a new conviction that the power realities required him to yield considerably more than he may have originally thought necessary. It is probable that Truman had this in mind when he noted that by early September "our possession of the secret of harnessing atomic energy already had far-reaching effects on our relations with other nations."[32]

Undoubtedly the best concise summary of the position taken by the West at Potsdam has been provided by General de Gaulle: "The Americans and British hoped to recover in application what they had conceded in principle." De Gaulle believed that "the rapidity of the Sovietization [of Eastern Europe] was only the inevitable result of what had been agreed upon at the Crimea Conference."[33] For this reason, although he strongly opposed the Yalta decisions, de Gaulle felt that "the regrets the British and Americans now expressed [at Potsdam] were quite uncalled for."[34] He concluded that "there was every reason to foresee that on no issue would the Potsdam Conference realize any durable entente"; and that there would be "unlimited friction between the Soviet and Anglo-American participants."[35]

Truman would not have agreed with this judgment. He believed that the United States had sufficient power to force Soviet acceptance of the American plan for lasting world peace. Above all, his policy

---

* Compare Deutscher: By the time of the Potsdam Conference "Stalin's figure loomed incomparably larger on the European horizon." And "Stalin may have reckoned with a more or less rapid withdrawal of American power from the Continent and consequently with the further growth of Russian predominance." (*Stalin*, p. 532.)

required a stable Europe based upon democratic governments and a sound Continental economy. There were two fundamental reasons why the President believed the atomic bomb would permit him to implement his plan: On the one hand, after a new symbolic showdown, the bomb seemed likely to force Soviet agreement to American economic and political plans for Eastern Europe; and, on the other, its power meant that there was no need to fear another German revival—the German economic contribution to Continental stability could be given priority over industrial disarmament schemes.

Truman's own argument that a stable Europe was vital to world peace and to American security reveals the error of the common opinion that America had little active interest in European affairs until the 1947 Truman Doctrine and Marshall Plan. The President's mid-1945 declaration to his staff was an accurate statement of American policy: "We were committed to the rehabilitation of Europe, and there was to be no abandonment this time."[36] Indeed, much more must be said, for the American commitment to Europe was not restricted to the Western regions of the Continent. As George F. Kennan, the author of the "containment policy," has emphasized, American policy was "by no means limited to holding the line."[37] And as Byrnes has repeatedly stressed, in 1945 and 1946 senior American officials were not primarily concerned with a Soviet political or military threat to Western Europe;[38] their eyes were focused on conditions in the Soviet-occupied zone. Byrnes has been quite explicit; his policy always aimed at forcing the Russians to yield in Eastern Europe, and in mid-1947 he still continued to argue that the United States had it in its power to force the Russians to "retire in a very decent manner."[*39]

There is no question that Byrnes's policy derived from the best

---

* Compare Harriman's previously quoted remark that only the lack of sufficient conventional forces made it impossible "to compel the Soviet Union to withdraw." (*Congressional Record*, Aug. 27, 1951, p. A5416.)

By the time the President accepted his resignation in early 1947, Byrnes had not achieved his objective. Though the Red Army had indeed withdrawn from Manchuria, Iran, Hungary, and Czechoslovakia, measured by his own standard he was a failure as Secretary of State—American policy had not been able to force Soviet withdrawal from the rest of Eastern Europe.

Byrnes left office complaining that the Russians "don't scare." With straightforward logic that illuminated the consistency of his basic view and the ironic tragedy of his idealism, he then attempted to convince his fellow countrymen that "measures of the last resort" were the only way to secure lasting world peace. As is often forgotten, Byrnes, who recently endorsed the Presidential candidacy of Senator Goldwater, was perhaps the most highly placed of those who urged a "preventive war" to force the Russians out of Europe. (Forrestal *Diaries*, p. 262; Byrnes, *Speaking Frankly*, p. 203.)

intentions and the highest ideals. And there is no reason to doubt Truman's statement that "the one purpose which dominated me in everything I thought and did was to prevent a third world war."[40] Nevertheless, the attempt to force Soviet withdrawal from Eastern Europe immediately after Hitler's invasion of Russia was an extremely difficult policy to implement. And, inevitably, the policy's problems were greatly multiplied when doubts were raised as to whether or not the industrial basis of German power would be weakened as had been agreed. It may well be true, as Walter Lippmann observed at the time, "that the best that was possible [was] an accommodation, a *modus vivendi,* a working arrangement, some simple form of cooperation, and that in demanding more than that we have been getting less than that, making the best the enemy of the good."[41]

Secretary Stimson seems to have shared this judgment and also to have recognized that the atomic bomb compounded the difficulties Truman's idealistic policy faced. By early September the Secretary of War had come full circle, concluding that "I was wrong" and that the attempt to use the atomic bomb to gain diplomatic objectives was "by far the more dangerous course."[42] In a profoundly ironic, but unsuccessful, attempt to change the policy he had launched, shortly before leaving office Stimson urged an immediate and direct approach to Moscow to attempt to establish international control of atomic energy which might head off "an armament race of a rather desperate character." Apparently greatly disturbed by the bombing of Hiroshima, and now openly opposed to Secretary Byrnes, he advised: *"If we fail to approach them now and merely continue to negotiate with them, having this weapon rather ostentatiously on our hip, their suspicions and their distrust of our purposes and motives will increase."**

At the same time Stimson offered this advice, Secretary Byrnes attempted to explain to Molotov that the United States was "not interested in seeing anything but governments friendly to the Soviet

---

* Stimson's emphasis. The Secretary of War recorded one of his last attempts to convince the President of what he now believed to be a fundamental error in his own previous advice and in American policy: "I described the talk that I had had with Byrnes and told him what our differences were. I told him that both my plan and Byrnes's plan contained chances which I outlined, and I said that I thought that in my method there was less danger than in his and also we would be on the right path towards world establishment of an international world, while on his plan we would be on the wrong path in that respect and (*Continued on next page*)

Union in adjacent countries." But the Soviet Foreign Minister was openly incredulous: "I must tell you I have doubts as to this, and it would not be honest to hide it."[43] Similarly, at this time former Soviet Foreign Minister Litvinov asked an American friend: "Why did you Americans wait till right now to begin opposing us in the Balkans and Eastern Europe? You should have done this three years ago. Now it is too late, and your complaints only arouse suspicions here."[44] And General Eisenhower, making a triumphal postwar visit to Moscow, sensed new and profound Soviet suspicions: "Before the atom bomb was used I would have said, yes, I was sure we could keep the peace with Russia. Now I don't know. . . . People are frightened and disturbed all over. Every one feels insecure again."[45]

To recall the judgments of Stimson and Eisenhower in the autumn of 1945 is to state the ultimate question of to what extent the atomic bomb affected the entire structure of postwar American-Soviet relations. But it is not possible at this juncture to test Secretary Stimson's September view that "the problem of our satisfactory relations with Russia [was] not merely connected with but [was] virtually dominated by the problem of the atomic bomb."[46] Nor can the issue of why the atomic bomb was used be conclusively resolved.

This essay has attempted to describe the influence of the atomic bomb on certain questions of diplomacy. I do not believe that the reverse question—the influence of diplomacy upon the decision to use the atomic bomb—can be answered on the basis of the presently available evidence. However, it is possible to define the nature of the problem which new materials and further research may be able to solve.

A fruitful way to begin is to note General Eisenhower's recollection of the Potsdam discussion at which Stimson told him the weapon would be used against Japan:

> During his recitation of the relevant facts, I had been conscious of a feeling of depression and so I voiced to him my grave misgivings,

---

(*Continued from preceding page*)
would be tending to revert to power politics." (Diary, Sept. 5, 1945.)

Stimson also reviewed the development of his thinking in a discussion with his successor, Robert P. Patterson: "I had a long talk with him. I told him how my view had been gradually formed; how in the beginning I was inclined to think we ought to hang on to the bomb . . . and its secrets; but first on the basis of my belief that Japan was already defeated and that dropping the bomb was completely unnecessary, and secondly because I thought that our country should avoid shocking world opinion by the use of a weapon whose employment was, I thought, no longer mandatory as a measure to save American lives. It was my belief that Japan was, at that very moment, seeking some way to surrender with a minimum loss of "face."

"It wasn't necessary to hit them with that awful thing," Eisenhower concluded.[47]

Perhaps the most remarkable aspect of the decision to use the atomic bomb is that the President and his senior political advisers do not seem ever to have shared Eisenhower's "grave misgivings."* As we have seen, they simply assumed that they would use the bomb, never really giving serious consideration to not using it. Hence, to state in a precise way the question "Why was the atomic bomb used?" is to ask why senior political officials did *not* seriously question its use as Eisenhower did.

The first point to note is that the decision to use the weapon did not derive from overriding military considerations. Despite Truman's subsequent statement that the weapon "saved millions of lives,"[48] Eisenhower's judgment that it was "completely unnecessary" as a measure to save lives was almost certainly correct. This is not a matter of hindsight; *before the atomic bomb was dropped each of the Joint Chiefs of Staff advised that it was highly likely that Japan could be forced to surrender "unconditionally," without use of the bomb and without an invasion.* Indeed, this characterization of the position taken by the senior military advisers is a conservative one.

General Marshall's June 18 appraisal was the most cautiously phrased advice offered by any of the Joint Chiefs: "The impact of

---

that gradually I had found that I was wrong and that that would be by far the more dangerous course than to make an effort with Russia particularly to get on terms with us of confidence in which we would eliminate the manufacture of such bombs for war purposes—eliminate the development of the atomic energy of the explosive kind, and confine ourselves to its use and the development of its more controllable smaller powers for commerce . . ." (Diary, Sept. 17, 1945.)

Stimson left office at the end of September deeply disturbed at having failed to change the direction of the strategy he had launched. (Diary, Sept. 21, 1945.) For a memorandum in which he offered his final detailed views to the President, see Appendix III.

* But see: "I must say that personally I am not at all sure that we were well advised to use it." (Atomic Energy Commission, *Oppenheimer Hearings*, p. 367.)

Russian entry on the already hopeless Japanese may well be the decisive action levering them into capitulation . . ."[49] Admiral Leahy was absolutely certain there was no need for the bombing to obviate the necessity of an invasion.[50] His judgment after the fact was the same as his view before the bombing: "It is my opinion that the use of this barbarous weapon at Hiroshima and Nagasaki was of no material assistance in our war against Japan. The Japanese were already defeated and ready to surrender . . ."[51] Similarly, through most of 1945 Admiral King believed the bomb unnecessary,[52] and Generals Arnold and LeMay defined the official Air Force position in this way: Whether or not the atomic bomb should be dropped was not for the Air Force to decide, but explosion of the bomb was not necessary to win the war or make an invasion unnecessary.*[53]

Similar views prevailed in Britain long before the bombs were used. General Ismay recalls that by the time of Potsdam, "for some time past it had been firmly fixed in my mind that the Japanese were tottering."[54] Ismay's reaction to the suggestion of the bombing was, like Eisenhower's and Leahy's, one of "revulsion."[55] And Churchill, who as early as September 1944, felt that Russian entry was likely to force capitulation,[56] has written: "It would be a mistake to suppose that the fate of Japan was settled by the atomic bomb. Her defeat was certain before the first bomb fell . . ."[57]

The military appraisals made before the weapons were used have been confirmed by numerous postsurrender studies. The best known is that of the United States Strategic Bombing Survey. The Survey's conclusion is unequivocal: "Japan would have surrendered even if the atomic bombs had not been dropped, even if Russia had not entered the war, and even if no invasion had been planned or contemplated."†[58]

(*Continued from preceding page*)
*At the time he argued against the use of the atomic bomb, Eisenhower advised the additional point that the war could easily be ended before Soviet entry. (Eisenhower, *Crusade in Europe*, pp. 441–42.)

† See also Marshall's postwar statement that the atomic bombs precipitated the surrender only "by months"; Bush's view that "the war would have ended before long in any case, for Japan had been brought nearly to her knees"; Curtis LeMay's opinion that the war would have ended in two weeks ("the atomic bomb had nothing to do with the end of the war"); Claire Chennault's view that the Russian declaration of war was the decisive factor; and the arguments of Morton, Baldwin, Blackett, and Craven and Cate, that the atomic bomb was not needed to force a surrender before an invasion. (J. P. Sutherland, "The Story General Marshall Told Me," *U.S. News & World Report*, Nov. 2, 1959, p. 52; Bush, V., *Modern Arms and Free Men*, p. 101; *New York Herald Tribune*, Sept. 21, 1945; *New York Times*, Aug. 15, 1945;

That military considerations were not decisive is confirmed—and illuminated—by the fact that the President did not even ask the opinion of the military adviser most directly concerned. General MacArthur, Supreme Commander of Allied Forces in the Pacific, was simply informed of the weapon shortly before it was used at Hiroshima.[59] Before his death he stated on numerous occasions that, like Eisenhower, he believed the atomic bomb was completely unnecessary from a military point of view.[60]

Although military considerations were not primary, as we have seen, unquestionably political considerations related to Russia played a major role in the decision; from at least mid-May American policy makers hoped to end the hostilities before the Red Army entered Manchuria. For this reason they had no wish to test whether Russian entry into the war would force capitulation—as most thought likely— long before the scheduled November invasion. Indeed, they actively attempted to delay Stalin's declaration of war.

Nevertheless, it would be wrong to conclude that the atomic bomb was used simply to keep the Red Army out of Manchuria. Given the desperate efforts of the Japanese to surrender, and Truman's willingness to offer assurances to the Emperor, it is entirely possible that the war could have been ended by negotiation before the Red Army had begun its attack. But, again, as we have seen, after Alamogordo neither the President nor his senior advisers were interested in exploring this possibility.

One reason may have been their fear that if time-consuming negotiations were once initiated, the Red Army might attack in order to seize Manchurian objectives. But, if this explanation is accepted, once more one must conclude that the bomb was used primarily because it was felt to be politically important to prevent Soviet domination of the area.

Such a conclusion is very difficult to accept, for American interests in Manchuria, although historically important to the State Department, were not of great significance. The further question therefore arises: Were there other political reasons for using the atomic bomb? In approaching this question, it is important to note that most of the men

Morton, "The Decision to Use the Atomic Bomb," *Command Decisions*, ed. K. R. Greenfield, p. 408; *Military and Political Consequences of Atomic Energy*, pp. 116– 30; Baldwin, *Great Mistakes of the War*, p. 84; Craven and Cate, *Air Forces in World War II*, Vol. V, p. 726.)

involved at the time who since have made their views public always mention *two* considerations which dominated discussions. The first was the desire to end the Japanese war quickly, which, as we have seen, was not primarily a military consideration, but a political one. The second is always referred to indirectly.

In June, for example, a leading member of the Interim Committee's scientific panel, A. H. Compton, advised against the Franck report's suggestion of a technical demonstration of the new weapon: Not only was there a possibility that this might not end the war promptly, but failure to make a combat demonstration would mean the 'loss of the opportunity to impress the world with the national sacrifices that enduring security demanded.'* The general phrasing that the bomb was needed 'to impress the world' has been made more specific by J. Robert Oppenheimer. Testifying on this matter some years later he stated that the second of the two "overriding considerations" in discussions regarding the bomb was "the effect of our actions on the stability, on our strength, and the stability of the postwar world."[61] And the problem of postwar stability was inevitably the problem of Russia. Oppenheimer has put it this way: "Much of the discussion revolved around the question raised by Secretary Stimson as to whether there was any hope at all of using this development to get less barbarous relations with the Russians."[62]

Vannevar Bush, Stimson's chief aide for atomic matters, has been quite explicit: "That bomb was developed on time . . . " Not only did it mean a quick end to the Japanese war, but "it was also delivered on time so that there was no necessity for any concessions to Russia at the end of the war."[63]

In essence, the second of the two overriding considerations seems to have been that a combat demonstration was needed to convince the Russians to accept the American plan for a stable peace. And the crucial point of this effort was the need to force agreement on the main questions in dispute: the American proposals for Central and Eastern Europe. President Truman may well have expressed the key consideration in October 1945; publicly urging the necessity of a more conventional form of military power (his proposal for universal military

---

* The words set off are a quotation of the paraphrase provided by the historians of the U.S. Atomic Energy Commission. (Hewlett and Anderson, *The New World,* p. 367.)

training), in a personal appearance before Congress the President declared: "It is only by strength that we can impress the fact upon possible future aggressors that we will tolerate no threat to peace . . ."[64]

If indeed the "second consideration" involved in the bombing of Hiroshima and Nagasaki was the desire to impress the Russians, it might explain the strangely ambiguous statement by Truman that not only did the bomb end the war, but it gave the world "a chance to face the facts."[65] It would also accord with Stimson's private advice to McCloy: "We have got to regain the lead and perhaps do it in a pretty rough and realistic way. . . . We have coming into action a weapon which will be unique. Now the thing [to do is] . . . let our actions speak for themselves."[66] Again, it would accord with Stimson's statement to Truman that the "greatest complication" would occur if the President negotiated with Stalin before the bomb had been "laid on Japan."[67] It would tie in with the fact that from mid-May strategy toward all major diplomatic problems was based upon the assumption the bomb would be demonstrated. Finally, it might explain why none of the highest civilian officials seriously questioned the use of the bomb as Eisenhower did; for, having reversed the basic direction of diplomatic strategy *because* of the atomic bomb, it would have been very difficult indeed for anyone subsequently to challenge an idea which had come to dominate all calculations of high policy.*

At present no final conclusion can be reached on this question. But the problem can be defined with some precision: Why did the American government refuse to attempt to exploit Japanese efforts to surrender? Or, alternatively, why did they refuse to test whether a Russian declaration of war would force capitulation? Were Hiroshima and Nagasaki bombed primarily to impress the world with the need to

---

* It might also explain why the sober and self-controlled Stimson reacted so strongly when Eisenhower objected to the bombing: "The Secretary was deeply perturbed by my attitude, almost angrily refuting the reasons I gave . . ." (Eisenhower, *Mandate for Change*, p. 313.) Stimson's post-Hiroshima reversal, and his repeated references to the gravity of the moral issues raised by the new weapon, are evidence of his own doubts. Eisenhower's searching criticism may well have touched upon a very tender point, namely, Stimson's undoubted awareness that Hiroshima and Nagasaki were to be sacrificed primarily for political, not military, reasons.

See also Williams, *The Tragedy of American Diplomacy*, p. 254, and Fleming, *The Cold War*, I, pp. 296–302. Compare Irving's account of the bombing of Dresden. See especially his discussion of the precisely parallel argument that Churchill felt it politically important to impress Stalin with overwhelming air power when Central and Eastern European issues were discussed at Yalta. (*The Destruction of Dresden*, pp. 86–102.)

accept America's plan for a stable and lasting peace—that is, primarily, America's plan for Europe? The evidence strongly suggests that the view which the President's personal representative offered to one of the atomic scientists in May 1945 was an accurate statement of policy: "Mr. Byrnes did not argue that it was necessary to use the bomb against the cities of Japan in order to win the war . . . Mr. Byrnes's . . . view [was] that our possessing and demonstrating the bomb would make Russia more manageable in Europe. . . ."[68]

The Polish Question: From Yalta to Truman

THE YALTA PROTOCOL INCLUDED an agreement on the Polish-Soviet border and on the organization of a new Polish government. Both issues were involved in the post-Yalta controversy.

With little debate the Yalta meeting approved the Curzon Line (with minor variations) as the new Polish-Soviet border. Although the heads of government had privately accepted the idea of the Line as early as the Teheran Conference,[1] the Yalta decision had a great impact upon the Polish exile groups in London. The extremely nationalistic Arciszewski government-in-exile refused any compromise on the border issue and denounced the Yalta agreement. Even the more moderate Peasant party leader and former Prime Minister, Mikolajczyk, was openly critical of the accord.[2]

The publication of the Yalta communiqué only underscored the hopeless predicament of the Polish exile government. Stalin had been abundantly clear about his postwar aims from the very first—he wanted the return of Russian lands given to Poland after the First World War and, as early as the winter of 1941, had asked Western approval of the Curzon Line.[3] Churchill also supported the Line originally suggested by a British foreign minister, but the issue had been postponed because of America's insistence that all territorial questions be held for settlement until after the war.[4] As a consequence, the Russian position became stronger with each day of the war. As the Red Army advanced through Poland, there could be little doubt that Stalin would have the final word on the Polish-Soviet border settlement.

Churchill believed that unless the Polish government-in-exile came to terms with Russia on the basis of the Curzon Line they could not hope to have a position of power in a postwar government. For this reason the Prime Minister urged acceptance of the Russian position. Churchill's support for the Line also acknowledged that the Russians could easily have taken more territory had they so desired. But the border issue had a significance beyond territorial matters. Acceptance of the Curzon Line by political leaders would establish their willingness to cooperate with the Soviet Union. Conversely, any Pole who opposed the border could not be termed "friendly" to the Soviet Union; and the Big Three were agreed that the new Poland would have to be led by men who were willing to cooperate with the Russians and who could be trusted to choose the Russian side in any future difficulties with Germany.

Throughout 1944, Churchill begged, bullied, harassed, and threatened the London Poles, trying to make them see that unless they accepted the border they would never regain power. However, the Prime Minister met with no success; and Stalin slowly began to build a new Polish governing group which would prove its "friendliness" to the Soviet Union. On January 1, 1944—three days before the Red Army crossed into Poland—the Soviet radio announced the formation of the *Lublin Committee* which was to help administer territories cleared of German troops.[5] As the Red Armies moved through Poland the Lublin Committee was given more power and, with the exile government still refusing to come to terms, the Committee proclaimed itself the Provisional Government of Poland on December 31, 1944.[6]

At each stage of the Lublin Committee's rise to power, Churchill had counseled the exile government that "everything hinges on one thing: the eastern frontier of Poland. If this is settled . . . agreement can be reached easily . . . [If not,] they will build up a rival government and gradually take over authority in Poland."[7] The Prime Minister soon bitterly denounced the exile government's stubbornness, pointing out: "It is your fault that the Lublin Poles have come into existence."[8] Churchill believed the London group "absolutely incapable of facing facts," and he told them that it was "absurd, pure Utopia" to cling to hope of a settlement on terms other than the Curzon Line.[9] Faced with the growing power of the Lublin Committee and the continued obstinacy of the government, Churchill declared that listening to the unrealistic proposals of the London Poles was "like being in a lunatic asylum."[10]

Though the growth of a new locus of political power in Poland was in large part the result of Polish stubbornness in the face of Soviet demands, this attitude derived not only from the lack of realism of the exiles. One of the main reasons for Polish intransigence was the ill-defined position of the United States government. Despite Roosevelt's general commitment to the Curzon principle, the President did not reveal his views to the Poles until the end of 1944. This was undoubtedly due to Roosevelt's fear of alienating the large bloc of Polish-American voters before the election of November 1944.[11] Because the President avoided the issue the Polish exile government came to believe that the American government might eventually champion their cause. So long as Roosevelt was uncommitted, it was possible to think that the Big Three might not endorse the Curzon Line.[12]

It was a great shock, therefore, when shortly after the election Roosevelt let it be known that he definitely would not support the exile government on the border issue.[13] At Yalta he quickly gave formal approval to the Curzon Line, thus leaving the London Poles in an untenable position, opposed not only to Stalin, but to the united stand of the Big Three. Now there could be no doubt: Polish opposition to the Yalta accord was an unmistakable sign of "unfriendliness" to the Soviet Union and unwillingness to cooperate in the big-power settlement.

Part of the Polish tragedy thus stems from the marriage of Roosevelt's evasiveness with the futile hopes of the Polish exile government. Another part stems from the demands of the war itself; for in the same way that Eisenhower demanded a recognized authority in France to establish order behind American lines,[14] Stalin demanded a group of "friendly" Poles who could act authoritatively as the Red Army struggled against the Germans.[15] To be sure, Stalin might have liked to establish a Soviet-dominated government in any case, but such a politically astute observer as Churchill was convinced that the Russians wanted a cooperative solution of the Polish problem.[16] In some respects, Stalin's willingness to dicker over the border issue during the long and bitter fight for Poland is remarkable, for it was only at the end of 1944 that he gave up hope of an agreement with the exile government.

When Roosevelt made his position clear, the then Prime Minister Mikolajczyk confronted his Cabinet with the necessity for some agreement with the Russians. However, the Peasant leader was unable to obtain support for a compromise position and, defeated on the issue, was replaced by Arciszewski.[17] Churchill understood that the new government was committed to a futile policy and refused to have anything to do with members of the government.[18] The end of the Mikolajczyk government was therefore a major turning point. From the Russian point of view, there was now no hope of an agreed settlement with the exile government. Despite Western protests, Stalin called attention to Mikolajczyk's resignation and recognized the Lublin Committee as the provisional government of Poland on January 5, 1945, a few days before the new Soviet offensive began in western Poland.[19] The Committee, now established in the Polish capital, was thereafter known as the Warsaw Provisional Government.

Thus, the inability of the powers to resolve the border issue in 1944 brought about a situation in which two governments claimed to represent Poland. Though the Western powers would have little to do with Arciszewski, their ambassadors were still accredited to the exile government. This set the conditions of the second major problem of the Yalta Polish negotiations: agreement had to be reached on the organization of a single Polish provisional government.

The West entered the negotiations in an extremely weak position. Roosevelt and Churchill had repeatedly promised to support a new Polish government "friendly" to the Soviet Union. (At Yalta, Roosevelt wrote Stalin: "The United States will never lend its support in any way to any provisional government in Poland that would be inimical to your interests.")[20] Unfortunately, the London Poles had all defined their position vis-à-vis the Soviet Union by their denunciation of the Curzon Line. In supporting these Poles, the West was fighting an uphill battle. Moreover, the failure to secure agreement on the border issue during the long period of Polish obstinacy weakened the Western claim that the Poles might easily be brought into "friendly" cooperation with the Russians.

From the Western point of view, the Arciszewski government was hopeless. The only possibility would be an attempt to fuse the Mikolajczyk Poles (now out of the government) with the Warsaw Provisional Government. It was hoped that both the exile government and the Warsaw government could be dissolved and the way cleared for a totally new government. This would draw its members from among the Mikolajczyk Poles, political leaders within Poland, and the Warsaw government. The new provisional government would be pledged to hold free elections as soon as possible.[21]

From the Soviet point of view, this plan represented a bold demand. Attempts to get the Western-oriented Poles to endorse the Curzon Line had failed throughout the war. To eliminate the Warsaw government would be tantamount to reversing the outcome of the long struggle over the border issue. However, at Yalta Stalin indicated that he was prepared to accept some additional Poles into the Warsaw government, provided they were "friendly" to the Soviet Union. With this concession, a long debate over the exact terms of a reorganization of the government began. The result was the Yalta agreement:

> A new situation has been created in Poland . . . This calls for the establishment of a Polish Provisional Government which can be more broadly based than was possible before the recent liberation of western Poland. The Provisional Government which is now functioning in Poland should therefore be reorganized on a broader democratic basis with the inclusion of democratic leaders from Poland itself and from Poles abroad. . . .

> M. Molotov, Mr. Harriman and Sir A. Clark Kerr are authorized as a Commission to consult in the first instance in Moscow with members of the present Provisional Government and with other Polish democratic leaders from within Poland and from abroad, with a view to the reorganization of the present Government along the above lines. . . .[22]

This was an extremely vague agreement, and Roosevelt was quite aware of its limitations.[23] Admiral Leahy believed it to be "so elastic that the Russians can stretch it all the way from Yalta to Washington without ever technically breaking it."[24] Still, the conservative and anti-Russian presidential adviser "was agreeably surprised" at Stalin's willingness to yield as much as he did, and the American Secretary of State regarded the agreement as a considerable concession by the Soviet Union.[25] Now the problem was to get agreement on the exact meaning of the vague formula which would establish a "more broadly based" government, by "reorganizing" the government "now functioning in Poland," in such a way as to create a "new" government.

The attempt to give content to these words began with the first meeting of the Moscow Commission on February 22.[26] Harriman, Molotov, and Clark Kerr began their work on a note of harmony, agreeing to invite a list of Poles to Moscow for consultations. Members of the London exile government were excluded (the government had not even been mentioned in the Yalta communiqué), but representatives from among the Mikolajczyk Poles, political leaders within Poland, and the Warsaw government were to be invited. The most important point about the initial decision was that an invitation went *first* to the Warsaw government. The government was also asked for comment on the other names suggested for consultations; thus the principle of prior consultation with the government "now functioning in Poland" was recognized.*[27]

On February 24, the Warsaw government objected to some of the names suggested for consultation. Warsaw observed that Mikolajczyk and others had publicly criticized the Yalta agreement, and therefore could not qualify to participate in consultations based upon that agreement. Molotov supported Warsaw's veto of Mikolajczyk.[28] The old issue was once more joined, and again the Western powers found themselves supporting groups publicly committed to an "unfriendly" policy toward the Russians. This situation immediately precipitated a split between British and American policy. London and Washington agreed that the only hope of preserving the influence of Western-oriented Poles lay with Mikolajczyk. Earlier the Peasant leader had been officially informed that he would have American support as a candidate for premier of a new government, and Eden had said that Britain would deal with no other Pole.[29] Now, however, Mikolajczyk's attitude on Yalta gave Western plans a severe setback.

Churchill's position was especially delicate, for Britain had gone to war over the question of Polish independence, and the government was under considerable pressure not to yield in the Polish negotiations.[30] Faced with a difficult problem, the Foreign Office took the

---

* This point has been obscured. Lane reports, vaguely, that at the first meeting of the Commission Harriman said the United States would not object to the Warsaw government's coming to Moscow for consultations ahead of the other Poles, *if* invitations were sent simultaneously to an agreed upon list. However, he immediately reveals that this statement was not binding by showing that Harriman agreed to a telegram inviting Warsaw *before* agreement had been reached on the other Poles. (*I Saw Poland Betrayed*, p. 57.) That the invitation did go out before agreement on the other issues is confirmed by Woodward. (*British Foreign Policy*, pp. 502–3.)

offensive. Disregarding Mikolajczyk's opposition to Yalta, Clark Kerr was instructed to demand that the invitation to the Warsaw government be held up until Mikolajczyk and others were also invited to Moscow. He refused to agree that the Warsaw government come to Moscow for prior consultations. He also asked that the great powers supervise the expected Polish elections.[31] Although the Foreign Office attempted to get American support for this position, Harriman was not instructed to go along with Clark Kerr's effort.[32] The American ambassador limited himself to the suggestion that although Warsaw had to be consulted, the government could not be accorded an absolute right of veto over a list of names suggested for consultation. He advised Washington that the best tactics would be to get the government to Moscow so that consultations could begin.[33]

Though this divergence among the powers appeared at the very outset of the talks, there was as yet no breakdown. In fact, at the second meeting of the Commission, on February 27, Molotov volunteered to allow British observers to enter Poland, although this had not been provided for in the Yalta agreement.[34] Reporting on Stalin's concessions at Yalta, Churchill had told the War Cabinet he had no doubts about Soviet willingness to find a harmonious solution to the Polish problem; now he found Molotov's suggestion "a friendly offer."[35] Nevertheless the Foreign Office instructed Clark Kerr to continue to oppose invitations to the Warsaw government until an agreed list of invitations had been sent out. The obstructionist strategy was quite simple; until Mikolajczyk was accepted, Britain would block further consultations. Thus the substantive work of the Moscow Commission came to a halt, for the Russians refused to accept a Pole openly hostile to the Curzon Line and the Yalta agreement. The Warsaw government, which had already been invited to Moscow, was asked to postpone its trip.*[36]

---

* The fact that the Moscow Commission was initially blocked by *unilateral* British action has often been obscured. The exact position taken by Harriman in the negotiations has not been made public. The point at issue is whether or not, between February 24 and March 18, Harriman changed his statement that the Warsaw government should be invited to Moscow without Mikolajczyk. (Woodward, *British Foreign Policy*, p. 502.) I have found no evidence that American policy switched to support the British position at this time. Using official British sources, Woodward shows that, on the contrary, the Foreign Office fought a losing battle to alter the American view. (*Ibid.*, p. 509.) Churchill also took the matter up directly with Roosevelt, continuing to hold up the invitation to Warsaw and repeating his view that any Pole (meaning, most particularly, Mikolajczyk), (*Continued on next page*)

THE DIPLOMACY OF STALEMATE

NOW AMERICAN POLICY WAS FACED with the obstinacy of Churchill and the stubbornness of Mikolajczyk. The Prime Minister and the Peasant leader had previously disagreed on many matters, but, from the American point of view, both were obstructing agreement on the Polish issue. To this challenge, Roosevelt's response was twofold. He undertook to bring Churchill to a more moderate stand, and he sent his agents to try to force Mikolajczyk to endorse the Yalta agreement.[37]

The debate with Churchill developed in the following manner: After the State Department had refused to support Clark Kerr, it was asked by London to hold up instructions to Harriman while Churchill approached Roosevelt directly.[38] In a cable on March 8, the Prime Minister defended his position and urged Roosevelt to join him. He opened his message with the veiled threat of a public statement in the Commons if his views were not accepted. Churchill urged a united approach to Stalin which would:

1. Reject the contention that the Warsaw government had an absolute right to prior consultation.
2. Demand that any Pole nominated by one of the three governments be invited to Moscow for consultations.

(*Continued from preceding page*)
if acceptable to at least one of the Big Three, should be invited to Moscow. Roosevelt countered: "I cannot believe that Molotov will accept the proposal . . . and I am opposed to putting forward such a suggestion at this time, as it would in my view almost certainly leave us in a stalemate." The President begged Churchill to agree so that "our Ambassadors may proceed with their instructions . . . "

The point is of considerable importance, for it reveals that the first post-Yalta controversy pitted Churchill against both Roosevelt and Stalin, not, as is often thought, Churchill and Roosevelt against Stalin; the American position was substantially the same as the Russian. There has been a good deal of confusion on this question and more than one author has made it appear that Britain and America were united in their stand. Feis, for example, slurs over the point at issue so as to suggest such a conclusion. (*Churchill, Roosevelt, Stalin,* p.

571–74.) Lane also passes over the point, making it seem that Britain and America were in accord. He says simply that "no agreement could be reached" on issuing invitations. (*I Saw Poland Betrayed,* p. 59.) It is true, of course, that Harriman reported Molotov's opposition to Mikolajczyk, that the State Department was unhappy about the situation, that Harriman urged that Warsaw be refused an absolute right to veto candidates, and that *at a later date,* American policy supported Britain. However, despite the vague language, a close reading of those who have used official American sources shows that no one has directly disputed the point that Clark Kerr stood alone in the actual negotiations. (Byrnes, *Speaking Frankly,* pp. 53–54; Lane, *I Saw Poland Betrayed,* pp. 57–59; Stettinius, *Roosevelt and the Russians,* pp. 312–13; Feis, *Churchill, Roosevelt, Stalin,* pp. 572–73.) For the subsequent change in American policy, see below, p. 262.

3. Provide that the reorganization of the government be arranged in discussions among the Poles themselves, with the Commission acting in "an impartial arbitral capacity."
4. Request the Soviet government to "use its utmost influence to prevent the Warsaw administration from taking any further legal or administrative action of a fundamental character affecting social, constitutional, economic, or political conditions in Poland."
5. Urge the Soviet government to arrange for Western observers to visit Poland.[39]

Following the advice of Harriman, who opposed a direct approach to Stalin, Roosevelt rejected this message: "I feel that our personal intervention would best be withheld." He also urged Churchill not to approach Stalin on his own: "I very much hope therefore that you will not send a message to Uncle Joe at this juncture, especially as I feel that certain parts of your proposed text might produce a reaction quite contrary to your intent."[40] Churchill agreed to postpone a direct approach to Stalin, but did not yield on the points at issue. On March 13, he cabled again, this time begging Roosevelt at least to allow the two ambassadors to raise the points with Molotov.[41] Once more he raised the threat of a public statement in the Commons which would "make it clear that we are in presence of a great failure and an utter breakdown of what was settled at Yalta." He urged "combined dogged pressure and persistence" on the five points of his earlier cable.[42]

The stream of cables from London, and the Prime Minister's obstruction of the Moscow talks apparently brought Roosevelt to the end of his patience. On March 16, he cabled: "I cannot but be concerned at the views you expressed in your message . . . *I cannot agree that we are confronted with a breakdown of the Yalta agreement* until we have made the effort to overcome the obstacles incurred in the negotiations at Moscow." Roosevelt went on to delineate his own views, point by point, on Churchill's position. The President:

1. Agreed that the Warsaw government was not entitled to an "absolute" right of prior consultation.
2. Opposed the proposal that any Pole whose name was suggested be invited.
3. Agreed that the Poles invited for consultation should discuss the composition of the government among themselves with the Commission presiding in an impartial arbitral capacity.

4. Continued to hold to an earlier suggestion of a "political truce" between the Polish groups, as opposed to Churchill's suggestion that Stalin be made responsible for stopping the Warsaw government's actions.*

5. Agreed that the question of observers in Poland might once more be raised.[43]

This cable summarized the main points at issue. In fact, however, four of the points involved subsidiary questions. Since the right of the Warsaw government to consult with the Commission "in the first instance" was not disputed, Churchill's insistence that there was no "absolute" right was trivial.† The suggestion that the Poles decide the composition of the new government by themselves was a matter of form rather than substance. Though the proposal reflected the view that the various Polish groups should be considered equal in status to the Warsaw government, the only reason for the Commission's existence was to arbitrate or dictate on disputed points. The matter of a "truce" or a request that Stalin stop the actions of the Warsaw government depended upon how quickly an agreement could be reached on a new government, for the Red Army was moving through Poland, and some form of administration was a practical necessity in the liberated areas. The "neutrality" of the administration would inevitably be a matter of judgment. The point about observers, too, was not a major one. Molotov himself had suggested it originally, but, as Roosevelt told Churchill, the Russian Foreign Minister "took fright when Clark Kerr revealed that you were thinking of a large special mission."‡[44]

---

* See below, p. 262.

† The point arose out of the controversy over whether or not the Yalta agreement required prior consultations with the Warsaw government. The British agreed that Warsaw had to be consulted "in the first instance" but argued that it would be going beyond the terms of the agreement if the Warsaw government arrived *in Moscow* before the other groups. The Russians believed Britain to be breaking the Yalta accord by insisting on a somewhat legalistic reading of language which provided for consultations with Warsaw "in the first instance in Moscow." Indeed, the British view seems to strain the meaning of the words, and the presumption in favor of the Russian view is even stronger in the Russian translation. Here consultations with Warsaw are to take place "*in Moscow* in the first instance." Harriman believed the point triv-ial; and the petty struggle over language is really more important as a reflection of the underlying stalemate over Mikolajczyk, the border solution, and the status to be accorded to the various contending Polish groups. In what is surely a strange exaggeration, Arthur Bliss Lane later wrote that the Russian interpretation was contrary to the "clear" wording of Yalta. (Woodward, *British Foreign Policy*, p. 502fn.; Lane, *I Saw Poland Betrayed*, p. 57; Churchill, *Triumph and Tragedy*, p. 487; *Stalin's Correspondence*, I, p. 207.)

‡ According to Woodward, two other factors led to the withdrawal of the offer to admit observers. One was the fact that Britain blocked the invitation to Warsaw. The second was a speech in the Commons by Eden which referred to the Warsaw government in contemptuous terms. (Woodward, *British Foreign Policy*, pp. 500, 503.)

The issue of real substance derived from Churchill's demand that any Pole suggested by one power be invited for consultations. This meant Mikolajczyk, and, in another form, it was the same question which, at Churchill's insistence, had caused the initial deadlock. Roosevelt cabled that "our chief purpose" is to "get the negotiations moving again, and tackle first of all the point on which they had come to a standstill. I cannot urge upon you too strongly the vital importance of agreeing without delay on instructions to our Ambassadors so that the negotiations may resume." On the issue of substance the President challenged Churchill directly: "I cannot believe that Molotov will accept the proposal . . . that any Pole can be invited unless all three members of the Commission object, and I am opposed to putting forward such a suggestion at this time, as it would in my view almost certainly leave us in a stalemate."[45] Evidently greatly annoyed with Churchill, on the same day Roosevelt told his Cabinet that "the British were perfectly willing for the United States to have a war with Russia at any time and that, in his opinion, to follow the British program would be to proceed toward that end."[46]

At the same time that he pleaded with Churchill to yield so that consultations could go forward, Roosevelt instructed his chargé d'affaires in London to urge Mikolajczyk to withdraw his opposition to Yalta. Following the American initiative, British representatives also approached the Peasant leader.[47] In Moscow, the American ambassador had already urged Molotov not to take an unyielding line on the principle of "absolute" prior consultations with Warsaw.[48]

It is important to understand the problem facing American policy makers following the deadlock of the Moscow Commission. The Red Army was moving relentlessly across Poland, at once liberating the country and consolidating administration behind the battlefront. Each day the influence of the London group waned and the power of the Warsaw government increased. Moreover, each day Soviet justification for giving power to Warsaw was greater, for the assault on Berlin required stability and order behind Red Army lines. Time was on the side of the Russians.

From the American point of view, it was absolutely essential to get agreement on a reorganized government as soon as possible. Moreover, there was a deadline: the charter meeting of the United Nations was to be held in San Francisco on April 25. It would be important to have a new government recognized by that time;[49] its presence in San Francisco would be a sign of its accepted legitimacy. From the Russian point of view, this deadline also imposed certain limits: if the United Nations meeting convened before agreement had been reached and the Conference went ahead *without* a representative from Warsaw, the legitimacy of the government "now functioning in Poland" would be called into question.

The only group which could gain from the deadlock was the London government-in-exile.* It believed that if matters could be stalled until the war's end the common purpose which united the Allies might disappear. Only then could it hope that the Western powers might champion its cause against the Russians. For this reason the exile government stressed delay, but the focal point of their efforts was also Mikolajczyk. The Peasant leader had already dissociated himself from the Arciszewski government, and, if he were to join in a reorganization of the Warsaw government, his action would at once increase the popularity of Warsaw and end the hopes of the London government. General Anders and others associated with the exile government attempted to keep Mikolajczyk with them, begging him not to go back to Poland.[50] Quite aware of this strategy, Eden had already discussed with Mikolajczyk what he would do if the London government followed a program which was "unrealistic—based on the principle of delay."[51] Mikolajczyk's initial response placed him between the Warsaw and London governments. He would not join Warsaw, and he criticized the Yalta agreement, but his criticism was a moderate one which left the door open to further change. However, his public attack on Yalta was enough to establish his opposition to the agreement, and, caught between contending forces, the Peasant leader stalled, hoping for better terms or greater support from the West. Roosevelt was unsuccessful in his efforts to obtain a statement in support of Yalta.[52]

---

* It is probable that Churchill also thought he could gain by delay. Apart from the fact that the Prime Minister faced great pressure not to yield in the Polish negotiations, it is known that he was making a tremendous effort to involve Roosevelt in a more active role against Soviet policy in Eastern Europe. It is probable that the Prime Minister, having failed to get American support for an invasion in the Balkans, believed it good tactics to stress—even exaggerate—a conflict on the Polish issue which had implications for Roosevelt's cherished United Nations project. Churchill's March 25 advice to Eden is illuminating: "We cannot press the case against Russia beyond where we can carry the United States. Nothing is more likely to bring them into line with us than any idea of the San Francisco Conference being imperilled." (Churchill, *Triumph and Tragedy*, p. 444.)

The stalemate which developed out of this situation opened the door to other complications. In Poland proper, the sheer force of the Russian assault gave more power, day by day, to the Soviet Union. The West grew apprehensive as each mile of Polish territory was wrenched from German hands and passed back to be administered by the Warsaw government. It was recognized that the Russians had to have order behind their front lines, but this requirement could also justify Soviet suppression of groups opposed to the Red Army.* In a country where anti-Russian sentiment was endemic there were many who were as violently antagonistic to the Russians as they were to the Germans. The Polish underground army—responsible to the exile government—had already come into conflict with the Red Army on a number of occasions.[53] Western leaders knew that the conservative and anti-Russian political figures involved in the underground army would give ample grounds for any action the Russians might take to suppress their activities.[54] Moreover, the Warsaw government announced a land reform at this time.[55] Churchill was especially concerned that the combination of popular social reforms and suppression of the opposition would prejudice the future political settlement. He urged Roosevelt to join him in a plea to Stalin to use his influence to hold back the Warsaw government, but Roosevelt was prepared only to suggest a "truce" which would acknowledge the responsibility of the right-wing groups harassing the Red Army as well as that of the Warsaw government. As the stalemate continued, Churchill's fears grew and he also continued to urge Roosevelt's support so that Western observers might enter the country.[56]

From the Russian point of view, the intolerable disturbances to the Red Army advance seemed to derive not only from the hostility of the Polish underground army; there were suspicious signs that the Poles were being aided by the British government and, to a lesser extent, by the Americans.[57] The most important fact, of course, was that the underground groups depended upon British airdrops for supplies,[58] but there were also incidents in which American forces aided the Poles. One instance involved American servicemen who disguised a Pole in

---

* Shortly after Yalta, Byrnes—who had advised Roosevelt at the conference—publicly declared: "It must be remembered that the Russians liberated Poland. The Russian position is that they do not want behind the Soviet Armies any government they cannot trust. The Russians cannot be looking back while they are going forward to Berlin." (Quoted in Mikolajczyk, *The Pattern of Soviet Domination*, p. 123.)

American military uniform and secretly flew him out of the country.*[59] In normal circumstances Anglo-American assistance might not have raised any problems, but since the Poles were often openly opposed to the Red Army, the Western efforts took on a more sinister cast. Inevitably it seemed that the West had ulterior motives in aiding Polish political groups. Stalin was soon to complain of efforts to resurrect a *cordon sanitaire*.[60]

A CRISIS OF CONFIDENCE

SUSPICIONS GREW ON BOTH SIDES, and the days after the stalemate in the Moscow Commission were some of the darkest in inter-Allied relations. General Deane, head of the United States Military Mission in Moscow, reports that at this time he "plumbed the depths of discouragement and despair."[61] But troubles in Poland and Moscow were relatively minor irritants compared with an event which at this time shattered confidence as had no other throughout the war. In late February, German officers made contact with Allied representatives in Switzerland and began to hint at the possibility of a surrender of German forces in Italy.[62] On March 8, a German general named Wolff appeared to discuss the possibility of negotiations with British and American military representatives in Bern, Switzerland.[63] Since the Russians, as allies, were entitled to participate in any actual surrender discussions with the common enemy, at Churchill's suggestion, information on the first contacts was given to Molotov on March 12.[64]

The Soviet Foreign Minister asked that Red Army representatives also be allowed to participate in the discussions. The British believed this to be proper procedure; it would eliminate the possibility of suspicions about a surrender in Italy which might facilitate German troop movements to the Russian front.[65] However, General Deane recommended refusal of the Soviet request. He argued that the Russians would introduce complications into the delicate meetings.[66] (Deane, whose relations with the Russians "were not going so well,"

---

* Such incidents led to a breakdown in arrangements to speed the release of American prisoners liberated by the Red Army in Poland. The Russians became wary of American military personnel behind Red Army lines and were reluctant to permit American access to Poland. (Deane, *The Strange Alliance*, pp. 197–99.)

later admitted there was a large element of "vindictiveness" in his recommendation.)[67] Ambassador Harriman, equally troubled in his relations with the Russians, supported the recommendation because he believed a firm stand would be a lesson to the Russians that they could not expect to get all that they requested.[68]

The recommendations from the top American officials in Moscow were accepted, and on March 15 Molotov was informed that the purpose of the Bern talks was only to make contact with a view to getting German military representatives to Allied Headquarters in Italy. If actual surrender talks could be arranged in Italy, Soviet representatives would be allowed to participate.[69] Greatly disturbed at this message, Molotov responded that the refusal to allow Soviet officers to come to Bern was "utterly unexpected and incomprehensible."[70] Molotov insisted that the talks be broken off until Soviet participation was accepted.[71] General Antonov informed Deane that the Soviet Union would not participate in later talks in Italy unless Soviet officers were in on the Bern discussions from the beginning.[72]

On March 21, Harriman and Clark Kerr told Molotov that he misunderstood the nature of the Bern talks; only arrangements for further negotiations were being discussed. But Molotov noted that the first information given to him (on March 12) was that the Bern talks would "discuss . . . the surrender of German armed forces," and he questioned the reassurances now given—"In this instance the Soviet Government sees not a misunderstanding but something worse."[73] He declared:

> Negotiations have been going on for two weeks at Bern (*sic*), behind the back of the Soviet Union which is bearing the brunt of the war against Germany. . . . The Soviet Government considers this absolutely impermissible. . . .[74]

Molotov's attitude stimulated a direct message from Roosevelt to Stalin. On March 25 the President repeated the assertion that Anglo-American representatives were only checking the accuracy of the report that surrender might be arranged. He continued to deny Soviet participation in the Bern talks, but promised that if a meeting to discuss the details of surrender could be arranged, Soviet representatives would be welcome.[75] This brought back a strongly worded cable from Stalin on March 29. The Soviet Premier said he could agree to discussions with the Germans only "if the opportunity for the Germans to maneuver and to use the talks for switching troops to other sectors, above all to the Soviet front, is precluded." Stalin claimed that "the Germans have already taken advantage of the talks . . . to move three divisions from Northern Italy to the Soviet front. . . . This circumstance irritates the Soviet Command and engenders distrust. . . . In a situation of this kind Allies should have nothing to conceal from each other."[76]

On April 1, Roosevelt responded: "There is no question of negotiating with the Germans in any way which would permit them to transfer elsewhere forces from the Italian front. . . . Your information about the time of the movements of German troops from Italy is in error." The President continued to refuse Soviet participation in the Bern talks. Stalin replied with a more serious charge: "My military colleagues . . . are sure that negotiations did take place and that they ended in an agreement with the Germans . . . to open the front to the Anglo-American troops and let them move east. . . . I think that my colleagues are not very far from the truth. If the contrary were the case the exclusion . . . of the Soviet Command from the Bern talks would be inexplicable."[77]

Roosevelt responded with "astonishment" to the assertion that a deal had been made with the Germans: "I am certain that there were no negotiations in Bern at any time. . . . Frankly, I cannot avoid a feeling of bitter resentment toward your informers, whoever they are, for such vile misrepresentations of my actions or those of my trusted subordinates."[78] Nevertheless, the President continued to refuse Soviet representatives. Stalin's final message was a bitter one: "A difference of views has arisen over what an ally may permit himself with regard to another and what he may not. We Russians believe that . . . in a situation in which the enemy is faced with inevitable surrender, whenever the representatives of one of the Allies meet the Germans to discuss surrender terms, the representatives of the other Ally should be enabled to take part in the meeting. . . . I still consider the Russian point of view to be the only correct one because it precludes mutual suspicions."[79]

These important exchanges have been quoted at length because they demonstrate that from mid-March—at the time when the Polish talks had broken down completely—the top Soviet leadership believed that the West was making an arrangement with the Germans which would have put the Red Army at a serious disadvantage. It is not difficult to discover the sources of this belief. The initial letter from the American ambassador stated that the Bern talks were to discuss surrender, not merely arrangements for a further meeting in Italy.[80] Moreover, and contrary to the American assertions at the time, it has since been established that the talks did go into the details of surrender terms,[81] and came very near to what must be termed negotiations. Even at the time, Churchill told Eden that "the Russians may have a legitimate fear of our doing a deal in the West to hold them well back in the East."[82] The Prime Minister was alive to the possibility that political affairs might be "trenched upon" and, indeed, was not certain himself that talks had "not already gone beyond" mere military matters.[83] Thus the Soviet fear that negotiations were going on was understandable. Inevitably, Soviet suspicions must have increased as the Bern talks—supposedly designed only to arrange further negotiations in Italy—continued for almost two months.*

The suspicion that the West was making a deal to end resistance on the western front and allow troop transfers to the Soviet front probably stemmed from two facts. In the last months the Germans allowed the Western Allies to advance as fast as possible into Germany while the Russians were faced with last-ditch resistance. Thus, in the month of February, 1,675 tanks and assault guns were sent to formations engaging the Russians. During that month the western front received only 67.[84] Hitler hoped to split the Allies by such tactics, or at least to give over more of Germany to troops whose homes had not been devastated by German occupation.[85] Inevitably, the German strategy must have seemed suspicious to the Russians. Moreover, at one stage German agents at Bern offered surrender terms which would have permitted German withdrawals from the Italian front.[86] If Soviet intelligence agents got wind of the offer, the combination of German actions and the Bern talks would have seemed extremely suspicious

---

* From late February to late April. (Feis, *Churchill, Roosevelt, Stalin*, p. 583; Ehrman, *Grand Strategy*, p. 128.)

indeed. Finally, the fact that German negotiators in Bern were responsible to Kesselring, who took over command of the entire western front in the midst of the Bern talks, must have increased fears that the discussions were not limited to the Italian surrender.[87]

It is against this background of profound Soviet suspicions that the Polish negotiations must be judged. The stalemate, which began with the British objection to consultations without Mikolajczyk, continued throughout March, and inevitably complications arose and questions of form and status came to dominate the negotiations. With issues of substance in abeyance, each side attempted to secure petty advantages for its favored group of Poles. The most important struggle of this kind developed on March 1, when invitations to the San Francisco Conference of the United Nations were issued to forty-four nations.[88] Poland was not among the nations invited. In London this caused great consternation, for the Polish government in exile was aware that the failure of the powers to include the government would undermine its claim to be the legitimate representative of the Polish nation. But this fight had long been lost.[89] The real struggle involved the status of the Warsaw government. The Russians wanted the existing government in Poland to be invited to San Francisco. Since the Yalta agreement provided that the government "now functioning in Poland" would be "reorganized," the Russians believed that to deny an invitation to Warsaw would unfairly diminish the government's claim to legitimate status. The Western powers understood the point but did not wish to increase the status of the Warsaw government before a reorganization had been arranged. In fact, an invitation to the San Francisco Conference was one of the few bargaining points the West could exercise in the Polish negotiations.

On March 5, the American Under Secretary of State, Joseph Grew, told the press that neither the London nor the Warsaw government would be invited to San Francisco.[90] On March 9, the Soviet ambassador in Washington asked that this position be reconsidered,[91] but by March 16, Roosevelt had reaffirmed the American view.[92] Once more the Soviet ambassador asked that the decision be changed, but his request was refused.[93] Thereupon Moscow let it be known that Molotov would not attend the United Nations meeting. His place would be taken by Ambassador Gromyko.[94] This move was a direct challenge to Roosevelt's ideal of a United Nations organization.

While it is clear that the Soviet action was related to the exclusion of the Warsaw government, it should be noted that the Russian decision to keep Molotov at home came just after the American decision to exclude Soviet representatives from the Bern talks. Thus, on the same day (March 25) that Roosevelt attempted to explain why the Russians could not come to Bern, he also begged Stalin to allow Molotov to come to San Francisco.[95] Similarly, at the same time that Stalin reiterated his demand for participation in the Bern talks, he reaffirmed the decision not to send Molotov.[96] Suspicions over Bern, the deadlock over Poland, and the fate of the United Nations meeting were now inevitably bound up in the more general problem of a crisis of confidence between the United States and the Soviet Union.

It is not the purpose of this essay to analyze the sources of this crisis. It may be noted, however, that in the last weeks of March a curious reversal of roles took place between Churchill and Roosevelt. Throughout the war, typically, Churchill urged Roosevelt to take a "firm" line with the Russians; the President usually sought to mediate between Churchill and Stalin. This attitude was strikingly evident in his handling of the Polish negotiations in the first half of March. However, with the Bern problem, it was Churchill who suggested that the Russians be allowed to join in the talks; the President took a firm and negative line. Although it is impossible to know the President's motives, it is probable that the new attitude was a result of Roosevelt's failing health and his increasing reliance on State Department and War Department advisers[97]—that is, upon men who had hitherto pressed unsuccessfully for a "firm" approach to the Russians.* Roosevelt was out of Washington for much of this period, and the Bern messages, in fact, were drafted by Admiral Leahy and General Marshall.[98] According to Harry Hopkins, most messages sent over the President's signature at this time were "not his own."[99] But the most striking example of the change of attitude came in a major reversal of American policy on the Polish question.

---

* Churchill claims that Roosevelt's health and strength "faded" earlier in March. He attributes Roosevelt's early opposition to his own firm line to this factor. (*Triumph and Tragedy*, pp. 419, 429.) It seems, however, that the more recognizable Roosevelt attitude—that of mediator and prudent compromiser—is represented in the early view, and that—to use Churchill's phrase—"various hands" drafted the later cables.

ROOSEVELT'S REVERSAL:
THE STALEMATE COMPOUNDED

ON MARCH 16, Roosevelt had minced no words in rejecting Churchill's attempt to get support for Mikolajczyk. ("I cannot believe that Molotov will accept the proposal . . . I am opposed to putting forward such a suggestion at this time, as it would in my view almost certainly leave us in a stalemate.")[100] Two days after these words were written, on March 18, the British ambassador and the State Department were able to get Presidential approval for a new instruction to Moscow.[101] The message (sent on March 19) urged that any Pole suggested by one of the powers be invited to Moscow for consultations! Now Britain and America were united in proposing that Mikolajczyk, an opponent of the Yalta agreement, should participate in consultations based upon that agreement. If we are to follow Roosevelt's earlier judgment, this new instruction would "almost certainly" account for the continued stalemate of the Moscow Commission until the President's death; for, despite Roosevelt's efforts to change his view, Mikolajczyk did not modify his opposition to Yalta.*

Roosevelt's March 19 instruction also took up a number of the minor issues of form and status which had dominated the talks as each side maneuvered for position. He affirmed Churchill's view on three of the remaining four points.†

1. The Warsaw government should not expect an "absolute" right of prior consultation.
2. The Poles consulted in Moscow should determine the composition of the reorganized government, with the Commission acting only in an impartial arbitral capacity.
3. The Soviet government should use its influence to stop the Warsaw government from actions which might prejudice the political situ-

---

* The precise terms of this message are not available. However, this paraphrase occurs in a subsequent message by Churchill: "There ought not to be a veto by one Power on all nominations." Churchill says: "Stalin will find all this set out . . . in our communication of March 19." (*Triumph and Tragedy*, pp. 434–35.) The precise wording is probably the same as that used by the President on March 29, although it is possible that the March 19 message was less definite. (*Ibid.*, p. 745; *Stalin's Correspondence*, II, pp. 210–14; Woodward, *British Foreign Policy*, p. 505; Lane, *I Saw Poland Betrayed*, pp. 59–61; Feis, *Churchill, Roosevelt, Stalin*, pp. 574–75.)

† For the controversy over Point 3, see p. 252.

ation in Poland. The West should attempt to restrain the anti-Russian Poles.

4. The Soviet government should arrange for Western observers to come to Poland.*

As Roosevelt had predicted, on March 23 Molotov refused to accept the view that any Pole suggested by one of the three powers should be invited for consultations. On the main issue the stalemate continued. On the minor points, Molotov offered four "rules" of procedure for the Commission:

1. They should recognize the Warsaw government as the basis for the new government with the inclusion of democratic leaders from Poland and abroad.
2. They should begin consultations in the first instance with the Warsaw government.
3. They should summon for consultation only Poles upon whom all three of the Commission agreed.
4. They should then decide upon other Polish leaders whom they wished to consult.[102]

This message ignored the suggestion that influence be used to halt repressive action and political change in Poland. Molotov also rejected the request that the Russians arrange for Western observers in Poland.[103] Nonetheless, both the American and British ambassadors believed Molotov's proposals might open the way to a resumption of negotiations. The Foreign Office, however, thought the proposals should be rejected out of hand. Eden now recommended a joint Anglo-American message to Stalin. Churchill agreed, and a new message was drafted and sent to Roosevelt for approval on March 27.[104]

Once more the Prime Minister raised the threat of a statement in

---

* As has been noted, the message has not been published. The points must be deduced from available materials. On points 1, 2, and 4, there is no doubt. (See Churchill, *Triumph and Tragedy*, pp. 422–23, 426–29, where negotiations between Roosevelt and Churchill on the wording are printed.) There is some doubt as to the exact wording of Point 3. In a later telegram, Churchill reminded Roosevelt that in the March 19 message they had "asked that the Soviet Government should use their influence with their friends in temporary power there." (*Ibid.*, p. 434.) It appears that this referred to the "truce" idea and not to Churchill's suggestion that the Russians should restrain only the Warsaw government, for on April 1, Churchill and Roosevelt did send a message asking for a "truce." (*Stalin's Correspondence*, II, p. 203.) It is unlikely that the American position, which became increasingly close to Churchill's as Roosevelt's death approached and his subordinates became more active, would have taken the more "firm" line on March 19 and the less "firm" line on April 1. (See also, Churchill, *Triumph and Tragedy*, pp. 424–25, 432; Woodward, *British Foreign Policy*, p. 505.)

Parliament. He then stressed the need for a more direct approach: "I am convinced it is no use trying to argue this any further with Molotov. . . . Is it not the moment now for a message from us both on Poland to Stalin?"[105] Churchill wished to reiterate the March 19 parallel instruction, laying emphasis upon the five points.[106]

Roosevelt, at first following the American and British ambassadors, suggested that Molotov's four rules might be accepted with certain modifications.[107] However the growing crisis of confidence apparently disturbed the President and he replied: "I agree with you however that the time has come to take up directly with Stalin the broader aspects of the Soviet attitude . . ."[108] The President agreed that any Pole might come to Moscow, despite Mikolajczyk's continued opposition to Yalta. He suggested that the Commission select Poles to be invited without allowing Warsaw a right of veto. He would agree to the Warsaw government's coming to Moscow for consultations first, if other invitations were issued before Warsaw arrived. The President proposed that "we should respectively use our influence" to ensure that "dissident groups cease any measures and counter-measures against each other." Finally, he asked that observers be permitted to enter the country. The message was substantially the same as the March 19 instruction. (Admiral Leahy dryly noted: "It does not appear likely that the messages sent today will have any beneficial effect.")[109] Together with a supporting message from Churchill, the President's April 1 message initiated the first exchange over Poland at the heads-of-government level since Yalta.[110]

Stalin's April 7 response came in two parts. He took up the substance of the main question in a reply to Churchill's separate demand that Mikolajczyk come to Moscow. Stalin complained that the Western ambassadors had insisted "on Mikolajczyk being invited to Moscow for consultation, and they do so in the form of an ultimatum, ignoring the fact that Mikolajczyk has openly attacked the Crimea Conference decisions on Poland." However, Stalin proposed a compromise solution: "If you deem it necessary, I shall try to induce the Provisional Polish Government to withdraw its objections to inviting Mikolajczyk, provided he publicly endorses the decisions of the Crimea Conference . . . and declares in favor of establishing friendly relations between Poland and the Soviet Union."[111] As is evident, Stalin's concessions on this key issue indicated substantially the same line of compromise that Roosevelt had been pursuing before March 19.*

Stalin also suggested a series of steps which might "break the deadlock and reach an agreed decision." They concerned the minor issues of status and form, and he urged that

1. The powers affirm that the reconstruction of the Warsaw government implies not abolition, but enlargement.
2. Eight Poles be invited to Moscow, five from Poland, three from London.
3. The Warsaw government be "consulted in all circumstances, that they be consulted in the first place."
4. Only leaders who have supported the Crimea decision be invited to Moscow.
5. Reconstruction should be effected by replacing a number of the present members of the Warsaw government by other Polish leaders.

In a concluding paragraph, Stalin suggested that "the ratio of old and new Ministers . . . might be established more or less on the same lines as was done in the Yugoslav Government." This meant that approximately four out of five Cabinet posts would remain in the hands of the Warsaw government.†[112]

This message was the last in the Polish negotiations before Roosevelt's death, and the divergence among the powers can now be summarized. Stalin's new proposal, as Churchill noted, "offered some hope of progress"; for a way out of the main impasse seemed possible.[113] If Britain and America could bring Mikolajczyk to support the Yalta agreement, Stalin would urge Warsaw to withdraw its objections. A concerted and united effort by the Big Three might turn the trick. After a month of squabbling, the approach originally attempted by Roosevelt seemed to offer promise.

On the minor issues there were still differences of opinion. Stalin's suggestion that he would urge Warsaw to withdraw its objection to Mikolajczyk indicated his view that Warsaw was entitled to veto candidates for the consultations. The Western Powers had argued that no absolute right of veto was permissible. Stalin wanted the Warsaw government to be "consulted in all circumstances," and in "the first

---

* See above, p. 250.   † See above, p. 20.

instance." Again the Western powers opposed an "absolute" right. Stalin asked that only leaders who had supported the Yalta decision be invited to Moscow. In backing Mikolajczyk, however, the West had refused to accept this as a "principle." Finally, Stalin had accepted neither the proposal that each side use influence to prevent hostilities within Poland, nor the proposal that Western observers be admitted to the country. Despite these differences, however, the distance between the positions had narrowed considerably. These relatively minor points could probably be settled if they could agree on the fundamental issues.

Perhaps the most important thing about Stalin's April 7 message, however, was that it showed the Soviet Union believed it was now necessary to come to terms on "fundamental issues." In suggesting the Yugoslav precedent as a basis for reorganization of the Warsaw government, Stalin cut through to the core of the dispute. Here was the issue of power distribution in the new government. The question had previously appeared only indirectly, in the struggle over Mikolajczyk and the minor points of status, but for some time it had been apparent that the Soviet and Western governments had differing views on the crucial question.

The suspicions which arose during the month-long stalemate apparently prompted Stalin to attempt to define the differences and reach agreement. His message contained a charge that the American and British ambassadors "have departed from the instructions of the Crimea Conference." Stalin pointed out that the Big Three had agreed that "the government now functioning in Poland . . . should be the core of a new Government." He complained that the Western ambassadors "ignore the Polish Provisional Government, pay no heed to it, and at best place individuals in Poland and London on a par with the Provisional Government." Stalin served notice that Warsaw had to be recognized as the basis of any reorganization.

That the Russians wanted a commitment on this point had also been apparent from Molotov's March 23 message. Responding to Molotov's suggestion that Warsaw be affirmed as the "basis" of a new government, Roosevelt had declared that Warsaw would play a "prominent role," but insisted that "a thinly disguised continuation of the present Warsaw regime would be unacceptable."[114] This was an extremely vague statement, and Roosevelt died before he was able to answer Stalin's more specific request that the Yugoslav precedent be adopted. However, his advice to Churchill at the end of March gives some indication of his general viewpoint:

> You will recall that agreement on Poland at Yalta was a compromise between the Soviet position that the Lublin government should merely be "enlarged" and our contention that we should start with a clean slate and assist in the formation of an entirely new Polish government. The wording of the resulting agreement reflects this compromise but if we attempt to evade the fact that we placed, as clearly shown in the agreement, somewhat more emphasis on the Lublin Poles than on the other two groups . . . I fear we will expose ourselves to the charge that we are attempting to go back on the Crimea decision.[115]

Although by the end of March each side feared the other was breaking the Yalta agreement, it seems that Roosevelt, like Stalin, believed the most important thing was to bring Churchill back into line with his Yalta commitment. Although the President's general sentiment is shown from this message, it is impossible to know how far he would have gone toward meeting Stalin's proposal at the Yugoslav ratio of four old ministers to each new one.

At Roosevelt's death on April 12 the dispute over Poland was still unresolved. For almost a month (February 23–March 19) the American position had been much closer to the Russian than the British. For a brief period at the end of March, Roosevelt had reversed his earlier stand and committed himself in support of Churchill. Now it appeared that Mikolajczyk might be brought to endorse the Yalta agreement. If so, this would remove the obstacle which impeded further negotiations, but would leave unresolved the major question of power in the reorganized government and a number of minor questions. In a sense, the fundamental issue which had produced the struggle over Mikolajczyk had simply been defined in more explicit terms. Nonetheless, progress had been made, and the British ambassador believed that the latest Soviet offer was a definite sign that Stalin wanted a cooperative solution to the Polish issue.[116] Apparently Roosevelt was equally optimistic, for a few hours before his death he advised Churchill to "minimize the general Soviet problem as much as possible, because these problems, in one form or another, seem to arise every day and most of them straighten out . . . ."[117]

TRUMAN'S POLISH PROBLEM

TRUMAN TOOK OFFICE facing three sets of Polish issues: the role of Mikolajczyk, the group of subsidiary status questions, and the fundamental matter of power distribution. Truman seems to have placed great faith in the advice of the State Department, for within twenty-four hours of his predecessor's death, the new President had agreed to another direct message to Stalin. He immediately endorsed the view that Mikolajczyk had to be invited to Moscow even though the Polish leader still opposed the Yalta decision. The claim to a right of veto over Poles suggested for consultations Truman deemed to be the "real issue."[118] The Prime Minister was highly pleased by Truman's enthusiastic support of the "firm" line, although he thought it "remarkable" that the President "felt able so promptly to commit himself to it."[119]

The draft message Truman endorsed was a response to Stalin's April 7 cable. Truman also accepted the idea that eight Poles be invited to Moscow, five from London, three from Warsaw; he named Mikolajczyk among the group. On the other minor questions, he was prepared to allow the Warsaw government to come to Moscow first, if the other invitations had gone out before the government arrived, and he also wanted the group of Poles to be able to suggest other names for the Moscow consultations. As is evident, on these minor questions the American and Russian positions were almost in agreement. On the remaining matter of substance, however, there was a great difference. Truman refused to take up the ratio of power in the new Cabinet in advance of the Moscow talks, and he specifically rejected the Yugoslav precedent.*[120]

On April 15, Churchill cabled that Mikolajczyk had finally agreed to endorse the Yalta decision. Though his endorsement was qualified, for all practical purposes this eliminated the major stumbling block which had held up consultations for more than a month and a half.[121] (Within a week Mikolajczyk removed the last qualification and pledged full support for the Yalta decision.)[122] Truman and the State

---

* After an exchange with Churchill, the joint message was sent on April 18. (Truman, *Year of Decisions*, pp. 25–26.)

Department were delighted with the news.[123] The "real issue," Truman pointed out to Churchill, was substantially resolved. The question of principle as to whether Warsaw had the theoretical right to veto candidates for consultations was still in dispute, but it was now only a minor quibble, since the point of the argument had disappeared with Mikolajczyk's new stand. Similarly, the questions of status were not matters of great import, and Truman considered that "minor questions" could be readily resolved.[124] However, there remained the substantive question of the power distribution; and, as had become evident shortly before the death of Roosevelt, the Russians now wanted the issue defined and resolved *before* the Moscow consultations began.

Stalin wished to leave no doubt that the Warsaw government was accepted by all the powers as the "core" of the reorganized government. Apparently he was especially adamant about the point, not only because of the signs that the West might be retreating from the Yalta formula,* but also because he gave up a powerful bargaining lever and status symbol just after Roosevelt's death. In a meeting with Stalin, Harriman suggested that it would be regarded as a friendly gesture and a sign that the Soviet Union wished to continue Roosevelt's policy of cooperation if Stalin would reverse his earlier decision and send Molotov to the United Nations.[125] Originally Stalin had refused to send Molotov, because the Warsaw government had not been invited to San Francisco and the absence of a representative from Warsaw would cast doubts on the government's legitimacy. Just after Roosevelt's death, however, Stalin accepted Harriman's suggestion and the Soviet Foreign Minister left for Washington despite the slur caused by the continued exclusion of Warsaw.[126]

Thus, when Truman met Molotov on April 23, the touchy question of the role and status to be accorded the Warsaw government was of increased importance to the Russians. Stalin pressed for a decision on the distribution of power in the new government, offering the Yugoslav precedent as a formula. Since the minor points would be of little consequence if this issue could be resolved, the outcome of the Polish dispute depended upon the view the new President took of Stalin's main proposal. As Admiral Leahy summed it up, this question was "the nub of the issue."[127]

---

* See Roosevelt's comment to Churchill, p. 267.

The Timing of Truman's Decisions and the Origin of the Hopkins Mission

ALTHOUGH AVAILABLE EVIDENCE establishes that Stimson recommended the delay of all disputes with Russia until the atomic bomb had been demonstrated, and that Truman followed this advice, the absence of complete information makes it difficult to pinpoint the exact dates on which the advice was offered and the decision was taken. The substance of the argument does not depend on this point, of course, but it may be useful to attempt to estimate the date from what is known.

The question is: When did Truman first decide to postpone diplomatic disputes until the weapon had been demonstrated? Theoretically the range of possible dates is from April 25 to June 6—*i.e.,* from the date on which Stimson first discussed the atomic bomb in detail with the President to the explicit reference to the decision in the available materials. On the latter date, Stimson's diary records that the Secretary of War reminded Truman "that the greatest complication was what might happen at the meeting of the Big Three" if the bomb had not yet been "laid on." Truman replied that he had "postponed [the meeting] until the 15th of July on purpose to give us more time."[1]

From the June 6 bench mark it is possible to move backward to a much earlier date. On May 16, Stimson's diary shows that he was fully satisfied that Truman had adopted the proper strategy and plans for the timing of the heads-of-government meeting. In the characteristically indirect way he used to discuss the secret project, Stimson wrote to Truman: "I believe that good and not harm would be done by the policy towards your coming meeting which you mentioned to me." Then, using the same words he had used in discussing the bomb in a preceding diary entry, Stimson commented on the reason he was satisfied with the President's policy: "We shall probably hold more cards in our hands later than now."[2]

Moving back one stage: on May 14, at the same time he pointed out to Eden that a delay in the meeting would not be dangerous, since the troop withdrawals from the Continent would be minimal, Stimson also "outlined to him the progress which we have made and the timetable as it stood now, and told him my own feeling as to [the atomic bomb's] bearing upon our present problems of an international character."[3]

The decision to postpone the confrontation with Stalin was taken earlier than this date, however. On May 10, Stimson records that Harriman told him he believed "Russia is . . . going to try to ride roughshod over her neighbors in Europe." In response, Stimson "talked over very confidentially our problem connected with [the atomic bomb] in this matter."[4]

But it was on May 9 that Truman told Churchill he could not meet with Stalin until early July—the time at which Stimson had originally stated the atomic bomb would be available.*[5]

Thus, the crucial decisions were probably taken in the two weeks between Stimson's April 25 talk with Truman and the May 9 message to Churchill. This is also the period of the greatest activity concerned with the establishment of the Interim Committee. During this time Stimson met with Truman on a number of occasions—at least on May 1, 2, 3, 4—to review preparations for a full discussion of the political and diplomatic implications of the new weapon.†

Within the period April 25–May 9 a still better approximation is possible. Almost immediately after meeting with Stimson, the President began to work on the Hopkins and Davies trips, and had summoned Davies by at least the evening of April 29.‡ That these missions were directly at odds with the tough line of policy accepted by Truman on April 23, and that they were opposed by the "firm" advisers, leaves little doubt that they were directly associated with the only line

---

* As is shown in Chapter IV, technical delays caused a second delay of the meeting, and it was also subsequently decided to delay not only until the bomb had been tested, but until it had been "laid on" Japan.

† See above, p. 59.

‡ When Truman met with Davies on the morning of April 30, he said that both he and Hopkins would be making special trips. (Truman, *Year of Decisions*, p. 110.)

of conciliatory strategy offered to the President—*i.e.*, Stimson's strategy of delay. Moreover, Truman's efforts to keep the trips secret from his top advisers strongly suggests the intimate relationship with the top secret atomic project and the discussions with Stimson.

Although as indicated in Chapter III Truman held on to his firm line of policy while he secretly prepared his new approach, all of the evidence suggests that the April 25 meeting was the crucial date on which Truman accepted Stimson's line of advice. This was the meeting the Secretary of War requested because the atomic bomb had "such a bearing on our present foreign relations and such an important effect upon all my thinking in this field that I think you ought to know about it without much further delay." This was also the meeting at which Stimson advised that the bomb would be (in Truman's words) "certain" to have a "decisive" effect on foreign relations. It was the meeting which Truman reports centered "specifically" on "the effect the atomic bomb might likely have on our future foreign relations."[6]

I have shown, in Chapters III and IV, how the decision to postpone a confrontation with Stalin illuminates the Hopkins mission. Once it was decided to wait for the atomic bomb, damage done during the initial showdown had to be repaired; further Soviet *faits accomplis* had to be forestalled, Stalin's suspicions had to be allayed, cooperation had to be re-established in Europe, and measures had to be taken to keep the door open to subsequent American influence. Thus, the new evidence regarding the atomic bomb provides an implicit rejection of other interpretations of the complicated events of the summer of 1945. Nevertheless, it may be useful to review the alternative theories to show that they do not explain even the previously available facts.

Probably because Truman maintained the greatest secrecy about his plans to send Harry Hopkins to Moscow, the literature on the subject is filled with a wide range of speculative, contradictory, and erroneous interpretations of the President's purpose. Broadly speaking, two major and three minor explanations have been offered for Truman's sudden conciliatory efforts after the showdown with Molotov. In order of importance these are:

1. The President thought the tension over European problems might lose Russian help in the war against Japan.

2. The President thought the tension was jeopardizing the San Francisco United Nations Conference.
3. The President sought to reduce tension and to try to get new assurances from Stalin on various Far Eastern matters.
4. The President simply wanted an evaluation of Stalin's attitude.
5. The President, nervous about difficulties with Russia, sent a special mission because he believed the British election would delay a heads-of-government meeting.

The first explanation has been offered by a scholar who has had access to most government materials. Feis has argued that a main reason for Truman's attempt to reduce tensions was: "The American military organization was still eager for Soviet entry in the Pacific War. . . ."*[7]

As I have shown, this explanation cannot be accepted for a number of reasons: (1) The fact is that in late April the military had reached the conclusion that Russian help was no longer needed for an invasion. (It was only two months later that they tentatively revised this judgment on the basis of new estimates of the shock value of a Russian declaration of war.)† (2) Moreover, Truman specifically rejected the military argument for a relaxation of tensions when it was presented to him by Marshall on April 23. There is no evidence that he changed his opinion in the few days before his decision to send Hopkins.‡ In fact, in his tough handling of the Trieste matter in mid-May (as I have shown in Chapter V) he again specifically rejected Marshall's argument. (3) In any case, throughout May the American military entertained few doubts about Stalin's intentions. In fact, the Polish showdown provided the best test of Russian plans, for at the height of the tensions there was every sign that the Red Army would enter the war at an early date. Even from this point of view there was no longer much need for conciliation.§ (4) Finally, if it were true that Truman wished to adopt a conciliatory attitude in order to ensure Soviet help in the war, there was no reason to keep his views from his advisers or from Churchill. Although the great mass of already available documents reveal countless facts of far greater secrecy, in none of the materials is Truman ever shown to offer this seemingly obvious justification for his policy.

---

* Hewlett and Anderson's imprecise argument could also be read as a statement of this view. (*The New World*, p. 351.)

† See above, pp. 118–119.
‡ See above, p. 70.
§ See above, pp. 104–106.

The second explanation has been offered by many scholars. Feis argues that another important reason for the Hopkins mission was: "The Secretary of State, from San Francisco, was advising [Truman] not to engage in acts of pressure or retaliation until the work of that conference was done and a charter written. . . ."[8] Similarly, Sherwood has written: "Less than a week after V-E Day, it seemed that the San Francisco Conference was going on the rocks . . . Harriman and Bohlen were on an airplane flying eastward across the continent with a sense of despair in their hearts. They asked each other whether there was any conceivable way of saving the situation. With considerable hesitancy, Bohlen suggested the possibility that President Truman might send Hopkins to Moscow . . ."[9]

This view must also be rejected: (1) Both Feis and Sherwood have gotten their dates wrong; Truman's decision to send Hopkins came in the last week of April (not the second week of May), at a time when the Secretary of State was reporting that the San Francisco Conference was off to a good start.[10] (2) Aside from the well-known fact that Truman had little respect for Secretary Stettinius (and decided to replace him a few days after taking office), the President did not even consult the Secretary of State about sending Hopkins.[11] (3) Indeed, the only advice he got from the State Department was from Acting Secretary Grew; this came at the last minute and was *against* the Hopkins mission.[12]

The third explanation has not been offered directly. Hewlett and Anderson report that Hopkins's mission was "to arrange a meeting of the Big Three, review the Polish tangle, discuss the future relations of the United States and Russia with China, and learn the approximate date of Soviet entry into the war."[13] Subsequently, however, by concentrating on the discussion of Far Eastern matters, these authors strongly suggest that such problems were the primary reason for the Hopkins mission.[14] Feis also suggests that the "main purpose" of the Hopkins mission was to explore the Russian attitude before fulfilling the Yalta agreement on the Far East.*[15] To set the record straight, it should be noted that Truman decided to send Hopkins to Moscow long before he came to any conclusions about the Far Eastern ques-

---

* Feis clouds this argument. He uses three pages to show that American policy makers considered the possibility of refusing to fulfill the Yalta agreement regarding the Far East. Having established the problem, inexplicably he concludes that "before going

tions. Indeed, the State and War Departments struggled over Far Eastern policy throughout the first half of May, and it was almost three weeks after Truman's decision to send Hopkins to Moscow that the President agreed to *add* the Far Eastern discussions to his primary tasks.*

The fourth view is offered by Truman and Feis. Truman states: "I wanted to be fully informed about the attitudes of Churchill and Stalin . . ."[16] Feis also argues that Hopkins was sent to "ascertain the truth about Soviet intentions."[17] In reality, of course, such general explanations beg the vital question; they ignore the fact that the Hopkins mission was not merely an exploratory venture, but a major reversal of policy which yielded the substance of the most important diplomatic issue in contest between the United States and Russia. To say that Truman only wanted to explore Stalin's attitudes is simply to ignore the fundamental debate over political strategy which resulted in the mission.

The fifth explanation is trivial. Woodward argues that "the possibility of a visit to Moscow by Mr. Hopkins . . . had been talked about vaguely for some time, though the decision had been taken abruptly and had been hastened by the belief that the British general election would delay a three-power meeting."[18] Aside from the fact that there is no evidence to suggest the British election had anything to do with Truman's decision, it hardly need be pointed out that Churchill fairly burned the trans-Atlantic cables begging Truman to hold the meeting at the earliest possible date.† The only merit of this explanation is that it recognizes that the decision to delay a three-power meeting was *the* crucial decision; though Woodward is mistaken in his view of why Truman delayed, he is right to point out that once delay had been decided upon, a mission of conciliation became a logical and political necessity.‡

---

ahead with . . . effectuation," Stalin was to be sounded out on issues *"both in Europe and in the Far East."* (*Between War and Peace*, p. 81.) Even on his own terms, Feis gives no reason to believe that "effectuation" of the *Far Eastern* accord depended upon Stalin's views of *European* issues. Feis apparently means that Hopkins sounded out Stalin on the Far Eastern issues before Truman decided whether to fulfill the Yalta accord. But Far Eastern problems were not the "main purpose" of the mission, and this

fact probably accounts for Feis's unexpected reference to European matters.

* See above, pp. 101–102.

† See above, pp. 66–67, 101.

‡ As will be noted, Feis has offered several different interpretations of the Hopkins mission. In fact, one can find each of the listed explanations (except the last) in his writing. See: *Churchill, Roosevelt, Stalin*, p. 637; *China Tangle*, pp. 308–9; *Between War and Peace*, pp. 81–83.

Stimson's Unsuccessful Attempt to Change the Strategy of Delay Before Leaving Office*

September 11, 1945

DEAR MR. PRESIDENT:

In handing you today my memorandum about our relations with Russia in respect to the atomic bomb, I am not unmindful of the fact that when in Potsdam I talked with you about the question whether we could be safe in sharing the atomic bomb with Russia while she was still a police state and before she put into effect provisions assuring personal rights of liberty to the individual citizen.

I still recognize the difficulty and am still convinced of the ultimate importance of a change in Russian attitude toward individual liberty but I have come to the conclusion that it would not be possible to use our possession of the atomic bomb as a direct lever to produce the change. I have become convinced that any demand by us for an internal change in Russia as a condition of sharing in the atomic weapon would be so resented that it would make the objective we have in view less probable.

I believe that the change in attitude towards the individual in Russia will come slowly and gradually and I am satisfied that we should not delay our approach to Russia in the matter of the atomic bomb until that process has been completed. My reasons are set forth in the memorandum I am handing you today. Furthermore, I believe that this long process of change in Russia is more likely to be expedited by the closer relationship in the matter of the atomic bomb

---

* Taken from Stimson and Bundy, *On Active Service*, pp. 642–46. The emphasis was added by Stimson in 1947. He considered the first italicized passage the heart of the memorandum, and the second the most important point of all. (*Ibid.*, pp. 644–45.)

which I suggest and the trust and confidence that I believe would be inspired by the method of approach which I have outlined.

Faithfully yours,
HENRY L. STIMSON,
Secretary of War

THE PRESIDENT
The White House

MEMORANDUM FOR THE PRESIDENT

11 September 1945

Subject: Proposed Action for Control of Atomic Bombs.

The advent of the atomic bomb has stimulated great military and probably even greater political interest throughout the civilized world. In a world atmosphere already extremely sensitive to power, the introduction of this weapon has profoundly affected political considerations in all sections of the globe.

In many quarters it has been interpreted as a substantial offset to the growth of Russian influence on the continent. We can be certain that the Soviet Government has sensed this tendency and the temptation will be strong for the Soviet political and military leaders to acquire this weapon in the shortest possible time. Britain in effect already has the status of a partner with us in the development of this weapon. Accordingly, unless the Soviets are voluntarily invited into the partnership upon a basis of co-operation and trust, we are going to maintain the Anglo-Saxon bloc over against the Soviet in the possession of this weapon. Such a condition will almost certainly stimulate feverish activity on the part of the Soviet towards the development of this bomb in what will in effect be a secret armament race of a rather desperate character. There is evidence to indicate that such activity may have already commenced.

If we feel, as I assume we must, that civilization demands that someday we shall arrive at a satisfactory international arrangement respecting the control of this new force, the question then is how long we can afford to enjoy our momentary superiority in the hope of achieving our immediate peace council objectives.

Whether Russia gets control of the necessary secrets of production in a minimum of say four years or a maximum of twenty years is not nearly as important to the world and civilization as to make sure that when they do get it they are willing and co-operative partners among the peace-loving nations of the world. It is true if we approach them now, as I would propose, we may be gambling on their good faith and risk their getting into production of bombs a little sooner than they would otherwise.

To put the matter concisely, I consider the problem of our satisfactory relations with Russia as not merely connected with but as virtually dominated by the problem of the atomic bomb. Except for the problem of the control of that bomb, those relations, while vitally important, might not be immediately pressing. The establishment of relations of mutual confidence between her and us could afford to await the slow progress of time. But with the discovery of the bomb, they became immediately emergent. *Those relations may be perhaps irretrievably embittered by the way in which we approach the solution of the bomb with Russia. For if we fail to approach them now and merely continue to negotiate with them, having this weapon rather ostentatiously on our hip, their suspicions and their distrust of our purposes and motives will increase.* It will inspire them to greater efforts in an all-out effort to solve the problem. If the solution is achieved in that spirit, it is much less likely that we will ever get the kind of covenant we may desperately need in the future. This risk is, I believe, greater than the other, inasmuch as our objective must be to get the best kind of international bargain we can—one that has some chance of being kept and saving civilization not for five or for twenty years, but forever.

The chief lesson I have learned in a long life is that the only way you can make a man trustworthy is to trust him; and the surest way to make him untrustworthy is to distrust him and show your distrust.

If the atomic bomb were merely another though more devastating military weapon to be assimilated into our pattern of international relations, it would be one thing. We could then follow the old custom of secrecy and nationalistic military superiority relying on international caution to prescribe the future use of the weapon as we did with gas. But I think the bomb instead constitutes merely a first step in a new control by man over the forces of nature too revolutionary and dangerous to fit into the old concepts. I think it really caps the climax of the race between man's growing technical power for destructiveness and his psychological power of self-control and group control—his moral power. If so, our method of approach to the Russians is a question of the most vital importance in the evolution of human progress.

Since the crux of the problem is Russia, any contemplated action leading to the control of this weapon should be primarily directed *to* Russia. It is my judgment that the Soviet would be more apt to respond sincerely to a direct and forthright approach made by the United States on this subject than would be the case if the approach were made as a part of a general international scheme, or if the approach were made after a succession of express or implied threats or near threats in our peace negotiations.

My idea of an approach to the Soviets would be a direct proposal after discussion with the British that we would be prepared in effect to enter an arrangement with the Russians, the general purpose of which would be to control and limit the use of the atomic bomb as an instrument of war and so far as possible to direct and encourage the development of atomic power for peaceful and humanitarian purposes. Such an approach might more specifically lead to the proposal that we would stop work on the further improvement in, or manufacture of, the bomb as a military weapon, provided the Russians and the British would agree to do likewise. It might also provide that we would be willing to impound what bombs we now have in the United States provided the Russians and the British would agree with us that in no event will they or we use a bomb as an instrument of war unless all three Governments agree to that use. We might also consider including in the arrangement a covenant with the U.K. and the Soviets providing for the exchange of benefits of future developments whereby atomic energy may be applied on a mutually satisfactory basis for commercial or humanitarian purposes.

I would make such an approach just as soon as our immediate political considerations make it appropriate.

I emphasize perhaps beyond all other considerations the importance of taking this action with Russia as a proposal of the United States— backed by Great Britain but peculiarly the proposal of the United States. Action of any international group of nations, including many small nations who have not demonstrated their potential power or responsibility in this war would not, in my opinion, be taken seriously by the Soviets. The loose debates which would surround such proposal, if put before a conference of nations, would provoke but scant favor from the Soviet. As I say, I think this is the most important point in the program.

After the nations which have won this war have agreed to it, there will be ample time to introduce France and China into the covenants and finally to incorporate the agreement into the scheme of the United Nations. The use of this bomb has been accepted by the world as the result of the initiative and productive capacity of the United States, and I think this factor is a most potent lever towards having our proposals accepted by the Soviets, whereas I am most skeptical of obtaining any tangible results by way of any international debate. I urge this method as the most realistic means of accomplishing this vitally important step in the history of the world.

HENRY L. STIMSON,
Secretary of War

Main Sources

GOVERNMENT PUBLICATIONS

Cline, R. S., *Washington Command Post: The Operations Division* (Vol. II of *The War Department* in the series *The United States Army in World War II*), Office of the Chief of Military History, U.S. Department of the Army, Washington, 1951.

Ehrman, J., *Grand Strategy, October 1944–August 1945* (Vol. VI of *History of the Second World War,* United Kingdom Series), London, 1956.

Great Britain. *Parliamentary Debates* (5th series). (Commons) Vol. 413. (1945) [Hansard].

Greenfield, K. R., ed., *Command Decisions,* U.S. Department of the Army, Washington, D.C., 1960.

U.S. Atomic Energy Commission, *In the Matter of J. Robert Oppenheimer. Transcript of Hearing before Personnel Security Board.* April 12–May 6, 1954.

U.S. Department of State. *Foreign Relations: Conference of Berlin (Potsdam) 1945,* 2 vols., U.S. Government Printing Office, 1960.

U.S. Department of State. *Foreign Relations of the United States: The Conferences at Malta and Yalta 1945.* U.S. Government Printing Office, 1955.

U.S. Department of State. *Postwar Foreign Policy Preparation: 1939–45.* U.S. Government Printing Office, 1950.

U.S. Department of State. *United States Relations with China 1944–49.* U.S. Government Printing Office, 1949.

U.S. House of Representatives, Committee on Banking and Currency. *Hearings: Export-Import Bank Act of 1945.* July 11, 12, 1945.

U.S. House of Representatives, Committee on Military Affairs. *Hearings: Atomic Energy Act.* October 9, 18, 1945.

U.S. House of Representatives, Committee on Military Affairs. *Hearings: The Demobilization of the Army of the United States.* August 28, 1945.

U.S. House of Representatives, Select Committee on Postwar Military Policy. *Hearings: Universal Military Training.* June 1945.

U.S. Senate, Committee on Appropriations. *Hearings: Wedemeyer Report.* December 17, 1947.

U.S. Senate, Committees on Armed Services and Foreign Relations. *Hearings: Military Situation in the Far East.* May, June 1951.

U.S. Senate, Committee on Banking and Currency. *Hearings: Export-Import Bank Act of 1945.* July 17, 18, 1945.

U.S. Senate, Committee on Foreign Relations. *A Decade of American Foreign Policy.* Document 123. 81st Cong., 1st Sess., 1950.

U.S. Senate, Committee on Military Affairs. *Hearings: Demobilization of the Armed Forces.* September 12, 13, 17, 18, 1945.

U.S. Senate, Special Committee on Atomic Energy. *Hearings: Atomic Energy Act of 1945*. January 1946.
United States Strategic Bombing Survey. *Japan's Struggle to End the War*. July 1, 1946.

BOOKS

Acheson, D., *Power and Diplomacy*, Cambridge, 1958.
Allen, H. C., *Great Britain and the United States*, London, 1954; New York, 1955.
Alsop, J. and S., *We Accuse! The Story of the Miscarriage of Justice in the Case of J. Robert Oppenheimer*, New York, 1954; London, 1955.
Amrine, M., *The Great Decision*, New York, 1959; London, 1960.
Anders, W., *An Army In Exile*, London, 1949.
Arnold, H. H., *Global Mission*, New York, 1949.
Ausubel, N., ed., *Voices of History, 1945–46*, New York, 1946.
Baldwin, H., *The Great Arms Race*, New York, 1958; London, 1959.
———, *Great Mistakes of the War*, New York, London, 1950.
Balfour, M., *Four-Power Control in Germany and Austria, 1945–46*, Royal Institute of International Affairs, *Survey of International Affairs, 1939–46*, London, 1956.
Barnet, R. J., *Who Wants Disarmament?*, New York, 1960.
Batchelder, R. C., *The Irreversible Decision*, Boston, 1962.
Bechhoefer, B. G., *Postwar Negotiations for Arms Control*, Washington, The Brookings Institution, 1961.
Bell, C., *Negotiation from Strength*, London, 1962.
Beloff, M., *Soviet Policy in the Far East* (issued under the auspices of the Royal Institute of International Affairs), London, 1953.
Betts, R. R., ed., *Central and South East Europe, 1945–48* (Royal Institute of International Affairs), Liverpool, 1950.
Blackett, P. M. S., *Atomic Weapons and East-West Relations*, Cambridge, 1956.
———, *Military and Political Consequences of Atomic Energy*, London, 1948.
———, *Studies of War*, Edinburgh and London, 1962.
Bradley, O. N., *A Soldier's Story*, New York, London, 1951.
Bryant, A., *Triumph in the West, 1943–46* (Based on diaries and autobiographical notes of Field Marshal Viscount Alanbrooke), London, 1959.
Brzezinski, Z. K., *The Soviet Bloc: Unity and Conflict*, Cambridge, 1960; New York, 1961.
Bundy, McG., ed., *The Pattern of Responsibility*, Boston, 1952.
Bush, V., *Modern Arms and Free Men*, Kingswood, 1950.
Butcher, H. C., *My Three Years with Eisenhower*, New York, London, 1946.
Butow, R. J. C., *Japan's Decision to Surrender*, Stanford, 1954; London, 1957.
Byrnes, J. F., *All in One Lifetime*, New York, 1958.
———, *Speaking Frankly*, New York, 1947.
Carr, E. H., *The Conditions of Peace*, London, 1945.
Churchill, W. S., *The Second World War*, Vol. VI, *Triumph and Tragedy*, Boston, 1953.

Ciechanowski, J., *Defeat in Victory*, New York, 1947.

Clark, M., *Calculated Risk*, New York, 1950.

Clark, R. W., *The Birth of the Bomb*, New York, 1961.

Clay, L. D., *Decision in Germany*, New York, London, 1950.

Compton, A. H., *Atomic Quest*, New York, 1956.

Connally, T., *My Name Is Tom Connally*, New York, 1954.

Craven, W. L., and Cate, J. L., eds., *The Army Air Forces in World War II*, Vol. V, *The Pacific: Matterhorn to Nagasaki, June 1944 to August 1945*, Chicago, 1953.

Current, R. N., *Secretary Stimson*, New Brunswick, 1954.

Dallin, A., *Soviet Conduct in World Affairs*, New York, 1960.

Daniels, J., *The Man of Independence*, Philadelphia, 1950; London, 1951.

Deane, J. R., *The Strange Alliance*, New York, 1947.

De Gaulle, C., *War Memoirs*, Vol. III, *Salvation*, New York and London, 1960.

Dennett, R., and Johnson, J. E., eds., *Negotiating with the Russians*, Boston, 1951.

Deutscher, I., *The Great Contest*, London, 1960.

———, *Russia: What Next?* New York, 1950.

———, *Stalin, A Political Biography*, New York, London, 1949.

Dewar, M., *Soviet Trade with Eastern Europe, 1945–49*, London, New York, 1951.

Dinnerstein, H. S., *War and the Soviet Union*, New York, 1959.

Djilas, M., *Conversations with Stalin*, Hammondsworth, 1963.

———, *The New Class*, New York, 1957.

Dulles, J. F., *War or Peace*, New York, London, 1950.

Eisenhower, D. D., *Crusade in Europe*, New York, 1948.

———, *The White House Years: Mandate for Change, 1953–56*, New York, 1963.

Feis, H., *Between War and Peace*, Princeton, 1960.

———, *The China Tangle*, Princeton, 1953.

———, *Churchill, Roosevelt, Stalin*, Princeton, 1957.

———, *Japan Subdued*, Princeton, 1961.

Finletter, T. K., *Power and Policy: U.S. Foreign Policy and Military Power in the Hydrogen Age*, New York, 1954.

Fleming, D. F., *The Cold War and Its Origins*, 2 vols., Garden City, 1961.

Forrestal, J. V., *The Forrestal Diaries*, W. Millis, ed., New York, 1951; London, 1952.

Frankel, J., *The Making of Foreign Policy*, London, 1963.

Freund, G., *Germany Between Two Worlds*, New York, 1961.

Garthoff, R. L., *The Soviet Image of a Future War*, Washington, 1959.

———, *Soviet Strategy in the Nuclear Age*, New York, 1958.

Goldwin, R., ed., *Readings in Russian Foreign Policy*, New York, 1959.

Gowing, M., *Britain and Atomic Energy*, Glasgow, 1964.

Grew, J. C., *Turbulent Era*, Vol. II, Boston, 1952.

Groves, L. R., *Now It Can Be Told: The Story of the Manhattan Project*, New York, 1962.

Harriman, W. A., *Peace with Russia?*, New York, 1959; London, 1960.

Hewlett, R. G., and Anderson, O. E., Jr., *The New World, 1939–46*, Vol. I, *A History of the United States Atomic Energy Commission*, University Park, 1962.

Hillman, W., *Mr. President*, New York, 1952.

Hull, C., *Memoirs*, Vol. II, New York, 1948.

Irving, D., *The Destruction of Dresden*, London, 1963.

Ismay, H., *The Memoirs of Lord Ismay*, London, 1960.

Jones, F. C., Borton, H., and Pearn, B. R., *The Far East, 1942–46*, Royal Institute of International Affairs, *Survey of International Affairs, 1939–46*, London, 1955.

Jones, J. M., *The Fifteen Weeks*, New York, 1955.

Jungt, R., *Brighter than a Thousand Suns*, New York, 1958.

Kase, T., *Eclipse of the Rising Sun*, London, 1951.

——, *Journey to the Missouri*, New Haven, 1950.

Kaufmann, W. W., ed., *Military Policy and National Security*, Princeton, 1956.

Kennan, G. F., *American Diplomacy, 1900–1950*, Chicago, 1951.

——, *Russia, the Atom, and the West*, London, 1958.

——, *Russia and the West Under Lenin and Stalin*, Boston, 1960.

Kertesz, S., ed., *The Fate of East-Central Europe: Hopes and Failures of American Foreign Policy* (University Committee on International Relations, International Studies), Notre Dame, 1956.

Keynes, J. M., *The General Theory of Employment, Interest and Money*, London, 1957.

King, E. J., and Whitehill, W. M., *Fleet Admiral King*, New York, 1952; London, 1953.

Kissenger, H. A., *The Necessity for Choice*, New York, 1961.

——, *Nuclear Weapons and Foreign Policy*, New York, 1957.

Knebel, F., and Bailey, C. W., II, *No High Ground*, New York, 1960.

Korbonski, S., *Warsaw in Chains*, London, 1959.

Lane, A. B., *I Saw Poland Betrayed*, Indianapolis, 1948. (Also published as *I Saw Freedom Betrayed*, London, 1949.)

Leahy, W. D., *I Was There*, New York, 1950.

Lee, A. G., *Crown against Sickle: The Story of King Michael of Rumania*, London, no date.

Leonhard, W., *Child of the Revolution*, Chicago, 1958.

Lippmann, W., *The Cold War: A Study in U.S. Foreign Policy*, New York, 1947.

Lukacs, J. A., *The Great Powers and Eastern Europe*, New York, 1953.

——, *History of the Cold War*, New York, 1961.

Mackintosh, J. M., *Strategy and Tactics of Soviet Foreign Policy*, London, 1962.

McCloy, J. J., *The Challenge to American Foreign Policy*, Cambridge, 1953.

McInnis, E., Hiscocks, R., Spencer, R., *The Shaping of Postwar Germany*, London, 1960.

McNeill, W. H., *America, Britain and Russia, 1941–46*, Royal Institute of International Affairs, *Survey of International Affairs, 1939–46*, London, 1953.

Mikolajczyk, S., *The Pattern of Soviet Domination*, London, 1948. (Also published as *The Rape of Poland*, New York, 1948.)

Millis, W., *Arms and the State*, New York, 1958.

Mills, C. W., *The Causes of World War III*, New York, 1959.

Moore, H. L., *Soviet Far Eastern Policy, 1941–45*, Princeton, 1948.

Morgenthau, H. J., *In Defense of the National Interest*, New York, 1951.

Morison, S. E., *Turmoil and Tradition*, Boston, 1960.

Morray, J. P., *From Yalta to Disarmament*, New York, 1961.

Murphy, R., *Diplomat Among Warriors*, New York, 1964.

Nettl, J. P., *The Eastern Zone and Soviet Policy in Germany, 1945–50*, London, 1951.

Nogee, J. L., *Soviet Policy Towards International Control of Atomic Energy*, Notre Dame, 1961.

Oppenheimer, J. R., *Science and the Common Understanding*, New York, London, 1954.

Patton, G. S., *War As I Knew It*, Boston, 1947; London, 1948.

Penrose, E. F., *Economic Planning for the Peace*, Princeton, 1953.

Ratchford, B. U., and Ross, W. D., *Berlin Reparations Assignment*, Chapel Hill, 1947.

Reitzel, W., Kaplan, M. A., and Coblenz, C. G., *United States Foreign Policy, 1945–55*, Washington, 1956.

Ridgway, M. B., *Soldier*, New York, 1956.

Roberts, H. L., *Rumania: Political Problems of an Agrarian State*, New Haven, 1951.

———, *Russia and America*, New York, 1956.

Rogow, A. A., *James Forrestal*, New York, 1964.

Roosevelt, E., *As He Saw It*, New York, 1946.

Roosevelt, F. D., *Victory and the Threshold of Peace: The Collected Papers of Franklin D. Roosevelt, 1944–45*, Compiled by S. I. Rosenman, New York, 1950.

Rothstein, A., ed., *Soviet Foreign Policy During the Patriotic War*, Vol. II, London, 1946.

Rozek, E. J., *Allied Wartime Diplomacy: A Pattern in Poland*, London, New York, 1958.

Seton-Watson, H., *The East European Revolution*, New York, 1961.

Sherwood, R. E., *Roosevelt and Hopkins: An Intimate History*, New York, 1950.

Slusser, R., ed., *Soviet Economic Policy in Postwar Germany*, New York, 1953.

Smith, W. B., *My Three Years in Moscow*, New York, 1950.

Snow, E., *Journey to the Beginning*, New York, 1959.

Stalin, J., *Stalin's Correspondence with Churchill, Attlee, Roosevelt and Truman, 1941–45*, Moscow, 1957.

Stettinius, E. R., Jr., *Roosevelt and the Russians*, New York, 1949.

Stillman, E., and Pfaff, W., *The New Politics: America and the End of the Postwar World*, New York, London, 1961.

Stimson, H. L., and Bundy, McG., *On Active Service in Peace and War*, New York, 1948.

Strang, W., *Home and Abroad*, London, 1956.

Strauss, L. L., *Men and Decisions*, New York, 1962.

Togo, S., *The Cause of Japan*, New York, 1956.

Toynbee, A. J., *The World and the West*, London, 1953.

Truman, H. S., *Mr. Citizen*, New York, 1960; London, 1961.

———, *Public Papers of the Presidents of the United States, April 12 to December 31, 1945*, Washington, 1961.

———, *Truman Speaks*, New York, 1960.

———, *Memoirs*, Vol. I, *Year of Decisions*, New York, 1955.

———, *Memoirs*, Vol. II, *Years of Trial and Hope*, New York, 1956.

Vandenberg, A. H., *The Private Papers of Senator Vandenberg*, A. H. Vandenberg, Jr., ed., Boston, London, 1952.

Warburg, J. P., *Germany, Key to Peace*, Cambridge, 1953; London, 1954.

Waskow, A. I., *The Limits of Defense*, New York, 1962.

Wedemeyer, A. C., *Wedemeyer Reports!*, New York, 1958.

Wheeler-Bennett, J. W., *John Anderson*, London, 1962.

Williams, F., *A Prime Minister Remembers*, London, 1961.

Williams, W. A., *The Tragedy of American Diplomacy*, New York, 1962.

———, *American-Russian Relations, 1781–1947*, New York, 1952.

Wilmot, C., *The Struggle for Europe*, London, 1963.

Wilson, Lord, *Eight Years Overseas*, London, 1948; New York, 1950.

Wolff, R. L., *The Balkans in Our Time*, Cambridge, 1950.

Woodward, L., *British Foreign Policy in the Second World War: History of the Second World War*, London, 1962.

Zacharias, E. M., *Secret Missions*, New York, 1946.

ARTICLES AND PERIODICALS

"The Atom and World Politics," University of Chicago *Roundtable*, No. 393, Sept. 30, 1945.

Attlee, C., "The Hiroshima Choice," *The Observer*, Sept. 6, 1959.

Black, C. E., "Soviet Policy in Eastern Europe," *Annals of the American Academy*, May 1949.

Brodie, D., "Atom Bomb as Policy Maker," *Foreign Affairs*, October 1948.

Brogan, D. W., "The Illusion of American Omnipotence," *Harper's* Magazine, December 1952.

Bundy, H. H., "Remembered Words," *The Atlantic*, March 1957.

Byrnes, J. F., "Actions Speak Louder than Words," *Vital Speeches*, April 1, 1948.

———, "Did 'Big 3' Give Russia Too Much?", *U.S. News and World Report*, Sept. 10, 1948.

Compton, A. H., "Hiroshima Revisited," *Science*, Vol. 134 (1961), pp. 1231–33.

Condon, E., Letter, *Science*, Dec. 4, 1959.

Cousins, N., and Finletter, T. K., "A Beginning for Sanity," *Saturday Review of Literature*, June 15, 1946.

Feis, H., "Diplomacy of the Dollar—1947," *The Atlantic*, January 1947.

———, Letter, *Science*, Dec. 4, 1959.

Franck, J., "A Report to the Secretary of War," *Bulletin of the Atomic Scientists,* May 1946.

Groom, A. J. R., "U.S.–Allied Relations and the Atomic Bomb in the Second World War," *World Politics,* October 1962.

Groves, L. R., Letter, *Science,* Dec. 4, 1959.

Haskins, C. P., "Atomic Energy and American Foreign Policy," *Foreign Affairs,* July 1946.

"If It Didn't Work?" *Newsweek,* April 17, 1961.

"Ike On Ike," *Newsweek,* Nov. 11, 1963.

Kawai, K., "Mokusatsu, Japan's Response to the Potsdam Declaration," *The Pacific Historical Review,* November 1950.

Knebel, F., and Bailey, C. W., "The Fight Over the A-Bomb," *Look,* Aug. 13, 1963.

Morgenthau, H. J., "The End of an Illusion," *Commentary,* November 1961.

Morison, S. E., "Why Japan Surrendered," *The Atlantic,* October 1960.

Mosely, P. E., "Dismemberment of Germany," *Foreign Affairs,* April 1950.

———, "Soviet-American Relations since the War," *Annals of the American Academy,* May 1949.

———, "The Occupation of Germany," *Foreign Affairs,* July 1950.

Oppenheimer, J. R., Letter, *Science,* Dec. 4, 1959.

———, "Niels Bohr and Atomic Weapons," *The New York Review of Books,* December 17, 1964.

Schoenfeld, H. F. A., "Soviet Imperialism in Hungary," *Foreign Affairs,* April 1948.

Smith, A., "Behind the Decision to Use the Atomic Bomb," *Bulletin of the Atomic Scientists,* October 1958.

Stimson, H. L., "The Decision to Use the Atomic Bomb," *Harper's* Magazine, February 1947.

Sutherland, J. P., "The Story Gen. Marshall Told Me," *U.S. News & World Report,* Nov. 2, 1959.

Szilard, L., "A Personal History of the Atomic Bomb," University of Chicago *Roundtable,* No. 601, Sept. 25, 1949, pp. 14–15.

Truman, H. S., Letter, *The Atlantic,* February 1947.

"Was A-Bomb on Japan a Mistake?" *U.S. News & World Report,* Aug. 15, 1960.

UNPUBLISHED MATERIAL

Grew, J. C., Papers, Houghton Library, Harvard University, Cambridge, Mass.

Hammond, P. Y., "Directives for the Occupation of Germany: The Washington Story," Twentieth Century Fund Study of Civil-Military Relations. (Typewritten.)

Kaplan, M. A., "Studies in State-Craft," University of Chicago. (Undated, mimeographed.)

Leahy, W. D., Diary (1945), Library of Congress, Washington.

Morgan, H. G., "Planning the Defeat of Japan: A Study of Total War Strategy," Office of the Chief of Military History, Department of the Army. (Mimeographed.)

Stimson, H. L., Diary, Yale University Library, New Haven.

U.S. Department of Defense, "The Entry of the Soviet Union into the War against Japan: Military Plans, 1941–45," Washington, September 1955. (Mimeographed.)

References

PREFACE (*pp. 11–15*)

1. Truman, *Year of Decisions*, p. 85.
2. *Ibid.*, pp. 85, 87.
3. Stimson Diary, May 16, 1945.
4. Feis, *Churchill, Roosevelt, Stalin*, pp. 599–600.
5. Byrnes, *All In One Lifetime*, p. 389.
6. Byrnes, *Speaking Frankly*, p. 104.
7. Feis, *Between War and Peace*, p. 180.
8. Stimson Diary, July 21, 1945.
9. Truman, *Year of Decisions*, p. 87.
10. Snow, *Journey*, p. 357.
11. Stimson, *On Active Service*, p. 644.
12. Truman, *Truman Speaks*, p. 67.
13. *Newsweek*, November 11, 1963, p. 107.
14. Keynes, *The General Theory*, p. viii.

CHAPTER I (*pp. 19–40*)

1. Leahy, *I Was There*, p. 352.
2. Woodward, *British Foreign Policy*, pp. xxxix, 519.
3. *Stalin's Correspondence*, I, p. 244; II, pp. 188–89.
4. *Conference of Berlin*, II, p. 1579.
5. Leahy, *I Was There*, p. 352.
6. Churchill, *Triumph and Tragedy*, p. 486.
7. *Stalin's Correspondence*, II, pp. 215–17.
8. Leahy, *I Was There*, pp. 315–16.
9. Feis, *Churchill, Roosevelt, Stalin*, p. 575.
10. Stettinius, *Roosevelt and the Russians*, p. 302.
11. Truman, *Year of Decisions*, p. 76.
12. *Ibid.*, pp. 70–72.
13. *Ibid.*, p. 70.
14. *Ibid.*, p. 71.
15. Forrestal, *Diaries*, p. 40.
16. Truman, *Year of Decisions*, p. 71.
17. Feis, *Churchill, Roosevelt, Stalin*, p. 598.
18. Forrestal, *Diaries*, p. 41; Truman, *Year of Decisions*, p. 15; *Conferences at Malta and Yalta*, pp. 310–12, 319, 323, 610.
19. Truman, *Year of Decisions*, p. 70.
20. *Ibid.*, p. 71.
21. *Ibid.*, p. 321.
22. *Ibid.*, p. 17.
23. Stimson Diary, May 10, 1945.
24. Forrestal, *Diaries*, p. 41; Vandenberg, *Papers*, p. 176; Grew memorandum of conversation, May 11–12, 1945.
25. Leahy, *I Was There*, p. 351; Leahy Diary, April 19, 1945.
26. Forrestal, *Diaries*, pp. 47–49.
27. Deane, *The Strange Alliance*, p. 9; Woodward, *British Foreign Policy*, p. xxxvi.
28. Byrnes, *Speaking Frankly*, p. 23.
29. Ehrman, *Grand Strategy*, p. 149.
30. Grew, *Turbulent Era*, II, p. 1485*fn.*
31. *Ibid.*, p. 1446.
32. *Ibid.*, p. 1485*fn.*
33. Stimson Diary, April 3, 1945.
34. Forrestal, *Diaries*, p. 51; Truman, *Year of Decisions*, p. 78.
35. Truman, *Year of Decisions*, p. 78.
36. Forrestal, *Diaries*, p. 50.
37. Truman, *Year of Decisions*, p. 78.
38. Leahy, *I Was There*, p. 351.
39. Stimson Diary, April 23, 1945.
40. Truman, *Year of Decisions*, p. 50.
41. *Ibid*, pp. 70–71.
42. *Ibid.*, p. 71.
43. *Ibid.*, p. 72; Woodward, *British Foreign Policy*, p. 509.
44. Forrestal, *Diaries*, p. 50.
45. *New York Times*, June 24, 1941.
46. Deane, *The Strange Alliance*, p. 265.
47. *Ibid.*, p. 262.
48. *Ibid.*, pp. 84–86, 98.
49. *Ibid.*, pp. 84–86.
50. Stimson Diary, April 23, 1945; Forrestal, *Diaries*, p. 40.
51. Deane, *The Strange Alliance*, p. 84.
52. *Ibid.*, p. 85.
53. *Ibid.*, pp. 85–86.
54. *Ibid.*, pp. 264–66.
55. *Ibid.*, p. 265; Feis, *Churchill, Roosevelt, Stalin*, pp. 599–600.
56. Deane, *The Strange Alliance*, pp. 261–65.

57. *Ibid.*, p. 263.
58. *Ibid.*, p. 265.
59. *Ibid.*, Department of Defense, "Entry of the Soviet Union into the War against Japan," pp. 60–61.
60. Deane, *The Strange Alliance*, p. 265.
61. Department of Defense, "Entry of the Soviet Union into the War against Japan," p. 61.
62. *Ibid.*, p. 50.
63. *Ibid.*, p. 67.
64. *Ibid.*
65. *Ibid.*, p. 68.
66. Deane, *The Strange Alliance*, p. 265.
67. Truman, *Year of Decisions*, p. 79.
68. *Ibid.*
69. Leahy, *I Was There*, p. 351.
70. Truman, *Year of Decisions*, p. 79.
71. *Ibid.*, p. 80.
72. Stettinius, *Roosevelt and the Russians*, p. 302.
73. Truman, *Year of Decisions*, p. 82.
74. *Ibid.*
75. *Ibid.*, pp. 80–82.
76. Leahy, *I Was There*, p. 352.
77. *Ibid.*, p. 413.
78. Leahy Diary, April 23, 1945, p. 63.
79. *Stalin's Correspondence*, II, pp. 219–20; Woodward, *British Foreign Policy*, p. 509.
80. Vandenberg, *Papers*, p. 176.
81. Truman, *Year of Decisions*, p. 109.
82. Feis, *Between War and Peace*, p. 223.
83. *Conference of Berlin*, II, p. 1580.
84. Woodward, *British Foreign Policy*, p. 511.
85. *Ibid.*
86. Truman, *Year of Decisions*, p. 24; Churchill, *Triumph and Tragedy*, pp. 424–26.
87. Lane, *I Saw Poland Betrayed*, p. 67; Woodward, *British Foreign Policy*, pp. 511–12.
88. Truman, *Year of Decisions*, p. 109.
89. *Ibid.*; Feis, *Between War and Peace*, p. 89; *Stalin's Correspondence*, II, pp. 228–29.
90. Grew memorandum of conversation, May 7, 1945; Truman, *Year of Decisions*, p. 255.
91. Forrestal, *Diaries*, p. 41.
92. Deane, *The Strange Alliance*, p. 98.
93. Leahy, *I Was There*, p. 351.
94. Deane, *The Strange Alliance*, pp. 84–86, 98.
95. Forrestal, *Diaries*, p. 41; *New York Times*, July 18, 1945; *Conference of Berlin*, I, p. 181.
96. Deane, *The Strange Alliance*, p. 86.
97. Grew memorandum of conversation, May 11, May 11–12, 1945; Leahy, *I Was There*, p. 351; Feis, *Between War and Peace*, p. 28; Stimson Diary, May 11, 1945.
98. Feis, *Between War and Peace*, pp. 27–28; Truman, *Year of Decisions*, p. 228.
99. Truman, *Year of Decisions*, p. 228.
100. Feis, *Between War and Peace*, pp. 28, 329.
101. Truman, *Year of Decisions*, p. 228.
102. Forrestal, *Diaries*, p. 41.
103. Grew memorandum of conversation, May 11, 1945.
104. Stimson Diary, May 11, 1945.
105. *Ibid.*, May 14, 1945.
106. Grew memorandum of conversation, May 11, 1945.
107. *Ibid.*
108. Truman, *Year of Decisions*, p. 228.
109. Feis, *Between War and Peace*, p. 331; *Conference of Berlin*, II, p. 341.
110. *Stalin's Correspondence*, II, p. 232.
111. Leahy, *I Was There*, p. 367.
112. *Conference of Berlin*, I, p. 13.
113. Churchill, *Triumph and Tragedy*, pp. 491–92.
114. *Ibid.*
115. *Ibid.*, pp. 456–57. Emphasis in original.
116. *Conference of Berlin*, I, pp. 5–9.
117. Churchill, *Triumph and Tragedy*, p. 503.
118. *Conference of Berlin*, I, p. 11.

CHAPTER II (*pp. 41–61*)

1. *Conference of Berlin*, I, p. 597.
2. Wilmot, *The Struggle for Europe*, pp. 798–800.
3. Feis, *Churchill, Roosevelt, Stalin*, pp. 633–34; Churchill, *Triumph and Tragedy*, p. 512.
4. Churchill, *Triumph and Tragedy*, pp. 511–12.
5. *Ibid.*, pp. 512–13.
6. *Ibid.*, p. 503; *Conference of Berlin*, I, p. 165.
7. Churchill, *Triumph and Tragedy*, p. 513.
8. Ehrman, *Grand Strategy*, pp. 152–53.
9. Churchill, *Triumph and Tragedy*, p. 513.
10. *Ibid.*, pp. 514–15.
11. Truman, *Year of Decisions*, p. 62.

12. Feis, *Between War and Peace*, p. 74; Feis, *Churchill, Roosevelt, Stalin*, p. 609.
13. Mosely, "The Occupation of Germany," p. 602.
14. Ehrman, *Grand Strategy*, p. 153.
15. Churchill, *Triumph and Tragedy*, p. 516; Truman, *Year of Decisions*, p. 214.
16. Truman, *Year of Decisions*, p. 215.
17. *Ibid.*
18. *Ibid.*, p. 217.
19. Bryant, *Triumph in the West*, p. 469.
20. Eisenhower, *Crusade in Europe*, p. 474.
21. Feis, *Churchill, Roosevelt, Stalin*, p. 623–24.
22. *Ibid.*, p. 624–25.
23. *Conference of Berlin*, I, p. 334.
24. *Ibid.*, pp. 334–35; Truman, *Year of Decisions*, p. 218.
25. Truman, *Year of Decisions*, p. 217; Feis, *Churchill, Roosevelt, Stalin*, pp. 623–25; Feis, *Between War and Peace*, p. 67.
26. Truman, *Year of Decisions*, p. 218; Churchill, *Triumph and Tragedy*, p. 519.
27. Churchill, *Triumph and Tragedy*, p. 502.
28. Truman, *Year of Decisions*, p. 218; *Conference of Berlin*, I, pp. 3–4.
29. *Conference of Berlin*, I, p. 4.
30. *Ibid.*, p. 5.
31. *Ibid.*, p. 9; Churchill, *Triumph and Tragedy*, p. 574.
32. Mosely, "Dismemberment of Germany," p. 497; Nettl, *The Eastern Zone and Soviet Policy in Germany*, p. 41; Smith, *My Three Years in Moscow*, p. 20; Leahy, *I Was There*, p. 363.
33. Feis, *Between War and Peace*, pp. 76–77.
34. *Ibid.*
35. Truman, *Year of Decisions*, p. 77.
36. See Stimson, *On Active Service.*
37. *Ibid.*, p. 604.
38. Truman, *Year of Decisions*, p. 78.
39. Forrestal, *Diaries*, p. 49.
40. Stimson Diary, April 23, 1945.
41. *Ibid.*, April 16, 1945.
42. *Ibid.*, April 26, 1945.
43. *Ibid.*
44. Truman, *Year of Decisions*, pp. 78–79; Forrestal, *Diaries*, p. 49.
45. Stimson Diary, April 23, 1945.
46. Truman, *Year of Decisions*, p. 79.
47. Stimson Diary, April 2, 1945.
48. *Ibid.*, April 3, 1945.
49. *Ibid.*
50. *Ibid.*, April 23, 1945.
51. *Ibid.*
52. *Ibid.*, May 16, 1945.
53. *Conference of Berlin*, II, p. 808–9.
54. Stimson, *On Active Service*, p. 589.
55. Truman, *Year of Decisions*, p. 236.
56. *Conference of Berlin*, II, p. 809.
57. *Ibid.*, p. 808.
58. Stimson, *On Active Service*, p. 571.
59. *Ibid.*, p. 573.
60. *Conference of Berlin*, II, pp. 754–57, 991.
61. *Ibid.*, p. 755.
62. Stimson, *On Active Service*, p. 567.
63. Truman, *Year of Decisions*, p. 102.
64. Forrestal, *Diaries*, p. 48.
65. Stimson, *On Active Service*, p. 583.
66. Stimson Diary, April 16, 1945.
67. *Ibid.*, April 4, 1945.
68. Feis, *Between War and Peace*, p. 77.
69. *Conference of Berlin*, II, p. 757.
70. Stimson Diary, April 30, 1945.
71. *Ibid.*, May 14, 1945.
72. Truman, *Year of Decisions*, p. 85.
73. Stimson, *On Active Service*, p. 635.
74. Byrnes, *All In One Lifetime*, p. 282; *Speaking Frankly*, p. 259; Truman, *Year of Decisions*, p. 87.
75. Hewlett and Anderson, *The New World*, p. 343.
76. *Ibid.*; Truman, *Year of Decisions*, p. 87.
77. Truman, *Year of Decisions*, p. 10.
78. *Ibid.*, p. 85.
79. *Ibid.*, p. 87.
80. Stimson Diary, March 15, 1945.
81. Truman, *Year of Decisions*, p. 85.
82. Stimson Diary, May 15, 1945.
83. *Ibid.*, May 16, 1945.
84. *Ibid.*, May 15, 1945.
85. *Ibid.*
86. *Ibid.*, May 10, 1945.
87. *Ibid.*, May 14, 1945.
88. Stimson, *On Active Service*, p. 643.
89. *Ibid.*, p. 635.
90. *Ibid.*
91. *Ibid.*, p. 636.
92. *Ibid.*
93. Hewlett and Anderson, *The New World*, p. 335.
94. *Ibid.*, p. 338.
95. Stimson, *On Active Service*, p. 636.
96. Truman, *Year of Decisions*, p. 87.
97. Stimson Diary, May 3, 1945.
98. Hewlett and Anderson, *The New World*, p. 345.

99. Stimson Diary, June 6, 1945.
100. *Ibid.*, May 14, 1945; Churchill, *Triumph and Tragedy*, p. 575.
101. Stimson Diary, May 16, 1945.
102. *Ibid.*, June 6, 1945.
103. *Ibid.*, May 14, 1945.

CHAPTER III (*pp. 62–90*)

1. Ehrman, *Grand Strategy*, p. 277.
2. Hewlett and Anderson, *The New World*, p. 345.
3. Stimson Diary, May 3, 1945.
4. Leahy, *I Was There*, p. 441; Leahy Diary, May 20, 1945, p. 85.
5. Truman, *Year of Decisions*, pp. 10–11.
6. Byrnes, *Speaking Frankly*, p. 261.
7. Truman, *Year of Decisions*, p. 87.
8. *Conference of Berlin*, I, pp. 6–7.
9. Forrestal, *Diaries*, p. 49.
10. Truman, *Year of Decisions*, p. 85.
11. *Ibid.*, p. 87.
12. *Ibid.*, p. 25; *Conference of Berlin*, I, p. 13.
13. Truman, *Year of Decisions*, p. 10.
14. *Conference of Berlin*, I, p. 4.
15. Stimson Diary, May 16, 1945.
16. *Conference of Berlin*, I, p. 13.
17. *Ibid.*, p. 8.
18. Churchill, *Triumph and Tragedy*, p. 575.
19. *Ibid.*, p. 574.
20. *Ibid.*, pp. 572–74; *Conference of Berlin*, I, pp. 8–9.
21. *Ibid.*, p. 13.
22. *Ibid.*, p. 11.
23. *Ibid.*, p. 10.
24. Stimson Diary, May 10, 14, 1945.
25. Churchill, *Triumph and Tragedy*, p. 575; *Conference of Berlin*, I, p. 13.
26. *Conference of Berlin*, I, p. 13.
27. Truman, *Year of Decisions*, p. 224.
28. Stimson Diary, May 16, 1945.
29. Truman, *Year of Decisions*, pp. 257–58.
30. Woodward, *British Foreign Policy*, p. 521.
31. Stettinius, *Roosevelt and the Russians*, p. 319.
32. Forrestal, *Diaries*, p. 58.
33. Lane, *I Saw Poland Betrayed*, pp. 68–71; Truman, *Year of Decisions*, p. 258.
34. Truman, *Year of Decisions*, pp. 22, 258.
35. Lane, *I Saw Poland Betrayed*, pp. 68–71.
36. Woodward, *British Foreign Policy*, p. 512; Sherwood, *Roosevelt and Hopkins*, p. 913.
37. Sherwood, *Roosevelt and Hopkins*, p. 913.
38. Truman, *Year of Decisions*, p. 110.
39. Lane, *I Saw Poland Betrayed*, p. 84.
40. Feis, *Churchill, Roosevelt, Stalin*, p. 650; Churchill, *Triumph and Tragedy*, p. 577.
41. Churchill, *Triumph and Tragedy*, p. 479.
42. *Ibid.*
43. Truman, *Year of Decisions*, p. 75.
44. *Ibid.*, p. 94.
45. Woodward, *British Foreign Policy*, p. 519; Truman, *Year of Decisions*, p. 333.
46. *Conference of Berlin*, I, pp. 8, 63, 65; Grew, *Turbulent Era*, II, p. 1463; Feis, *Churchill, Roosevelt, Stalin*, p. 649; Butcher, *Three Years with Eisenhower*, p. 712.
47. Truman, *Year of Decisions*, pp. 110, 257.
48. Woodward, *British Foreign Policy*, p. 512; Churchill, *Triumph and Tragedy*, p. 555.
49. *Conference of Berlin*, I, pp. 21–22, 63.
50. *Ibid.*, p. 22; Grew memorandum of conversation, May 21, 1945; Leahy Diary, May 20, 1945, p. 86; Lane, *I Saw Poland Betrayed*, p. 71.
51. Forrestal, *Diaries*, p. 58.
52. Lane, *I Saw Poland Betrayed*, p. 71.
53. Forrestal, *Diaries*, pp. 66–67.
54. Truman, *Year of Decisions*, p. 259.
55. Sherwood, *Roosevelt and Hopkins*, p. 888.
56. *Ibid.*, p. 890.
57. *Ibid.*, pp. 890, 899, 909.
58. *Ibid.*, p. 890.
59. *Ibid.*, p. 889.
60. *Ibid.*, p. 892.
61. *Conference of Berlin*, I, p. 28.
62. *Ibid.*
63. Sherwood, *Roosevelt and Hopkins*, p. 893.
64. *Conference of Berlin*, I, p. 32.
65. Sherwood, *Roosevelt and Hopkins*, p. 894.
66. *Conference of Berlin*, I, pp. 33–38.
67. Sherwood, *Roosevelt and Hopkins*, p. 898.
68. *Ibid.*, pp. 905–6.

69. *Conference of Berlin*, I, pp. 55–56.
70. *Ibid.*, p. 40.
71. Feis, *Between War and Peace*, p. 103.
72. *Ibid.*, p. 105.
73. Sherwood, *Roosevelt and Hopkins*, p. 908.
74. Leahy, *I Was There*, p. 377; Forrestal, *Diaries*, p. 68; Byrnes, *Speaking Frankly*, pp. 63–64.
75. Feis, *Between War and Peace*, p. 208.
76. *Ibid.*; Mikolajczyk, *The Pattern of Soviet Domination*, pp. 140–43.
77. Sherwood, *Roosevelt and Hopkins*, p. 909.
78. *Stalin's Correspondence*, I, p. 326; II, p. 216.
79. Mikolajczyk, *The Pattern of Soviet Domination*, p. 128; Rozek, *Allied Wartime Diplomacy*, pp. 384–86.
80. Sherwood, *Roosevelt and Hopkins*, pp. 908–10.
81. *Ibid.*, pp. 909–10.
82. *Conference of Berlin*, I, p. 716.
83. *Ibid.*, pp. 716, 722–23.
84. *Ibid.*, p. 735.
85. *Ibid.*
86. Truman, *Year of Decisions*, p. 17.
87. *Ibid.*, p. 45.
88. Forrestal, *Diaries*, p. 48.
89. Truman, *Year of Decisions*, p. 102.
90. *Ibid.*, p. 105.
91. *Ibid.*, p. 308.
92. *Ibid.*, pp. 236–38; Stimson Diary, May 16, 1945.
93. Truman, *Year of Decisions*, p. 45.
94. *Ibid.*, p. 496.
95. Truman, *Years of Trial and Hope*, p. 68.
96. Truman, *Year of Decisions*, p. x.
97. *Ibid.*, p. 308.
98. *Ibid.*, p. 464.
99. *Ibid.*, p. 46.
100. *Ibid.*, p. 262.
101. *Ibid.*, p. 236.
102. *Ibid.*, p. 306.
103. *Ibid.*, p. 235; Grew memorandum of conversation, May 10, 1945.
104. Feis, *Between War and Peace*, p. 56fn; Clay, *Decision in Germany*, p. 16; Hammond, "Directives for the Occupation of Germany," p. 312.
105. Truman, *Year of Decisions*, pp. 105–6.
106. *Ibid.*, p. 308.
107. Stimson Diary, July 2, 1945.
108. Truman, *Year of Decisions*, p. 300.
109. Feis, *Between War and Peace*, p. 77.
110. Sherwood, *Roosevelt and Hopkins*, p. 891.
111. *Conference of Berlin*, I, pp. 28–29.
112. Sherwood, *Roosevelt and Hopkins*, p. 891.
113. *Ibid.*, pp. 901–2.
114. Feis, *Between War and Peace*, p. 140.
115. *Conference of Berlin*, I, p. 51.
116. Mosely, "The Occupation of Germany," pp. 599–603; Truman, *Year of Decisions*, p. 302; Feis, *Between War and Peace*, p. 142.
117. Feis, *Between War and Peace*, pp. 52–56.
118. *Conference of Berlin*, I, p. 39.
119. Truman, *Year of Decisions*, p. 301.
120. Churchill, *Triumph and Tragedy*, p. 557.
121. Feis, *Between War and Peace*, p. 141.
122. *Conference of Berlin*, I, p. 53.
123. Truman, *Year of Decisions*, p. 302; Feis, *Between War and Peace*, p. 141; Clay, *Decision in Germany*, pp. 22–23.
124. *Conference of Berlin*, I, p. 348.
125. Truman, *Year of Decisions*, p. 301.
126. *Ibid.*, p. 302.
127. Churchill, *Triumph and Tragedy*, p. 604.
128. Feis, *Between War and Peace*, p. 142.
129. *Ibid.*, p. 142fn.
130. Truman, *Year of Decisions*, p. 302.
131. *Ibid.*, pp. 303–4.
132. *Ibid.*, p. 303.
133. *Stalin's Correspondence*, II, pp. 245–46; Leahy, *I Was There*, p. 382.
134. Mosely, "The Occupation of Germany," p. 601; Feis, *Between War and Peace*, p. 144.
135. *Conference of Berlin*, I, p. 348fn.
136. *Ibid.*, II, p. 244.
137. Feis, *Between War and Peace*, p. 241.
138. Grew Papers, message dated June 6, 1945.
139. Forrestal, *Diaries*, p. 68.
140. Grew, *Turbulent Era*, II, p. 1518.
141. Leahy, *I Was There*, p. 383. See also Byrnes, *Speaking Frankly*, p. 61.
142. *Conference of Berlin*, I, p. 62.

143. Churchill, *Triumph and Tragedy,* pp. 576–81.
144. Truman, *Year of Decisions,* p. 229.
145. Sherwood, *Roosevelt and Hopkins,* p. 897; Feis, *Between War and Peace,* p. 101*fn.*
146. Feis, *Between War and Peace,* pp. 329–30.
147. *Ibid.,* p. 138*fn.;* Woodward, *British Foreign Policy,* p. 527.
148. Feis, *Between War and Peace,* pp. 60, 137–38.
149. *Conference of Berlin,* I, p. 36.
150. *Ibid.,* p. 562*fn.*
151. *Ibid.,* p. 33.
152. *Ibid.,* pp. 33–34.
153. *Ibid.,* p. 53.
154. *Ibid.,* p. 157.
155. Feis, *Between War and Peace,* p. 330.
156. Truman, *Year of Decisions,* p. 310; *Conference of Berlin,* II, p. 940.
157. *Conference of Berlin,* I, p. 563.
158. Truman, *Year of Decisions,* p. 233.
159. *New York Times,* Jan. 18, Mar. 2, 3, April 2, May 9, 1946.
160. *Conference of Berlin,* I, p. 181.
161. *Ibid.,* pp. 785–87.
162. *Ibid.,* pp. 786–87.
163. *Ibid.,* p. 726.
164. *Ibid.,* pp. 788–89.
165. *Ibid.,* p. 784.
166. *Ibid.,* p. 715.
167. Szilard, "A Personal History of the Atomic Bomb," pp. 14–15. See also "Was A-Bomb on Japan a Mistake?", p. 69.
168. Leahy, *I Was There,* p. 441.
169. Stimson Diary, June 6, 1945.
170. *Ibid.*
171. Truman, *Year of Decisions,* p. 321.
172. Grew, *Turbulent Era,* II, pp. 1464–65. Emphasis added.
173. *Conference of Berlin,* I, p. 728.
174. Grew Papers, letter to Paul V. Bacon, June 4, 1945.

CHAPTER IV (*pp. 91–126*)

1. Grew, *Turbulent Era,* II, pp. 1455–56; Department of State, *Relations with China,* pp. 113–14.
2. *Conference of Berlin,* I, p. 860.
3. *Congressional Record,* Aug. 27, 1951, p. A5413.
4. *Ibid.;* Leahy, *I Was There,* p. 318.
5. *Congressional Record,* Aug. 27, 1951, p. A5412.
6. Leahy, *I Was There,* p. 318.
7. Deutscher, *Stalin,* pp. 399–402; Beloff, *Soviet Policy,* p. 36.
8. Department of State, *Relations With China,* p. 99.
9. *Ibid.,* p. 96.
10. Truman, *Year of Decisions,* pp. 280–81.
11. Feis, *Japan Subdued,* p. 168.
12. Feis, *China Tangle,* 286*fn.*
13. Ehrman, *Grand Strategy,* p. 214.
14. Feis, *China Tangle,* pp. 280–85; Department of State, *Relations With China,* pp. 95–96.
15. Truman, *Year of Decisions,* p. 66.
16. *Ibid.,* p. 76.
17. Department of State, *Relations With China,* pp. 97–98; *Congressional Record,* Aug. 27, 1951, p. A5414.
18. Department of Defense, "Entry of the Soviet Union into the War Against Japan," p. 67.
19. Truman, *Year of Decisions,* pp. 84–85.
20. *Congressional Record,* Aug. 27, 1951, p. A5414; Feis, *China Tangle,* p. 304.
21. Forrestal *Diaries,* p. 55.
22. Leahy Diary, May 11, 1945, p. 82.
23. Forrestal *Diaries,* p. 56.
24. *Ibid.*
25. Grew, *Turbulent Era,* II, pp. 1455–57; Department of Defense, "Entry of the Soviet Union into the War against Japan," pp. 68–70.
26. Truman, *Year of Decisions,* p. 85.
27. *Ibid.,* p. 266.
28. Grew, *Turbulent Era,* II, pp. 1460–61.
29. Stimson Diary, May 13, 1945.
30. *Ibid.,* May 14, 1945.
31. *Ibid.,* May 15, 1945.
32. Grew, *Turbulent Era,* II, pp. 1457–59.
33. Feis, *Between War and Peace,* pp. 80–81.
34. Grew, *Turbulent Era,* II, pp. 1457–59.
35. *Ibid.*
36. *Conference of Berlin,* I, p. 14.
37. Hewlett and Anderson, *The New World,* p. 351.
38. *Ibid.;* Stimson Diary, May 15, 16, 1945.
39. Stimson Diary, May 15, 1945.
40. *Conference of Berlin,* I, pp. 13–14.
41. Stimson Diary, May 16, 1945.
42. *Ibid.,* June 6, 1945.
43. Atomic Energy Commission, *Oppenheimer Hearings,* p. 31.

44. *Ibid.;* Feis, *Japan Subdued,* p. 32.
45. *Conference of Berlin,* I, p. 19.
46. Hewlett and Anderson, *The New World,* p. 375.
47. *Ibid.,* p. 352; *Conference of Berlin,* I, p. 87.
48. Stimson Diary, June 6, 1945.
49. *Conference of Berlin,* I, pp. 19–20; *Stalin's Correspondence,* I, p. 361.
50. *Ibid.,* pp. 361–63; Woodward, *British Foreign Policy,* p. 523.
51. *Conference of Berlin,* I, pp. 41–52.
52. Department of Defense, "Entry of the Soviet Union into the War against Japan," p. 73.
53. *Conference of Berlin,* I, p. 62.
54. Stimson Diary, June 6, 1945.
55. Department of Defense, "Entry of the Soviet Union into the War against Japan," p. 72.
56. Feis, *China Tangle,* pp. 311–12.
57. *Conference of Berlin,* I, p. 162.
58. Stimson Diary, May 15, 1945.
59. Leahy, *I Was There,* p. 318.
60. Deane, *The Strange Alliance,* p. 247; Forrestal, *Diaries,* p. 12; Churchill, *Triumph and Tragedy,* p. 218.
61. Churchill, *Triumph and Tragedy,* pp. 229, 238.
62. Department of Defense, "Entry of the Soviet Union into the War against Japan," p. 35.
63. Leahy, *I Was There,* p. 335.
64. Feis, *China Tangle,* p. 285.
65. Truman, *Year of Decisions,* p. 76.
66. *Ibid.,* p. 79; Forrestal *Diaries,* pp. 12, 55; Deane, *The Strange Alliance,* p. 247; Leahy, *I Was There,* p. 369.
67. *Congressional Record,* Aug. 27, 1951, p. A5415; Stimson Diary, May 15, 1945.
68. Stimson Diary, May 15, 1945.
69. Feis, *Between War and Peace,* pp. 80–81.
70. Department of Defense, "Entry of the Soviet Union into the War against Japan," p. 72.
71. Forrestal, *Diaries,* p. 79.
72. Hewlett and Anderson, *The New World,* p. 348.
73. Craven and Cate, *Air Forces in World War II,* Vol. V, p. 644.
74. *Ibid.,* pp. 617, 756.
75. Knebel and Bailey, *No High Ground,* p. 111.
76. Craven and Cate, *Air Forces in World War II,* Vol. V, p. 728.
77. *Ibid.,* p. 740.
78. Feis, *Japan Subdued,* pp. 168–69; Butow, *Japan's Decision,* pp. 82–85.
79. Butow, *Japan's Decision,* pp. 58–59, 77, 85–86; Craven and Cate, *Air Forces in World War II,* Vol. V, pp. 728, 729.
80. Feis, *Japan Subdued,* pp. 168–73; Butow, *Japan's Decision,* pp. 77–78; Forrestal, *Diaries,* p. 20.
81. Forrestal, *Diaries,* p. 89; Jones *et al., The Far East 1942–46,* pp. 126–27.
82. U.S. Senate, *Military Situation in the Far East,* pp. 2432–33.
83. Butow, *Japan's Decision,* pp. 65–66.
84. *Ibid.,* pp. 86–91; Feis, *Japan Subdued,* pp. 168–73.
85. Feis, *Japan Subdued,* pp. 168–77; Butow, *Japan's Decision,* pp. 30–166.
86. U.S. Senate, *Military Situation in the Far East,* p. 561; *Strauss, Men and Decisions,* p. 188; Stimson, *On Active Service,* pp. 617–18; Grew, *Turbulent Era,* II, p. 1423*fn.*
87. Department of Defense, "Entry of the Soviet Union into the War against Japan," p. 68.
88. Churchill, *Triumph and Tragedy,* pp. 154, 215.
89. Department of Defense, "Entry of the Soviet Union into the War against Japan," p. 49.
90. Cline, *Washington Command Post,* p. 343.
91. Feis, *Japan Subdued,* p. 15*fn.*
92. Department of Defense, "Entry of the Soviet Union into the War against Japan," p. 64.
93. Stimson, *On Active Service,* pp. 626–28; Ehrman, *Grand Strategy,* pp. 302–4.
94. Cline, *Washington Command Post,* p. 343.
95. Leahy, *I Was There,* pp. 384–85; *Conference of Berlin,* I, p. 909.
96. Grew, *Turbulent Era,* II, pp. 1438–42.
97. *Conference of Berlin,* I, pp. 891–92.
98. Feis, *Japan Subdued,* p. 169; King, *Fleet Admiral King,* pp. 597–99, 623; Butow, *Japan's Decision,* pp. 58, 76.
99. Ehrman, *Grand Strategy,* pp. 284–85.
100. *Conference of Berlin,* I, pp. 875–76.
101. Forrestal, *Diaries,* p. 74.
102. Leahy, *I Was There,* p. 419; Grew, *Turbulent Era,* II, p. 1406.
103. Grew, *Turbulent Era,* II, p. 1458; *Conference of Berlin,* I, pp. 44–45; "Entry of the Soviet Union into the War against Japan," p. 74.

104. Cline, *Washington Command Post*, p. 344.
105. *Conference of Berlin*, I, p. 905.
106. *Ibid.*, II, p. 36*fn*.
107. Truman, *Year of Decisions*, p. 416; Grew, *Turbulent Era*, II, pp. 1421–23, 1434.
108. Grew, *Turbulent Era*, II, p. 1434.
109. Department of Defense, "Entry of the Soviet Union into the War against Japan," p. 63.
110. *Conference of Berlin*, I, p. 892; Leahy, *I Was There*, pp. 384–85; Forrestal, *Diaries*, pp. 68–69; Grew, *Turbulent Era*, II, p. 1429.
111. Truman, *Year of Decisions*, p. 417; King, *Fleet Admiral King*, pp. 396, 398; Sutherland, "The Story General Marshall Told Me."
112. Leahy, *I Was There*, p. 245.
113. *Conference of Berlin*, I, p. 906.
114. *Ibid.*, p. 909.
115. McCloy, *Challenge to American Foreign Policy*, p. 41; Forrestal, *Diaries*, p. 68.
116. Leahy, *I Was There*, pp. 318, 336, 385.
117. Deane, *The Strange Alliance*, pp. 263–65; King, *Fleet Admiral King*, p. 606; Morton, "The Decision to Use the Atomic Bomb," *Command Decisions*, K. R. Greenfield, ed., p. 509; Forrestal, *Diaries*, pp. 55, 68, 69, 70, 78–79; Byrnes, *All in One Lifetime*, pp. 291, 298, 300; Grew, *Turbulent Era*, II, pp. 1444–46; Byrnes, *Speaking Frankly*, p. 208; Truman, *Year of Decisions*, p. 425; Stimson Diary, Aug. 10, 1945.
118. Byrnes, *Speaking Frankly*, p. 208.
119. Byrnes, *All in One Lifetime*, p. 300. Emphasis added.
120. "Was A-Bomb on Japan a Mistake?" *U.S. News and World Report*, Aug. 15, 1960, p. 66.
121. Cline, *Washington Command Post*, p. 345.
122. Byrnes, *Speaking Frankly*, p. 208.
123. Ehrman, *Grand Strategy*, p. 214.
124. Blackett, *Military and Political Consequences*, p. 117.
125. Ehrman, *Grand Strategy*, pp. 276, 297.
126. Truman, *Year of Decisions*, p. 419; Wilson, *Eight Years Overseas*, p. 259; Churchill, *Triumph and Tragedy*, p. 639.
127. U.S. Senate, *Military Situation in the Far East*, p. 563.

128. Feis, *Japan Subdued*, pp. 10–11; Sutherland, "The Story General Marshall Told Me."
129. Byrnes, *Speaking Frankly*, p. 260; Hewlett and Anderson, *The New World*, p. 356.
130. Hewlett and Anderson, *The New World*, pp. 356–60; Leahy, *I Was There*, pp. 440–41.
131. Stimson, *On Active Service*, p. 617.
132. U.S. Senate, *Military Situation in the Far East*, p. 562.
133. Compton, *Atomic Quest*, p. 238.
134. *Ibid.*, p. 230; Department of Defense, "Entry of the Soviet Union into the War against Japan," p. 72.
135. Smith, "Behind the Decision to Use the Atomic Bomb," p. 297; Feis, *Japan Subdued*, pp. 44–45.
136. Hewlett and Anderson, *The New World*, pp. 356–60.
137. *Ibid.*, p. 358.
138. *Ibid.*, p. 352; Stimson Diary, May 29, 1945.
139. Stimson, *On Active Service*, p. 617.
140. *Ibid.* Emphasis added.
141. Hewlett and Anderson, *The New World*, pp. 365, 692.
142. Byrnes, *All in One Lifetime*, p. 286; Byrnes, *Speaking Frankly*, p. 262.
143. Byrnes, *Speaking Frankly*, p. 262.
144. Truman, *Year of Decisions*, p. 420.
145. Byrnes, *Speaking Frankly*, p. 262.
146. Craven and Cate, *Air Forces in World War II*, Vol. V, p. 709.
147. Truman, *Year of Decisions*, p. 262.
148. Ehrman, *Grand Strategy*, p. 223.
149. Truman, *Year of Decisions*, p. 235.
150. *Ibid.*, pp. 235–37; Feis, *Japan Subdued*, p. 38; Stimson Diary, May 16, 1945.
151. Stimson Diary, May 15, 1945.
152. Stimson, *On Active Service*, p. 618: King, *Fleet Admiral King*, p. 621.
153. Forrestal, *Diaries*, p. 70.
154. *Ibid.*, p. 83; Hewlett and Anderson, *The New World*, p. 364.
155. *Conference of Berlin*, I, p. 909.
156. Grew, *Turbulent Era*, II, p. 1458.
157. Leahy, *I Was There*, p. 383; King, *Fleet Admiral King*, pp. 395–96.
158. Department of Defense, "Entry of the Soviet Union into the War against Japan," p. 61.
159. *Ibid.*, p. 67.
160. Leahy, *I Was There*, p. 385; *Conference of Berlin*, I, p. 911.

161. *Conference of Berlin,* I, pp. 194–95; Department of Defense, "Entry of the Soviet Union into the War against Japan," p. 72.
162. *Conference of Berlin,* I, p. 910.
163. Byrnes, *All in One Lifetime,* p. 291.
164. *Ibid.*
165. *Ibid.,* p. 300.
166. Forrestal, *Diaries,* p. 70; Truman, *Year of Decisions,* p. 314.
167. Grew, *Turbulent Era,* II, p. 1465.
168. Grew memorandum of conversation, June 11, 1945.
169. Feis, *China Tangle,* p. 313.
170. *Ibid.,* p. 314.
171. *Ibid.*
172. Grew, *Turbulent Era,* II, p. 1468.
173. *Conference of Berlin,* I, p. 176.
174. *Ibid.,* p. 201.
175. Truman, *Year of Decisions,* p. 269; Feis, *China Tangle,* p. 315.
176. Feis, *China Tangle,* p. 312.
177. *Ibid.*
178. *Ibid.,* p. 315; Truman, *Year of Decisions,* pp. 318–19.
179. Feis, *China Tangle,* p. 316.
180. Truman, *Year of Decisions,* p. 319.
181. *Congressional Record,* Aug. 27, 1951, p. A5415. Emphasis added.
182. *Ibid.*
183. Feis, *China Tangle,* p. 317; Truman, *Year of Decisions,* pp. 315–16.
184. Department of State, *Relations with China,* p. 117.
185. Truman, *Year of Decisions,* pp. 316–17.
186. *Congressional Record,* Aug. 27, 1951, p. A5414.
187. Truman, *Year of Decisions,* p. 315.
188. *Ibid.,* p. 316.
189. *Ibid.,* pp. 315–18; Department of State, *Relations with China,* pp. 116, 123; *Congressional Record,* Aug. 27, 1951, p. A5414.
190. *Conference of Berlin,* I, p. 867.
191. Truman, *Year of Decisions,* p. 317.
192. Byrnes, *Speaking Frankly,* p. 205.
193. *Ibid.*
194. Truman, *Years of Trial and Hope,* p. 64.
195. Feis, *China Tangle,* p. 319.
196. Truman, *Year of Decisions,* p. 317.
197. *Ibid.,* pp. 317–18.
198. *Conference of Berlin,* I, p. 231.
199. Feis, *China Tangle,* p. 319; *Congressional Record,* Aug. 27, 1951, p. A5415.
200. Knebel and Bailey, *No High Ground,* p. 122.
201. Ehrman, *Grand Strategy,* p. 298; *Conference of Berlin,* I, p. 941.
202. Department of Defense, "Entry of the Soviet Union into the War against Japan," p. 75; Feis, *Between War and Peace,* p. 28.
203. *Conference of Berlin,* II, p. 34.
204. *Congressional Record,* Aug. 27, 1951, p. A5415.
205. Feis, *China Tangle,* pp. 318–19.
206. *Ibid.,* p. 319; Truman, *Year of Decisions,* p. 319.
207. Feis, *China Tangle,* p. 319; *Conference of Berlin,* I, pp. 862–63.
208. *Conference of Berlin,* I, p. 231.
209. Feis, *Japan Subdued,* p. 61.
210. Feis, *China Tangle,* p. 320.
211. *Ibid.; Conference of Berlin,* I, pp. 231, 862–63.
212. *Conference of Berlin,* I, p. 864.
213. Daniels, *Man of Independence,* p. 266.
214. Department of Defense, "Entry of the Soviet Union into the War against Japan," pp. 54, 67; Truman, *Year of Decisions,* p. 417.
215. Department of State, *Relations with China,* p. 93.

CHAPTER V *(pp. 127–156)*

1. Grew, *Turbulent Era,* II, p. 1464.
2. Leahy, *I Was There,* p. 382; Leahy Diary, June 15, 1945.
3. *Conference of Berlin,* II, pp. 1097–98.
4. *New York Times,* July 6, 1945.
5. *Conference of Berlin,* I, p. 704.
6. Grew, *Turbulent Era,* II, p. 1488.
7. *Conference of Berlin,* I, p. 181. Emphasis in original. See also *New York Times,* Feb. 15, 1950.
8. House Committee on Banking and Currency, *Hearings: Export-Import Bank Act of 1945;* Senate Committee on Banking and Currency, *Hearings: Export-Import Bank Act of 1945.*
9. *New York Times,* July 18, 1945; Senate Committee on Banking and Currency, *Hearings: Export-Import Bank Act of 1945,* p. 6.
10. Woodward, *British Foreign Policy,* pp. 539–40; *Conference of Berlin,* I, pp. 171, 359; II, pp. 633–34.
11. Truman, *Year of Decisions,* p. 415.

12. Daniels, *Man of Independence*, p. 266.
13. Truman, *Year of Decisions*, p. 245.
14. *Conference of Berlin*, I, pp. 257, 369, 373.
15. *Ibid.*, pp. 360–62.
16. Senate Committee on Banking and Currency, *Hearings: Export-Import Bank Act of 1945*, p. 9. House Committee on Banking and Currency, *Hearings: Export-Import Bank Act of 1945*, pp. 51–54.
17. *Conference of Berlin*, I, pp. 357–62.
18. McNeill, *America, Britain, and Russia, 1941–46*, pp. 325–26, 417, 421, 425, 476, 609; Woodward, *British Foreign Policy*, pp. 516–18.
19. Lukacs, *The Great Powers and Eastern Europe*, p. 658; *Conference of Berlin*, I, p. 358fn.
20. *Conference of Berlin*, I, pp. 334–35.
21. Feis, *Churchill, Roosevelt, Stalin*, p. 569; Betts, *Central and South-East Europe*, pp. 50, 170, 178. See also *Conference of Berlin*, I, p. 318.
22. *Conference of Berlin*, II, p. 193.
23. *Ibid.*, I, p. 728; II, pp. 1130–31.
24. Byrnes, *Speaking Frankly*, p. 294.
25. *New York Times*, March 4, 1945; McNeill, *America, Britain, and Russia, 1941–46*, p. 476.
26. *Conference of Berlin*, I, p. 262.
27. *Ibid.*
28. *Ibid.*, pp. 169–70, 361–62.
29. Churchill, *Triumph and Tragedy*, pp. 227–33.
30. Woodward, *British Foreign Policy*, pp. 293–94; Churchill, *Triumph and Tragedy*, p. 77; Hull, *Memoirs*, II, p. 1458; Dennett and Johnson, *Negotiating with the Russians*, pp. 176–77.
31. Feis, *Churchill, Roosevelt, Stalin*, pp. 415–16, 450–51; Allen, *Great Britain and the United States*, pp. 870–73; Churchill, *Triumph and Tragedy*, pp. 75–77; McNeill, *America, Britain, and Russia, 1941–46*, p. 493.
32. Woodward, *British Foreign Policy*, p. 307; Sherwood, *Roosevelt and Hopkins*, pp. 833–34.
33. Feis, *Churchill, Roosevelt and Stalin*, pp. 450–51.
34. *Ibid.*, pp. 415–16.
35. *Conference of Berlin*, I, p. 215.
36. Kennan, *Russia and the West*, p. 366; Feis, *Churchill, Roosevelt, Stalin*, pp. 415–16; *Conferences of Malta and Yalta*, p. 445; Senate Committee on Foreign Relations, *A Decade of American Foreign Policy*, pp. 482, 487, 494.
37. *A Decade of American Foreign Policy*, p. 455; *Conferences at Malta and Yalta*, p. 246.
38. *A Decade of American Foreign Policy*, pp. 487–91.
39. Woodward, *British Foreign Policy*, p. 308.
40. Churchill, *Triumph and Tragedy*, pp. 283–325.
41. *Ibid.*, p. 293.
42. *Ibid.*, p. 420.
43. *Ibid.*
44. Hull, *Memoirs*, II, pp. 1458–61.
45. *Conferences at Malta and Yalta*, pp. 97–108.
46. *Ibid.*, pp. 97–99.
47. Byrnes, *Speaking Frankly*, p. 33.
48. *Conferences at Malta and Yalta*, p. 503.
49. Byrnes, *Speaking Frankly*, p. 33.
50. *Conferences at Malta and Yalta*, pp. 503, 977; Byrnes, *Speaking Frankly*, pp. 32–33.
51. *Conferences at Malta and Yalta*, pp. 873, 909; Byrnes, *Speaking Frankly*, pp. 32–33; Lukacs, *The Great Powers and Eastern Europe*, p. 649; Kertesz, *Fate of East-Central Europe*, p. 266.
52. Dennett and Johnson, *Negotiating with the Russians*, p. 180.
53. *Conference of Berlin*, I, p. 374; Byrnes, *Speaking Frankly*, p. 50; Feis, *Churchill, Roosevelt, Stalin*, pp. 565–67.
54. *Conference of Berlin*, I, p. 398fn.
55. Byrnes, *Speaking Frankly*, p. 53; *Conference of Berlin*, I, p. 374.
56. Stimson Diary, May 10, 1945.
57. *Ibid.*
58. Grew memorandum of conversation, May 2, 1945.
59. Clark, *Calculated Risk*, pp. 442–48.
60. *Ibid.*; Truman, *Truman Speaks*, pp. 70–71.
61. Grew memorandum of conversation, May 14, 1945.
62. *Ibid.*, May 2, 1945.
63. *Ibid.*
64. *Ibid.*, May 4, 1945.
65. Truman, *Year of Decisions*, p. 254.
66. Grew memorandum of conversation, May 10, 1945; *Conference of Berlin*, I, pp. 158–59, 169–70, 210–11.
67. *Conference of Berlin*, I, pp. 367, 369–70; Betts, *Central and South-East Europe*, p. 207.

68. Betts, *Central and South-East Europe*, p. 29.
69. *Conference of Berlin*, II, p. 729.
70. Betts, *Central and South-East Europe*, p. 29.
71. Feis, *Churchill, Roosevelt, Stalin*, p. 567.
72. *Ibid.*, p. 568; *Conference of Berlin*, I, p. 365.
73. McNeill, *America, Britain and Russia, 1941-46*, p. 422.
74. Roberts, *Rumania*, p. 260.
75. *Conference of Berlin*, I, p. 413.
76. *Ibid.*, p. 374.
77. *Ibid.*, pp. 422-23.
78. *Ibid.*, pp. 364*fn.*, 368, 372*fn.*
79. Woodward, *British Foreign Policy*, p. 517; Churchill, *Triumph and Tragedy*, pp. 76-79.
80. *Conference of Berlin*, I, pp. 393-94.
81. *Ibid.*, pp. 372*fn.*, 687; II, pp. 582, 1494.
82. Deane, *The Strange Alliance*, p. 268.
83. *Conference of Berlin*, II, p. 582.
84. Grew memorandum of conversation, May 10, 1945.
85. Grew, *Turbulent Era*, II, p. 1465; Roberts, *Rumania*, p. 264.
86. Dennett and Johnson, *Negotiating with the Russians*, p. 181.
87. *Stalin's Correspondence*, II, p. 239.
88. Feis, *Between War and Peace*, p. 110.
89. *Stalin's Correspondence*, II, pp. 241-42; *Conference of Berlin*, I, p. 358*fn.*
90. *Conference of Berlin*, I, p. 358*fn.*; *Stalin's Correspondence*, II, pp. 243-44; Churchill, *Triumph and Tragedy*, p. 115.
91. *Conference of Berlin*, I, p. 182; *Stalin's Correspondence*, II, pp. 248-49.
92. *Stalin's Correspondence*, II, p. 250; *Conference of Berlin*, I, p. 387.
93. *Conference of Berlin*, I, p. 417.
94. Stimson Diary, June 6, 1945.
95. *Ibid.*
96. Atomic Energy Commission, *Oppenheimer Hearings*, pp. 32, 33. Emphasis added.
97. Craven and Cate, *Air Forces in World War II*, Vol. V, p. 709; Hewlett and Anderson, *The New World*, pp. 374-80.
98. Truman, *Year of Decisions*, p. 331.
99. *Ibid.*, p. 338.
100. *Conference of Berlin*, II, pp. 643-44.
101. *Ibid.*, I, pp. 400, 413.
102. *Speaking Frankly*, Byrnes, pp. 67-68.
103. *Conference of Berlin*, II, pp. 150-55.
104. Truman, *Year of Decisions*, p. 384.
105. Leahy, *I Was There*, p. 428.
106. *Conference of Berlin*, II, p. 8.
107. *Ibid.*, p. 1361.
108. *Ibid.*, p. 1360.
109. Stimson Diary, July 16, 1945.
110. Leahy Diary, p. 110, July 17, 1945.
111. McNeill, *America, Britain and Russia, 1941-46*, p. 615; Byrnes, *Speaking Frankly*, p. 31.
112. *Conference of Berlin*, II, pp. 53, 643-44.
113. *Ibid.*, pp. 52-63.
114. *Ibid.*, p. 56.
115. *Ibid.*, pp. 1360-61, Hewlett and Anderson, *The New World*, p. 386.
116. Stimson Diary, July 18, 1945; *Conference of Berlin*, II, p. 1361.
117. *Conference of Berlin*, II, p. 106.
118. *Ibid.*, p. 127.
119. Churchill, *Triumph and Tragedy*, p. 636.
120. *Conference of Berlin*, II, pp. 146-55, 698, 1044.
121. *Ibid.*, p. 151.
122. *Ibid.*
123. *Ibid.*, pp. 151-55.
124. *Ibid.*, p. 186.
125. Stimson Diary, July 21, 1945; *Conference of Berlin*, II, p. 1361. Emphasis added.
126. *Conference of Berlin*, II, p. 207.
127. *Ibid.*
128. Stimson Diary, July 22, 1945; *Conference of Berlin*, II, p. 225.
129. *Conference of Berlin*, II, pp. 1492-94.
130. Leahy, *I Was There*, p. 428.
131. Stimson Diary, July 23, 1945.
132. *Ibid.*, July 24, 1945.
133. *Conference of Berlin*, I, p. 413.
134. *Ibid.*, pp. 413-14.
135. Churchill, *Triumph and Tragedy*, p. 636.
136. *Hansard*, 413, H. C. Deb. 5s. (1945), pp. 78-79.
137. *Conference of Berlin*, II, pp. 361-64; Woodward, *British Foreign Policy*, 539*fn.*
138. Bryant, *Triumph in the West 1943-46*, pp. 477-78.
139. *Ibid.*, p. 478.
140. Stimson Diary, July 22, 1945.
141. Hewlett and Anderson, *The New World*, pp. 367-69.

142. *Ibid.*, p. 367.
143. *Ibid.;* Feis, *Japan Subdued*, pp. 40–43.
144. Hewlett and Anderson, *The New World*, p. 369.
145. Stimson Diary, July 3, 1945; Hewlett and Anderson, *The New World*, p. 372.
146. *Conference of Berlin*, I, p. 942.
147. Hewlett and Anderson, *The New World*, p. 384; Stimson Diary, July 17, 1945; *Conference of Berlin*, II, p. 47.
148. Churchill, *Triumph and Tragedy*, p. 641.
149. Truman, *Year of Decisions*, p. 416.
150. Churchill, *Triumph and Tragedy*, pp. 668–70.
151. *Ibid.*, pp. 669–70; *Conference of Berlin*, II, p. 379.
152. Byrnes, *Speaking Frankly*, p. 263; Leahy, *I Was There*, p. 429. See also Craven and Cate, *Air Forces in World War II*, Vol. V, pp. 712–13.

CHAPTER VI (pp. *157–187*)

1. *Conference of Berlin*, II, p. 367.
2. *Ibid.*, p. 330.
3. McNeill, *America, Britain and Russia, 1941–46*, p. 622.
4. Stimson Diary, July 24, 1945.
5. *Ibid.*, July 23, 1945.
6. *Ibid.*, July 24, 1945.
7. Forrestal, *Diaries*, p. 78.
8. Byrnes, *Speaking Frankly*, p. 72.
9. *Ibid.*, p. 79.
10. *Ibid.*, p. 68.
11. Feis, *Between War and Peace*, p. 241–44; *Conference of Berlin*, II, pp. 72–76, 94.
12. *Conference of Berlin*, II, p. 795.
13. *Ibid.*, I, p. 611.
14. *Conferences at Malta and Yalta*, p. 983.
15. *Ibid.*
16. *Ibid.*, p. 982.
17. *Ibid.*, pp. 622, 937, 971.
18. *Ibid.*, p. 322.
19. *Ibid.*, p. 909.
20. Stimson, *On Active Service*, pp. 572–83.
21. *Conferences at Malta and Yalta*, p. 632.
22. *Ibid.*, p. 628.
23. *Conference of Berlin*, I, p. 504; see also Byrnes, *Speaking Frankly*, p. 37.
24. Stimson, *On Active Service*, p. 581; see also Churchill, *Triumph and Tragedy*, p. 156.
25. *Conference of Berlin*, I, pp. 228, 507; II, pp. 752, 832, 869, 1484.
26. Penrose, *Economic Planning for the Peace*, p. 268.
27. Byrnes, *Speaking Frankly*, p. 181.
28. Stimson, *On Active Service*, p. 573.
29. Hammond, "Directives for the Occupation of Germany," p. 213; Leahy, *I Was There*, p. 219; Balfour, *Four-Power Control of Germany, 1945–46*, p. 145; Churchill, *Triumph and Tragedy*, p. 351.
30. Byrnes, *Speaking Frankly*, p. 26.
31. *Conference of Berlin*, II, p. 281.
32. Stimson, *On Active Service*, p. 583; Diary, May 16, 1945.
33. *Conference of Berlin*, I, p. 524fn.
34. Truman, *Year of Decisions*, p. 327.
35. *Ibid.*, p. 496; *Conference of Berlin*, I, p. 612–13.
36. Truman, *Year of Decisions*, p. 323.
37. *Ibid.*, p. 398.
38. *Conference of Berlin*, I, p. 520fn.
39. Truman, *Year of Decisions*, p. 309; see also *Conference of Berlin*, I, p. 452–53.
40. *Conference of Berlin*, I, pp. 520–21.
41. *Ibid.*, p. 510; Truman, *Year of Decisions*, pp. 310–11.
42. Stimson, *On Active Service*, p. 582; *Conference of Berlin*, I, pp. 539, 540, 547–48; II, pp. 833, 896.
43. *Conference of Berlin*, I, p. 547.
44. *Ibid.*, pp. 468–71, 524–25.
45. *Ibid.*, p. 540; II, pp. 870, 896.
46. *Ibid.*, I, pp. 530–31.
47. *Ibid.*, p. 510.
48. *Ibid.*, pp. 510–11.
49. *Ibid.*, pp. 519–20.
50. *Ibid.*, pp. 522–23.
51. *Ibid.*, pp. 530–31; II, pp. 870–71.
52. *Ibid.*, I, p. 532; II, p. 871.
53. *Ibid.*, II, p. 809; Byrnes, *Speaking Frankly*, pp. 68, 82; Leahy, *I Was There*, pp. 395–96; Truman, *Year of Decisions*, p. 341.
54. Truman, *Year of Decisions*, p. 357; *Conference of Berlin*, II, pp. 873–76.
55. *Conference of Berlin*, II, pp. 428, 871.
56. *Ibid.*, pp. 754–57, 808–9; Stimson Diary, July 2, 1945.
57. *Conference of Berlin*, II, p. 755.
58. *Ibid.*, pp. 754–56, 808.
59. Stimson Diary, July 23, 1945.

60. *Conference of Berlin*, II, p. 279–80.
61. *Ibid.*, p. 280–81.
62. *Ibid.*, pp. 279, 810.
63. *Ibid.*, pp. 277–78.
64. *Ibid.*, p. 275; Byrnes, *Speaking Frankly*, pp. 83–84.
65. *Conference of Berlin*, II, pp. 428–31, 490–91, 947.
66. *Ibid.*, pp. 872, 877–85, 900.
67. *Ibid.*, p. 430.
68. *Ibid.*, p. 901.
69. *Ibid.*, pp. 900–1.
70. *Ibid.*, pp. 275, 296–97.
71. *Ibid.*, p. 428.
72. *Ibid.*, p. 429.
73. *Ibid.*
74. *Ibid.*
75. Byrnes, *Speaking Frankly*, p. 82; *Conference of Berlin*, II, p. 297.
76. *Conference of Berlin*, I, pp. 510–11.
77. *Ibid.*, II, pp. 451–52.
78. *Ibid.*, p. 473.
79. *Ibid.*, pp. 473–76.
80. *Ibid.*, pp. 486–87, 841, 855, 877–78, 880, 884.
81. *Ibid.*, pp. 473, 886–87.
82. *Ibid.*, pp. 473, 487.
83. *Ibid.*, p. 487.
84. *Ibid.*, pp. 877–85, 892.
85. *Ibid.*, p. 892.
86. *Ibid.*, p. 926.
87. Leahy Diary, July 26, 27, 1945, pp. 126, 130.
88. Truman, *Year of Decisions*, pp. 389, 394; *Conference of Berlin*, II, p. 471.
89. *Conference of Berlin*, II, pp. 471–77.
90. *Ibid.*, pp. 484–85.
91. *Ibid.*, p. 510; Byrnes, *Speaking Frankly*, p. 85.
92. *Conference of Berlin*, II, p. 514.
93. *Ibid.*, pp. 510–14.
94. Penrose, *Economic Planning for the Peace*, p. 287.
95. Leahy, *I Was There*, p. 427.
96. Byrnes, *Speaking Frankly*, p. 82.
97. *Conference of Berlin*, I, pp. 228, 507; II, pp. 752, 775–80, 832, 869, 1484.
98. *Ibid.*, I, p. 50; II, pp. 183–84, 482.
99. *Ibid.*, I, pp. 520–21; Truman, *Year of Decisions*, p. 309.
100. *Conference of Berlin*, II, p. 756.
101. De Gaulle, *Salvation*, U.K., pp. 285–86.
102. *Conference of Berlin*, II, pp. 1481–85.
103. *Ibid.*, p. 251.
104. *Ibid.*, pp. 515, 1486.
105. *Ibid.*, pp. 52, 186, 609–10, 1479–80.
106. Churchill, *Triumph and Tragedy*, p. 672.
107. *Conference of Berlin*, II, pp. 1086, 1492–93.
108. McNeill, *America, Britain and Russia, 1941–46*, pp. 627–28.
109. Leahy, *I Was There*, p. 428.
110. De Gaulle, *Salvation*, U.K., p. 230.
111. Forrestal, *Diaries*, p. 78; see also Truman, *Year of Decisions*, p. 411.
112. Byrnes, *Speaking Frankly*, p. 87.
113. *Ibid.*, p. 72.
114. Byrnes, *All in One Lifetime*, p. 303.
115. *Conference of Berlin*, I, p. 879.
116. *Ibid.*, I, pp. 879–80.
117. *Ibid.*, II, p. 1249.
118. *Ibid.*, p. 1250.
119. *Ibid.*, p. 1260.
120. *Ibid.*, p. 1261.
121. Eisenhower, *Mandate for Change*, p. 313.
122. Truman, *Year of Decisions*, p. 417; Grew, *Turbulent Era*, II, pp. 1423, 1434; *Conference of Berlin*, II, p. 1272fn.
123. *Conference of Berlin*, II, p. 1294.
124. *Ibid.*, pp. 1260–64.
125. *Ibid.*, pp. 1260–61.
126. *Ibid.*, p. 1266.
127. *Ibid.*, pp. 87, 1588.
128. *Ibid.*, pp. 45, 1585.
129. Department of Defense, "Entry of the Soviet Union into the War against Japan," p. 106; see also Ehrman, *Grand Strategy*, p. 303; Leahy, *I Was There*, p. 397.
130. Ehrman, *Grand Strategy*, p. 291.
131. Truman, *Truman Speaks*, pp. 67, 93.
132. *Ibid.*, p. 93; Truman, *Year of Decisions*, p. 419.
133. *Conference of Berlin*, I, pp. 941–42.
134. Churchill, *Triumph and Tragedy*, p. 639; see also Wilson, *Eight Years Overseas*, p. 259.
135. Stimson Diary, July 22, 1945; *Conference of Berlin*, II, p. 1373fn.
136. *Conference of Berlin*, II, p. 1374.
137. Stimson Diary, July 24, 1945.
138. Knebel and Bailey, *No High Ground*, pp. 124–25; Hewlett and Anderson, *The New World*, p. 394.
139. Truman, *Year of Decisions*, p. 421.
140. *Conference of Berlin*, II, pp. 87, 1587–88.
141. *Ibid.*, pp. 1587–88.
142. *Ibid.*, p. 81; Ehrman, *Grand Strategy*, pp. 302–3.

143. Bryant, *Triumph in the West 1943–46*, pp. 477; Feis, *Between War and Peace*, p. 172.
144. Ehrman, *Grand Strategy*, p. 292; *Conference of Berlin*, II, p. 276.
145. Byrnes, *Speaking Frankly*, p. 206.
146. Stimson Diary, July 23, 1945.
147. *Ibid.*, July 24, 1945.
148. Forrestal, *Diaries*, pp. 78–79; Byrnes, *All in One Lifetime*, p. 297; Hillman, *Mr. President*, p. 123; Truman, *Year of Decisions*, p. 411; "Was A-Bomb on Japan a Mistake?" *U.S. News and World Report*, Aug. 15, 1960, pp. 62–76.
149. *Conference of Berlin*, I, p. 889; Stimson Diary, June 19, 1945; Hewlett and Anderson, *The New World*, p. 365, and *especially* p. 403.
150. Cline, *Washington Command Post*, p. 345; Morton, "The Decision to Use the Atomic Bomb," *Command Decisions*, K. R. Greenfield, ed., p. 499.
151. *Conference of Berlin*, I, pp. 173, 891.
152. *Ibid.*, pp. 893, 897.
153. *Ibid.*, II, p. 1267; Stimson Diary, June 19, 1945.
154. *Conference of Berlin*, I, pp. 889–90.
155. *Ibid.*, II, pp. 449–50, 460, 1284.
156. *Ibid.*, I, pp. 110, 125.
157. *Ibid.*, II, pp. 449–50, 460, 1284; Byrnes, *Speaking Frankly*, p. 207.
158. Byrnes, *Speaking Frankly*, pp. 207–9; Truman, *Year of Decisions*, pp. 401–4; *Conference of Berlin*, II, p. 476; Byrnes, *All in One Lifetime*, pp. 297–98.
159. Byrnes, *All in One Lifetime*, p. 298; *Speaking Frankly*, p. 208.
160. Byrnes, *All in One Lifetime*, p. 298.
161. Truman, *Year of Decisions*, pp. 403–4; *Conference of Berlin*, II, pp. 1333–34.
162. *Conference of Berlin*, II, pp. 1333–34.
163. Deane, *The Strange Alliance*, pp. 267–68.
164. Forrestal, *Diaries*, p. 78.
165. Deane, *The Strange Alliance*, p. 270.
166. *Conference of Berlin*, II, pp. 276, 1241; Byrnes, *All in One Lifetime*, p. 291.
167. Byrnes, *All in One Lifetime*, p. 291.
168. *Conference of Berlin*, II, pp. 43–47, 1582–87.
169. *Ibid.*, pp. 1223–24, 1240–41, 1586.
170. *Ibid.*, pp. 1227–30.
171. *Ibid.*, p. 460.
172. *Ibid.*
173. *Ibid.*, p. 1293.
174. *Ibid.*, p. 1293*fn.*
175. Hewlett and Anderson, *The New World*, p. 396; Butow, *Japan's Decision*, pp. 140–41, 143–49.
176. *Conference of Berlin*, II, pp. 1292–93.
177. Strauss, *Men and Decisions*, p. 189; Feis, *Japan Subdued*, p. 103–4; Ehrman, *Grand Strategy*, p. 308.
178. Hewlett and Anderson, *The New World*, p. 401; Truman, *Year of Decisions*, p. 420.
179. Truman, *Year of Decisions*, pp. 423–24; Byrnes, *All in One Lifetime*, p. 304; Hewlett and Anderson, *The New World*, p. 398; Feis, *China Tangle*, pp. 330–31; *Congressional Record*, Aug. 27, 1951, p. A5415.
180. Leahy, *I Was There*, p. 430; Hewlett and Anderson, *The New World*, p. 401.

CHAPTER VII (pp. *188–225*)

1. Byrnes, *Speaking Frankly*, p. 264; Truman, *Year of Decisions*, pp. 421–22; Leahy, *I Was There*, p. 430.
2. Truman, *Year of Decisions*, p. 421.
3. *New York Times, New York Herald Tribune*, Aug. 7, 1945.
4. *Ibid.; New York Times*, Aug. 8–10, 1945.
5. Morton, "The Decision to Use the Atomic Bomb," *Command Decisions*, Greenfield, ed., p. 516; Truman, *Year of Decisions*, p. 425; Hewlett and Anderson, *The New World*, p. 403.
6. Stimson Diary, Aug. 10, 1945.
7. *Ibid.*, Aug. 8–10, 1945; Byrnes, *All in One Lifetime*, p. 305.
8. Byrnes, *All in One Lifetime*, p. 305; Truman, *Year of Decisions*, pp. 427–29; Stimson Diary, Aug. 10, 1945.
9. Stimson Diary, Aug. 10, 1945; Truman, *Year of Decisions*, p. 428; Byrnes, *All in One Lifetime*, p. 305.
10. Byrnes, *All in One Lifetime*, p. 305; Forrestal, *Diaries*, p. 83.
11. Forrestal, *Diaries*, p. 95; Truman, *Year of Decisions*, p. 428; Hewlett and Anderson, *The New World*, pp. 404–5; Stimson Diary, Aug. 10, 1945.

12. Byrnes, *All in One Lifetime*, pp. 305–6.
13. *Ibid.;* Hewlett and Anderson, *The New World*, p. 405.
14. Byrnes, *All in One Lifetime*, p. 306; Truman, *Year of Decisions*, p. 430–31.
15. Truman, *Year of Decisions*, p. 432.
16. Byrnes, *Speaking Frankly*, p. 210; *All in One Lifetime*, p. 306.
17. Byrnes, *All in One Lifetime*, pp. 305–7.
18. Truman, *Year of Decisions*, p. 205.
19. Byrnes, *Speaking Frankly*, p. 210.
20. Truman, *Year of Decisions*, p. 425.
21. *Ibid.*, pp. 142, 432, 439.
22. Stimson Diary, Aug. 10, 1945.
23. Truman, *Year of Decisions*, pp. 430–31; Byrnes, *All in One Lifetime*, p. 306.
24. Byrnes, *All in One Lifetime*, p. 306; Truman, *Year of Decisions*, p. 439.
25. Truman, *Year of Decisions*, pp. 440–43; *Stalin's Correspondence*, II, pp. 266–68.
26. Byrnes, *Speaking Frankly*, pp. 213–15; Dennett and Johnson, *Negotiating with the Russians*, p. 120.
27. Dennett and Johnson, *Negotiating with the Russians*, p. 121.
28. *New York Times*, Aug. 17, 1945; Senate Committee on Foreign Relations, *A Decade of American Foreign Policy, 1941–49*, p. 628.
29. Truman, *Year of Decisions*, p. 423; Feis, *China Tangle*, pp. 342–45; Department of State, *Relations with China*, p. 117.
30. Department of State, *Relations with China*, p. 589.
31. *Ibid.*, p. 594.
32. *Ibid.*, p. 120; Feis, *China Tangle*, pp. 344–47.
33. Department of State, *Relations with China*, p. 118*fn.*
34. *Ibid.*, pp. ix, 99, 120; *Congressional Record*, Aug. 27, 1951, p. A5413.
35. Feis, *China Tangle*, p. 347; *New York Times*, Aug. 28, 1945.
36. Truman, *Public Papers of the Presidents*, I, p. 248; Department of State, *Relations with China*, p. 121.
37. U.S. Senate, *Military Situation in the Far East*, p. 2934.
38. Department of State, *Relations with China*, pp. 119, 137, 147; Beloff, *Soviet Policy*, p. 37.
39. Truman, *Year of Decisions*, p. 448.
40. Department of State, *Relations with China*, pp. 119, 122, 124, 137, 147, 149.
41. *Ibid.*, pp. 123–24.
42. *Ibid.*, Truman, *Year of Decisions*, p. 424; Beloff, *Soviet Policy*, pp. 39–40; Wedemeyer, *Wedemeyer Reports!*, p. 347.
43. Department of State, *Relations with China*, p. ix.
44. *Ibid.*, pp. 118–19; Feis, *China Tangle*, pp. 342–43; Truman, *Year of Decisions*, pp. 423–24.
45. Department of State, *Relations with China*, p. 118.
46. Feis, *China Tangle*, pp. 342, 349–50.
47. *Ibid.*, pp. 349–50; Department of State, *Relations with China*, pp. 118–19.
48. Byrnes, *Speaking Frankly*, p. 92.
49. *New York Times*, Aug. 23, 1945; see also Truman, *Year of Decisions*, p. 483.
50. Truman, *Year of Decisions*, p. 423; *Public Papers of the Presidents*, I, p. 199.
51. Truman, *Public Papers of the Presidents*, I, pp. 212–13.
52. Hewlett and Anderson, *The New World*, p. 407.
53. Truman, *Year of Decisions*, p. 524.
54. Stimson, *On Active Service*, p. 616; Diary, March 15, 1945.
55. Hewlett and Anderson, *The New World*, p. 357.
56. *Ibid.*
57. *Ibid.*
58. *Ibid.*
59. *Ibid.*, pp. 357–58.
60. *Ibid.*, pp. 357–58, 360–61; Stimson Diary, June 6, 1945.
61. Stimson Diary, June 6, 1945; Hewlett and Anderson, *The New World*, pp. 360–61.
62. Hewlett and Anderson, *The New World*, p. 355.
63. *Ibid.*, p. 368.
64. *Ibid.*, pp. 398–99; Truman, *Year of Decisions*, pp. 422–23.
65. Stimson Memo, April 25, 1945.
66. *Ibid.*, Aug. 12–Sept. 5; Sept. 11, 12; Dec. 11, 1945; Hewlett and Anderson, *The New World*, pp. 357–58, 417, 456, 458–59, 460–61, 469.
67. *Ibid.*, pp. 355, 417, 418; Truman, *Year of Decisions*, p. 87; Stimson Diary, Aug. 12–Sept. 3; Sept. 5, 1945; Szilard, "A Personal History

of the Atomic Bomb"; "Was A-Bomb on Japan a Mistake?" *U.S. News and World Report*, Aug. 15, 1960, p. 69.

68. Byrnes, *Speaking Frankly*, p. 179.
69. *Ibid.*, pp. 87, 179, 203; *All in One Lifetime*, p. 303; Senate Committee on Foreign Relations, *A Decade of American Foreign Policy, 1941–49*, pp. 51–58.
70. Byrnes, *Speaking Frankly*, p. 261; *All in One Lifetime*, p. 283.
71. Byrnes, *All in One Lifetime*, p. 284.
72. *Conference of Berlin*, II, p. 82; Churchill, *Triumph and Tragedy*, p. 641.
73. Truman, *Year of Decisions*, p. 525.
74. Hewlett and Anderson, *The New World*, p. 388; Stimson Diary, July 19–22, 1945; *Conference of Berlin*, II, pp. 1155–57.
75. *Ibid.*, p. 1156*fn.*; Stimson, *On Active Service*, p. 642.
76. *Conference of Berlin*, II, p. 1155–56; Stimson Diary, July 20, 1945.
77. Stimson Diary, July 20, 1945; *Conference of Berlin*, II, p. 1156*fn.*
78. Truman, *Year of Decisions*, p. 525.
79. Hewlett and Anderson, *The New World*, p. 401.
80. Truman, *Year of Decisions*, p. 526.
81. *Ibid.*, p. 525.
82. Hewlett and Anderson, *The New World*, pp. 455–56, 458–59; Stimson Diary, Sept. 21, 1945; de Gaulle, *Salvation*, U.K. pp. 207, 287.
83. Truman, *Year of Decisions*, p. 524.
84. Hewlett and Anderson, *The New World*, p. 417.
85. *Ibid.*
86. Atomic Energy Commission, *Oppenheimer Hearings*, p. 33.
87. Hewlett and Anderson, *The New World*, p. 724.
88. *Ibid.*, p. 417.
89. Truman, *Public Papers of the Presidents*, I, p. 214.
90. *Ibid.*, p. 207.
91. For details see *ibid.*, or *New York Times*, Aug. 10, 1945.
92. Deane, *The Strange Alliance*, p. 212; Smith, *Moscow Mission*, pp. 10–12; Eisenhower, *Crusade in Europe*, pp. 438, 444; Clay, *Decision in Germany*, pp. 33–34.
93. Clay, *Decision in Germany*, p. 34; Nettl, *The Eastern Zone and Soviet Policy in Germany*, pp. 65, 260,

262–63; Balfour, *Four-Power Control in Germany and Austria, 1945–46*, p. 17.
94. Clark, *Calculated Risk*, p. 461.
95. Truman, *Year of Decisions*, p. 354; *Conference of Berlin*, II, p. 1491.
96. *Conference of Berlin*, II, pp. 403, 419.
97. *Ibid.*, pp. 193, 506; Lane, *I Saw Poland Betrayed*, pp. 179–82; *New York Times*, Aug. 25, 1945.
98. Truman, *Public Papers of the Presidents*, I, p. 210.
99. Truman, *Year of Decisions*, p. 87.
100. Grew, *Turbulent Era*, II, p. 1465.
101. *New York Times*, Aug. 26, 1945.
102. *Hansard*, 413, H.C. Deb. 5s. (1945), p. 102.
103. *Ibid.*, pp. 291–92.
104. *Ibid.*
105. *Ibid.*, pp. 82–85.
106. *Ibid.*, p. 79.
107. *Conference of Berlin*, II, pp. 1494–95.
108. *Ibid.*
109. *Ibid.*, p. 690; Lukacs, *The Great Powers and Eastern Europe*, p. 632; Seton-Watson, *The East European Revolution*, pp. 104–5.
110. *Conference of Berlin*, I, pp. 367, 370.
111. Fleming, *The Cold War*, I, p. 310; *New York Times*, Aug. 30, 1945.
112. *Conference of Berlin*, II, pp. 687, 690.
113. *New York Times*, Aug. 30, 1945; Fleming, *The Cold War*, I, p. 310.
114. Fleming, *The Cold War*, I, p. 310; Seton-Watson, *The East European Revolution*, p. 193; McNeill, *America, Britain and Russia, 1941–46*, p. 702; Betts, *Central and South East Europe*, p. 105.
115. Betts, *Central and South East Europe*, pp. 31–32; *New York Times*, June 3, 1945.
116. Seton-Watson, *The East European Revolution*, p. 213; Dennett and Johnson, *Negotiating with the Russians*, p. 187; Betts, *Central and South East Europe*, p. 29.
117. Betts, *Central and South East Europe*, p. 31; Seton-Watson, *The East European Revolution*, p. 213.
118. Seton-Watson, *The East European Revolution*, pp. 213–15; Betts, *Central and South East Europe*, p. 31.
119. Betts, *Central and South East Europe*, p. 32.

120. Senate Committee on Foreign Relations, *A Decade of American Foreign Policy, 1941–49*, pp. 484–85.

121. Seton-Watson, *The East European Revolution*, p. 212; Betts, *Central and South East Europe*, pp. 31, 32.

122. Betts, *Central and South East Europe*, p. 32; Seton-Watson, *The East European Revolution*, pp. 213–14.

123. *Conference of Berlin*, II, p. 729.

124. *Ibid.*

125. *Ibid.*, pp. 730–31; Betts, *Central and South East Europe*, p. 32.

126. Betts, *Central and South East Europe*, p. 32; Seton-Watson, *The East European Revolution*, p. 213.

127. *Ibid.*

128. *Ibid.*

129. *Ibid.*

130. *New York Times*, June 3, 1945; *Conference of Berlin*, I, p. 384.

131. *Conference of Berlin*, I, pp. 357–67.

132. *Daily Telegraph*, May 21, 1945; Truman, *Year of Decisions*, p. 50; *New York Times*, March 11, 1945.

133. *New York Herald Tribune*, June 18, 1945; Betts, *Central and South East Europe*, p. 32; Seton-Watson, *The East European Revolution*, p. 214.

134. Seton-Watson, *The East European Revolution*, p. 212; Fleming, *The Cold War*, I, p. 311; Woodward, *British Foreign Policy*, pp. 516–18.

135. *Conference of Berlin*, II, p. 731.

136. *Ibid.*, p. 723; Seton-Watson, *The East European Revolution*, p. 214.

137. *Conference of Berlin*, II, pp. 716–18, 730.

138. *Ibid.*, I, p. 383.

139. *Ibid.*, pp. 383–84.

140. *Ibid.*, p. 384.

141. *Ibid.*

142. *Ibid.*, I, p. 384; II, p. 695.

143. *Ibid.*, II, p. 730.

144. *Ibid.*, pp. 716–18.

145. *Ibid.*, pp. 694–95.

146. *Ibid.*, I, p. 403.

147. *Ibid.*, II, p. 731.

148. *Ibid.*, pp. 730–31.

149. *Ibid.*, pp. 722–25.

150. *Ibid.*, p. 730.

151. *Ibid.*, p. 735; Dennett and Johnson, *Negotiating with the Russians*, p. 189.

152. *Conference of Berlin*, II, p. 734.

153. *Ibid.*, p. 731.

154. Dennett and Johnson, *Negotiating with the Russians*, p. 190.

155. *New York Times*, Aug. 19, 1945; Wolff, *The Balkans in Our Times*, p. 296; Betts, *Central and South East Europe*, p. 33.

156. Betts, *Central and South East Europe*, p. 33; *New York Times*, Aug. 19, 1945; Wolff, *The Balkans in Our Times*, p. 296; State Dept. *Bulletin*, Aug. 19, 26, 1945.

157. *New York Herald Tribune*, Aug. 22, 1945; Betts, *Central and South East Europe*, p. 33; Seton-Watson, *The East European Revolution*, p. 214.

158. Dennett and Johnson, *Negotiating with the Russians*, p. 190.

159. London *Times*, Aug. 24, 1945.

160. *Ibid.*, Aug. 20, 1945; *Manchester Guardian*, Aug. 20, 1945; *New York Times*, Aug. 17, 18, 1945.

161. *New York Times*, Aug. 17, 18, 1945; *Daily Telegraph*, Aug. 17, 1945.

162. *Daily Telegraph*, Aug. 17, 1945; *New York Times*, Aug. 18, 1945; Dennett and Johnson, *Negotiating with the Russians*, p. 189; *New York Herald Tribune*, Aug. 20, 1945.

163. *New York Herald Tribune*, Aug. 20, 1945.

164. *New York Times*, Aug. 20, 1945.

165. *Manchester Guardian*, Aug. 20, 1945.

166. *Conference of Berlin*, I, p. 383.

167. *New York Herald Tribune*, Aug. 16, 1945.

168. London *Times*, Aug. 21, 1945.

169. *New York Times*, Aug. 26, 1945.

170. London *Times*, Aug. 21, 1945.

171. *New York Herald Tribune*, Aug. 22, 1945.

172. *Ibid.*, Sept. 16, 1945; *New York Times*, Aug. 26, 1945.

173. *New York Times*, Aug. 26, 1945; Wolff, *The Balkans in Our Time*, p. 296; Seton-Watson, *The East European Revolution*, p. 214; *New York Herald Tribune*, Aug. 26, 1945; London *Times*, Aug. 27, 1945; Betts, *Central and South East Europe*, p. 33.

174. Dennett and Johnson, *Negotiating with the Russians*, p. 190.

175. *New York Herald Tribune*, Aug. 26, 1945.

176. Dennett and Johnson, *Negotiating with the Russians*, p. 190.
177. *New York Herald Tribune*, Aug. 30–31, 1945; *New York Times*, Sept. 4–10, 1945.
178. *New York Times*, Sept. 4–10, 1945; *New York Herald Tribune*, Aug. 30–31, 1945.
179. *New York Herald Tribune*, Aug. 29, 1945; *New York Times*, Sept. 7, 1945.
180. *New York Times*, Sept. 10, 1945.
181. *Conference of Berlin*, II, pp. 1492–93; State Department *Bulletin*, Aug. 26, 1945, pp. 283–84.
182. Betts, *Central and South East Europe*, pp. 33–34; *New York Times*, Sept. 10, 1945; Dennett and Johnson, *Negotiating with the Russians*, p. 190; Seton-Watson, *The East European Revolution*, p. 214.
183. Dennett and Johnson, *Negotiating with the Russians*, p. 190.
184. *New York Times*, Sept. 10, Nov. 20, 1945.
185. *Ibid.*, Sept. 10, 1945.
186. *New York Herald Tribune*, Aug. 30, 1945.
187. *Ibid.*, Aug. 31, 1945; *New York Times*, Sept. 8, 1945; Betts, *Central and South East Europe*, p. 33.
188. *New York Herald Tribune*, Aug. 30, 1945.
189. *Ibid.*, Aug. 31, Sept. 10, 1945; Betts, *Central and South East Europe*, p. 33.
190. *New York Times*, Sept. 9, 1945.
191. *Ibid.*, Sept. 20, 1945.
192. Seton-Watson, *The East European Revolution*, p. 97; Betts, *Central and South East Europe*, p. 29; Lukacs, *The Great Powers and Eastern Europe*, p. 616.
193. Churchill, *Triumph and Tragedy*, p. 233; Fleming, *The Cold War*, I, p. 251; Betts, *Central and South East Europe*, p. 2.
194. Betts, *Central and South East Europe*, pp. 2, 203.
195. *Ibid.*, p. 203; Roberts, *Rumania*, pp. 264–65.
196. Roberts, *Rumania*, pp. 264–65, *Conferences at Malta and Yalta*, p. 248; Lee, *Crown against Sickle*, pp. 111–12.
197. Lee, *Crown against Sickle*, pp. 110–12; Betts, *Central and South East Europe*, p. 7.
198. *New York Times*, March 23, 1945.
199. *Conference of Berlin*, II, p. 714.
200. *Ibid.*, pp. 700, 714–15.
201. *Ibid.*, p. 700; *Senate Committee on Foreign Relations: A Decade of American Foreign Policy 1941–49*, pp. 483–84.
202. *Conference of Berlin*, II, p. 700.
203. *Ibid.*
204. *Ibid.*
205. *Ibid.*
206. *Ibid.*, pp. 700–1, 714.
207. *Ibid.*, p. 701.
208. *Ibid.*, p. 714.
209. *Ibid.*
210. *Ibid.*
211. *Ibid.*
212. *Ibid.*, pp. 714–15.
213. Churchill, *Triumph and Tragedy*, p. 76.
214. Byrnes, *Speaking Frankly*, p. 98.
215. Seton-Watson, *The East European Revolution*, p. 207; Lee, *Crown against Sickle*, pp. 121–22.
216. Lee, *Crown against Sickle*, pp. 109–10; Feis, *Between War and Peace*, p. 191.
217. Lee, *Crown against Sickle*, pp. 122–24, 126, 129.
218. *Ibid.*, p. 122; London *Times*, *New York Times*, *New York Herald Tribune*, Aug. 23–24, 1945.
219. *New York Herald Tribune*, *New York Times*, London *Times*, Aug. 23, 24, 1945; Seton-Watson, *The East European Revolution*, p. 207; Lee, *Crown against Sickle*, p. 123; Betts, *Central and South East Europe*, p. 9.
220. Betts, *Central and South East Europe*, p. 9; Seton-Watson, *The East European Revolution*, p. 207; Lee, *Crown against Sickle*, p. 123.
221. *New York Times*, Sept. 19, 1945.
222. Betts, *Central and South East Europe*, p. 9.
223. Lee, *Crown against Sickle*, p. 124.
224. *Ibid.*, pp. 124, 126; State Department *Bulletin*, Aug. 26, 1945, p. 281; London *Times*, Aug. 23, 1945; *New York Herald Tribune*, Aug. 25, 1945; *Daily Telegraph*, Aug. 23, 1945; *New York Times*, Aug. 23, 1945.
225. *New York Times*, Aug. 27, 1945.
226. Betts, *Central and South East Europe*, p. 9; Grew memorandum of conversation, Aug. 6, 1945.

227. *New York Times*, Aug. 24, 1945; *Christian Science Monitor*, Aug. 23, 1945.
228. London *Times*, Aug. 29, 1945.
229. *New York Times*, Aug. 29, 1945; Lee, *Crown against Sickle*, p. 127.
230. Lee, *Crown against Sickle*, p. 128; *New York Times*, Sept. 5, 1945; *New York Herald Tribune*, Sept. 9, 1945; Betts, *Central and South East Europe*, p. 9.
231. London *Times*, Sept. 5, 1945.
232. *Manchester Guardian*, Sept. 6, 1945; Lee, *Crown against Sickle*, p. 128.
233. *New York Times*, Sept. 9, 1945.
234. London *Times*, Sept. 13, 20, 1945.
235. *New York Herald Tribune*, Sept. 13, 1945.
236. Byrnes, *All in One Lifetime*, p. 309.
237. McNeill, *America, Britain and Russia, 1941–46*, p. 691; *New York Times*, Oct. 1, 1945, Jan. 18, March 2, 3, April 2, 20, 21, May 9, 1946; *Wall Street Journal*, March 18, 20, 21, 1946; Truman, *Year of Decisions*, pp. 475–76; see also Byrnes, *Speaking Frankly*, pp. 113–14.
238. Truman, *Public Papers of the Presidents*, I, p. 227; *New York Times*, Aug. 17, 1945.
239. Truman, *Year of Decisions*, p. 510.
240. Stimson Diary, Aug. 12–Sept. 3, 1945.
241. *Ibid.*, Sept. 4, 1945.
242. Leahy, *I Was There*, p. 431.
243. Byrnes, *All in One Lifetime*, pp. 313–14; *Speaking Frankly*, pp. 97–101, 105, 107, 108.
244. Byrnes, *Speaking Frankly*, p. 105.

CONCLUSIONS (pp. 226–242)

1. Byrnes, *Speaking Frankly*, p. 104.
2. *Ibid.*, p. 105.
3. *Ibid.; All in One Lifetime*, p. 317; *New York Times*, Oct. 7, 1945.
4. Hewlett and Anderson, *The New World*, p. 456.
5. Leahy, *I Was There*, p. 416.
6. *Ibid.*, p. 429.
7. *Conference of Berlin*, II, p. 1361fn.
8. *Conferences at Malta and Yalta*, p. 319.
9. Truman, *Year of Decisions*, p. 71.
10. Churchill, *Triumph and Tragedy*, pp. 72, 76, 77, 78.
11. *Ibid.*, p. 76.
12. *Ibid.*, p. 238.
13. *Conferences at Malta and Yalta*, p. 234.
14. *Ibid.*, p. 95.
15. Dennett and Johnson, *Negotiating with the Russians*, p. 178.
16. Black, "Soviet Policy in Eastern Europe," p. 155. Emphasis in original.
17. Bryant, *Triumph in the West 1943–46*, pp. 477–78.
18. Truman, *Year of Decisions*, p. 87.
19. *Conference of Berlin*, I, p. 10.
20. Truman, *Year of Decisions*, p. 87.
21. *New York Times*, Feb. 15, 1950.
22. Woodward, *British Foreign Policy*, p. 519.
23. Truman, *Year of Decisions*, p. 71.
24. Byrnes, *Speaking Frankly*, p. 104.
25. Churchill, *Triumph and Tragedy*, pp. 457, 574; emphasis in original.
26. *Conference of Berlin*, I, p. 7.
27. Churchill, *Triumph and Tragedy*, p. 503.
28. *Ibid.*, pp. 637, 649, 650, 655, 672; *Conference of Berlin*, I, pp. 295, 359, 380, 417; Feis, *Between War and Peace*, pp. 223–24, 238.
29. Feis, *Between War and Peace*, pp. 155–56.
30. *Conference of Berlin*, I, p. 295.
31. *Hansard*, 413, H. C. Deb. 5s (1945), p. 78.
32. Truman, *Year of Decisions*, p. 524.
33. De Gaulle, *Salvation*, U.K., pp. 229–30.
34. *Ibid.*, p. 230.
35. *Ibid.*
36. Truman, *Year of Decisions*, p. 262.
37. Kennan, *American Diplomacy 1900–1950*, p. 123.
38. See for example, Byrnes, *Speaking Frankly*, pp. 294–95.
39. *Ibid.*, p. 295.
40. Truman, *Year of Decisions*, p. x.
41. *New York Herald Tribune*, Nov. 27, 1945.
42. Stimson Diary, Sept. 17, 1945.
43. Byrnes, *Speaking Frankly*, p. 98.
44. Snow, *Journey*, p. 357.
45. *Ibid.*, p. 361.
46. Stimson, *On Active Service*, p. 643.
47. Eisenhower, *Mandate for Change*, pp. 312–13; "Ike on Ike," *Newsweek*, Nov. 11, 1963, p. 107.
48. Truman, *Truman Speaks*, p. 67.
49. *Conference of Berlin*, I, p. 905.
50. Leahy, *I Was There*, pp. 245, 259, 269, 384–85.
51. *Ibid.*, p. 441.

52. King and Whitehill, *Fleet Admiral King*, p. 621.
53. Knebel and Bailey, *No High Ground*, p. 111; Craven and Cate, *Air Forces in World War II*, Vol. V, pp. 711, 741.
54. Ismay, *Memoirs*, p. 401.
55. *Ibid.*
56. Churchill, *Triumph and Tragedy*, p. 215.
57. *Ibid.*, p. 646.
58. U.S. Strategic Bombing Survey, *Japan's Struggle to End the War*, p. 13.
59. Knebel and Bailey, *No High Ground*, pp. 73, 89, 141–42, 222.
60. See for example, *New York Times*, Aug. 22, 1963.
61. U.S. Atomic Energy Commission, *Oppenheimer Hearings*, p. 34.
62. *Ibid.*
63. *Ibid.*, p. 561.
64. State Department *Bulletin*, Oct. 28, 1945, p. 659.
65. Craven and Cate, *Air Forces in World War II*, Vol. V, pp. 712–13.
66. Stimson Diary, May 14, 1945.
67. *Ibid.*, June 6, 1945.
68. L. Szilard, "A Personal History of the Atomic Bomb," University of Chicago *Roundtable*. No. 601 (Sept. 25, 1949), pp. 14–15. Byrnes has not denied this statement, but see his recollection of a different aspect of the conversation with Dr. Szilard. (*All in One Lifetime*, pp. 284–85.) See also Hewlett and Anderson, *The New World*, p. 355; and *U.S. News and World Report*, Aug. 15, 1960, p. 69.

APPENDIX I (*pp. 243–269*)

1. Rozek, *Allied Wartime Diplomacy*, pp. 162–63, 274–75, 286, 313, 338.
2. Anders, *An Army in Exile*, pp. 261–62; Feis, *Churchill, Roosevelt, Stalin*, p. 573; Rozek, *Allied Wartime Diplomacy*, pp. 352–53.
3. Rozek, *Allied Wartime Diplomacy*, p. 107.
4. *Ibid.*, p. 108; Hull, *Memoirs*, II, p. 1172.
5. Rozek, *Allied Wartime Diplomacy*, p. 183.
6. *Ibid.*, p. 326.
7. *Ibid.*, p. 278.
8. *Ibid.*, p. 280.
9. *Ibid.*, p. 307.
10. *Ibid.*, p. 283.
11. *Ibid.*, pp. 298–302.
12. *Ibid.*, p. 298.
13. *Ibid.*, pp. 301–2, 313.
14. McNeill, *America, Britain and Russia*, p. 420.
15. *Stalin's Correspondence*, II, pp. 180–81.
16. Rozek, *Allied Wartime Diplomacy*, pp. 303–14; Woodward, *British Foreign Policy*, p. 500.
17. Rozek, *Allied Wartime Diplomacy*, p. 313; Mikolajczyk, *The Pattern of Soviet Domination*, p. 118.
18. Rozek, *Allied Wartime Diplomacy*, pp. 333, 337; Anders, *An Army in Exile*, p. 260; *Stalin's Correspondence*, I, p. 289.
19. Rozek, *Allied Wartime Diplomacy*, pp. 328–29; Lukacs, *The Great Powers and Eastern Europe*, p. 641.
20. *Stalin's Correspondence*, II, pp. 188–89.
21. Rozek, *Allied Wartime Diplomacy*, pp. 338–56.
22. *Conference of Berlin*, II, p. 1579.
23. Lukacs, *The Great Powers and Eastern Europe*, p. 652; Leahy, *I Was There*, p. 316.
24. Lukacs, *The Great Powers and Eastern Europe*, p. 652.
25. Leahy, *I Was There*, p. 307; Stettinius, *Roosevelt and the Russians*, p. 303.
26. Feis, *Churchill, Roosevelt, Stalin*, p. 572; Woodward, *British Foreign Policy*, p. 502; Lane, *I Saw Poland Betrayed*, p. 57.
27. Woodward, *British Foreign Policy*, p. 502.
28. *Ibid.*, pp. 502–3; Lane, *I Saw Poland Betrayed*, pp. 57–59.
29. Rozek, *Allied Wartime Diplomacy*, p. 337.
30. Churchill, *Triumph and Tragedy*, pp. 424–26.
31. Woodward, *British Foreign Policy*, pp. 502–3.
32. *Ibid.*
33. Feis, *Churchill, Roosevelt, Stalin*, p. 573; Woodward, *British Foreign Policy*, pp. 502–3.
34. Woodward, *British Foreign Policy*, p. 503; Feis, *Churchill, Roosevelt, Stalin*, p. 573; Lane, *I Saw Poland Betrayed*, pp. 58–59.
35. Woodward, *British Foreign Policy*, pp. 500, 503; Lane, *I Saw Poland Betrayed*, pp. 58–59.

36. Woodward, *British Foreign Policy*, pp. 502–3.
37. Rozek, *Allied Wartime Diplomacy*, pp. 363–64.
38. Woodward, *British Foreign Policy*, p. 504.
39. Churchill, *Triumph and Tragedy*, pp. 422–23.
40. *Ibid.*, pp. 424–25; Woodward, *British Foreign Policy*, pp. 503–4.
41. Churchill, *Triumph and Tragedy*, p. 425; Woodward, *British Foreign Policy*, pp. 503–5.
42. Churchill, *Triumph and Tragedy*, p. 426.
43. *Ibid.*, pp. 426–28; Woodward, *British Foreign Policy*, pp. 503–5.
44. Churchill, *Triumph and Tragedy*, p. 428.
45. *Ibid.*, p. 427.
46. Forrestal, *Diaries*, p. 36.
47. Rozek, *Allied Wartime Diplomacy*, pp. 363–64.
48. Woodward, *British Foreign Policy*, p. 502.
49. Lane, *I Saw Poland Betrayed*, p. 57.
50. Rozek, *Allied Wartime Diplomacy*, pp. 357–58.
51. *Ibid.*, p. 333.
52. *Ibid.*, pp. 363–64.
53. Truman, *Year of Decisions*, p. 24.
54. *Ibid.;* Churchill, *Triumph and Tragedy*, pp. 425–26.
55. Churchill, *Triumph and Tragedy*, p. 424.
56. *Ibid.;* Woodward, *British Foreign Policy*, pp. 504–5.
57. Deane, *The Strange Alliance*, p. 138.
58. Churchill, *Triumph and Tragedy*, p. 652.
59. Deane, *The Strange Alliance*, p. 123.
60. Sherwood, *Roosevelt and Hopkins*, p. 890.
61. Deane, *The Strange Alliance*, p. 202.
62. Feis, *Churchill, Roosevelt, Stalin*, p. 583.
63. Ehrman, *Grand Strategy*, pp. 122–23; Feis, *Churchill, Roosevelt, Stalin*, p. 583; Churchill, *Triumph and Tragedy*, p. 442.
64. Churchill, *Triumph and Tragedy*, pp. 441–42; Feis, *Churchill, Roosevelt, Stalin*, pp. 583–84; Leahy Diary, March 13, 1945, p. 42.
65. Churchill, *Triumph and Tragedy*, p. 441.
66. Deane, *The Strange Alliance*, p. 163.
67. *Ibid.*, p. 164.
68. Feis, *Churchill, Roosevelt, Stalin*, p. 584.
69. *Ibid.*, pp. 585–6.
70. *Ibid.*, p. 586.
71. *Stalin's Correspondence*, II, p. 297; Ehrman, *Grand Strategy*, pp. 123–24.
72. Feis, *Churchill, Roosevelt, Stalin*, p. 587.
73. Ehrman, *Grand Strategy*, p. 124; Feis, *Churchill, Roosevelt, Stalin*, pp. 588–89; *Stalin's Correspondence*, II, p. 297.
74. *Stalin's Correspondence*, II, p. 297.
75. *Ibid.*, pp. 198–99.
76. *Ibid.*, pp. 200–1.
77. *Ibid.*, pp. 204–6.
78. *Ibid.*, p. 208.
79. *Ibid.*, pp. 208–9.
80. *Ibid.*, p. 297; Feis, *Churchill, Roosevelt, Stalin*, p. 585.
81. Feis, *Churchill, Roosevelt, Stalin*, pp. 591, 594; *New York Times, Washington Post,* July 14, 1964.
82. Churchill, *Triumph and Tragedy*, p. 442.
83. *Ibid.*, pp. 445–46.
84. Wilmot, *The Struggle for Europe*, pp. 758–59.
85. *Ibid.*, p. 798.
86. Feis, *Churchill, Roosevelt, Stalin*, p. 591.
87. *Ibid.*, pp. 591–92.
88. Woodward, *British Foreign Policy*, p. 528.
89. Anders, *An Army in Exile*, p. 264.
90. Lane, *I Saw Poland Betrayed*, p. 60.
91. Grew memorandum of conversation, March 9, 1945.
92. Woodward, *British Foreign Policy*, pp. 503–5.
93. Grew memorandum of conversation, March 23, 1945.
94. Woodward, *British Foreign Policy*, p. 506.
95. *Stalin's Correspondence*, II, pp. 197–99.
96. *Ibid.*, pp. 299–301.
97. Ehrman, *Grand Strategy*, p. 149.
98. Leahy, *I Was There*, pp. 333–34, 336.
99. Woodward, *British Foreign Policy*, p. 505*fn.*
100. Churchill, *Triumph and Tragedy*, p. 427.

101. Leahy, *I Was There*, p. 336; Woodward, *British Foreign Policy*, p. 505.
102. Churchill, *Triumph and Tragedy*, p. 432; Lane, *I Saw Poland Betrayed*, p. 59; Woodward, *British Foreign Policy*, pp. 505–6.
103. Woodward, *British Foreign Policy*, pp. 505–6.
104. *Ibid.*, p. 506.
105. Churchill, *Triumph and Tragedy*, p. 433.
106. *Ibid.*, pp. 432–35, 633–35; Woodward, *British Foreign Policy*, p. 506.
107. Woodward, *British Foreign Policy*, p. 506.
108. Churchill, *Triumph and Tragedy*, pp. 435, 743.
109. Leahy Diary, March 29, 1945, p. 49.
110. *Stalin's Correspondence*, I, p. 309; II, pp. 198–202.
111. *Ibid.*, I, p. 313.
112. *Ibid.*, pp. 315–16; II, pp. 211–13.
113. Churchill, *Triumph and Tragedy*, p. 439.
114. *Stalin's Correspondence*, II, p. 202.
115. Feis, *Churchill, Roosevelt, Stalin*, p. 575.
116. Woodward, *British Foreign Policy*, p. 508.
117. Byrnes, *Speaking Frankly*, p. 59.
118. Woodward, *British Foreign Policy*, p. 508.
119. Churchill, *Triumph and Tragedy*, p. 486.
120. Truman, *Year of Decisions*, pp. 25–26; *Stalin's Correspondence*, II, pp. 215–17.
121. *Stalin's Correspondence*, I, pp. 322–24; Churchill, *Triumph and Tragedy*, p. 488.
122. *Stalin's Correspondence*, I, p. 329.
123. Churchill, *Triumph and Tragedy*, p. 484.
124. Truman, *Year of Decisions*, p. 76.
125. Feis, *Churchill, Roosevelt, Stalin*, p. 576.
126. *Ibid.*, p. 576.
127. Leahy, *I Was There*, p. 352.

APPENDIX II (*pp. 270–275*)

1. Stimson Diary, June 6, 1945; Hewlett and Anderson, *The New World*, p. 352.
2. Hewlett and Anderson, *The New World*, p. 351; Stimson Diary, May 16, 1945.
3. Stimson Diary, May 14, 1945; Churchill, *Triumph and Tragedy*, p. 575.
4. Stimson Diary, May 10, 1945.
5. *Conference of Berlin*, I, p. 4.
6. Truman, *Year of Decisions*, pp. 85, 87.
7. Feis, *Churchill, Roosevelt, Stalin*, p. 637.
8. *Ibid.*
9. Sherwood, *Roosevelt and Hopkins*, p. 885.
10. Truman, *Year of Decisions*, p. 104; Woodward, *British Foreign Policy*, p. 523.
11. Grew memorandum of conversation, May 21, 1945.
12. Truman, *Year of Decisions*, p. 258.
13. Hewlett and Anderson, *The New World*, p. 351.
14. *Ibid.*, p. 352.
15. Feis, *Between War and Peace*, p. 81.
16. Truman, *Year of Decisions*, pp. 110, 257.
17. Feis, *Between War and Peace*, p. 81.
18. Woodward, *British Foreign Policy*, p. 521.

Index

Alanbrooke, Viscount, 153–54, 175 *fn.*, 180, 186 *fn.*
Anders, Gen. Wladyslaw, 254
Anderson, Sir John, 56 *fn.*
Antonov, General, 257
Arciszewski, M., 243, 246, 254
Arnold, Gen. Henry H., 116, 119 *fn.*, 124, 190 *fn.*, 238
Atlantic Charter, 177
atomic bomb: its role in diplomacy, 11–14, 55–58, 97–104, 130, 151–54, 157, 158, 164–65, 171–73, 191, 192, 195, 210, 211, 236, 240; Stimson's and Byrnes's views on, 12–13, 55–56, 62–63, 88, 89, 144, 164–65, 203, 229, 235, 276–79; basis for delayed-showdown strategy, 57–61, 64–66, 70, 80, 84, 85, 89, 116–18, 125, 126, 143–46, 150, 176, 181, 183, 186, 203, 210, 211, 230–33, 241, 270–73; postwar Europe and Asia, 201, 203, 204, 216, 217, 223–29, 234, 242; its use decided or assumed, 14, 56, 113, 116, 179–81, 236–41; its use not necessary, 14, 110, 236–39; test blast, 56, 59, 65, 101, 118, 125, 127, 128, 130, 144, 145, 147–53, 158, 164–65, 172, 173, 176, 180, 183, 232, 233; its use on Japan, 56, 101, 110, 112–18, 124, 155, 157, 181, 183, 184, 186–92, 237–40, 242; monopoly or international control, 58–60, 63, 88–89, 100, 154, 155, 195–200, 235, 276–79; Interim Committee, 59, 62, 63, 114–16, 117 *fn.*, 144, 154–56, 196–98, 200, 240, 271; demonstrations suggestion, 115; postwar development of, 200
Atomic Energy Commission, 197 *fn.*, 198 *fn.*, 227 *fn.*, 237 *fn.*, 240 *fn.*
Attlee, Clement, 149 *fn.*, 203, 227
Augusta, U.S.S., 125, 186, 188
Austria, 42–48, 53–55, 80, 82, 83, 130–31, 201

Baldwin, Hanson W., 238 *fn.*
Balkans, 47, 89, 132 *fn.*, 136, 175; diplomatic recognition, 130, 142, 143, 149–52, 232; spheres of influence in, 132–38, 140–41, 146, 149, 151, 153, 211, 217, 219; British policy on, 133–35, 140–41, 143, 148, 151–53; armistice

agreements, 134, 1⸱ 5, 140–41, 149, 204, 205; U.S. interven⸱ion in, 137–38, 140, 144, 146–52, 158, 165, 170, 192 *fn.*, 202–5, 214, 223, 225, 227, 231, 236; *see also* BULGARIA; GREECE; RUMANIA; YUGOSLAVIA
Bard, Ralph A., 117 *fn.*
Barnes, Maynard, 206–14 *passim*
Batchelder, R. C., 111 *fn.*
Belgium, 25, 79, 131
Beloff, Max, 112 *fn.*, 194 *fn.*
Benes, Eduard, 131
Berlin, 44, 83, 198, 253
Bern, Switzerland, 256–61 *passim*
Betts, R. R., 201 *fn.*, 211 *fn.*, 215 *fn.*
Bevin, Ernest, 149 *fn.*, 171 *fn.*, 203
Blackett, P. M. S., 112 *fn.*
Bohlen, Charles E., 19 *fn.*, 67, 274
Bratianu, Constantin, 218, 222, 223
Brenner Pass, 137
Bryant, A., 138 *fn.*, 175 *fn.*
Bucharest, 218
Budapest, 205
Bulgaria: Soviets' predominant influence in, 50, 132–34, 136 *fn.*, 138–42, 148, 149, 153, 205, 211, 217, 218; postwar government, 130, 138–43, 148, 149, 153, 158, 171, 202–16; armistice agreement, 134, 136 *fn.*, 139, 140, 149; Allied Control Commission, 134, 140, 141, 204, 205, 210, 211; diplomatic recognition, 143, 149–51, 203, 211, 213; U.S. demands for reorganization, 148, 149, 153, 158, 171, 202, 204 *fn.*, 214–16, 226; U.S. intervention in, 205–17, 220, 221, 223, 226, 233; postwar elections, 207–16
Bulletin of the Atomic Scientists, 155 *fn.*
Bush Vannevar, 240
Butow, R. J. C., 107 *fn.*, 178 *fn.*
Byrnes, James F., 13, 53 *fn.*, 197, 202, 203, 205, 223, 234, 235; and the atomic bomb, 13, 63, 112–16, 144, 147, 150, 156, 172, 180–81, 188, 195–200, 202, 203, 224–26, 229, 231, 234, 235, 242; and Interim Committee, 59, 62, 63, 115, 196, 200; postwar Germany, 81, 158, 159, 161, 164–74; policy in the Far East, 111, 112, 120, 123, 125, 178–84, 190, 191, 194; Potsdam Confer-